Green parties in Europe

The emergence of green parties throughout Europe during the 1980s marked the arrival of a new form of political movement, challenging established models of party politics and putting new issues on the political agenda. Since their emergence, green parties in Europe have faced different destinies; in countries such as Germany, Belgium, Finland, France, and Italy, they have accumulated electoral successes, participated in governments, implemented policies and established themselves as part of the party system. In other countries, their political relevance remains very limited.

After more than 30 years on the political scene, green parties have proven to be more than just a temporary phenomenon. They have lost their newness, faced success and failure, power and opposition, grassroots enthusiasm and internal conflicts. *Green Parties in Europe* includes individual case studies and a comparative perspective to bring together international specialists engaged in the study of green parties. It renews and expands our knowledge about the green party family in Europe.

Emilie van Haute is Lecturer at the Université libre de Bruxelles (ULB) and a member of the Centre d'étude de la vie politique (Cevipol). Her main research interests include party membership, intra-party dynamics, participation, elections, and voting behaviour.

Party Families in Europe

Emilie Van Haute, Université Libre de Bruxelles, Belgium

The concept of party families is central to comparative party politics. Looking systematically at individual party families, their origins, development, ideology, policy positions, organizational structure, and/or sociological composition, this series investigates the nature of families of political parties. Themes are systematically developed through case studies and comparative chapters to consider key issues around:

- Electoral performance and composition: the electoral fate of each party family, differences among national, sub-national and European elections, common patterns in the electoral development and the composition of the electorate of each party family.
- Participation to power: how the relationship to power has evolved for each party family. How their origins affect their capacity to enter government. What type of governmental coalitions or alliances they favour and which policies they develop once in power.
- Ideology and policy positions: how the ideological positioning of each party family evolved. How electoral performances, participation to power, or leadership change contribute or not to major programmatic evolutions.
- Party organization: how the intra-party organizational feature of each party family has evolved. Are these features homogeneous within each family? Is each family unique in their organizational choices?

Aimed at scholars and students of comparative politics, with a specific appeal for those interested in political parties and party systems, representation and elections, voting behaviour and public opinion the comparative nature of titles in the series will appeal to readers throughout the world. Bringing together expert authors, editors and contributors it renews and expands our knowledge of political parties and party families in Europe.

Forthcoming titles:

Regionalist Parties in Europe
Edited by Oscar Mazzoleni and Sean Mueller

Green parties in Europe

Edited by Emilie van Haute

Routledge
Taylor & Francis Group

LONDON AND NEW YORK

First published 2016
by Routledge

2 Park Square, Milton Park, Abingdon, Oxfordshire OX14 4RN
52 Vanderbilt Avenue, New York, NY 10017

Routledge is an imprint of the Taylor & Francis Group, an informa business

First issued in paperback 2019

British Library Cataloguing in Publication Data
A catalogue record for this book is available from the British Library

Library of Congress Cataloging-in-Publication Data
A catalog record for this book has been requested

ISBN: 978-1-4724-3443-2 (hbk)
ISBN: 978-0-367-28140-3 (pbk)

Typeset in Times New Roman
by Apex CoVantage, LLC

Contents

Figures

Tables

Notes on contributors

Lynn Bennie is Reader in Politics in the Department of Politics and International Relations, School of Social Science, University of Aberdeen. Her research interests span the areas of elections and political parties, political participation and Green politics. She has published books and articles on the membership of the Liberal Democrats, the Greens and the Scottish National Party.

Roberto Biorcio is Professor of Political Science at the University of Milano Bicocca. His research interests are in political participation, social movements, parties and electoral behaviour. His recent books include *Politica a 5 stelle: Idee, storia e strategie del movimento di Grillo* (Feltrinelli, 2013), *La rivincita del Nord: La Lega dalla contestazione al governo* (Laterza, 2010) and *Sociologia politica: Partiti, movimenti sociali e partecipazione* (Il Mulino, 2003)

Niklas Bolin is Senior Lecturer in Political Science at the Mid Sweden University, Sundsvall. His research interests include political parties, party system change and parliamentary government with a special focus on Scandinavia. Previously he has published in journals like *West European Politics* and *Scandinavian Political Studies*.

Nathalie Brack holds a PhD in Political Science from the Université libre de Bruxelles (ULB) and was Postdoctoral Fellow at the University of Oxford between 2013 and 2014. She is currently FNRS postdoctoral researcher at the Cevipol (ULB). Her research interests include the European Parliament, political representation, party politics and legislative studies as well as Euroscepticism. She recently published 'Euroscepticism at the supranational level: The case of the 'untidy right' in the European Parliament', *Journal of Common Market Studies*, 2013, 51(1).

Dr Sebastian Bukow is Assistant Professor (Akademischer Rat a.Z.) at the Institute of Social Science, Heinrich-Heine-University Düsseldorf (Comparative Politics; Chair: Prof Dr Thomas Poguntke). He is Research Fellow at the Düsseldorf Party Research Institute (PRuF) and spokesman of the standing group 'political parties' of the German Political Science Association (DVPW, AK Parteienforschung). His research interests are party organisations, party systems and parliaments.

Caroline Close holds a PhD in Political Science from the Université libre de Bruxelles (ULB). She is currently FNRS postdoctoral researcher at the Centre d'Etude de la Vie Politique (Cevipol). Her research interests include political representation, party politics and factionalism and legislative studies.

Pascal Delwit is Professor of Political Science at the Université libre de Bruxelles (ULB) and member of the Centre d'Etude de la Vie Politique (Cevipol). His research interests include political parties and electoral processes in Europe. He recently edited *Les Partis Politiques en France* (Editions de l'Université de Bruxelles, 2014) and published *PTB: Nouvelle Gauche, Vieille Recette* (Editions Luc Pire, 2014).

Martin Dolezal is a postdoctoral researcher at the Department of Government, University of Vienna. He has published on various aspects of party competition, electoral behaviour and 'unconventional' modes of political participation. Dolezal is coauthor of *West European Politics in the Age of Globalization* (2008) and *Political Conflict in Western Europe* (2012).

E. Gene Frankland is Professor of Political Science at Ball State University, Muncie, Indiana, USA. His research has focussed on European Green parties, especially the German Greens (*Bündnis 90/Die Grünen*). He is coeditor/coauthor of *Green Parties in Transition: The End of Grassroots Democracy?* (Ashgate, 2008) and of the *International Encyclopedia of Environmental Politics* (Routledge, 2002).

Camille Kelbel is a PhD student in the 'PartiRep' project and a member of the Centre d'Etude de la Vie Politique (Cevipol), Université libre de Bruxelles (ULB). Prior to joining the ULB, Camille Kelbel was an academic assistant at the College of Europe, in Bruges. Her PhD dissertation deals with candidate selection processes for European elections. Her other current research interests lie in EU politics, political parties and elections.

Conor Little is a Postdoctoral Researcher at the Department of Political Science in the University of Copenhagen. He received his PhD from the European University Institute in Florence. He has worked as a Research Associate on the ESRC-funded *Climate Policy and Political Parties* project in Keele University and as a Teaching Fellow in University College Dublin. His research interests include political parties, political careers, the politics of climate change and Irish politics.

Paul Lucardie is (semiretired) researcher at the Documentation Centre Dutch Political Parties, at the University of Groningen (The Netherlands). He coedited, with Benoît Rihoux and Gene Frankland, *Green Parties in Transition* (Farnham: Ashgate, 2008) and, with Gerrit Voerman, *Van de straat naar de staat? GroenLinks 1990–2010* (Amsterdam: Boom, 2010).

Jean-Benoit Pilet is Professor of Political Science at the Université libre de Bruxelles (ULB). He works mainly on electoral systems, party politics and elections. He has recently coedited (with William Cross) *The Selection of Party Leaders in Parliamentary Democracies* (Routledge, 2014).

Gareth Price-Thomas recently completed his PhD at the University of Manchester, where he continues to teach. His thesis was a study of the contemporary ideology of Green parties in Britain, France and Germany. He has taught on comparative and European politics, and political economy; and his research interests include Green politics, ideology, political parties of the left and the thought of Antonio Gramsci.

Benoît Rihoux is Full Professor of Political Science at the Université catholique de Louvain (Belgium). His research interests include Green parties, party organisations, new social movements, political change, policy processes, configurational comparative methods and QCA (Qualitative Comparative Analysis). He has published extensively on Green parties (among which *Greens in Transition: The End of Grass-Roots Democracy?*, Ashgate, ed., with E. Gene Frankland and Paul Lucardie, 2008) and configurational comparative methods/QCA.

Emilie van Haute is Lecturer at the Université libre de Bruxelles (ULB) and a member of the Centre d'Etude de la Vie Politique (Cevipol). Her main research interests include party membership, intraparty dynamics, participation, elections and voting behaviour.

Bruno Villalba is Professor of Political Science at AgroParisTech. He is member of the Ceraps (Lille Centre for Politics and Administration, CNRS). His areas of research are political ecology, sustainable development and environmental sociology. He is the Director of the Reading Committee of the review *Etudes Rurales* and Member of the Reading Committee of the digital review *Sustainable Development and Territories*.

Gerrit Voerman is historian and director of the Documentation Centre Dutch Political Parties of the University of Groningen and, since 2011, Professor of 'Development and Functioning of the Dutch and European Party System' at this university. He has published widely on political parties, especially on party history; organisation, membership and identity and on candidate selection. Since 2008, he has served as editor of a series on the political parties in the Netherlands. With Paul Lucardie, he published *Van de straat naar de staat? GroenLinks 1990–2010* (Amsterdam: Boom, 2010).

Marie-Catherine Wavreille is a PhD student and Fonds National de la Recherche Scientifique (FRS-FNRS) research fellow at the Centre d'Etude de la Vie Politique (Cevipol), Université libre de Bruxelles (ULB) since 2012. Her dissertation focuses on state-level initiatives and referendum campaigns in the United States in the last ten years (2004–2014). Her research interests lie in democratic innovation, campaigns, political parties and US politics.

Acknowledgements

This book is the continuation of the conference on 'Green Parties in Europe' held in Brussels (Belgium) in March 2013. We would like to thank the participants to this event, as well as its sponsors, the Fonds National de la Recherche Scientifique (FRS-FNRS) and The Greens – European Free Alliance in the European Parliament.

We are grateful to the Routledge team for their professional and human collaboration and to the referees for their very constructive remarks.

Introduction

Emilie van Haute

The emergence of Green parties throughout Europe during the 1980s marked the arrival of a new form of political movement, which challenged established models of party politics and raised new issues on the political agenda. Since their emergence, Green parties have faced different destinies throughout Europe. In some countries such as Germany, Belgium, Finland or France, they have accumulated electoral successes, participated in governments and/or implemented policies. They have established themselves as part of the party system. In other European countries, their political relevance is still very limited, especially in Central and Eastern Europe. The European elections in 2014 have confirmed the uneven success of Green parties. Yet, after more than 30 years of presence on the political scene, Green parties have proven to be more than just a passing experience. They have lost their newness; they have faced successes and failures, power and opposition, grassroots enthusiasm, internal conflicts and divisions.

This volume reflects on the evolution of Green parties in Europe. There have been comparative exercises conducted in the past, with edited volumes focusing on the emergence of Greens parties (Müller-Rommel, 1989; Richardson and Rootes, 1995; O'Neill, 1997) and volumes analysing one specific dimension of Green parties: electoral (Kitschelt, 1988; Müller-Rommel, 1994), organisational (Kitschelt, 1989; Poguntke, 1989; Rihoux, 2001), ideological (Burchell, 2001) or governmental (Müller-Rommel and Poguntke, 2002). This volume's ambition is to combine these dimensions, using the concept of party family as an analytical framework. It raises two main questions: (1) is this concept relevant for the study of Green parties in Europe? and (2) if it is, how can we characterise the Green party family today: have Green parties reached adulthood or are they eternal teenagers?

Framework of analysis

The concept of party family is central in comparative party politics, as it has been used to classify parties across countries and time. Mair and Mudde (1998) identify four approaches to classify parties in families: name; transitional federations; origins and sociology, and policy and ideology. In this volume, we have combined and expanded the various approaches identified by Mair and Mudde in order to identify potential Green parties, to assess whether they can be classified as belonging to one single party family and to highlight their core common characteristics and differences.

Name and transnational federations

The most straightforward strategy is to identify Green parties based on their name or their affiliation to a transnational federation of parties. As noted by Mair and Mudde (1998), this strategy presents the advantages of being easy to apply and of respecting the parties' own choices. However, they point at some difficulties linked to this approach: not all parties are affiliated to a transnational grouping (especially in the case of smaller or more marginal parties); party labels may cover very diverse ideological currents, and parties identifying with an ideology may choose to avoid referring to it in their name.

Researchers are confronted to these difficulties when trying to identify Green parties in Europe. Given their relative small size and low level of institutionalisation in some countries, not all Green parties are stable enough to start building transnational bonds with other Green parties. Transnational groupings themselves may struggle to exist on their own. For instance, Green representatives in the European Parliament (EP) have allied with (mainly) regionalist parties under the Green/EFA alliance to form a parliamentary group. In Europe, the development of Europarties creates incentives for this transnational federation to identify at least one agent in each member state. It may push them, including the European Green Party (EGP), to invite and involve parties that they would not have recognised as siblings under other circumstances.

Labels can be misleading too when trying to identify Green parties. By focusing on two labels (Green and party), one may miss a lot of parties from the same ideological strand that decided to adopt other labels. The Green label is sometimes discarded to the benefit of other references such as sustainable, ecological, environmental or even progressive or alternative; even the term 'party' is debated, and some organisations tend to favour terms referring to looser forms of collective organisation such as movement, forum, list, league, club, and so forth.

Therefore, this straightforward strategy may lead researchers to include parties that do not belong to the Green family or to exclude parties that could be considered as members of the family. Nevertheless, as we will see in this volume, names and federations tell us something about the parties' strategies and how they perceive themselves.

Origins and sociology

The classification of parties based on their origins is an important criterion identified by Mair and Mudde (1998). Referring to the classic study of Lipset and Rokkan (1967, 2008), they propose a classification of party families based on four cleavages, linking parties to the conflict from which they originated (Seiler, 1980). Parties that originated from a specific structural conflict dividing society would

then see this reflected in their sociological composition. They would mainly organise specific segments of society.

This approach is praised for its clear theoretical anchorage. However, it was
developed for the Western European context, and its applicability to Central and
Eastern Europe has been debated (De Waele, 2004). Furthermore, this approach
does not take into consideration changes, realignments and the emergence of new
parties.

Applied to Green parties, this approach generates even more debate, as Green
parties have emerged after the development of the theory. Their development
generated the debate on the 'defreezing' of cleavages and the emergence of
new cleavage(s) (Dalton, et al., 1984; Shamir, 1984; Bartolini and Mair, 1990;
Hottinger, 1995). Three competing views are opposed (Seiler, 1999). The first sees
Green parties as the sign of the emergence of a new, fifth cleavage opposing new
and old politics, or materialists and postmaterialists. The second view classifies
Green parties in the existing typology. It connects them to the rural side of the
urban–rural cleavage stemming from the industrial revolution. Finally, the third
view assumes a reactivation and a transformation of the rural–urban cleavage in
the postindustrial era, into an opposition between market and nature (Seiler, 1999).

This approach combines the challenges of being geographically narrow, synchronic and dated. Nevertheless, we will see in this volume that looking at the
origins of parties and at their social composition is a very useful approach to
identify the potential members of the Green party family.

Ideology and policy positions

The last approach pointed by Mair and Mudde (1998) to identify party families is
based on ideological congruence between parties. It indirectly refers to the previous approach that sees parties from the same family as sharing a common project,
defending similar interests located on one specific side of societal conflicts.

Mair and Mudde stress that this approach presents the advantage of data availability, which has even improved since then, and the development of new data
management software. They also underline the methodological difficulties connected to this approach, due to the variety of sources and material from which
deriving the parties' ideology and policy positioning, and the very contextual
nature of party positioning that makes transnational comparison more difficult.

Regarding Green parties in particular, the question is even more crucial. First,
transnational data-gathering processes have not systematically integrated Green
parties in their case selection, given their relatively small electoral size or parliamentary representation in some countries. Second, some data-gathering processes
on policy positioning of parties, such as the Comparative Manifesto Project, began
before the emergence of Green parties. The coding scheme has progressively
evolved to integrate new themes, but it is rather a reactive process.

Therefore, there is still work to be done in terms of comparative analysis of
Green parties' ideological positioning, of the level of congruence among Green

parties or the evolution of policy positioning over time and the impact of electoral performances and participation to power on programmatic evolutions over time.

These approaches are systematically developed in this volume, with some adaptation to address the critics and difficulties pointed by Mair and Mudde (1998). The first main addition is the integration of a more longitudinal perspective, to avoid the synchronic view of party origins in Lipset and Rokkan's theory. In this volume, we investigate how Green parties originated and discuss whether their origins can be linked to existing or new cleavages. We go further by expanding the geographical scope to see whether the same mechanisms applied in all European countries. Finally, we take Mair and Mudde's warning seriously, that 'an approach that focuses exclusively on the origins of parties as the key to their contemporary classification risks neglecting more than it can offer' (1998, p. 216). Therefore, we look beyond party origins and discuss the development of these parties over time. In order to do so, we use the party lifespan approach proposed by Pedersen (1982) and identify the four main phases in the parties' development:

- The threshold of declaration, which corresponds to the parties' origins, when they declare their first participation to elections;
- The threshold of authorisation, which refers to the meeting of legal regulations or requirements in order to participation in elections;
- The threshold of representation, that is, the gaining of the first seats in parliament;
- The threshold of relevance, which corresponds to an impact on government formation and policy output.

The second main addition is the discussion of party organisations. If the concept of party family mainly refers to a common project or sociological base, scholars also tend to associate it loosely with organisational types. Therefore, this volume integrates party organisation as an additional criterion on which to evaluate the existence of a Green party family that would share common organisational features.

In accordance with these adjustments, four major themes are developed in this volume, each raising a number of questions:

(1) Origins and development: following Lipset and Rokkan's theory but also Pedersen's lifecycle approach, we investigate the birth of Green parties, their electoral performances and their experience of governmental participation over time. We try to identify common or divergent patterns in their electoral development, and we investigate their relationship to power and its evolution over time: have their origins as social movements inhibited their capacity to enter governments? What type of governmental coalitions or alliances do they favour? To develop which policies?

(2) Sociological composition: following Lipset and Rokkan's theory, we analyse the electorate of Green parties and try to highlight the similarities and differences in their profiles. We want to stress whether Green parties encapsulate

similar segments of the electorate across national contexts, or if their respective electorate significantly differs across countries.

(3) Ideology and policy positions: we analyse whether Green parties share congruent policy positions and whether ideological positions have become more or less congruent over time. We relate this to electoral performances and participation to power, to see if the parties' electoral and governmental fate affects programmatic choices.

(4) Organisational structure: we investigate the uniqueness of Green parties' organisational choices. More specifically, we discuss whether the participatory perspective of Green parties has sustained over time and whether oligarchic tendencies have developed, especially in the case of governing parties.

Comparative strategy and book structure

The book proposes two types of contributions. The first part of the book consists of case studies, for which contributors present the major developments of national Green parties on the four aspects.

The volume covers a large geographical spectrum of no less than 30 countries and 70 parties. The book provides longer developments and analyses on 25 countries and 37 parties (Table I.1). Some case studies are presented in a full chapter when the development of Green parties requires it. Other case studies are grouped together when relevant in order to be as comprehensive as possible in terms of geographical coverage. Depending on the weight and relevance of Green parties in their respective systems, chapters cover one single-country experience (Belgium, France, Germany, the Netherlands) or multiple countries organised in geographical blocs (Austria and Switzerland; Sweden and Finland; Southern Europe – Italy, Spain, Portugal and Greece –; the United Kingdom and the Republic of Ireland; and Central and Eastern Europe). The Green group in the European Parliament is also considered as a case study.

The case studies provide an overview of the development, challenges and opportunities of Green parties in various settings. These chapters provide information on the four crucial aspects linked to the study of party families as developed in our framework of analysis: the origins and development of the parties, their ideology or policy positions, their organisational structure, and their sociological composition.

Each chapter starts by describing the main events or developments of the party since its foundation, chronologically. The chronology lists the main developments of the party in the party system, following the four phases identified by Pedersen (1982). It also includes the main intraparty events (relevant leadership contests or crises, main organisational changes, scissions, fusions, name changes); electoral performances (with a main emphasis on the results for the lower chamber at the national level, although other levels might be of relevance in case of major discrepancy with the lower chamber) and the relation of the party towards participation to power at various levels.

The second section presents the position of the party on main cleavages or issues: socio-economic issues, religious, moral or cultural issues, centre-periphery issues

Table 1.1 List of parties

Country	Party acronym/ short name	Full name in original language	English translation	Previous name(s)	Chapters
AT	Grüne	Die Grünen – Die Grüne Alternative	The Greens – The Green Alternative	Grüne Alternative (until 1993)	1, 11, 14
AT	VGÖ	Vereinten Grünen Österreichs	United Greens of Austria		1, 11
AT	ALÖ	Alternative Liste Österreichs	Alternative List of Austria		1, 11
BE	Ecolo	Écologistes Confédérés pour l'organisation de luttes originales	Confederated Ecologists for the Organisation of Original Struggles	Wallonie-Écologie	2, 11, 12, 14
BE	Groen	Groen	Green	Agalev (until 2003), Groen! (until 2012)	2, 11, 12, 14
BG	ZPB	Zelena Partija Bulgaria	Bulgarian Green Party		3, 11
BG	Zelenite	Zelenite	The Party of the Greens		3, 11
BG	PC Ecoglasnost	Ecoglasnost	Political Club Ecoglasnost		3
HR	ZL	Zelena Lista	Green List		3, 11
HR	ORaH	Održivi Razvoj Hrvatske	Croatian Sustainable Development Party		3, 11
HR	HSZ	Hrvatska Stranka Zelenih	Croatian Green Party		3
HR	ZS	Zelena Stranka	Green Party		3
HR	Zeleni HR	Zeleni Hrvatske	Greens of Croatia		3
CY	KOP	Kinima Oikologon Perivallontiston	Ecological and Environmental Movement		11
CZ	SZ	Strana Zelených	Green Party		3, 11, 12
DK	De Grønne	De Grønne	The Greens		11, 12
DK	SF	Socialistisk Folkeparti	Socialist People's Party		11

EE	EER	*Erakond Eestimaa Rohelised*	Estonian Greens	Eestimaa Rahvaliit – (until 1990); Eesti Roheline Partei and Eesti (until 1991); Roheline Erakond (until 1991); Eesti Rohelised	3, 11
FI	VL	*Vihreä Liitto*	Green League		7, 11, 12, 14
FR	EELV	*Europe Écologie – Les Verts*	Europe Ecology – The Greens	Mouvement d'écologie politique (until 1982); Les Verts-Parti écologiste (until 1984); Les Verts (until 2008) – Europe Écologie (until 2010)	4, 11, 12, 13, 14
FR		*Les Alternatifs*	The Alternatives	Alternative rouge et verte – Arev (until 1989)	4
FR	GE	*Génération Écologie*	Generation Ecology		4
FR	CES	*Convergence écologie solidarité*	Convergence Ecology Solidarity		4
FR		*Écologie bleue*	Blue Ecology		4
FR		*Mouvement écologiste indépendant*	Independent Ecology Movement		4
DE	DG	*Bündnis 90/Die Grünen*	Alliance 90/The Greens		5, 11, 12, 13, 14
EL	OP	*Oikologoi Prasinoi*	Green Ecologists	Federation of Ecologists Alternatives (until 2002)	8, 11
HU	LMP	*Lehet Más a Politika*	Politics Can Be Different		3, 11
HU	MZP	*Magyarorszagi Zold Part*	Hungarian Green Party		3
HU	ZB	*Zöld Baloldal*	Green Left	Zöld Alternativa (until 2000); Zöld Demokraták Szövetsége (until 2008)	3
HU	PM	*Párbeszéd Magyarországért*	Dialogue for Hungary		3
IE		*Comhaontas Glas*	The Green Party	Ecology Party of Ireland (until 1983); Green Alliance (until 1987)	9, 11, 12, 14
IT	FV	*Federazione dei Verdi*	Federation of the Greens	*Federazione delle Liste Verdi* and *Verdi Arcobaleno* (until 1990)	8, 11, 12, 14

(Continued)

Table I.1 (Continued)

Country	Party acronym/ short name	Full name in original language	English translation	Previous name(s)	Chapters
LV	LZP	Latvijas Zala Partija	Latvian Green Party		3, 11
LT	LZP	Leutuvos Žaliųjų Partija	Lithuanian Green Party		3, 11
LT	LVŽS	Lietuvos valstiečių ir žaliųjų sąjunga	Lithuanian Peasant and Greens Union	Lietuvos valstiečių liaudininkų sąjunga	3
LU	DG	Déi Gréng – Les Verts	The Greens	Gréng Alternativ Partei	11, 12, 14
MT	AD	Alternattiva Demokratica	Democratic Alternative		11
NL	GL	GroenLinks	Green Left		6, 11, 14
NL		De Groenen	The Greens		11, 14
NO	MDG	Miljøpartiet de Grønne	The Greens		11
PL	Zieloni	Zieloni	Greens		3, 11
PL	FE	Forum Ekologiczny	Ecological Forum		3
PT	PEV	Partido Ecologista Os Verdes	Ecologist Party The Greens	Movimento Ecologista Português – Partido 'Os Verdes'	8, 11
RO	PER	Partidul Ecologist Român	Romanian Ecological Party		3
RO	PV	Partidul Verde	Green Party		3, 11
RO	FER	Federaţia Ecologistă Română	Romanian Ecologist Federation	Mişcarea Ecologista din Romania	3
RO	MVDA	Mişcarea Verzilor – Democraţi Agrarieni	Green Movement – Agrarian Democrats	Mişcarea Verzilor (until 2011)	3, 11
SK	SZ	Strana Zelených	Green Party	Strana Zelených na Slovensku	3, 11
SK	SZA	Slovenska Zelena Alternative	Slovak Green Alternative		3
SI	SMS–Zeleni	Stranka mladih–Zeleni Evrope	The Youth Party – European Greens	Stranka mladih Slovenije (until 2009)	3, 11
SI	ZS	Zeleni Slovenije	The Greens of Slovenia		3, 11
SI	TRS	Stranke za Trajnostni Razvoj Slovenije	Party for Sustainable Development		3

SI	ZESS	*Zeleni Ekološko Socialna Stranka*	*Ecological Social Party*		3
SI	ZA	*Zelena Alternativa*	*Green Alternative Party*		3
ES		*Equo*			8
ES	LV	*Confederación de los Verdes*	*Confederation of The Greens*	*Los Verdes (until 1995)*	8, 11
ES	AV	*Alternativa Verda*	*Green Alternative*		8
ES	ICV	*Iniciativa per Catalunya Verds*	*Initiative for Catalonia Greens*		8, 11
SE	MP	*Miljöpartiet de Gröna*	*Green Party*		7, 11, 14
CH	GPS	*Grüne – Grüne Partei der Schweiz; Les Verts – Parti écologiste Suisse; I Verdi – Partito ecologista svizzero*	*Greens – Green Party of Switzerland*	Föderation der grünen Parteien der Schweiz – GFS (until 1986)	1, 11, 14
CH	GLP	*Grünliberale Partei Schweiz; Parti vert libéral Suisse; Partito Verde Liberale svizzero*	*Green Liberal Party Switzerland*		1
CH	MPE	*Mouvement populaire pour l'environnement*	*Popular Movement for the Environment*		1
CH	GPE	*Groupement pour la protection de l'environnement*	*Grouping for the Protection of the Environment*		1
CH	POCH	*Progressive Organisationen der Schweiz*	*Progressive Organisations of Switzerland*		1
CH	GBS	*Grünes Bündnis Schweiz*	*Green Alliance Switzerland*	*Grüne Alternative Schweiz*	1
UK	GPEW	Green Party of England and Wales	Green Party of England and Wales	People (until 1975); Ecology Party (until 1985)	9, 11, 13, 14
UK	SGP	Scottish Green Party	Scottish Green Party		9, 11
UK	GPNI	Green Party of Northern Ireland	Green Party of Northern Ireland		9, 11
EU	EGP	European Green Party	European Green Party	European Green Coordination (until 1993); European Federation of Green Parties (until 2004)	10

Note: Italics indicate smaller parties mentioned only in country case studies or in Chapter 11 but not systematically developed throughout the volume.

(or structure of the state), environment, law and order, immigration and Europe. It also discusses the main developments or shifts across time when necessary.

The third section presents the party organisation and structure. It starts by describing the main party bodies and their competences (with a specific focus on leadership selection, candidate selection, and policy position formulation) and points to evolutions over time when necessary. It then presents the evolution of party membership figures and elements of profiles when available. Lastly, it describes the formal and informal links between the party and social movements.

Finally, the chapter concludes with a short analysis of the main challenges and opportunities for the party in the future.

The chapter on the Green/EFA group in the European Parliament follows a somewhat different structure. The first part explores the evolution of the Greens in the EP since 1979. The second part considers the cohesion of the group across time and across issues. The third section analyses the factors behind the cohesiveness of the group. This chapter constitutes a nice transition from the case study perspective to the comparative part of the book.

The second part of the book is dedicated to a comparative perspective. Each chapter presents the major evolutions related to one of the four core themes in a comparative perspective, and thereby contributes to the discussion of the concept of party family.

In Chapter 11, Caroline Close and Pascal Delwit discuss the electoral fate of Green parties in Europe as well as the evolution of the profile of Green party voters. The chapter distinguishes the performances between national, sub-national and European elections. It tries to find common patterns in the electoral development of Green parties. It also presents comparative elements regarding the composition of the electorate (socio-demographic characteristics and political positioning).

In Chapter 12, Conor Little looks at how the relationship to power has evolved for Green parties. The chapter provides a comparative overview of Green parties' participation in national governments. It investigates whether their origins as social movements have inhibited their capacity to enter governments and what type of governmental coalitions or alliances they tend to favour. It analyses the policy output of Green parties when in power and how long Green parties tend to last in power. The goal is to provide an understanding of the differences and similarities of Green parties in governments.

In Chapter 13, Gareth Price-Thomas addresses the question of the existence of a single ideology that is common to contemporary Green parties. It looks at contemporary party manifestos and policy positions on various issues. It also investigates how has the ideological positioning of Green parties evolved over time.

Finally, in Chapter 14, Benoît Rihoux discusses whether Green parties constitute a distinct party organisation type. The chapter also looks at the evolution of Green parties from social movements to political parties and analyses the potential factors of organisational change and organisational development.

These four comparative chapters contribute to the genealogic, sociological, ideational and organisational approaches to the notion of party family.

Based on the country chapters and the comparative perspective, the conclusion looks back at the initial discussion of the notion of the party family and concludes on its application to Green parties in Europe. As part of a series on party families in Europe, it connects this question to the general debate on party families. Furthermore, it looks at the impact of the presence of these (not so new anymore) Green parties on politics and policies in Europe.

By bringing together the best specialists engaged in the study of Green parties, this book aims at renewing and expanding our knowledge on Green parties in Europe. In doing so, the book can also be considered a unique discussion on the notion of the party family in Europe.

References

Bartolini, S., and Mair, P., 1990. *Identity, Competition, and Electoral Availability*. Cambridge: Cambridge University Press.

Burchell, J., 2001. Evolving or conforming? Assessing organisational reform within European Green parties. *West European Politics*, 24(3), pp. 113–134.

Dalton, R., Flanagan, S., and Beck, P. eds, 1984. *Electoral Change in Advanced Democracies*. Princeton: Princeton University Press.

De Waele, J.-M., ed., 2004. *Les clivages politiques en Europe centrale et orientale*. Brussels: Editions de l'Université de Bruxelles.

Frankland, G., Lucardie, P., and Rihoux, B. eds, 2008. *Green Parties in Transition: The End of Grass-Roots Democracy?* Farnham: Ashgate.

Hottinger, J.-T., 1995. Le dégel des clivages ou une mauvaise interprétation de la théorie de Lipset et Rokkan. *Revue internationale de politique comparée*, 2(1), pp. 47–59.

Kitschelt, H., 1988. Left-libertarian parties: Explaining innovation in competitive party systems. *World Politics*, 40(2), pp. 194–234.

Kitschelt, H., 1989. *The Logics of Party Formation: Ecological Politics in Belgium and West Germany*. New York: Cornell University Press.

Lipset, S. M., and Rokkan, S., 1967. *Party Systems and Voter Alignments: Cross-National Perspectives*. Toronto: The Free Press.

Lipset, S. M., and Rokkan, S., 2008. *Structures de clivages, systèmes de partis et alignement des électeurs: une introduction*. Brussels: Editions de l'Université de Bruxelles, coll. UBLire.

Mair, P., and Mudde, C., 1998. The party family and its study. *Annual Review of Political Science*, 1, pp. 211–229.

Müller-Rommel, F., ed., 1989. *New Politics in Western Europe: The Rise and Success of Green Parties and Alternative Lists*. London and Boulder, CO: Westview Press.

Müller-Rommel, F., 1994. Green parties under comparative perspective. *ICPS Working Papers* 99.

Müller-Rommel, F., and Poguntke, T. eds, 2002. *Green Parties in National Governments*. London and Portland, OR: Frank Cass.

O'Neill, M., 1997. *Green Parties and Political Change in Contemporary Europe*. Aldershot: Ashgate.

Pedersen, M., 1982. Towards a new typology of party lifespan and minor parties. *Scandinavian Political Studies*, 5(1), pp. 1–16.

Poguntke, T., 1989. The 'new politics dimension' in European Green Parties. In: F. Müller-Rommel, ed., *New Politics in Western Europe: The Rise and Success of Green Parties and Alternative Lists*. London and Boulder, CO: Westview Press. pp. 175–194.

Richardson, D., and Rootes, C., 1995. *The Green Challenge: The Development of Green Parties in Europe*. London and New York: Routledge.

Rihoux, B., 2001. *Les partis politiques: Organisations en changement: Le test des écologistes*. Paris: L'Harmattan.

Seiler, D.-L., 1980. *Partis et familles politiques*, Paris: PUF.

Seiler, D.-L., 1999. Comment classer les partis verts en Europe? In: P. Delwit and J.-M. De Waele, eds., *Les partis verts en Europe*. Bruxelles: Complexe. pp. 43–70.

Shamir, M., 1984. Are Western European Party Systems 'Frozen'? *Comparative Political Studies*, 17, pp. 35–79.

Part I
Case studies

1 The Greens in Austria and Switzerland

Two successful opposition parties

Martin Dolezal

Introduction

The Austrian and Swiss Greens belong to the successful members of the Green party family. Since 1979 and 1986 (Switzerland and Austria, respectively), they have been represented in the national parliament. Their vote shares are close to (Switzerland) or even above (Austria) 10 per cent, and they are also represented in several governments at the regional and local levels. However, government participation at the national level has been so far out of reach.

This chapter covers the two parties' electoral, programmatic and organisational developments. As regards the contextual factors that influence these developments, Austria and Switzerland are federal countries whose political elites often follow inclusive strategies towards challengers. Especially in the beginning of their development, the Greens benefited from open political opportunity structures. The central role of direct democracy is a unique feature of Swiss politics, but both countries share other relevant characteristics: Populist radical right parties are extremely strong (McGann and Kitschelt, 2005), and immigration and European integration are major issues for which the Greens and the Populist radical right present genuinely different answers (Kriesi, et al., 2008, 2012).

The main focus of this chapter will be on the two parties that have dominated the Green political spectrum since the late 1980s at the national level: *Die Grünen – Die Grüne Alternative* (Greens) in Austria and the *Grüne – Grüne Partei der Schweiz* (GPS) in Switzerland. Until the 1990s, both had to deal with competing Green parties before they achieved a dominant position. While the Austrians have not experienced any Green challenger since then, their Swiss sister party has been confronted with a relevant splinter party since the mid-2000s, the *Grünliberale Partei Schweiz* (GLP).[1]

The chapter proceeds as follows: it first briefly summarises the origins and development of Green parties in both countries. Subsequently, it deals with the Greens' ideology and policy positions, as well as their organisation. Finally, the chapter discusses some of the main challenges that both parties face in the near and mid-term future.

Origins and development

In Austria, the early development of the Greens until the mid-1980s was characterised by two major and finally successful instances of public protest. In 1978,
opposition against the use of nuclear energy led to the world's first national referendum on this topic. A thin majority (50.5 per cent) voted against bringing into
service an already completed power plant in Zwentendorf, near Vienna. While
at that time opposition to nuclear energy was also tactically directed against the
government led by the Social Democrats (SPÖ), it later turned into a kind of
'state doctrine'. A few years later, in the winter of 1984–1985, protests stopped
the construction of a hydroelectric power station on the Danube near Hainburg,
close to the then Czechoslovak Socialist Republic (now Slovakia). First, the government declared a 'Christmas peace' and postponed further forest clearances;
later, the area became a national park. In the electoral arena, by contrast, the first
Green breakthrough happened in the west of the country. Already in 1977, the
Bürgerliste Salzburg won two seats in the local council.

In 1982, veterans of the antinuclear movement founded first Green party at the
national level: the *Vereinte Grüne Österreichs* (VGÖ). These 'pure Green' reformists were a rare example of a conservative Green party (Poguntke, 1989). A second
party was founded the same year, the *Alternative Liste Österreichs* (ALÖ). Contrary to the VGÖ, this party represented the left-wing and radical part of the Green
movement. However, the relative weakness of new social movements in Austria
severely limited its impact (Dolezal and Hutter, 2007). Because of programmatic
and personal differences, the two parties competed separately in the 1983 national
election (Table 1.1). This division prevented them from gaining parliamentary
representation: had they competed together, they could have won at least five seats
(Haerpfer, 1989).

The protests against the Danube power station and the first successes in regional
elections in which the Greens had combined their forces[2] led to new efforts to
build a common Green candidacy at the national level. In 1985, prominent Green
activists formed a loose organisation called *Bürgerinitiative Parlament* (BIP). In
spring 1986, they nominated Freda Meissner-Blau as candidate for the presidential election. In the first round of this poll, the 59-year old 'Grande Dame' of
Austria's environmental movement won 5.5 per cent of the votes. In the early parliamentary election held in November, Meissner-Blau led a united Green list (*Die
Grüne Alternative – Liste Freda Meissner-Blau*), which was backed by a majority
of both the ALÖ and VGÖ. The Greens won 4.8 per cent and secured 8 out of
183 seats in the *Nationalrat* (Table 1.1). Since then, they have continuously been
represented in parliament. Since 2001, they have also been present in the – largely
irrelevant – second chamber (*Bundesrat*).

Shortly after the 1986 election, a new party was founded: the *Grüne Alternative* (GA). It successfully absorbed the ALÖ (Haerpfer, 1989). However, the
heterogeneity of the Green movement immediately led to struggles in the parliamentary party and to a rival candidacy by the VGÖ in 1990, which again
split the Green vote. Subsequently, the VGÖ moved ever more to the right and
became insignificant. Apart from the conflict with the VGÖ, the first half of the

Table 1.1 Election results in Austria and Switzerland – federal (% votes and N seats)

Austria					Switzerland				
	Die Grünen – Die Grüne Alternative (Grüne)		Other Green/ alternative parties			Grüne Partei der Schweiz (GPS)		Other Green/ alternative parties	
Year	%	Seats (183)	%	Seats (183)	Year	%	Seats (200)	%	Seats (200)
1983	–	–	3.4	0	1975	0.1*	0	1.0	0
1986	4.8	8	0.1	0	1979	0.6*	1	1.9	2
1990	4.8	10	2.0	0	1983	1.9	3	3.2	3
1994	7.3	23	0.1	0	1987	4.9	9	3.7	4
1995	4.8	9	–	–	1991	6.1	14	1.5	1
1999	7.4	14	–	–	1995	5.0	8	1.5	2
2002	9.5	17	–	–	1999	5.0	8	0.3	1
2006	11.1	21	–	–	2003	7.4	13	0.5	1
2008	10.4	20	–	–	2007	9.6	20	1.6	3
2013	12.4	24	–	–	2011	8.4	15	5.4	12

Notes: Others in Austria: 1983 = ALÖ and VGÖ; 1986 = Only regionally based splinter groups in Vienna and Carinthia; 1990, 1994 = VGÖ; Switzerland: * Parties that became founding members of the GFS/GPS in 1983; Others in 1975 = POCH; 1979, 1983, 1987, 1991 = POCH and FGA (Feminist and Green Alternative Groups – umbrella term); 1995, 1999, 2003 = FGA; 2007 = FGA and GLP; 2011 = GLP.

Sources: Federal Ministry of the Interior (Austria); Federal Office of Statistics (Switzerland).

1990s was characterised by important organisational adaptations that turned the Greens into a 'normal' and more professional party and gave it its current name (see below).

The national elections held in 1994 and 1995 already demonstrated a higher professionalisation as the Greens had for the first time a real top candidate: Madeleine Petrovic. In 1990, they had been led by a team of four. After success in 1994 (7.3 per cent), the Greens lost in 1995 (4.8 per cent) because this sudden election was dominated by a strong polarisation between the major parties, the Social Democrats (SPÖ) and the Conservatives (ÖVP). Additionally, the Liberal Forum, a left-libertarian scission from the Populist radical right (FPÖ), proved to be attractive for many potential Green voters (Table 1.1). Petrovic resigned but remained head of the parliamentary party. In a close vote at the subsequent party congress, Christoph Chorherr was elected the new party leader. But he resigned after less than two years due to internal conflicts on the Greens' programmatic orientation (Williams, 2000).

Since the late 1990s, the Greens managed to stabilise under a new party leader, Alexander Van der Bellen. They increased their vote shares in almost every election. In the three most recent polls, they won above 10 per cent (Table 1.1).

While their results have been above the average of European Green parties, government participation at the national level has remained out of reach. In 2002, they held initial talks with the ÖVP, which immediately provoked strong internal opposition from the party's left wing (Lauber, 2003). Nevertheless, in recent elections, the Greens did not rule out a coalition with either the SPÖ or the ÖVP. Given the secular decline of both traditional parties, the Greens' plan for the 2013 election was to join a three-party coalition. But the 'old' parties secured a short majority and finally built another grand coalition, which consigned the Greens again to the opposition benches (Dolezal and Zeglovits, 2014).

Contrary to the national level, the Greens had already participated in several governments at the *Land* level (Table 1.2). They entered a *Land* government for the first time in Tyrol (1994–1999), which then still used a system of 'proportional government' that distributed executive offices among all parties with a certain share of seats in the legislature. Since 2003, the Greens have governed with the ÖVP in Upper Austria (within another 'proportional government'); since 2010, they have been in power with the SPÖ in the city-state of Vienna. After highly successful elections in the first half of 2013, the Greens joined three additional coalitions and were thus represented in five out of nine regional governments (Dolezal, 2014).

Compared to the Austrians, the Swiss Greens do not share a major common or even 'mythical' event such as the above-mentioned referendum on Zwentendorf or the protests in Hainburg (see Table 1.4 at the end of this section). Nevertheless, new social movements were comparatively strong in the 1970s and 1980s, and they had similar close linkages with the Greens (Kriesi, et al., 1995). Overall, the Swiss Greens' history is even more complex than the Austrians' and is heavily influenced by some unique features of Switzerland's political system.

The Greens' development began in the French-speaking part of the country (Seitz, 2008). In 1971, opponents of a planned motorway on the lakefront of Neuchâtel founded the *Mouvement populaire pour l'environnement* and entered the city's assembly in the following year. In 1978, the *Groupement pour la protection de l'environnement* achieved representation in the cantonal legislature of Vaud where one year later Daniel Brélaz was elected into the *Nationalrat* (Ladner, 1989). He was the first Green representative in a national parliament worldwide.[3] Since then, 'moderate' Greens have been represented in parliament; since 2007 also in its equally important second chamber (*Ständerat*) (Table 1.1).

In 1983, thus one year after Austria, two parties were founded at the national level: the moderate *Föderation der grünen Parteien der Schweiz* (GFS) and the more radical *Grüne Alternative Schweiz* (GRAS). In addition, the radical left *Progressive Organisationen der Schweiz* (POCH) mobilised on ecological matters (Ladner, 1989). This split of the Green movement resembled the situation in Austria, but because of a lower threshold of representation,[4] the GFS nevertheless secured three seats in the 1983 national elections by winning just 1.9 per cent of the votes. In 1987, both parties ran again separately. The moderate Greens had renamed themselves into the *Grüne Partei der Schweiz* (GPS); the radicals operated as *Grünes Bündnis Schweiz* (GBS). Both parties managed to (re)enter parliament.

In the 1990s, the GPS became the dominant Green party in Switzerland. All cantonal organisations of the alternative Greens were integrated step by step into

Table 1.2 Government experience at the *Land* level in Austria

Land	Period	Type of government	Parties in government	Green member(s)	Portfolio(s)
Carinthia	2013–	Proportional	SPÖ-ÖVP-Greens & [FPÖ, Team Stronach]	Rolf Holub	Environment/ energy/public transport
Salzburg	2013–	Majority	ÖVP-Greens-Team Stronach	Astrid Rössler	Environment/ planning
				Martina Berthold	Science/family/ women/ integration
				Heinrich Schellhorn	Welfare/culture
Tyrol	1994– 1999	Proportional	ÖVP & [SPÖ, FPÖ, Greens]	Eva Lichtenberger	Environment
	2013–	Majority	ÖVP-Greens	Ingrid Felipe	Environment/ transport
				Christine Baur	Welfare/women
Upper Austria	2003– 2009	Proportional	ÖVP-Greens & [SPÖ]	Rudi Anschober	Environment
	2009–	Proportional	ÖVP-Greens & [SPÖ, FPÖ]	Rudi Anschober	Environment
Vienna	2010–	Majority*	SPÖ-Greens	Maria Vassilakou	Planning/ environment/ participation

Notes:
Parties: SPÖ, ÖVP, FPÖ, Team Stronach (populist).
Period: The legislative period lasts five years; in Upper Austria, six.
Type of government: Apart from Vorarlberg and Vienna, executive offices at the *Land* level were tra-ditionally distributed among all relevant parties represented in the legislature. Since the 1990s, these 'proportional' governments were replaced by majority governments in Tyrol and Salzburg.
Parties in government: Parties in square brackets are automatically included in 'proportional govern-ments' but do not belong to the *de facto* coalition built by some of the government parties. In Tyrol 1994–1999, the ÖVP had an absolute majority.
Portfolios: The titles of the portfolios are not official and summarise various offices and competences.
* This only refers to 'Executive City Councillors', thus to councillors with a portfolio. Because Vienna is also a municipality for which the system of 'proportional government' is recommended by the fed-eral constitution there are additional members without a portfolio. The Greens had one such councillor from 1991–1996, 1996–2001 and 2001–2005 and two such councillors from 2005–2010.

Sources: Jordan (2013) and websites of *Land* governments. Reference date: 31 December 2013

the federal party in a long process that had already started with the *Demokratische Alternative Bern* in 1985 (Seitz, 2008) and that finally ended with the canton of Zug in 2009 (Grüne/Les Verts, 2013b). In the beginning of 2014, the GPS was present in 24 out of 26 cantons.[5] The incorporation of the alternative branches changed the Greens' profile and moved the party towards the left. In the 1980s, by contrast, the GPS was dominated by moderate 'conservationists' and thus rather resembled the Austrian VGÖ (Poguntke, 1989).

Although parliamentary representation at the national level was secured, no real electoral breakthrough occurred in the 1990s. Additionally, government participation was – and still is – out of reach. In 1993, a party conference declared a basic commitment to join the *Bundesrat*, the federal executive. In advance of the 1995 election, the GPS advocated the building of a centre-left government. However, involvement in government would require a break with Switzerland's tradition of consociationalism according to which the same four parties have always formed the government since 1959.[6] Both in 2003 and in 2007, the GPS presented candidates but withdrew them before the actual election of the members of the *Bundesrat* by a joint session of the two chambers (*Vereinigte Bundesversammlung*). In the most recent election of 2011, the Greens experienced a drop to 8.4 per cent (−1.2 per cent), which put a damper on their governmental ambitions.

Nevertheless, like their Austrian sister party, the GPS has entered several governments at the cantonal level (Table 1.3). Here, the Swiss Greens operate in a specific political context because the members of these executives are directly elected by the people. In 1986, two Green candidates were elected into the government of Bern, which then consisted of nine *Regierungsräte* (Ladner, 1989); nowadays, most cantons elect seven executive offices. In 2013, the Greens were represented in 9 out of 26 cantonal governments.

Table 1.3 Government experience at the cantonal level in Switzerland

Canton	Election	Period	Seats (total)	Name (portfolio)	Name (portfolio)
Aargau	30 November 2008	2009–2012	1 (5)	Susanne Hochuli (health & social affairs)	
	21 October 2012	2013–2016	1 (5)	Susanne Hochuli (health & social affairs)	
Basel-Stadt	28 November 2004	2005–2008	1 (7)	Guy Morin (justice)	
	14 September 2008	2009–2013	1 (7)	Guy Morin (president of government)	
	28 October 2012	2013–2017	1 (7)	Guy Morin (president of government)	
Basel-Landschaft	27 March 2011	2011–2015	1 (5)	Isaac Reber (security)	
Bern	11 May 1986	1986–1990	2 (9)	Benjamin Hofstetter (police)	Leni Robert (education)
	9 April 2006	2006–2010	1 (7)	Bernhard Pulver (education)	
	28 March 2010	2010–2014	1 (7)	Bernhard Pulver (education)	

Canton	Election	Period	Seats (total)	Name (portfolio)	Name (portfolio)
Fribourg	4 December 2011	2012–2016	1 (7)	Marie Garnier (institutions & agriculture)	
Geneva	16 November 1997	1997–2001	1 (7)	Robert Cramer (interior, agriculture, environment, energy)	
	11 November 2001	2001–2005	1 (7)	Robert Cramer (interior, agriculture, environment)	
	13 November 2005	2005–2009	2 (7)	Robert Cramer (regional planning)	David Hiler (finances)
	15 November 2009	2009–2013	2 (7)	David Hiler (finances)	Michèle Künzler (interior, mobility, environment)
	10 November 2013	2013–2018	1 (7)	Antonio Hodgers (regional planning, housing, energy)	
Neuchâtel	10 April 2005	2005–2009	1 (5)	Fernand Cuche (regional planning)	
Nidwalden	15 March 1998	1998–2002	1 (7)	Leo Odermatt (health and social affairs)	
	3 March 2002	2002–2006	1 (7)	Leo Odermatt (health and social affairs)	
	26 March 2006	2006–2010	1 (7)	Leo Odermatt (health and social affairs)	
Schaffhausen	25 August 1996	1997–2000	0–1 (5)	Herbert Bühl (health, social affairs, environment)	
	27 August 2000	2001–2004	1 (5)	Herbert Bühl (health, social affairs, environment)	
Vaud	20 March 1994	1994–1998	1 (7)	Philippe Biéler (security, environment)	
	15 March 1998	1998–2003	1 (7)	Philippe Biéler (infrastructure, personnel)	

(Continued)

Table 1.3 (Continued)

Canton	Election	Period	Seats (total)	Name (portfolio)	Name (portfolio)
	30 November 2003	2003–2007	1 (7)	Francois Marthaler (infrastructure, personnel)	
	1 April 2007	2007–2012	1–2 (7)	Francois Marthaler (infrastructure, personnel)	Béatrice Métraux (interior)
	1 April 2012	2012–2017	1 (7)	Béatrice Métraux (interior)	
Zug	11 November 1990	1991–1994	1 (7)	Hanspeter Uster (justice, police)	
	13 November 1994	1995–1998	1 (7)	Hanspeter Uster (justice, police)	
	25 October 1998	1999–2002	1 (7)	Hanspeter Uster (security)	
	27 October 2002	2003–2006	1 (7)	Hanspeter Uster (security)	
	29 October 2006	2007–2010	2 (7)	Patrick Cotti (education, culture)	Manuela Weichelt-Picard (interior)
	3 October 2010	2011–2014	1 (7)	Manuela Weichelt-Picard (interior)	
Zurich	2 April 1995	1995–1999	1 (7)	Verena Diener (health)	
	18 April 1999	1999–2003	1 (7)	Verena Diener (health)	
	6 April 2003	2003–2007	1–0 (7)	Verena Diener (health)	
	3 April 2011	2011–2015	1 (7)	Martin Graf (justice, interior)	

Notes: This summary only refers to the GPS and affiliated groups; some of them only later joined the GPS.

Period: Legislative periods are fixed. The election takes place either in the first year of the period or in the year before.

Seats: The size of the executive is fixed.

Name (portfolios): Council members are directly elected by the people. The portfolios refer to the beginning of the period.

Neuchâtel: Cuche, like all other candidates, did not win the required majority. Two days after the election the parties agreed upon a 'silent election' and withdrew all but the five strongest candidates.

Schaffhausen, 1997–2000: Bühl won a by-election (26 September 1999).

Vaud, 2007–2012: Métraux won a by-election (18 December 2011).

Zurich, 2003–2007: In 2004, Diener changed her affiliation to the Green Liberals.

Source: Grüne/Les Verts (2013a; 2013b), Federal Office of Statistics, websites of cantonal governments, literature cited in chapter, media reports. Reference date: 31 December 2013.

Direct democracy, another Swiss peculiarity, influenced the Greens' development too. The GPS was initially rather 'timid' in its strategic use of direct democratic procedures (Church, 1995) not least because launching initiatives or referenda, for which signatures have to be collected, requires resources. The GPS initiated its first referendum on its own only in 1991. It was directed against the building of a huge system of railway tunnels through the Alps. In 1993, the GPS launched its first initiatives: One demanded a shift of taxation from labour to energy, the other a more flexible pension age. However, all three efforts were subsequently declined by the electorate (Zürcher, 2008). Apart from these 'own' efforts, the Greens have also been expected to recommend how their supporters should decide on other votes. From 1983 to 2007, the GPS had to decide on 217 of such *Parolen*. Because of their internal heterogeneity, the Greens were less able than other parties to decide and recommended a 'free vote' in 13 cases (Zürcher, 2008). From 2008 to 2013, the party had to decide on 49 cases and failed to do so in 2: in 2010, on the regulation of research on humans and, in 2012, on a social security issue.[7]

Contrary to the Austrian Greens, the GPS could not maintain its status as the only relevant Green party at the national level. In 2004, some members of the Zurich branch who had criticised the left turn of the party formed a new one,

Table 1.4 Chronology of the main developments of Green parties in Austria and Switzerland

Austria		Switzerland	
1982	VGÖ and ALÖ founded	1979	Daniel Brélaz elected into national parliament (first Green worldwide)
1983	VGÖ and ALÖ fail to enter national parliament	1983	GFS and GRAS founded
1986	A united Green list wins first seats in national parliament		GFS wins three seats in national parliament
1987	*Grüne Alternative* founded	1986	GFS renamed GPS
1992	Major reform of party organisation	1993	GPS renamed: *Grüne – Grüne Partei der Schweiz*
1993	Party renamed: *Die Grünen – Die Grüne Alternative*	2007	Green Liberals (GLP) founded
2001	First Green seat in *Bundesrat* (second chamber)*		GPS wins two seats in *Ständerat* (second chamber), GLP one**
2002	Unsuccessful coalition negotiations with ÖVP		

Notes:
* The members of the *Bundesrat* are delegated by the nine *Land* parliaments. After the 2001 election in Vienna, the Greens received one of this *Land*'s 11 seats.
** The members of the *Ständerat* are directly elected; each canton elects two representatives. In 2007, GPS candidates won in Geneva and Vaud, two French-speaking cantons. The GLP candidate won in Zurich.

Source: Author's own compilation.

the *Grün-Liberale Zürich* (GLiZ), which combined ecological stances with market liberal positions. Initially, they wanted to become a member of the GPS, which is possible as the party statutes allow for more than one party per canton. But, the GPS rejected an immediate accession and proposed – backed by the party statutes – a one-year observer status. Additionally, it also criticised a lack of programmatic clarity. The GLiZ responded by cancelling its application in 2005. Consequently, the *Grünliberale Partei* (GLP) was established in several cantons and became a national party in 2007 when it also entered the national parliament (Ladner, 2012; Seitz, 2013). In the 2011 election, the liberal Greens achieved 5.4 per cent of the votes, against 8.4 per cent for the GPS. At the beginning of 2014, the GLP had 18 cantonal sections, but it was not represented in any government. With respect to parliamentary representation at the cantonal level, the GLP is also weaker than the GPS: in March 2014, the liberal Greens were represented in 14 out of 26 cantons;[8] the GPS in 22. The Austrian Greens, by contrast, have been represented in all nine regional parliaments since 2004.

Ideology and policy positions

As a matter of fact, for the Austrian and Swiss Greens, ecological concerns are the core feature of their programmatic basis; these issues also highly motivate their voters (Dolezal, 2010). Opposition to nuclear energy has been especially important in both countries: Swiss voters decided on several occasions on this topic, but only in 1990 did an antinuclear majority emerge, deciding on a ten-year moratorium on the building of new stations. After the disaster of Fukushima in 2011, the government proposed a slow phase-out, but so far no final decision has been reached. In Austria, the electorate had already done so in a 1978 referendum. As a consequence, the Greens directed their efforts against stations in neighbouring countries.

In terms of their general ideological position, both parties have often tried to define themselves beyond 'old' politics. In its statutes, the GPS even declares to aim for 'overcoming the traditional left–right-scheme' (Grüne/Les Verts, 2014, §3.1.). Nevertheless, both parties are clearly situated at the left side of the political spectrum. The expert survey by Benoit and Laver (2006) puts the Austrian Greens at 5.4 and the Swiss at 4.2 on a scale from 1 (left) to 20 (right). The Austrians were placed as the most leftist party in their system, the Swiss were placed to the right of the communist PdA (Dolezal, 2008).[9] The most recent Chapel Hill expert survey from 2010 used a shorter scale (from 0 to 10) and placed the Austrian Greens at 2.3, the GPS at 1.9 and the GLP at 5.3 (Bakker, et al., 2015). According to the experts, the liberal Greens are thus situated in the centre of the Swiss party system, far away from the GPS.

To examine the Greens' programme beyond their general left–right position, content analyses of election manifestos are a valuable source. They are especially suited to assess the saliency of environmental matters and thus to test the 'single issue' hypothesis. While the Austrians also agreed upon a comprehensive basic

Table 1.5 Green election manifestos: Saliency of major policy areas in three decades (%)

	Decade	ENV	ECO	WEL	EUR	INT	CUL	DEMO	LST	OTH
A	1980s	21.7	13.1	13.0	0.1	4.8	3.0	18.6	15.0	10.7
	1990s	19.0	14.3	13.4	3.8	5.0	0.6	14.2	14.0	15.7
	2000s	13.2	17.1	18.8	5.4	6.9	10.8	9.4	13.7	4.7
	All years	17.5	15.1	15.3	3.5	5.7	5.0	13.5	14.1	9.7
	Other parties	6.3	26.5	13.5	2.8	5.5	7.5	7.6	16.3	12.1
CH	1980s	36.8	8.8	14.7	0.0	10.3	0.0	10.3	16.2	2.9
	1990s	21.7	8.3	17.8	3.6	11.3	3.9	11.0	14.6	7.8
	2000s	38.8	17.5	16.1	1.7	7.8	0.8	7.2	6.8	2.1
	All years	29.9	11.4	16.7	2.4	10.0	2.2	9.6	12.2	4.2
	Other parties	7.1	26.0	12.9	2.8	6.8	5.0	9.5	18.9	8.9

Notes: Elections included: Austria in 1986, 1990, 1994, 1995, 1999, 2002, 2006, 2008; Switzerland in 1987, 1991, 1995, 1999, 2003, 2007. Other parties: The percentages are based on the weighted (by vote share) issue saliencies attributed by all other parties since 1986 (Austria) and 1987 (Switzerland), respectively.

The aggregation of categories was done by the author: ENV = environment (416, 501), ECO = economy (401–415, 701–704), WEL = welfare (503–505), EUR = Europe (108, 110), INT = international (101–107, 109), CUL = culture and education (502, 506, 507), DEMO = democracy (201–204, 301, 302), LST = lifestyle (601–608, 705, 706), OTH = others (303–305). A = Austria, CH = Switzerland.

Source: Volkens, et al., 2013.

programme in 2001 (*Grünes Grundsatzprogramm*) (Dachs, 2006), the Swiss only produced a short *Manifest* in 2002. The *Programmplattform* of 1991, which was then interpreted as an initial point for further discussions, was never extended into a comprehensive basic programme. Using data collected by the manifesto project, Table 1.5 compares the saliency of various policy areas in election manifestos.

Both parties strongly emphasise environmental issues. Especially the Swiss, but also the Austrian Greens are high above the average saliency that the other parties attribute to this topic. In the 2000s, almost 40 per cent of the GPS manifestos dealt with environmental matters, far more than those of the Austrian Greens. With respect to the 'old politics' of socio-economic issues, both parties refer less to economic policies than their competitors. The saliency of welfare, by contrast, is above the other parties' manifestos.

New cultural issues such as immigration and European integration are of crucial importance in both countries (Kriesi, et al., 2008, 2012). In this dimension of conflict, the Greens vehemently oppose the Populist radical right, in Austria primarily the FPÖ, in Switzerland the Swiss People's Party (SVP). While, unfortunately, immigration issues are not well captured by this data source, Table 1.5 shows that the Austrian Greens give more room to European issues than their competitors. Austria joined the European Union (EU) in 1995; Switzerland is a nonmember but strongly integrated through a system of bilateral treaties. Originally, both Green parties were Eurosceptic and declined accession, which they interpreted as a threat to their countries' standards in environmental policies, its status of neutrality and – in Switzerland – to direct democratic rights.

In advance of the Austrian accession referendum in June 1994, a party congress recommended a 'no' by an overwhelming 87.3 per cent of the delegates' votes. However, some prominent Greens announced to vote against the party's official course. While the electorate supported accession by a clear two-thirds majority, about 60 per cent of the Green supporters followed their party and declined Austria's accession (Pelinka and Greiderer, 1996). Nevertheless, the Green representatives in the national parliament argued for accepting the people's mandate and supported accession in a concluding vote in the legislature (Fallend, 2008). Since the mid-1990s, the Greens' position towards the EU has dramatically changed. They gradually discovered the advantages of European integration and even became its strongest supporters in the 2000s. Figure 1.1, which is based on several expert surveys, mirrors this dramatic policy change over a quarter century.

Figure 1.1 shows that the Austrian Greens were not the only ones who changed their position: the Swiss Greens also abandoned their Eurosceptic stances (Seitz, 2008).[10] In 1990, a party conference passed a resolution that criticised the then European Community as a threat to the environment and as a centralistic institution; a 'Europe of Regions' was propagated as alternative. One year later, the party demanded an end of the negotiations to join the European Economic Area (EEA). In addition, the GPS rejected an eventual EC-membership application. These positions, however, were not uniformly supported. At a party conference in 1992, in which the GPS had to decide their recommendation for the EEA referendum, representatives of the French-speaking cantons advocated a 'yes' vote. Thanks

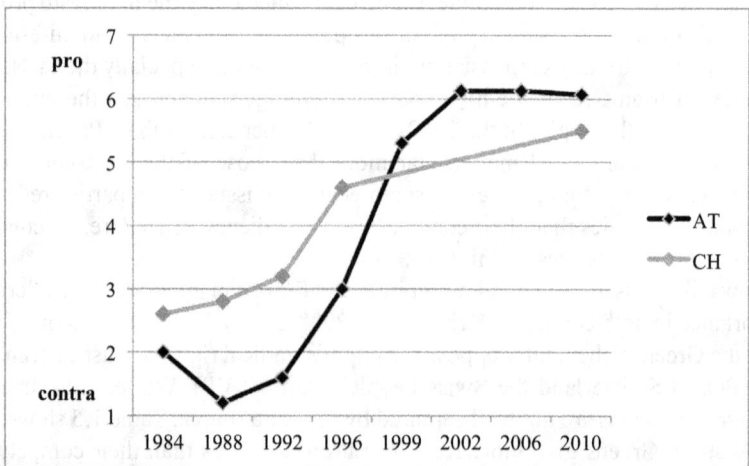

Figure 1.1 The changing positions of the Greens towards European integration, 1984–2010
Source: Expert surveys from Ray, 1999; Bakker, et al., 2015.

to the numerical power of the German-speaking cantonal parties, the delegates decided with 82:30 to recommend a 'no' vote. Nevertheless, the French-speaking Greens capitalised on their autonomy and stuck to their dissenting opinion in the actual campaign. The famous *Röstigraben*, the conflict between the German- and French-speaking parts of the country named after a typical meal, reignited also within the GPS (Seitz, 2008).

After the Swiss electorate had rejected the EEA, the GPS dramatically changed its policy position and argued in favour of Switzerland's accession to the EU. Consequently, the Greens supported the *Ja zu Europa* initiative in 2001, which demanded immediate access negotiations. However, this initiative was defeated by two-thirds of the people and all cantons. Because the electorate rejected full membership, the Greens supported the government's alternative strategy to negotiate a system of bilateral treaties even though they still favour Swiss accession.[11] In all referenda, the GPS backed the bilateral treaties and was also in line with a majority of the voters. In February 2014, the GPS opposed the SVP's successful initiative *Gegen Masseneinwanderung* (against mass migration), which endangered Switzerland's relations with the EU.

Both parties followed the overall pro-European turn of the Green party family and they rearranged their positions towards the attitudes of their own voters who had become pro-European after the mid-1990s. In both countries, the Green Eurosceptics were confronted with the same dilemma: the Populist radical right parties dominate the negative discourse of the EU, and the prevalence of identity-related arguments does not leave much room for a genuine Green critique (Höglinger, et al., 2012).

Structure and organisation

Especially in the 1980s – and most prominently in Germany (Poguntke, 1993) – Green parties have defined themselves by new organisational principles and practices. A system of 'grassroots democracy' should differentiate them from the established parties. However, when analysing their organisational development, the national context is also an important factor.

First, the two countries fundamentally differ with respect to the role of parties. In Austria, parties are extremely strong and well-funded political actors; the Greens almost exclusively depend on subventions from the state (Sickinger, 2009). Swiss parties are comparatively weaker (Ladner, 2014). Because they do not receive public funding – only parliamentary groups get subsidies – their organisations are much smaller and less professional. In the most recent national elections, for example, the Austrian Greens spent about 3 million Euros, the Swiss only about 0.8 million Euros.[12] A further example is the size of the parties' federal headquarters: in March 2014, the GPS had 7 full-time positions (and 10 employees), the Austrians had 11 (and 14 employees).[13]

In addition, the different degrees of federalism in the two countries influence the organisation of the parties. The Austrian party statutes (Die Grünen/Die Grüne Alternative, 2012) define the regional party organisations as being autonomous 'within their realm' (§13.1). The GPS, by contrast, operates in an extremely decentralised political system and defines itself as 'a federation of groups, movements and political parties which act at the cantonal level' (Grüne/Les Verts, 2014, §1.2). As mentioned above, the GPS even, allows for more than one member party per canton (§4.1.2); in February 2014, there were three cantons where the GPS had two members.[14] The Austrian Greens' structure, by contrast, resembles the state structure, which is why there are nine *Land* parties.

Main party structures

Since the foundation of the Austrian Greens in 1987, the *Bundeskongress* (federal congress) has been the party's highest decision-making body. According to the current statutes (Die Grünen/Die Grüne Alternative, 2012), the *Bundeskongress* meets at least once a year. It is composed of delegates from the *Land* parties plus representatives of ethnic minorities.[15] Since the major party reform of 1992 (see below), Green members of legislatures and executives as well as from the party executives have voting rights. Apart from electing the party executive and deciding on major policy and organisational changes, the *Bundeskongress* plays an important role in the selection of candidates for national[16] and European elections. Contrary to other Austrian parties, there is very often an actual competition for list positions. Only the top candidate is normally appointed in advance and thus faces no challenger in the formal nomination process. Nevertheless, this candidate has also to be elected – or at least confirmed – by a secret vote.

The *Bundesvorstand* (federal executive committee) runs the daily business of the party. Until 1992, there were two *Bundesgeschäftsführer* (federal party managers) as party spokespersons, one of them responsible for 'external affairs'. However, due to strong incompatibility rules regarding public and party offices, the Greens' public face was rather the head of the parliamentary party who was not allowed to be a member of the *Bundesvorstand,* as in the case of all public office holders. A major reform in 1992 abandoned these incompatibility rules and introduced a nominal party leader, officially called 'speaker of the federal executive committee' (*Bundessprecher* or *Sprecher des Bundesvorstands*). Additionally, the former *Bundesausschuss* (federal committee), in which all nine *Land* parties and the ethnic minorities were equally represented, was replaced by a new organ called *Erweiterter Bundesvorstand* (extended federal executive committee). More professional politicians are represented in this new intermediate organ. In 1993, the party also changed its name from *Grüne Alternative* to *Die Grünen – Die Grüne Alternative* (Frankland, 1995; Lauber, 2008).

Organisational matters have generated fewer debates in Switzerland. The GPS does not fundamentally differ from other Swiss parties with respect to the low degree of professionalisation and the highly decentralised structures (Ladner and Brändle, 2008). For a long time, the GPS' organisation was hardly formalised (Ladner, 2012). However, this might have changed after a complete revision of the party statutes in January 2014 (Grüne/Les Verts, 2014) – which was unanimously supported by a concluding vote at a party conference.[17]

The GPS' *Delegiertenversammlung* is the highest decision-making body. According to the current statutes, it meets at least thrice a year (§6.2.1), thus more frequently than the Austrian party conference. As in the Austrian case, the Swiss *Delegiertenversammlung* consists, not only of delegates of the cantonal parties but also includes, amongst others, all Green members of cantonal executives and the national legislature. Contrary to the Austrian Greens, the *Delegiertenversammlung* does not decide on candidates, as there is none of them at the national level. However, the conference is responsible for the election manifesto. A very important task is to decide on *Parolen*, recommendations for direct democratic votes. Media reports on *Delegiertenversammlungen* usually focus only on this topic. Until 2014, decisions on *Parolen* and other important topics required a double majority of delegates and cantons. This resembled the decision-making process in the direct democratic arena in which a majority of both the people (*Volk*) and cantons (*Stände*) is required for constitutional amendments (Ladner and Brändle, 2008). In addition, the *Delegiertenversammlung* also elects the party leaders, the members of the *Präsidium* (see below). Until 1989, they were elected by the *Ausschuss*, a committee in which all members of the party federation had one seat and were thus equally represented. Since then, the statutes give more weight to the bigger cantons.

Apart from the *Präsidium,* the day-to-day business is run by the small *Geschäftsleitung* (directorate), which includes the *Präsidium*, the head of the parliamentary party and a general secretary. Similar to the *Erweiterter Bundesvorstand* in Austria, the GPS' *Vorstand* (executive committee) includes the members of the *Geschäftsleitung*, representatives from all cantonal parties and representatives from additional groups (for example, the party's youth organisation).

Coming back to organisational principles, gender parity has always been an important matter for many Green parties. The Austrian Greens have developed very strict rules demanding a minimum share of 50 per cent of women in all elected organs and functions (§7.3). In 1996, the GPS decided a 40 per cent quota for women in the *Vorstand* (old statutes §7.1) but later relaxed this rule and nowadays refers to 'seeking to achieve a just gender distribution' (§7.3.2). Additionally, the cantonal parties are asked to seek such a 'just representation' in party offices and on lists of candidates (§4.1.6). Table 1.6 shows the share of women in party offices as well as in the parliamentary parties in March 2014.

Even though the Swiss party statutes are not as strict as the Austrian ones, this does not result in a weaker representation of women. Figures presented in Table 1.6 show that the presence of women is equally strong in both parties. Comparative data for party offices are hardly available, but with respect to the representation of women in parliament, both Green parties are clearly above the national shares. In March 2014, the proportion of female representatives in Austria was 32.2 per cent (29.5 per cent in the second chamber) and 31.0 per cent in Switzerland (19.6 per cent). While the Austrian Greens had the highest share of women in both chambers, the Swiss Greens were shortly behind the Social Democrats who had a 50 per cent share in the first chamber.[18] However, the two Green parties differ in the representation of women in regional executives. The Austrian Greens placed six

Table 1.6 Representation of women in party organisation and parliamentary party (March 2014)

Party-	Austria			Switzerland		
		% women	Total		% women	Total
Leader(s)	Bundessprecher	100.0	1	Co-Präsidium	100.0	2
	Stellvertretender Bundessprecher	100.0	1	Vize-Präsidium	25.0	4
Executive	Bundesvorstand	50.0	14	Geschäftsleitung	50.0	8
	Erweiterter Bundesvorstand*	54.8	31	Vorstand**	60.4	48
Parliament						
1st Chamber	Nationalrat	54.2	24	Nationalrat	46.7	15
2nd Chamber	Bundesrat	50.0	4	Ständerat	0.0	2

Note:
* If four co-opted members are included, the share of women increases to 57%;
** When this research was carried out, the seat of the cantonal party of Zug was vacant.

Sources: Websites of parties (www.gruene.at; www.gruene.ch); author's own data.

women in the ten positions they have had since 1994, whereas the share of women in Switzerland was far lower. In 41 Green victories, women won the executive office in only 12 cases (29.3 per cent). This 'deficit in representation' has been a topic within the GPS (Schneider, 2008, p. 161). However, research has shown that female candidates are in general less successful in majority elections (McAllister and Studlar, 2002).

Party leadership

The introduction of the office of *Bundessprecher* in 1992 and the abandonment of former incompatibility rules has led to a much stronger leadership in the Austrian Greens. The speaker is elected by the *Bundeskongress* for a two-year term, and re-elections are possible. Petrovic, the most prominent Green politician in the mid-1990s, was the first to combine party leadership (1994–1996) with leadership of the parliamentary party (1992–1999) and set a precedent (Table 1.7). Van der Bellen led both offices for nine years; his successor Eva Glawischnig assumed both from the very beginning of her term. Contrary to the elections of the *Bundesgeschäftsführer* before 1992, only 2 of the so far 13 elections of party speaker were actually competitive: both in 1992 and in 1996, the 'reformer' beat the 'functionary'. Petrovic (1994), Van der Bellen (1997–2008) and Glawischnig (since 2009), by contrast, were always elected without (formal) challengers.

The Swiss Greens have always had a *Parteipräsidium*. Interestingly, the party conference is free to elect either one president or two co-presidents for a two-year

Table 1.7 Party leaders in Austria (1987–2013)

Office(s)	Date of (re-)election	Candidates	Mode of election (always at party conference)	Round	Result (%)	(Re-)elected	Date of resignation	Years in office	Reason for resignation
2 Bundes-geschäfts führer (federal party managers)	15 February 1987	5	Majority, delegates have two votes	1st	57.7	Werner Haslauer	15.05.1988	1.2	End of term
					57.7	Manfred Stadlmann			—
	15 May 1988	4	Plurality, separate vote for each office	1st	65.7	Johannes Voggenhuber	09.12.1990	2.6	End of term
				2nd	42.4	Pius Strobl			End of term
	9 December 1990	6	Majority, separate vote for each office	2nd	51.8	Franz Floss	11.10.1992	1.8	End of term
				3rd	57.3	Franz Renkin			End of term
Sprecher des Bundes vorstands (Speaker of the federal party executive)	11 October 1992	2	Majority	1st	65.6	Peter Pilz	20.11.1994	2.1	End of term
	20 November 1994	1	Majority	1st	83.5	Madeleine Petrovic	31.03.1996	1.4	Election result
	31 March 1996	2	Majority	1st	51.3	Christoph Chorherr	13.12.1997	1.7	Various internal conflicts
	13 December 1997	1	Majority	1st	82.3	Alexander Van der Bellen			
	22 January 2000	1	Majority	1st	83.7	Alexander Van der Bellen			

(Continued)

Table 1.7 (Continued)

Office(s)	Date of (re-)election	Candidates	Mode of election (always at party conference)	Round	Result (%)	(Re-)elected	Date of resignation	Years in office	Reason for resignation
	20 January 2002	1	Majority	1st	90.5	Alexander Van der Bellen			
	24 January 2004	1	Majority	1st	83.6	Alexander Van der Bellen			
	4 March 2006	1	Majority	1st	86.7	Alexander Van der Bellen			
	4 May 2008	1	Majority	1st	80.7	Alexander Van der Bellen	03.10.2008	10.8	Election result
	3 October 2008	–			–	Eva Glawischnig			
	17 January 2009	1	Majority	1st	97.4	Eva Glawischnig			
	11 September 2010	1	Majority	1st	96.0	Eva Glawischnig			
	1 December 2012	1	Majority	1st	93.4	Eva Glawischnig	(In office)	(5.2)	

Notes: Reason for resignation: Except for 'end of term', these are assessments based on media reports. 1987: Stadlmann resigned shortly after his election because the party had to reduce the compensation for this office. Mode of election 1988: The candidates first had to stand for a 'vote of confidence', which all four won unanimously; 1990: All six candidates ran for the party manager responsible for 'external affairs'. Floss won a head-off against Renkin, who was subsequently elected party manager for 'internal' affairs; 2008: Glawischnig first became acting speaker of the party executive before she was officially elected at the party conference in January 2009. Reference date: 31 December 2013.

Source: Minutes of the *Bundeskongress* (party conference); media reports.

period. Also the candidates can decide whether they run for president or co-president (and, in the latter case, also with whom they prefer to collaborate). The current statutes allow for three re-elections (§9.3.3) so that a (co-)president might theoretically be in office for eight years. In elections with only one (team of) candidate(s), the *Delegiertenversammlung* often did not conduct a proper election but decided 'by acclamation'. The new party statutes, by contrast, demand an election by ballot (§6.10).

Most of the GPS leadership elections were not competitive, as in Austria (Table 1.8). Open contests happened only twice: first, in 1997, after the resignation of Hanspeter Thür, when the election of Ruedi Baumann, who beat two rivals, affirmed the pragmatic and especially pro-European course of the GPS (Seitz, 2008). Second, after the disappointing election of 2011, when five candidates ran for office in April 2012. With Regula Rytz and Adèle Thorens, the delegates elected two female co-presidents who represented both major languages. Contrary to Austria, the offices of party president and head of the parliamentary party have always been led by different persons even though no specific rule exists in the statutes. This gives the president a weaker role than his Austrian counterpart. In addition, the Swiss electoral system reduces the personalisation of Green politics, as there is no top candidate at the national level.

Party members

Austria and Switzerland strongly differ with respect to the number of party members. In the late 2000s, no less than 17 per cent of the Austrian electorate were party members; in Switzerland, about five per cent (Van Biezen, et al., 2012). Unfortunately, little systematic information on Green party members exists, especially for Austria. Meaningful membership figures are available only for the 2000s onwards; for earlier years, we can only rely on estimates (Table 1.9). The Austrian Greens organise only about 1 per cent of their electorate with currently about 6,000 members. Since 2012, the party publishes figures on the gender of their members, who are disproportionally male. About 60 per cent of Green voters, by contrast, are female (Johann, et al., 2014). We know less about the attitudes and activities of the members. Based on a survey among party members, Müller and Stefou (2003) found a comparatively strong support for Europe and a belief in the government's capacity to solve (economic) problems.[19]

Membership figures for Switzerland are equally difficult to collect. Official figures are available since 2003; the numbers for earlier years are rough estimates or are based on surveys of local parties. In 2013, the GPS had about 7,000 members, thus about 1,000 more than the Austrian Greens which contradicts the country differences mentioned above. The Swiss thus organise a much larger share of their voters: almost 4 per cent in 2011. Thanks to surveys of local party organisations, some information is available on the profiles of Green members. Between 1990 and 2003, the Greens became significantly older and ideologically more oriented towards the left (Ladner and Brändle, 2008).

Table 1.8 Party leaders in Switzerland (1983–2013)

Office(s)	Date of (re-)election	Candidates	Mode of election (by Ausschuss, since 1990 Delegiertenversammlung)	Round	Result (%)	(Re-)elected	Date of resignation	Years in office	Reason for resignation
President	28 May 1983					Laurent Rebeaud	16.11.1985	2.5	End of term
	6 November 1985					Monica Zingg	18.12.1986	1.1	Internal conflict
	17 January 1987		[Interim]			Laurent Rebeaud	21.03.1987	0.2	[Interim leader]
	21 March 1987	1				Peter Schmid			
	29 April 1989	1				Peter Schmid	27.10.1990	3.6	End of term
	27 October 1990	1				Irène Gardiol	10.10.1992	2.0	End of term
	10 October 1992	1		1st	100	Verena Diener	01.07.1995	2.7	Elected into Zurich executive
	1 July 1995					Hanspeter Thür	25.10.1997	2.3	Internal conflict
	25 October 1997	3	Majority required	1st	59.3	Ruedi Baumann			
	5 February 2000	1	Per acclamation			Ruedi Baumann	27.10.2001	4.0	Personal reason (moved to France)
2 Co-presidents	27 October 2001	2			100	Patrice Mugny / Ruth Genner	10.01.2004	2.2	Elected into Geneva executive

Office	Date		Method		%	Elected	Until	Years
President	10 January 2004	1	Per acclamation			Ruth Genner		
	4 March 2006	1				Ruth Genner	26.04.2008	7.2
	26 April 2008	1				Ueli Leuenberger		
	8 May 2010	1			100	Ueli Leuenberger	21.04.2012	4.0
2 Co-presidents	21 April 2012	5	Delegates have two votes	1st	58.3	Regula Rytz	(In office)	(1.7)
					83.9	Adèle Thorens	(In office)	(1.7)

Notes: 1989: Schmid was re-elected 'without dissenting votes but with some abstentions' (*Neue Zürcher Zeitung*, 2 May 1989, p. 19); 2006: Genner was re-elected with one dissenting vote; years in office include her years as co-president; 2008: Leuenberger was elected 'by a large majority'; 2012: Percentages are based on the 218 delegates present. Reference date is 31 December 2013.

Source: Grüne/Les Verts (2013a); minutes of the *Delegiertenversammlung* (party conference); media reports; *Année Politique Suisse* (various volumes).

Table 1.9 Party members in Austria and Switzerland (1983–2013)

Year	Austria (Greens)		Switzerland (GPS)	
	Members (M)	M/V (%)	Members (M)	M/V (%)
1983	–	–	1,000	
1984	–	–		
1985	–	–		
1986	–	–		
1987	2,000			
1988	2,000			
1989	2,000		4,500	
1990	2,000		3,225/5,000*	
1991			6,000	
1992				
1993				
1994				
1995	2,000			
1996				
1997			4,240	
1998				
1999				
2000				
2001				
2002	1,810	0.4		
2003	3,298		4,779	3.0
2004	3,493		5,240	
2005	4,839		4,757	
2006	4,007	0.8	5,077	
2007	4,028		5,559	2.5
2008	4,573	0.9	6,140	
2009	4,907		6,746	
2010	5,257		7,075	
2011	5,383		7,599	3.7
2012	5,719		7,476	
2013	6,088	1.0	7,043	

Note: The quality of these data varies considerably; the round figures are (partly crude) estimates only. M/V = members/voters * 100. This calculation is done only for years with official data on membership. Given some peculiarities of Swiss elections (voters have different numbers of votes in each canton) the number of voters is based on 'notional voters' (*fiktive Wählende*).

Sources: Austria 1987–1990: Müller (1992); 1995: Mair and Van Biezen (2001); 2002–2013: official figures provided by the federal party, since 2003 always referring to August. The 2002 data do not include the regional party organisation of Vorarlberg. Switzerland 1983 and 1989: Ladner (1989); 1990; and 1997: Ladner and Brändle (2008), 1990* Universität Bern/Institut für Politikwissenschaft (o.J.); 1991: Mair and Van Biezen (2001); 2003–2013: official figures provided by the federal party, since 2006 always referring to January.

Main challenges for the future

The Austrian and Swiss Greens have managed to establish themselves as an integral part of their respective party systems. In terms of vote shares, the Austrian Greens belong to the strongest European Green parties, but the Swiss GPS also receives larger shares than many of its sister parties. Both parties have developed a stable organisation and a clear programmatic profile. Nevertheless, when summarising this comparative analysis there are three interrelated challenges the Greens have to deal with.

First, while both parties have established themselves as a governing party at the regional and local levels, government participation at the national level has so far been out of reach. This reduces the impact of the Greens on policymaking and might discourage their voters and their party officials. While both parties are confronted with this task, the national context makes this challenge very different: in Austria, the Greens have already demonstrated their willingness to govern and – based on the experiences at the *Land* level – they are accepted as potential partners by both major parties. For this reason, the Greens just need a favourable numeric constellation. Winning a majority with one of the two major parties is rather unlikely. A more realistic perspective would be a loss of their combined majority. In such a situation, the Greens are a likely partner in a three-party coalition. The Swiss Greens' entry into government, by contrast, is severely hindered by the country's tradition of government formation. To challenge the contemporary system, the Greens must win more votes than the smallest party in government. Apart from the Conservative Democratic Party of Switzerland (BDP), the split-off from the SVP that is smaller than the Greens, the GPS was four points behind the Christian Democrats (CVP) in 2011. If the GPS manages to overtake the CVP, the legitimacy of the current system would be challenged, although the CVP is the strongest party in the second chamber.

A second challenge for the Greens is their strategic position in the party system. With respect to 'internal' competition for the Green vote, the Austrians enjoy a monopoly. After the breakdown of the VGÖ, no other Green party has appeared on the political scene. However, the Greens have to compete with other parties that are attractive for left wing and/or libertarian voters: the SPÖ is a potential coalition partner but also an opponent – especially in elections with a bipolar constellation. To prevent a right-wing victory, Green-leading voters might switch to the Social Democrats. Another challenger could come from the political centre, the newly founded liberal NEOS that surprisingly entered parliament in the 2013 election. In the 1990s, the Greens had to compete with the Liberal Forum for highly educated urban and liberal voters; in the 2000s, they had a quasi-monopoly in this voter segment. However, it remains to be seen whether NEOS will be able to establish itself. In Switzerland, by contrast, the Greens are confronted with a competitor: the GLP. The emergence of the liberal Greens has obviously stopped the GPS' growth and has weakened its libertarian wing. A further shift to the left might endanger its competitive position.

In terms of their programmatic development, both parties highlight environmental issues, especially the Swiss Greens. Nevertheless, the GPS is not a single-issue party. Particularly on the cultural dimension of conflict, both parties position themselves as a polarising force and have developed a left-libertarian, culturally open and pro-European profile. Given the ongoing impact of climate change and – especially in Switzerland – the struggle against nuclear energy, Green issues will remain on the political agenda. However, the saliency of economic issues is always a potential threat as the Greens are seen as less competent in this realm. Austria and Switzerland were hit by the Global Financial Crisis of 2007–2008 as well as by the subsequent Eurozone Crisis, but both countries still belong to the richest countries worldwide. A major backlash to 'materialist' concerns is rather unlikely.

Notes

1   In multilingual Switzerland, the GPS additionally operates under the name *Les Verts.* *Parti écologiste Suisse* as well as *I Verdi – Partito ecologista svizzero.* The French and Italian names of the GLP are *Parti vert libéral Suisse* and *Partito Verde Liberale svizzero*, respectively.
2   For an overview, see Schandl and Schattauer (1996).
3   Source: Global Greens (www.globalgreens.org/officeholders, accessed 12 February 2014).
4   The seats in the first chamber are proportionally distributed at the cantonal level without using thresholds. Access is thus easy in large cantons such as Zurich where 34 seats are at stake (out of 200). By contrast, there are six cantons electing only one seat each.
5   The only remaining are two small German-speaking cantons: Obwalden and Appenzell Innerrhoden.
6   After a split of the Swiss People's Party (SVP), a fifth party is represented since 2007: the Conservative Democratic Party of Switzerland (BDP).
7   Source: www.gruene.ch/web/gruene/de/waehlen_stimmen/parolen_und_ergebnisse. html, accessed on 19 February 2014.
8   One cantonal legislature (Appenzell Innerrhoden) is not composed of partisans.
9   The Austrian communists (KPÖ) who are not represented in parliament since 1959 were not included in the survey.
10   The following discussion is additionally based on various issues of the *Année Suisse Politique*.
11   The 2011 election manifesto demands the start of accession negotiations at an 'opportune moment' (Grüne/Les Verts 2011, p. 19).
12   The Austrian figure is based on data collected by Media Focus, a market research enterprise. These data sum up all advertising expenditure, yet they do not include any discounts. For Switzerland, see Lutz (2012, p. 687).
13   Sources: Switzerland (www.gruene.ch/web/gruene/de/die_gruenen/partei/sekretariat. html, accessed on 5 March 2014); Austria (personal information).
14   These three cantons were Bern, Basel-Stadt and Zurich.
15   In Austria, there are some small minorities, mainly Slovenes and Croatians.
16   Because the electoral system allocates seats on three tiers, the *Land* parties decide on the candidates in 39 regional and 9 *Land* constituencies. However, these decisions have to be confirmed by the *Bundeskongress* (§8.9.a).
17   Source: Minutes of the *Delegiertenversammlung* in Delémont (25 January 2014).
18   Sources: www.parlament.gv.at; www.parlament.ch.
19   This survey was part of the European Green Parties Membership Survey.

References

Bakker, R., de Vries, C., Edwards, E., Hooghe, L., Jolly, S., Marks, G., Polk, J., Rovny, J., Steenbergen, M., and Vachudova, M. A., 2015. Measuring party positions in Europe: The Chapel Hill expert survey trend file, 1999–2010. *Party Politics*, 21(1), pp. 143–152.

Benoit, K., and Laver, M., 2006. *Party Policy in Modern Democracies*. London: Routledge.

Church, C. H., 1995. Switzerland: Greens in a Confederal Polity. In: D. Richardson and C. Rootes, eds, *The Green Challenge: The Development of Green Parties in Europe*. London: Routledge. pp. 146–167.

Dachs, H., 2006. Grünalternative Parteien. In: H. Dachs, P. Gerlich, H. Gottweis, H. Kramer, V. Lauber, W. C. Müller and E. Tálos, eds, *Politik in Österreich: Das Handbuch*. Wien: Manz. pp. 389–401.

Die Grünen/Die Grüne Alternative, 2012. *Satzungen der Partei: Beschlossen vom 33. Bundeskongress der GRÜNEN – der GRÜNEN ALTERNATIVE am 1./2. Dezember 2012*. Wien: Die Grünen – Die Grüne Alternative.

Dolezal, M., 2008. Kein Sonderfall. Die Schweizer Grünen im internationalen Vergleich. In: M. Baer and W. Seitz, eds, *Die Grünen in der Schweiz: Ihre Politik, ihre Geschichte, ihre Basis*. Zürich: Rüegger Verlag. pp. 135–149.

Dolezal, M., 2010. Exploring the stabilization of a political force. The social and attitudinal basis of Green parties in the age of globalization. *West European Politics*, 33(3), pp. 534–552.

Dolezal, M., 2014. Five more years in opposition? The Austrian Greens in the 2013 parliamentary election. *Environmental Politics*, 23(3), pp. 525–530.

Dolezal, M., and Hutter, S., 2007. Konsensdemokratie unter Druck? Politischer Protest in Österreich, 1975–2005. *Österreichische Zeitschrift für Politikwissenschaft*, 36(3), pp. 338–352.

Dolezal, M., and Zeglovits, E., 2014. Almost an earthquake: The Austrian national election 2013. *West European Politics*, 37(3), pp. 644–652.

Fallend, F., 2008. Euroscepticism in Austrian Political Parties: Ideologically Rooted or Strategically Motivated? In: A. Szczerbiak and P. Taggart, eds, *Opposing Europe? The Comparative Party Politics of Euroscepticism: Volume 1. Case Studies and Country Surveys*. Oxford: Oxford University Press. pp. 201–220.

Frankland, E. G., 1995. The Austrian Greens: From Electoral Alliance to Political Party. In: W. Rüdig, ed., *Green Politics Three*. Edinburgh: Edinburgh University Press. pp. 192–216.

Grüne/Les Verts, 2011. *Wahlplattform der Grünen Partei Schweiz 2011*. Bern: Grüne Partei der Schweiz.

Grüne/Les Verts, 2013a. *Geschichte der Grünen in der Schweiz – Grüne Persönlichkeiten (Aktualisierung April 2013)*. Bern: Grüne Partei der Schweiz.

Grüne/Les Verts, 2013b. *Geschichte der Grünen in der Schweiz (Aktualisierung April 2013)*. Bern: Grüne Partei der Schweiz.

Grüne/Les Verts, 2014. *Statuten der Grünen Partei der Schweiz (Totalrevision am 25. Januar 2014)*. Bern: Grüne Partei der Schweiz.

Haerpfer, C., 1989. Austria: The 'United Greens' and the 'Alternative List/Green Alternative'. In: F. Müller-Rommel, ed., *New Politics in Western Europe: The Rise and Success of Green Parties and Alternative Lists*. Boulder, CO: Westview Press. pp. 23–38.

Höglinger, D., Wüest, B., and Helbling, M., 2012. Culture Versus Economy: The Framing of Public Debates Over Issues Related to Globalization. In: H. Kriesi, E. Grande, M. Dolezal, M. Helbling, S. Hutter, D. Höglinger and B. Wüest, eds, *Political Conflict in Western Europe*. Cambridge: Cambridge University Press. pp. 229–253.

Johann, D., Glantschigg, C., Glinitzer, K., Kritzinger, S., and Wagner, M., 2014. Das Wahlverhalten bei der Nationalratswahl 2013. In: S. Kritzinger, W. C. Müller and K. Schönbach, eds, *Die Nationalratswahl 2013: Wie Parteien, Medien und Wählerschaft zusammenwirken*. Wien: Böhlau. pp. 191–214.

Jordan, G., 2013. *Chronik der Grünen Alternative: Die Grüne Alternative als Parlamentspartei (1986–2013) (Stand: Dezember 2013)*. Wien: Grüner Klub im Rathaus.

Kriesi, H., Grande, E., Dolezal, M., Helbling, M., Hutter, S., Höglinger, D., and Wüest, B., 2012. *Political Conflict in Western Europe*. Cambridge: Cambridge University Press.

Kriesi, H., Grande, E., Lachat, R., Dolezal, M., Bornschier, S., and Frey, T., 2008. *West European Politics in the Age of Globalization*. Cambridge: Cambridge University Press.

Kriesi, H., Koopmans, R., Duyvendak, J. W., and Giugni, M., 1995. *New Social Movements in Western Europe: A Comparative Analysis*. Minneapolis: University of Minnesota Press.

Ladner, A., 1989. Switzerland: The 'Green' and 'Alternative Parties'. In: F. Müller-Rommel, ed., *New Politics in Western Europe: The Rise and Success of Green Parties and Alternative Lists*. Boulder, CO: Westview Press. pp. 155–165.

Ladner, A., 2012. Switzerland's Green liberal party: A new party model for the environment? *Environmental Politics*, 21(3), pp. 510–515.

Ladner, A., 2014. Politische Parteien. In: P. Knoepfel, Y. Papadopoulos, P. Sciarini, A. Vatter and S. Häusermann, eds, *Handbuch der Schweizer Politik – Manuel de la politique suisse*. Zürich: Verlag Neue Zürcher Zeitung. pp. 53–85.

Ladner, A., and Brändle, M., 2008. Switzerland: The Green Party, Alternative and Liberal Greens. In: G. E. Frankland, P. Lucardie and B. Rihoux, eds, *Green Parties in Transition: The End of Grass-Roots Democracy?* Farnham and Burlington, VT: Ashgate. pp. 109–128.

Lauber, V., 2003. The Austrian Greens after the 2002 elections. *Environmental Politics*, 12(3), pp. 139–144.

Lauber, V., 2008. Struggling to Become Competitive: The Organizational Evolution of the Austrian Greens. In: G. E. Frankland, P. Lucardie and B. Rihoux, eds, *Green Parties in Transition: The End of Grass-Roots Democracy?* Farnham and Burlington, VT: Ashgate. pp. 129–141.

Lutz, G., 2012. The 2011 Swiss federal elections: Right-wing defeat and increased fractionalisation. *West European Politics*, 35(3), pp. 682–693.

Mair, P., and van Biezen, I., 2001. Party membership in twenty European democracies, 1980–2000. *Party Politics*, 7(1), pp. 5–21.

McAllister, I., and Studlar, D. T., 2002. Electoral systems and women's representation: A long-term perspective. *Representation*, 39(1), pp. 3–14.

McGann, A. J., and Kitschelt, H., 2005. The radical right in the Alps. Evolution of support for the Swiss SVP and Austrian FPÖ. *Party Politics*, 11(2), pp. 147–171.

Müller, W. C., 1992. Austria (1945–1990). In: R. S. Katz and P. Mair, eds, *Party Organizations: A Data Handbook on Party Organizations in Western Democracies, 1960–90*. London: Sage. pp. 21–120.

Müller, W. C., and Stefou, P., 2003. Green grassroots: What makes Austrian Green party members tick. *ECPR Joint Sessions of Workshops*, Edinburgh.

Pelinka, A., and Greiderer, S., 1996. Austria: The referendum as an instrument of internationalisation. In: M. Gallagher and P. V. Uleri, eds, *The Referendum Experience in Europe*. Houndmills: Macmillan Press. pp. 20–32.

Poguntke, T., 1989. The 'new politics dimension' in European Green parties. In: F. Müller-Rommel, ed., *New Politics in Western Europe: The Rise and Success of Green Parties and Alternative Lists*. Boulder, CO: Westview Press. pp. 175–194.

Poguntke, T., 1993. *Alternative Politics: The German Green Party*. Edinburgh: Edinburgh University Press.

Ray, L., 1999. Measuring party orientations towards European integration: Results from an expert survey. *European Journal of Political Research*, 36(2), pp. 283–306.

Schandl, F., and Schattauer, G., 1996. *Die Grünen in Österreich: Entwicklung und Konsolidierung einer politischen Kraft*. Wien: Promedia.

Schneider, M., 2008. Die Grünen in Zahlen. Analyse der Wahlergebnisse 1975 bis 2007. In: M. Baer and W. Seitz, eds, *Die Grünen in der Schweiz: Ihre Politik. Ihre Geschichte. Ihre Basis*. Zürich: Rüegger Verlag. pp. 151–163.

Seitz, W., 2008. 'Melonengrüne' und 'Gurkengrüne'. Die Geschichte der Grünen in der Schweiz. In: M. Baer and W. Seitz, eds, *Die Grünen in der Schweiz: Ihre Politik. Ihre Geschichte. Ihre Basis*. Zürich: Rüegger Verlag. pp. 15–37.

Seitz, W., 2013. Die Grünliberale Partei (GLP): Sind die Grünliberalen eine Rechtsabspaltung der Grünen? In: O. Mazzoleni and O. Meuwly, eds, *Die Parteien in Bewegung: Nachbarschaft und Konflikte*. Zürich: Verlag Neue Zürcher Zeitung. pp. 123–155.

Sickinger, H., 2009. *Politikfinanzierung in Österreich*. Wien: Czernin Verlag.

Universität Bern/Institut für Politikwissenschaft. o.J. *Grüne Partei der Schweiz und Gruppierungen, die teilweise in ihr aufgegangen sind (Grünes Bündnis, POCH, SAP)*. Bern: Universität Bern/Institut für Politikwissenschaft.

van Biezen, I., Mair, P., and Poguntke, T., 2012. Going, going, . . . gone? The decline of party membership in contemporary Europe. *European Journal of Political Research*, 51(1), pp. 24–56.

Volkens, A., Lehmann, P., Merz, N., Regel, S., and Werner, A., 2013. *The Manifesto Data Collection: Manifesto Project (CMP). Version 2013b*. Berlin: Wissenschaftszentrum Berlin für Sozialforschung.

Williams, M., 2000. The changing fortunes of the Austrian Greens. *Environmental Politics*, 9(4), pp. 135–140.

Zürcher, R., 2008. Grosse Chance für eine kleine Partei. Die Grünen und die direkte Demokratie. In: M. Baer and W. Seitz, eds, *Die Grünen in der Schweiz: Ihre Politik, ihre Geschichte, ihre Basis*. Zürich: Rüegger Verlag. pp. 103–117.

2 The Greens in Belgium's federal landscape

Divergent fates

Marie-Catherine Wavreille and Jean-Benoit Pilet

Introduction

This chapter covers the developments of two of the most successful Green parties in Europe: *Ecolo* and *Groen*.[1] The two parties have gained access to governmental positions at federal and regional levels. They have been able, at least for the French-speaking *Ecolo*, to stabilise around 10 to 15 per cent of the electorate. They both have developed a stable organisation that has helped them to persist for about 30 years now. In terms of programme, they have exerted a considerable and effective influence on the political agenda, imposing their core issues such as climate change and sustainable development, but also other topics like gender parity in politics, political transparency and democratic renewal.

Yet, their 30-year existence has not been a quiet journey. The two parties have experienced episodes of major electoral victories but also severe electoral defeats. Moreover, in the last ten years, they have faced different fates. In French-speaking Belgium, *Ecolo* has remained one of the four major parties and has participated in regional governments. In Flanders, on the other hand, *Groen* has become a junior party and has not truly played a significant role in the building of governing coalitions.

This chapter attempts to better understand why *Ecolo* and *Groen* have gone through periods of success and defeat but also why their fates have diverged in the last ten years. In the next sections, we succinctly review the electoral performances of the two parties, their programmatic evolution and their organisational development. We examine how these dimensions contribute to a better understanding of the evolution of the Belgian Green parties in the last three decades.

Origins and development

The starting point of this section is the 'party lifespan approach' developed by Pedersen (1982). According to this model, political parties are mortal organisations that pass through a 'lifespan' composed of four distinct phases or thresholds. In applying this concept, we can sketch the evolution and the main developments of the Greens in Belgium since their foundation in the early 1980s (Table 2.1).

Table 2.1 Chronology of the main developments of *Ecolo* and *Groen* in Belgium

Ecolo		Groen	
Year	*Developments*	*Year*	*Developments*
1980	Creation of *Ecolo*	1981	First seats won by *Agalev* in the national parliament
1981	First seats won by *Ecolo* in the national parliament	1982	Creation of *Agalev*
1982	First participation to power at local level	1982	First participation to power at local level
1999	First participation to power at national and regional levels	1999	First participation to power at national and regional levels
2003	Severe electoral defeat	2003	Severe electoral defeat (*Agalev* lost all parliamentary representation)
2004	*Ecolo* enters the regional government in Brussels	2003	*Agalev* is renamed *Groen!* (Green!)
2009	Big electoral victory at the regional and European elections (18.5 per cent of the votes in Wallonia and 20.2 in Brussels, its second best electoral performance ever).	2004	Electoral recovery (around 7.6 per cent of the votes in Flanders at the EU and regional elections).
2009	*Ecolo* participates to regional governments in Brussels and Wallonia	2009	*Groen!* participates to the regional government in Brussels
		2012	*Groen!* is renamed *Groen*

Source: Authors' own compilation.

The Green parties in Belgium have passed the first threshold of declaration and authorisation in the 1970s, with both parties affirming their intention to participate in elections and meeting the requirements to do so. In Flanders, the origins of the Greens are closely linked to a broad basis of new social movements and civil society (Dandoy, 2011a). In the early 1970s, the 'Live Differently' movement (*Anders Gaan Leven*) was created. The movement initially decided to back candidates with ecological views on existing lists in 1974 and 1976 but did not run for elections itself (Kitschelt, 1989). In French-speaking Belgium, the foundation of a first Green party took a slightly different path. Various local movements that were both ecologists and calling for democratic renewal were created in the 1970s and ran for elections in a few districts. The political movement New Democracy (*Démocratie nouvelle* – DN) fielded candidates in both the 1974 national elections and the 1976 local elections in the electoral district of Namur (Rihoux, 1993). At the 1977 and 1978 national elections, lists were fielded under the label of Wallonia Ecology *(Wallonie-écologie* – WE), along with other ecologist groupings. These movements were the foundations on which *Ecolo* would eventually be founded.

The relative success of these lists backed by Green movements was crucial in the decision to create genuine Green political parties in Flanders, Wallonia and

Brussels. A turning point was reached at the first European elections of 1979. In Wallonia, *Europe Écologie*, the only Green list supported by *Wallonie-écologie* won nearly 5 per cent in Wallonia and 3.3 per cent in the Brussels district (Buelens and Delwit, 2008). In Flanders, the lists supported by the ecologists won 2.3 per cent of the votes.

These two unexpected (relative) successes were central in the transformation of these young Green movements into genuine Green parties. The *Ecolo* movement was formally created as a party during two assemblies in March 1980 (Delwit and De Waele, 1996). In addition, in November 1982, a Green party was also founded in Flanders under the name *Agalev*.

The second threshold in Pedersen's model is the threshold of representation that is reached when a party wins its first seats in parliament. In the Belgian case, the two Green parties quickly passed this threshold. In the legislative elections of 1981, both *Ecolo* and *Groen* gained their first Members of Parliament (MPs). That year, *Groen* crossed the threshold of representation for the first time and obtained 2.6 per cent of the votes in Flanders and two seats at the national parliament. In French-speaking Belgium, the early years of *Ecolo* were characterised by a direct electoral take-off. The party made its first breakthrough in the 1981 legislative elections, gathering 5.1 per cent in Wallonia and in the Brussels-Halle-Vilvoorde district (Pilet and Schrobiltgen, 2011). This enabled both Green parties to cross the third threshold by having their first MP and senatorial seats in the federal parliament. In the subsequent electoral contests, both Green parties systematically crossed the threshold of representation, with the main exception of *Groen* in 2003 (Table 2.2). This corroborates Pedersen's argument that parties may have to cross thresholds several times (1982, p. 11).

The next stage in the life of a party is its accession to government responsibilities. This next threshold was crossed rapidly at the local level (Delwit and van Haute, 2008). By 1982, *Ecolo* had already taken part in four local governments, including in Liège (the second largest city in Wallonia).

Reaching the threshold of relevance at other levels of power appeared to be more complex. It was only in the late 1990s that the two Belgian Green parties came into power for the first time at the national and regional levels (Table 2.3). In between, the two parties remained on the opposition benches, and the question of whether the party should participate to government was recurrently and intensively debated within both *Ecolo* and *Groen*. *Ecolo* was deeply divided internally on the issue. In the 1980s, the party was invited twice to join a possible coalition at the Walloon regional level. The first occasion occurred in the mid-1980s, when *Ecolo* accepted an offer to take part in the regional government in Wallonia (Buelens and Deschouwer, 2002; Delwit and van Haute, 2008), although only a small majority of its members (50.7 per cent) approved the governmental participation. In 1986, the French-speaking Liberals and Christian Democrats invited *Ecolo* for a second time to support the governmental majority, but *Ecolo* denied this invitation. The question of how to deal with these offers created significant internal tensions within *Ecolo* with two opposing

Table 2.2 Electoral results of *Ecolo* and *Groen*, Lower Chamber (federal), 1978–2010 (% votes and N seats)

Year	Ecolo		Groen	
	% votes	*Seats (N)*	*% votes*	*Seats (N)*
1978	0.6	0	0.2	0
1981	2.5	2	2.6	2
1985	2.5	5	3.7	4
1987	2.6	3	4.5	6
1991	5.1	10	4.9	7
1995	4.0	6	4.8	5
1999	7.4	11	7.0	9
2003	3.1	4	2.5	0
2007	5.1	8	4.0	4
2010	4.8	8	4.4	5
2014	3.3	6	5.3	6

Note: In 1995, the total number of seats in the Lower Chamber was reduced from 212 to 150.

Source: Cevipol.

factions: a 'fundamentalist-environmentalist' faction and a 'generalist-social' faction. They disagreed on the project (single issue vs. societal project) and the strategy (opposition vs. participation) (Delwit and van Haute, 2008). The position of the party towards participation to power was a central source of internal disputes and was unsettled until the late 1990s. The party managed to reach some kind of compromise after a series of political forums held between 1996 and 1998.

For the Flemish Greens, the question came a bit later on the agenda (Buelens and Deschouwer, 2002). Following the 1991 elections, the Flemish Greens were for the first time invited by the Liberals to form a national government with the Socialists. However, this 'purple' coalition failed to be formed.

In 1992, *Ecolo* and *Groen* experienced an unusual situation of quasi-participation. They took part in the institutional negotiations leading to the transformation of the country into a full-fledged federal system and joined a temporary two-thirds majority necessary for the reform to be passed (Buelens and Rihoux, forthcoming). Even though the involvement of the Greens was not genuine governmental participation, signing the 'Saint-Michel Agreement' demonstrated that both parties had governing potential and were able to accept compromises (Buelens and Deschouwer, 2002).

By 1998–1999, the leaders of *Ecolo* were eager to gain access to executive power. Their willingness was clearly stated, both internally and externally (Buelens and Delwit, 2008). On 15 March 1998, Jacky Morael, then secretary-general, stated that 'we are candidates to power' (*Nous sommes candidats au pouvoir*). One year

Table 2.3 Government experience of *Ecolo* and *Groen* in Belgium

Level	Party	Period	Portfolios/number of municipal mayors
National	*Ecolo*	1999–2003	1 VP (Durant) 1 M – Mobility and Transport (Durant) 1 SS – Energy and Sustainable Development (Deleuze)
	Groen	1999–2003	1 VP (Aelvoet) 1 M – Health, Consumer Affairs and Environment (Aelvoet) 1 SS – Development Co-operation (Boutmans)
Regional (Wallonia)	*Ecolo*	1999–2004	2 M – Social Affairs and Health (Detienne); Transport, Energy and Mobility (Daras)
Regional (Wallonia)	*Ecolo*	2009–2014	2 M – Sustainable Development (Nollet); Environment, Planning and Mobility (Henry)
Regional (French-speaking community)	*Ecolo*	1999–2004	2 M – Primary Education (Nollet); Social Affairs (Maréchal)
Regional (French-speaking community)	*Ecolo*	2009–2014	2 M – Childcare, Research and Public Administration (Nollet); Youth Policy (Huytebroeck)
Regional (German community)	*Ecolo*	1999–2004	1 M – Youth and Family, Social Affairs and Historic Buildings (Niessen)
Regional (Flanders)	*Groen*	1999–2004	2 M – Welfare, Health and Equal Opportunities (Vogels); Agriculture and Environment (Dua)
Regional (Brussels)	*Ecolo*	2004–2009	1 M – Environment, Energy and Water Policy (Huytebroeck)
Regional (Brussels)	*Ecolo*	2009–2014	1 M – Environment, Energy, Water Policy and Housing (Huytebroeck) 1 SS – Housing Policy (Doulkeridis)
Regional (Brussels)	*Groen*	2009–2014	1 SS – Transport, Equality and Public Administration (De Lille)
Local	*Ecolo*	2000–2006	3*
		2006–2012	2
		2012–2018	6
	Groen	2000–2006	2**
		2006–2012	2
		2012–2018	5

Note: VP = Vice Prime Minister; M = Minister; SS = Secretary of State; * There are 262 municipalities in Wallonia. ** There are 308 municipalities in Flanders.

Source: Authors' own compilation.

later, in 1999, *Ecolo* and *Groen* came into power for the first time at the national and regional levels (except in Brussels) after their biggest electoral victory so far. *Ecolo* almost doubled its electoral results, from 4.0 per cent in 1995 to 7.4 per cent in 1999. It became the second major party in the metropolitan area of Brussels (above the Socialists and the Christian Democrats) and the third party in Wallonia (above the Christian Democrats). In Flanders, *Groen* polled 6.9 per cent and gathered nine seats in the lower chamber. Part of the Green parties' success was probably caused by a heightened awareness about environmental security and food safety in the final weeks of the campaign (Hooghe and Rihoux, 2000). At the national level, they decided to enter an unusual coalition with the Socialists and Liberals. Both Green parties opted for 'a strategy of "all or nothing"', according to which neither would step alone into the national government and neither would join the national government if the other Green party did not join its own regional government (Hooghe and Rihoux, 2000). Therefore, despite a rather linear trajectory as stable parliamentary parties since 1981 (Rihoux, 2006), *Ecolo* and *Groen* have experienced 18 years of opposition before joining a coalition at the national level. This made the Belgian Greens holding the longest uninterrupted period of representation in national parliament in comparison with their Western European counterparts (Müller-Rommel, 2002).

Comparative analyses point out that participation in government usually leads to an electoral defeat for Green parties (Rihoux, 2006; Rüdig, 2006). The Greens in Belgium are no exception (Hooghe and Rihoux, 2008). In 2003, after their first participation in government, both *Ecolo* and *Groen* suffered a major electoral setback. The former kept only 4 of its 11 seats in the Lower Chamber (Delwit and Pilet, 2005), while *Groen* lost all of its 9 national MPs, bringing an end to 22 years of continuous parliamentary presence at the national level (Hooghe and Rihoux, 2003). This was partly due to the newly established electoral threshold of 5 per cent (Hooghe and Rihoux, 2003). With no representation in the national parliament, the Flemish Greens had to significantly reduce their staff. The electoral defeat left *Groen* in financial disarray, with almost its entire income being lost due to the link between electoral results and public funding for parties. Change was needed in order to survive. As a reaction, the party adopted a new name, and a new political secretary was elected.

At the 2004 European and regional elections, *Groen* managed to obtain six regional MPs, which helped the party to survive its deepest crisis (Buelens and Delwit, 2008). For *Ecolo*, 2004 largely confirmed the 2003 electoral defeat. The French-speaking Greens returned to the opposition benches at all levels – national, regional and community levels, except in Brussels where the party joined the regional government in an 'olive tree' coalition with the French-speaking Socialists (PS) and Christian Democrats (CDH) (Delwit and van Haute, 2008). Interestingly, this was the only executive *Ecolo* had not yet participated in (Delwit and Pilet, 2005). Following these consecutive defeats, the resource base of the party was considerably weakened (Hooghe and Rihoux, 2008).

After being voted out in 2003, *Groen* re-entered the national parliament in 2007, gaining four seats in the lower chamber. *Ecolo* did remarkably well too by doubling their number of seats from four to eight. However, their electoral performances went down again at the national elections in 2010, with 12.3 per cent of the votes in Wallonia and 12 per cent in Brussels. In Flanders, *Groen* was the only party not to have lost any percentage of the votes in comparison with the other established Flemish parties. With 7.1 per cent of the votes, *Groen* even obtained an additional parliamentary seat. Even though *Ecolo* and *Groen* took part in the 2010–2011 negotiations that have led to the 'Butterfly Agreement' on the sixth reform of the state, it did not translate into governmental participation.

Ideology and policy positions

This section portrays how *Ecolo* and *Groen* position themselves on the main political issues and how these positions have evolved since the early 1980s. In this respect, two approaches can be adopted. The first approach emphasises issue saliency; it looks at the relative importance of the main political issues in the electoral manifestos of the Belgian Green parties in order to distinguish which topics are most extensively covered. The other approach stresses issue ownership; it identifies the core issues on which the Belgian Greens differentiate themselves from other parties. The two perspectives produce a different portrayal of the Greens in Belgium.

In terms of issue saliency, the two parties do not considerably differ from the other parties. They are not and have never really been single-issue parties. In his study based on data from the Comparative Manifesto Project, Dandoy shows that environmental issues never exceeded around 15 per cent of the total length of their manifestos (Dandoy, 2011b). Other more traditional issues like economic growth or the welfare state have always been extensively covered. For example, for the 2003 elections, the most salient issues in *Ecolo*'s manifesto were the welfare state (27.9 per cent) and the economy (16.3 per cent); the environment only came third (10.8 per cent) (Dandoy, 2007). Nevertheless, the way *Ecolo* and *Groen* address environmental issues is different from the other parties. Their strategy has been to focus on the concept of sustainable development and to present it as a transversal notion that would be applicable to a large range of issues in society, from the economy to education, and from democratic renewal to immigration or foreign affairs (Rihoux, 2003).

Yet, the approach of issue ownership highlights the environmentalist component of the two parties. Between 1981 and 2007, *Ecolo* and *Groen* have dedicated a rather stable proportion of their party manifestos to environmental issues, around 10 to 15 per cent (Dandoy, 2011b). This proportion has almost never exceeded 5 per cent for the other parties. This gap translates into the perception of voters who clearly and without any contestation attribute the ownership of the environmental issue to *Ecolo* and *Groen* (Walgrave, et al., 2012).

A third approach to apprehend the programmatic profile of *Ecolo* and *Groen* is to observe how they position themselves on the main issues that dominate the Belgian political landscape and to what extent they differentiate themselves from the other parties. First, on the socio-economic left–right divide, both parties have from the beginning adopted a left-leaning profile. They were, to use their own words, against a contemporary economic model based upon strong productivism and permanent growth at the expense of natural resources and of the quality of life.[2] Their positions were fundamentally radical, calling for a completely new economic model. Yet, the two parties faced difficulties with the traditional left–right cleavage. They often claimed that they were neither left, nor right, and that they were just radically new and different.

With years, this radical profile has gradually evolved towards a more classical positioning on the left side of the political spectrum. The two parties have developed closer ties with trade unions and have become the main competitor on the left for the two Socialist parties (Castanheira and Noury, 2007). Today, they both accept being portrayed as a left-wing party. In 2002, *Ecolo* signed a sort of pre-electoral agreement with the French-speaking Socialists to facilitate the making of left-wing coalition governments. Yet, with the electoral defeat of 2003, this strategy of organised partnership was put to an end.

The positioning of the Greens to the left of the political spectrum goes beyond socio-economic issues. On many other political dimensions, *Ecolo* and *Groen* are on the left, and often the most left wing of the parties represented in the Belgian Parliament (Castanheira and Noury, 2007). Such is the case on issues like immigration and on moral issues. On immigration, *Ecolo* and *Groen* have close ties with social movements that call for more open immigration policies and for an easier legal settlement for illegal migrants who have long been residing in Belgium. *Ecolo* and *Groen* were also the first parties in Belgium to mobilise in favour of voting rights for non-EU citizens, a right that was eventually granted in 2004. On moral issues, the two parties have been the most progressive parties on same-sex marriage and on adoption by same-sex couples. Together with the Socialists and to some extent the Liberals, they have actively pushed legislation on these issues that was adopted in Belgium in the early twenty-first century.

Two other issues are of importance in the manifestos of *Ecolo* and *Groen*: Europe and Belgian federalism. Regarding European integration, the Greens have, since their creation, been strongly in favour of more integration. They have been Euro-federalists from the beginning. In addition, they call for providing a greater say to citizens in EU decision-making processes. It has translated into demands for expanding the role of the European Parliament and for the adoption of European treaties through EU-wide referendums (Delwit, 2001). Yet, in recent years, both *Ecolo* and *Groen* have become more critical towards European integration. They remain in favour of a federal and democratic Europe, but the current evolution of the European Union does not satisfy the two Green parties for two main reasons. First, they are uncomfortable with the growing influence of the European Council at the expense, they argue, of the European Parliament. More importantly, like many other left-wing parties, they face increasing difficulties with many of the decisions of the European Commission and of the European Council (Delwit, et al., 2005; Pilet and van Haute, 2007). The malaise was already palpable in the 1990s surrounding discussions about the Maastricht Treaty but has become more salient in the late 2000s with the economic crisis and the austerity measures defended by EU institutions.

Finally, like any other party in Belgium, *Ecolo* and *Groen* have had to define their position on the organisation of the Belgian federal state and on the relations between regions and linguistic communities. This issue has never been a central priority for the two parties. In their founding years, members of regionalist movements joined *Ecolo* and *Groen*. This led the two parties to adopt positions favourable to more regional autonomy, mostly because regional autonomy was perceived as more efficient in order to bring politics closer to the citizens. Yet, since the 1990s, the two parties have gradually become more moderate and have actually become strong advocates of the Belgian federal system. As we will show below, while the Belgian party system is rigorously divided along linguistic lines, the Greens are the only parties in Belgium to form a joint parliamentary group within the national parliament. They claim for a balanced approach of Belgian federalism that would imply transfers of competencies to the regions, but also transfers back to the federal state. This positioning is common for a French-speaking party but is much less frequent in Flanders. In that respect, *Groen* is undoubtedly the Flemish party with the most moderate position of regional autonomy (Dandoy, et al., 2013). It is also the Dutch-speaking party for which the issue is the least salient (Franck, 2005).

Structure and organisation

Main party structures

The organisational structures of *Ecolo* and *Groen* are very similar. Both parties are structured in three territorial layers: federal, regional and local. The federal level corresponds to the linguistic community covered by the party: Flanders for *Groen*, Wallonia and Brussels for *Ecolo*. The regional units correspond to the constituencies (either provincial or sub-provincial). The local units coincide with the municipalities. At each level, there are four main decision bodies: the general assembly composed of all party members, the party council made of a smaller group of party delegates (and of MPs and ministers), the party bureau and the party presidency.

Beyond this classical model of party organisation that does not contrast considerably from the other Belgian parties, three crucial elements differentiate *Ecolo* and *Groen* from other party organisations in Belgium.

First, the two parties were created with the aim to differentiate themselves from other parties by introducing stronger mechanisms of intraparty democracy. In particular, party members were given strong prerogatives in order to avoid the party to be controlled by a small elite (Rihoux, 2001). This remains a characteristic of the two Belgian Green parties today. The role of party members is still larger than in most other parties in Belgium. The difference does not lie in their formal rights and duties. Like in almost all other Belgian parties, members of *Ecolo* and *Groen* have the right to vote for the selection of the party leader(s) and candidates, for the adoption of the electoral manifesto and on the participation to ruling coalitions at all levels. Yet, unlike in other Belgian parties, these rights and duties are not purely formal. While in other parties the party elite easily controls general assemblies of party members, it is not the case for *Ecolo* and *Groen*. In 1999, party leaders had approved participation in the Brussels regional government, but the general assembly of members rejected it. When it comes to the selection of party leaders, imposing a candidate preselected by the party elite is very difficult (see below). Members also have a real say in the selection of candidates and the composition of the electoral lists.

The second distinctive characteristic of the two Green parties is their fear of strong leadership. Therefore, they have adopted party structures promoting collective leadership. In the case of *Ecolo*, party leadership was divided between several coleaders elected individually. Gradually, their number was lowered to three, and then to two. *Groen* opted for a single party leader elected together with a strong deputy leader.

Finally, the two parties have been very reluctant to the professionalisation of politics. Again, they feared the emergence of closed party elites. The role of MPs and, later on, of ministers, was limited within the party structure. The function of party leader was incompatible with that of MP; strict term limits were imposed both for positions within the party and parliamentary mandates. However, the severe electoral defeats of 2003 and 2004 were partly attributed to this lack of professionalisation. Since then, *Ecolo* and *Groen* have evolved. Party staff has increased and has become more professional. The role of ministers and MPs has been strengthened within the party. The control of the party elite over party members in general assemblies or within the party councils has also increased.

Party leadership

As mentioned above, *Ecolo* presents the peculiarity of having been led by coleaders rather than by a single person for most of its history. *Ecolo* started with a team of five to eight secretaries-general elected individually (Table 2.4). In 1994, the party shifted to the joint election of a team of three secretaries-general. In 2007, the party opted for the joint election of two copresidents, one man and one woman, one from Brussels and one from Wallonia. *Groen* has also functioned during most of its history with a collective leadership. In its very first years, the entire party bureau formally chaired the party. Yet, this collective body had a spokesperson that gradually imposed themselves as the leader of the party. In 1986, *Groen* changed its structure, and party leadership was divided between a party secretary (in charge of the internal party organisation) and a political secretary (in charge of the representation of the party in the media and in public offices). Finally, in 2003, *Groen* abandoned dual leadership and opted for a single-party president.

Regarding the leadership selection, *Ecolo* and *Groen* give complete power to their party members. Both parties have adopted the full members' vote system for the selection of their leaders like almost all other Belgian parties (Wauters, 2013). Yet, *Ecolo* and *Groen* present two singularities. First, the vote is organised neither in local polling stations, nor by postal or electronic ballot. Instead, party members have to attend a general assembly, during which the leadership vote is

Table 2.4 Party leaders, *Ecolo* and *Groen* in Belgium (1980–2012)

Party	Year	Candidates	Results	Length in office	Reason for resigning
Ecolo	1980	5 party secretaries	n.a.	2 years	End of term
	1982	8 party secretaries	n.a.	2 years	End of term
	1984	5 party secretaries	n.a.	2 years	End of term
	1986	Morael, Lannoye, Dardenne, Sadoine, Comblain	n.a.	2 years	End of term
	1988	Morael, Dardenne, Jonckheer, Nagy, Trussart	n.a.	2 years	End of term
	1990	Morael, Cheron, Adriaen, Miraglia, Paternotte	n.a.	2 years	End of term
	1992	Burnotte, Decroly, Lateur, Libois	n.a.	2 years	End of term
	1994	Morael, Josse, Durant	61.8%, 38.1%	4 years	End of term
	1998	Morael, Josse, Durant	92.9%	1 year	Durant became federal minister, Morael resigned after rebuff as regional minister
	1999	Defeyt, Baudouin, Ernst	55.7%, 44.3%	3 years	Voluntary resignation (Baudouin)
	2002	Defeyt, Hordies, Ernst	96.7%	1 year	Electoral defeat
	2003	Javaux, Huytebroeck, Brouir	61.9%, 38.1%	1 year	Huytebroeck became regional minister
	2004	Javaux, Durant, Brouir	n.a.	3 years	Statutory shift to 2 copresidents
	2007	Javaux, Durant	n.a.	2 years	Durant became vice-president of the EP
	2009	Javaux, Turine	Unanimity	2 years	End of term
	2012	Deleuze, Hoyos	55.3%; 46.7%	n.a.	n.a.
Groen	1982	Leo Cox	n.a.	7 years	n.a.
	1989	John Malcorps	n.a.	6 years	Voluntary resignation
	1995	Wilfried Bervoets	80.8%	3 years	Force majeure (death)
	1998	Jos Geysel	77.3%	5 years	Forced resignation (Electoral defeat)
	2003	Dirk Holemans	n.a.	1 year	Forced resignation (Electoral defeat)
	2004	Vera Dua	94.0%	3 years	Voluntary resignation
	2007	Mieke Vogel	58.0%, 42.0%	2 years	Voluntary resignation
	2009	Wouter van Besien	89.7%	n.a.	n.a.

Note: n.a. = Information not available; Full Member Vote (FMV) in general assembly is used for the leadership elections; For *Groen*, we only report the political secretary until 2003. After 2003, we report the party presidents.

Source: Wauters and Pilet (2014) and Political Party Database, (www.politicalpartydb.com).

held. Secondly, contests for experienced leadership tend to be more competitive, at least for *Ecolo* (Table 2.4). *Ecolo* has known several contested elections. First, in most contests, there is more than one candidate, which is not the case for the majority of party leadership races in Belgium (Wauters and Pilet, 2014). Second, there have been a few races with a contender winning more than one-third of the votes. It has always happened at crucial moments in the life of the party, after several electoral defeats (1997, 2003) or when the party entered government for the first time (1999). *Groen* has had much less contested races, with only one tight race in 2007.

Party membership

Interestingly enough, while *Ecolo* and *Groen* are probably the Belgian parties granting the most comprehensive powers to their members, they also attract fewer members. Lower membership figures are greatly due to the barriers at entry. While in other Belgian parties registering as party member can be reduced to a few clicks on the party website and the annual payment of a fee, *Ecolo* and *Groen* impose on their members genuine involvement in the life of the party and require strict conditions to become a full member (Rihoux, 2001). Citizens who wish to join the party will first be granted the status of 'associated members' and will be allowed to take part to the activities of the party, either at the local level or in thematic groups at the national level. After a few months, their application to become full member will have to be approved by a membership commission that will consider to what extent they are committed to the activities of the party and whether they are in line with the party ideology. As pointed out by Buelens and Rihoux, the consequences of these rules of entry are that 'In both Belgian Green parties, a "party member" was defined as an activist: thus there were only activists and no passive members' (forthcoming). After the 2003 electoral defeat, the implementation of these rules of entry has become more flexible. Yet, the general idea of active membership remains.

Consequently, the number of party members remains limited in both *Ecolo* and *Groen*. In a sense, the development of membership illustrates the successive crises and successes that both Green parties encountered. During the first 10 to 15 years, the two parties experienced a slow but gradual increase of their membership, from around 1,000 members in 1982 to more than 2,000 for *Groen* and about 1,200 for *Ecolo* in 1990 (Table 2.5). A first peak in the mid-1990s was followed by a massive increase after the electoral victory of 1999. After the 2003–2004 electoral defeats, *Ecolo* noticed a fairly solid loss of members, but this rose again gradually from 2005 onwards. *Groen*, on the other hand, was able to retain most of the membership bonus gained after the access to the national government and to stabilise its membership around 5,000 (Buelens and Rihoux, forthcoming). Finally, in the most recent period, we may observe a new rise in membership figures that is to be linked with the recent electoral recoveries of both *Ecolo* and *Groen*. The former reached more than 6,000 members for the first time in 2010, and the latter achieved over 7,000 for the first time in 2012.

Table 2.5 Party members, *Ecolo* and *Groen* in Belgium (1982–2012)

Year	Ecolo		Groen	
	Members (M)	*M/V (%)*	*Members (M)*	*M/V (%)*
1982	900	0.68	870	0.63
1983	n.a		n.a.	
1984	808		835	
1985	959	0.63	925	0.41
1986	836		1,123	
1987	617	0.39	1,373	0.50
1988	891		3,000	
1989	1,403		2,499	
1990	1,212		2,130	
1991	1,360	0.44	2,038	0.68
1992	1,876		2,529	
1993	1,934		1,897	
1994	2,347	0.81	3,375	0.98
1995	2,367	0.97	3,985	1.48
1996	1,968		3,272	
1997	2,237		3,404	
1998	2,591		3,690	
1999	2,903	0.63	4,281	0.99
2000	4,050		6,171	
2001	4,057		6,158	
2002	4,463		5,354	
2003	3,751	1.87	6,078	3.75
2004	3,208	1.34	6,153	2.04
2005	3,051		5,405	
2006	4,231		5,462	
2007	4,890	1.44	5,623	1.75
2008	5,002		4,459	
2009	5,870	1.04	4,997	2.12
2010	6,029	1.93	5,075	1.77
2011	5,742		6,249	
2012	6,233		7,855	

Note: The number of voters is the number of voters nationwide for the lower chamber of the national parliament. For the 2004 and 2009 elections, the number of voters is the number of voters nationwide for European elections.

Source: Cevipol, Université libre de Bruxelles (ULB), published on the Members and Activists of Political Parties (MAPP) website (www.projectmapp.eu).

Although these most recent figures show a real increase in membership over 30 years, with 6 to 7 times more members nowadays, the ratio of party members to party voters (M/V) is still very small compared to the traditional Belgian parties (van Haute, et al., 2013); it remains around 2 to 3 per cent.

Relation to social movements

The ties between the Green parties and social movements have always been strong. As mentioned above, the two parties emerged from new social movements. Ecologist organisations, peace movements, international cooperation movements and associations calling for more direct citizen participation were the pool from which the founding leaders, members and voters of *Ecolo* and *Groen* were recruited in the 1980s. Yet, over the years, these ties have somehow weakened. First, the widening of the electoral basis of the two Green parties has reduced the relative weight of these social movements among Green voters. Second, although many rank-and-file members remain members of these social movements, their intraparty influence has somehow diluted. Nowadays, less than 20 per cent of all members of the two parties are also members of environmental organisations (Buelens and Rihoux, forthcoming). Moreover, today, the leaders of *Ecolo* and *Groen* are less often former leaders of social movements. Dual membership remains, but can mainly be found among rank-and-file. Finally, *Ecolo* and *Groen* have developed ties with other social movements, and with trade unions in particular. In the 2000s, around 50 per cent of the members of *Ecolo* were also members of a trade union (Pilet and Schrobiltgen, 2011). It could partially explain why *Ecolo* and *Groen* have nowadays a more traditional left-wing image than during their first few years.

Main challenges and opportunities for the future

The life of *Ecolo* and *Groen* in the last 30 years has not been a quiet ride. The two parties have experienced fluctuating electoral fortunes, alternating between major electoral victories like in 1999 and spectacular defeats like in 2003 and 2004. In addition, they have been involved in governments at national and regional levels but were out of the game in the most recent episodes of government formation, at least in Flanders. In order to assess their main challenges, one could examine the conditions under which both Green parties seem to be performing better electorally. Another strategy would be to compare the situation since the 2009 regional and European elections, where the fate of the two parties has differed greatly. *Ecolo* was very successful in 2009, reaching almost its best electoral score in history and entering government in Wallonia and Brussels, while *Groen* remained very modest electorally and was never really seen as a viable coalition partner for the Flemish regional government.

Three factors seem to be crucial: the capacity of the party to attract beyond a single issue, the salience of environmental issues and the image of the party in government. First, although they have expanded their programmatic basis, *Ecolo* and *Groen* still have difficulties in presenting themselves as more than parties focusing mostly on the environment. Their image remains very much associated with the environment. As demonstrated by Walgrave, et al. (2012), both *Ecolo* and *Groen* remain by far the first parties that voters spontaneously associate with the environmental issue. However, when one looks at voters' motivation in 2009, *Ecolo* and *Groen* differ. The most important issue raised by *Groen* voters is the environmental issue; this is not the case for *Ecolo*, who attracts more voters mentioning the financial crisis as their most significant motive.[3] Interestingly, in an analysis of electoral loyalty among Brussels voters between 2009 and 2010, Delwit et al. note that, while *Groen* was able to keep 63 per cent of its electorate between the two contests, this proportion was considerably lower for *Ecolo* (Delwit, et al., 2010). The pattern is similar in Wallonia, where *Ecolo* was able to keep only half of its voters (52 per cent).

Secondly, in the same way as most parties that were created around a specific issue, *Groen* faces difficulties when the issue the party is most associated with – in this case, environment – is not high on the political agenda. In 1999, the environment was one of the main priorities on the agenda due to the food safety crisis. In 2003, that was much less the case. *Ecolo* faces the same problem, and it partly explains its severe defeat in 2003 (Hino and Rihoux, 2007). However, *Ecolo* is able to go beyond this specific issue and to capitalise for example on the question of democratic renewal. In 2009, the campaign in Wallonia was animated by several political scandals affecting the French-speaking Socialists, which benefited *Ecolo*. These scandals were not present in Flanders, but even if they would have been, *Groen* would have had to face other parties more able to attract dissatisfied voters (Hooghe, et al., 2011).

Finally, the first governmental participation between 1999 and 2003–2004 seems to have been more difficult for *Groen* than for *Ecolo*. Both parties have faced many challenges during their participation, partly due in part to their lack of professionalisation. They have both adapted gradually. Yet, *Groen* still experiences difficulties in convincing the other parties and the electorate of its ability to be a credible coalition partner. *Ecolo*, on the other hand, was able to regain more rapidly credibility among voters.

Drawing from this brief comparison between *Ecolo* and *Groen* at the end of the 2000s, we can probably conclude that the three main challenges for the two parties for the future are to broaden their credibility among voters on a wider range of issues, to be able to impose their own issues on the agenda and to maintain their credibility as potential coalition partners.

Notes

1 For matters of consistency, in this chapter, we refer to the Dutch-speaking ecologist party as *Groen* even though, as emphasized in Table 2.1, the name of the party has evolved since its foundation, from *Agalev* to *Groen!* and finally *Groen*.
2 'Déclaration de Peruwelz-Louvain-la-neuve experimant les principes fondamentaux du Mouvement Ecolo', made publicly available on 1 July 1985. Almost 30 years later, on 23 June 2013, Ecolo adopted the 'Manifeste politique d'Ecolo – Pour une transition écologique de la société', replacing the foundational text of the party.
3 Press release, PartiRep Election Study 2009.

References

Buelens, J., and Delwit, P., 2008. Belgium: Ecolo and Agalev (Groen!): Two Institutional-ized Green Parties with Parallel but Different Stories. In: G. E. Frankland, P. Lucardie and B. Rihoux, eds, *Green Parties in Transition: The End of Grass-Roots Democracy?* Farnham and Burlington, VT: Ashgate. pp. 75–92.

Buelens, J., and Deschouwer, K., 2002. The Belgian Greens in Government. In: F. Müller-Rommel and T. Poguntke, eds, *Green Parties in National Government:* London: Frank Cass. pp. 112–132.

Buelens, J., and Rihoux, B., forthcoming. Green Party Members in Belgium: Twins in Contrasted Sub-National Communities. In: W. Rüdig, ed., *Green Party Members*. Cambridge, MA: MIT Press.

Castanheira, M., and Noury, A., 2007. Les positions politiques des partis belges. *Reflets et perspectives de la vie économique*, Tome XLVI (1), pp. 13–29.

Dandoy, R., 2007. L'analyse des programmes de partis. In: A.-P. Frognier, L. De Winter and P. Baudewyns, eds, *Elections: Le Reflux? Comportements et attitudes lors des élections en Belgique*. Bruxelles: De Boeck. pp. 141–156.

Dandoy, R., 2011a. Groen! In: P. Delwit, J.-B. Pilet and E. van Haute, eds, *Les partis poli-tiques en Belgique*. Brussels: Éditions de l'Université de Bruxelles. pp. 163–177.

Dandoy, R., 2011b. Party manifestos and party competition in Belgium: The environ-mental issue. *Association Française de Science Politique, XIème Congrès*, 31 August–1 September.

Dandoy, R., Matagne, G., and Van Wynsberghe, C., 2013. L'avenir du fédéralisme belge: une analyse des programmes électoraux et des accords de gouvernement. In: R. Dandoy, G. Matagne and C. Van Wynsberghe, eds, *Le fédéralisme Belge: Enjeux institution-nels, acteurs socio-politiques et opinions publiques*. Louvain-la-Neuve: Academia – L'Harmattan. pp. 87–109.

Delwit, P., 2001. La Belgique et l'Union Européenne. In: D. Reynié and B. Cautrès, eds, *L'opinion Européenne 2001. Espaces Européens.* Paris: Presses de Science Po. pp. 173–197.

Delwit, P., and De Waele, J.-M., 1996. *Ecolo: les verts en politique.* Brussels: De Boeck.

Delwit, P., Gassner, M., and van Haute, E., 2010. Les mouvements de voix dans la Région de Bruxelles-Capitale entre l'élection régionale de juin 2009 et le scrutin fédéral du 13 juin 2010. *Brussels Studies*, 41, pp. 1–18.

Delwit, P., Kulahci, E., Hellings, B., Pilet, J.-B., and van Haute, E., 2005. L'Européanisation de la représentation communautaire: le cas des partis francophones belges. *Politique Européenne*, 16, pp. 83–102.

Delwit, P., and Pilet, J.-B., 2005. Regional and European election in Belgium: The Greens still at low tide. *Environmental Politics*, 14(1), pp. 112–117.

Delwit, P., and van Haute, E., 2008. Greens in a Rainbow: The Impact of Participation in Government of the Green Parties in Belgium. In: K. Deschouwer, ed., *New Parties in Government: In Power for the First Time*. London: Routledge. pp. 104–120.

Franck, E., 2005. Convergentie in het gedachtegoed van de Vlaamse politieke partijen: waarheid of illusie? *PSW-Paper*, 7. Antwerpen: Universiteit Antwerpen.

Hino, A., and Rihoux, B., 2007. Le vote Ecolo: les raisons de la colère. In: A.-P. Frognier, L. De Winter and P. Baudewyns, eds, *Elections: le Reflux? Comportements et attitudes lors des élections en Belgique*. Brussels: De Boeck. pp. 65–94.

Hooghe, M., Marien, S., and Pauwels, T., 2011. Where do distrusting voters turn if there is no viable exit or voice option? The impact of political trust on electoral behaviour in the Belgian regional elections of June 2009. *Government and Opposition*, 46(2), pp. 245–273.

Hooghe, M., and Rihoux, B., 2000. The Green breakthrough in the Belgian general election of June 1999. *Environmental Politics*, 9(3), pp. 129–136.

Hooghe, M., and Rihoux, B., 2003. The harder the fall . . . the Greens in the Belgian general elections of May 2003. *Environmental Politics*, 12(4), pp. 120–126.

Hooghe, M., and Rihoux, B., 2008. No place at the table: Green parties in the 2007–2008 political crisis in Belgium. *Environmental Politics*, 17(5), pp. 822–827.

Kitschelt, H., 1989. *The Logics of Party Formation: Ecological Politics in Belgium and West Germany.* Ithaca, NY: Cornell University Press.

Müller-Rommel, F., 2002. The lifespan and the political performance of Green parties in Western Europe. *Environmental Politics*, 11(1), pp. 1–16.

Pedersen, M. N., 1982. Towards a new typology of party lifespans and minor parties. *Scandinavian Political Studies*, 5(1), pp. 1–16.

Pilet, J.-B., and Schrobiltgen, M.-H., 2011. Ecolo. In: P. Delwit, J.-B. Pilet and E. van Haute, eds, *Les partis politiques en Belgique*. Brussels: Éditions de l'Université de Bruxelles. pp. 179–200.

Pilet, J.-B., and van Haute, E., 2007. Les réticences à l'Europe dans un pays Europhile. Le cas de la Belgique. In: J. Lacroix and R. Coman, eds, *Les résistances à l'Europe: Cultures nationales, idéologies et stratégies d'acteurs*. Brussels: Éditions de l'Université de Bruxelles. pp. 211–225.

Rihoux, B., 1993. Emergence et développement des deux partis écologistes belges: Ecolo et Agalev. *Université Catholique de Louvain, Working Paper 77.*

Rihoux, B., 2001. *Les partis politiques: organisations en changement: Le test des écologistes.* Paris: L'Harmattan.

Rihoux, B., 2003. La percée d'Ecolo au 13 juin 1999: un effet-dioxine, et des électeurs moins "verts"? In: A.-P. Frognier and A.-M. Aish, eds, *Elections: La rupture? Le comportement des belges face aux élections de 1999*. Brussels: De Boeck. pp. 44–53.

Rüdig, W., 2006. Is government good for Greens? Comparing the electoral effects of government participation in Western and East-Central Europe. *European Journal of Political Research*, 45, pp. 127–154.

van Haute, E., Amjahad, A., Borriello, A., Close, C., and Sandri, G., 2013. Party members in a pillarized partitocracy. An empirical overview of party membership figures and profiles in Belgium. *Acta Politica*, 48(1), pp. 68–91.

Walgrave, S., Lefevere, J., and Tresch, A., 2012. The associative dimension of issue ownership. *Public Opinion Quarterly*, 76(4), pp. 771–782.

Wauters, B., 2013. Democratising party leadership selection in Belgium: Motivations and decision makers. *Political Studies*, 62, pp. 1–20.

Wauters, B., and Pilet, J.-B., 2014. The Selection of Party Leaders in Belgium. In: J.-B. Pilet and W. Cross, eds, *The Selection of Party Leaders in Parliamentary Democracies.* London: Routledge. pp. 30–46.

3 Central and Eastern European Green parties

Rise, fall and revival?

E. Gene Frankland

Introduction

Central and Eastern European (CEE)[1] Green parties can be traced back to the rise during the 1980s of environmental activism against the pollution and destruction caused by the industrial development policies of the communist governments. During 1988–1990, Green and Ecologist parties emerged, and most joined national 'umbrella' movements of democratic opposition to the communist regimes. As a result of the first postcommunist elections (1990–1992), CEE Greens not only entered parliaments but also in several countries joined coalition governments. However, in contrast to West European (WE) Green parties, their electoral support rapidly faded with almost all falling below Pedersen's (1982) threshold of relevance by the end of the decade (Table 3.1).

There are many explanations of the decline of CEE Green parties. For example, Jordan (1998) cites six external factors: the post-1992 emphasis on economic questions; the low level of postmaterialistic values; the rise of postindependence nationalism; the appropriation of environmental issues by other parties; the West's material support of Christian democratic, liberal and social democratic parties; and the electoral law hurdles that forced Green parties into awkward alliances. Jordan lists one internal factor: Green party splits and interest conflicts, such as between movement and party activists. Waller and Millard (1992) note how environmental 'champions' went into government but soon shifted their allegiances to other parties. Early on, Greens had to contend with not only the infiltration of communists within their organisations but also the misappropriation of the 'Green' label by 'fake groups' (Frankland, 2002). Rüdig in his comparative study of Greens in government (2006) describes CEE Greens during the 1990s as 'proto-parties . . . without stable structures, loyal members and activists, and [with] an ideology limited to environmentalism'. More consolidated parties might have coped with the disappearance of their core issues from the policy agenda, but even then it would have been a huge challenge.

Today's CEE Green parties includes survivors and newcomers. Some parties have shared power at the national level while most have had little direct policy impact. Some have maintained a 'postmaterialist' or centre-left identity while others have positioned themselves as centre-right, especially on economic issues.

Table 3.1 Central and Eastern European Green parties

Country	Party	Year founded	Parliamentary representation once or more	Government participation once or more	Last national election results (%)	2014 EP election results (%)
Bulgaria	ZPB	1989	Yes	Yes	0.01	0.4
	Zelenite	2008	No	No	0.7	0.6
Croatia	ZL	2004	No	No	0.4	a
	ORaH	2013	No	No	a	9.4
Czech Republic	SZ	1989	Yes	Yes	3.2	3.8
Estonia	EER	2006*	Yes	No	3.8	0.3
Hungary	LMP	2009	Yes	No	5.3	5.0
	ZB	1993	No	No	?	?
Latvia	LZP	1990	Yes	Yes	3.7	b
Lithuania	LZP	2011**	Yes (c)	No	c	3.5
Poland	Zieloni	2004	No	No	b	b
Romania	PER	1990	Yes	No	0.8	1.1
	PV	2006	Yes	No	1.0 (d)	0.3
Slovakia	SZ	1989	Yes	Yes	0.3	?
Slovenia	SMS-Zeleni	2000	Yes	No	?	?
	ZS	1989	Yes	Yes	0.5	?

Notes: *EER is ER's successor, **LZP is successor of old LZP, a = nonparticipation in last election, b = ran within a coalition, c = LZP member elected as independent district candidate, d = PV estimate reported by EGP.

Sources: EGP documents, state election commissions and party websites.

Some parties have built up multi-level organisations while others revolve around personalities. Some parties have enjoyed financial support from the state budget while others have had to seek out private 'sponsors'. Most are full members of the European Green Party (EGP), but a few are not.

The objectives of this chapter are to review the origins and development of CEE Green parties, to highlight their distinguishing structural and programmatic characteristics and to assess opportunities and challenges in their national circumstances. We focus our survey first on the Green parties of East Central Europe (Poland, the Czech Republic, Slovakia and Hungary), which are located in a historically strategic region and have in recent decades maintained relatively close contacts with WE Greens, especially the German and/or Austrian Greens. Secondly, we consider the Green parties of the Baltic States (Estonia, Latvia and Lithuania). Lastly, we turn to the less well-known Green parties of Southeast Europe (Slovenia, Croatia, Bulgaria and Romania). The chapter concludes that, while most CEE Green parties are likely to remain marginal actors, there are recent developments with positive implications for the future.

East Central Europe

The communist regimes of this region varied over time and cross-nationally in the tolerance shown toward environmental activism. Environmental groups flourished during the 1980s in Poland. Some were officially associated with the government, others were dissident groups and still others were like the Polish Ecology Club (*Polski Klub Ekologiczny* – PKE), which was formed in 1980, grew to 25,000 members and organised protests within the letter of the law. As of 1987, there were all together 2,000 local environmental groups (Waller and Millard, 1992) in Poland. In December 1988, Zygmunt Fura (from the PKE) founded the first Green party in Poland and in East Central Europe. The Polish Green Party reported a membership of 4,000. Soon there were two more Green or Ecologist parties claiming thousands of members. Green parties elected 120 local officials in the 1990 elections. Jordan (2010) counts seven Green parties/movements as participants in the 1991 elections for the *Sejm* (lower house of parliament); all together, they won 2 per cent of the votes but no seats. By 1995, there were as many as 17 Green parties in Poland, but none succeeded in establishing a national profile (Grzybek and Szwed, 2008) or winning parliamentary seats. In 1997, members of the Polish Green Party joined the list of the Democratic Left Alliance (SLD) (Bugajski, 2002), but won no seats.

Other activists from the PKE formed the Ecological Forum (*Forum Ekologiczny* – FE) within the post-Solidarity Democratic Union (UD), which after a merger became the Freedom Union (UW). While the FE claimed 200 members, only 6 of the UW members of parliament elected in 1993 were from the FE. The UW was part of the centre-right government (1997–2000) in which Radoslaw Gawlik (FE) served as deputy minister of environmental protection.[2] FE members were elected to three seats in the *Sejm* and one in the Senate. The UW failed to clear the 5 per cent threshold in 2001. According to Ferry (2002), the FE was a marginal, rarely united group within the UW.

In 2003 Polish activists from environmental, feminist, human rights, antiwar and other nongovernmental groups, former members of the FE and the 'Freedom and Peace' movement, as well as representatives from the PKE, Amnesty International and others debated the advantages of creating a new broad social movement or a new Green party. Those arguing for the latter prevailed: *Zieloni* (Greens) was registered as a new party (Grzybek and Szwed, 2008). *Zieloni* did not get off to a good start. Failing to get sufficient signatures to run candidates all across the country, it won only 0.3 per cent of the votes for the Polish seats in the 2004 European Parliament. In 2005, *Zieloni* ran in an alliance with a splinter leftist party and failed to win any parliamentary seats; it ended up with only 0.2 per cent of the votes. In the 2009 European Parliament elections, *Zieloni* ran as part of a coalition that won 2.4 per cent of the votes (no seats). Not until the local elections of 2010 did party leaders dare speak of a 'breakthrough' (Kozek, 2013). As the result of *Zieloni*'s alliance with the Democratic Left Alliance (SLD), it won one local council seat (out of 39,838), two city council seats (out of 6,280) and two regional council seats (out of 561) in the 2010 elections. *Zieloni* won no seats in the parliamentary elections of 2011.

The *Zieloni* 2004 party statute delineates the role of and expectations for members and describes its multi-level organisational structure. The Congress is the supreme authority, but the statute allows for membership referenda on program issues. The party statute is explicit about the obligation of membership dues and expects activism from members. As of 2009, the reported membership of *Zieloni* was 3,500 (van Biezen, et al., 2012). This number is likely a bit inflated; the party co-chair in a recent interview (Ostolski, 2013) replied, 'We have a total of only a few hundred members'. *Zieloni* elects a male co-chair and a female co-chair and utilises a gender quota system in drawing up its candidate lists.

The Green Manifesto of 2003 provides the basic framework for *Zieloni*'s policies. It lists the party's basic goals as:

> respect for human rights abiding by the principles of balanced social, environmental and economic development . . . social justice and solidarity, civil society and state protection of the environment and its resources for future generations, equal status regardless of gender and age . . . respect for the rights of minorities, nonviolent conflict resolution.
>
> (Quoted in Grzybek and Szwed, 2008, p. 23)

The Manifesto includes a provision giving women the right to choose, which caused some founding members in heavily Catholic Poland to withdraw from the party. While *Zieloni*'s environmental policies follow the general direction of WE Greens, there are special considerations of Polish circumstances; for example the Polish Greens 'want no immediate and complete departure from coal' (Ostolski, 2013). The party has in recent years formulated more detailed policy documents regarding social, economic and health policies. This can be seen as a step toward a more social ecology by those who aspire to see *Zieloni* become a significant force within a New Left in Poland (Zakowski, 2008), which seems a project for a new generation.

In contrast to Poland, the communist regime in Czechoslovakia was rigid and stable. There had been no mass democratic opposition during the 1980s and no large autonomous environment groups like the PKE. Toward the end of the regime, small groups of ecological and peace activists played an important role in the emergence of the Civic Forum and in Slovakia of the Public against Violence (Hloušek and Kopeček, 2010). The Green Party (*Strana Zelených* – SZ) was founded on 21 November 1989 with 5,200 members. Its membership was to triple in only a few months. Three regional party groups emerged: one for Prague, whose leaders were 'unknown' to the environmental movement; one for Bohemia and Moravia; and one for Slovakia. At the SZ's first national congress in Brno, the Prague group failed to take over the party leadership; delegates approved the loose regional structure of the party, and former Communist Party members were banned from standing as SZ candidates. In the 1990 parliamentary elections, the Greens received 4.1 per cent of the votes but no seats (due to the required threshold of 5 per cent). The Slovakian Greens (who faced an initial lower threshold of 3 per cent) won 3.5 per cent and six seats in the Slovak National Council.

In the parliamentary and (later) local elections of 1990, the SZ won 5 per cent or more of the votes only in the highly polluted areas of northwestern Bohemia (Jehlička and Kostelecký, 1992).

To contest the 1992 parliamentary elections, the Czech Greens joined the Liberal Social Union (LSU) with the Czech Socialist Party and the Agrarian Party. Although the LSU won sufficient votes to qualify for seats with three going to the SZ, many members were uncomfortable with the move to the left, and over a third of the original members of the SZ dropped out of the party. Czechoslovakia was peacefully dissolved on 1 January 1993, and the Czech Republic and Slovakia officially became independent states. The LSU collapsed in 1993, leaving the SZ with only one member of the Czech parliament. The party did not participate in the 1996 parliamentary elections, and in the 1998 parliamentary elections, it won only 1.1 per cent of the votes (not enough to qualify for state funding) and no seats. In 1998–1999, it claimed to have 1,800 members and 142 local councillors (Bugajski, 2002).

After a series of political scandals, the party was running low on money and was down to 239 members in 2001. Jehlička and Kostelecký (2003) credit chairperson Miroslav Rokos's positive response to a proposal to allow civil society activists to run on the Green Party list with preventing the demise of the SZ. Journalists began to provide positive coverage of the party, which gained credibility and 150 new members. In the 2002 parliamentary elections, the SZ won 2.4 per cent of the votes (no seats), enough to qualify for state funding. In spring 2003, Jan Beranek, who had been elected SZ leader thanks to the votes of the new members, rewrote the party's program and constitution. The organisational changes to centralise power in a party that advocates more democracy stirred factional strife. Personal rivalries intensified until 2005, when Martin Bursik, a media-savvy politician who had been a Christian Democrat minister of the environment, ousted Beranek.

In the 2006 parliamentary campaign, the new leadership attempted to project the image of a 'flexible, pragmatic party' (Deets and Kouba, 2008, pp. 815–821). The SZ won 6.3 per cent of the votes and six seats. After lengthy negotiations, the Greens agreed to join a centre-right governing coalition with the Civic Democrats (ODS) and the Christian Democrats (KDU–ČSL). They obtained four cabinet positions, including the minister of the environment, as well as a special agreement not to expand nuclear power. The party's left wing had favoured instead a Social Democratic (ČSSD) minority government. As junior partner, the SZ shared responsibility for policies that contradicted the Greens' manifesto, especially the government's support for a US missile radar facility on Czech soil, which most Czechs opposed. The Greens' popularity dropped in the polls, and two Green deputies joined the opposition in bringing down the government with a vote of no confidence (Jehlička, et al., 2011). In the 2010 parliamentary elections, the Greens were overshadowed by the rise of two new centre-right parties. The SZ won only 2.4 per cent of the votes, losing all its seats and most of its state funding. In the 2012 elections for the Senate, the Greens won 1 seat (out of 81) by running a popular judge as their candidate; they also won 6 regional council seats (out of 675) and 323 local council seats (out of 62,178). In the 2013 parliamentary elections, the

Greens won 3.2 per cent of the votes but no seats. Centre-right volatility continued as a new Populist party Yes (ANO), formed by the country's second richest billionaire, finished second with 18.7 per cent of the votes and 47 seats.

The four established Czech parties have had large memberships and dense organisational networks. TOP09, one of the two new (as of 2010) centre-right parties with Public Affairs (VV), has been the more successful in building up membership and organisation. In 2011, TOP09 lead the Greens (SZ) in membership (4,250 to 1,874), in local organisations (193 to 190), district organisations (84 to 0) and employees (41 to 5). After joining the centre-right government in 2007, the Green Party had 2,500 members (Bakke, 2011) – so the trend has been downward since its electoral setback in 2010. The weak institutionalisation of the party in 2003 had allowed 'outsiders' to take over its leadership. A more charismatic leader was welcomed, but his concentration of powers and policy compromises soon fuelled dissension within the membership. The party has long suffered from a lack of resources so the leadership has been working to build a network of individual contributors (Cisar, 2011).

The SZ platform of the late 1990s was based on 'sustainable development', which meant 'the protection and reasonable use of natural resources' while incorporating a social democratic perspective that sought also 'to meet the social and cultural needs of people' (Bugajski, 2002, p. 48). The collapse of the liberal Freedom Union (US–DEU) meant that there was a centre-right opening within the Czech party system. Accordingly the new SZ leadership in the 2006 campaign emphasised quality of life, good governance, community control of schools and better local land use to appeal to urban middle-class voters (Deets and Kouba, 2008). The SZ manifesto embraced economic incentives, Green consumerism and integration of environmental protection into other policy areas. A noteworthy difference with other parties was the Greens' special attention to minority rights (Jehlička, et al., 2011). A quantitative analysis of the electoral manifestos of three Green parties in the 2000s (Carter, 2013) found that economic goals were the biggest concern of the Czech Greens' 2010 manifesto, followed by environment and then by welfare state expansion.

The Greens' future will be largely dependent on its competitive circumstances once the Czech party system restabilises. The Greens remain committed to a 'new' (bottom-up) style of politics, but they have been overshadowed lately by 'new' (top-down) parties, which have both Populist slogans and wealthy sponsors. The Greens should draw encouragement from Bolleyer's research on new parties (2013), which finds that nearly 79.7 per cent of new parties that experienced sustained success were socially rooted compared to 21.3 per cent of those that were formed by 'entrepreneurs'. However, in the meantime, the challenge for the Czech Greens is to hold on to their postmaterialist supporters while reaching out to young, middle-class, centre-right voters during a time of economic insecurity.

The rise of nationalism in the early 1990s split the Slovak Greens. The party returned to its original name, the Green Party in Slovakia (*Strana Zelených na Slovensku* – SZS), with its majority favouring an independent Slovakia and its minority forming an intraparty platform in favour of federalism. Prior to the June 1992 parliamentary elections, the profederal Slovakian Greens reintegrated with the federal Green Party. In the elections, they won only 1.1 per cent of the votes in Slovakia while the proindependence Green Party won 2.1 per cent. Neither won seats. Even if they had remained united, they would have been without seats because the Federal Assembly had raised the electoral threshold for representation to 4 per cent. Following Czechoslovakia's dissolution on 1 January 1993, profederal Slovak Greens reorganised as the Green League. Later they merged with the centre-right Democratic Party (DP) and constituted an intraparty group until 2001 (Kopeček, 2009).

The development of the Slovak Greens (*Strana Zelených na Slovensku* – SZS) has been more complicated. The major division of the 1990s involved diverging attitudes toward Vladimír Mečiar, nationalist leader of the Movement for a Democratic Slovakia (HZDS), whose critics saw as a threat to democracy. The HZDS had provided the Greens with a no-interest loan before the 1992 elections, and some party activists favoured cooperating with it (Kopeček, 2009). However, more activists leaned toward working with the postcommunist party of the Democratic Left (SDL), which was anti-Mečiar and closer to the SZS on environmental issues. Pro-Mečiar Greens left the party and formed the Slovak Green Alternative (*Slovenska Zelena Alternative* – SZA) whose chair was elected in 1994 to parliament from the HZDS's party list.[3] For the 1994 parliamentary elections, the Greens (SZS) joined the centre-left Common Cause coalition, which ended up in the opposition after winning 10.4 per cent of the votes and 18 seats, 2 of which went to the SZS. Later in the year, the party managed to win 206 seats in local councils (0.6 per cent of total seats). For the 1998 parliamentary elections, the SZS joined a heterogeneous anti-Mečiar coalition, the Slovak Democratic Coalition (SDK), which won 26.3 per cent of the votes and constructed a parliamentary majority with other opposition parties. The Greens received three seats in parliament and the post of deputy minister of the environment.

Although Mečiar's HZDS had been blocked from power and the SZS had become a junior partner in a governing coalition, there were fears that the Greens' distinctive identity had become submerged within the SDK. Most of the Greens rejected merger into the successor party of the SDK, and alternative alliances proved impossible. With polls indicating very low public interest in environmental issues, the SZS ran separately in the 2002 parliamentary elections and won 0.99 per cent of the votes. In the local elections later in the year, the Greens won 121 council seats (0.5 per cent of the total) (Kopeček, 2009). For the 2004 European Parliament elections, the SZS allied with Direction–Social Democracy (SMER–SD), a Populist party established in 1999. SMER had emerged as the main opponent of the centre-right government. A leading member of the SZS ran on the SMER list. Although she failed to receive a seat, she argued that the campaign was worthwhile because it had shown that the Greens stand for more than environmental protection (Záhumenská, 2004).

In 2005, a surge of new members doubled the SZS's size to 1,200 members. They voted in a new leadership, which changed the party's name to *Strana*

Zelených (SZ). A new program was adopted that expanded the party's concerns into new areas, such as the 'information economy and multi-cultural society'. The SZ turned away from SMER and toward the (liberal) Free Forum for the 2006 parliamentary elections. The Free Forum won 3.5 per cent of the votes (no seats). Kopeček (2009) attributes its disappointing performance mainly to public feuding by leaders of the alliance right before the elections. A 'new' Green party emerged and took up the name of the old party (SZS) to compete against the SZ in the local elections in late 2006; not surprisingly, neither party did well. For the 2009 European Parliament elections, the SZ's list of candidates was opened to environmental and civil society activists. It received 2.1 per cent of the votes (no seats). A different strategy was used for the 2010 parliamentary elections: the SZ placed its candidates on the Democratic Left's (SDL) list. But the combined list received only 2.4 per cent of the votes (no seats). On 28 November 2010, the SZ elected 6 mayors and 58 city or district councillors, which was heralded by the European Green Party as a 'historical success'.[4] In the 2012 parliamentary elections, the SZ running alone managed to win 0.3 per cent of the votes (less than ten years before).

The Greens (SZ) have left behind the nationalism of the 1990s and have incorporated the core program of the European Green Party: sustainable development, democracy, human rights, environmental protection and social justice (Blum, 2004). A recent election manifesto differentiated the SZ from traditional left and right parties as a party whose orientations are focussed on long time horizons and whose policies seek sustainable and balanced development in all areas. In contrast to SMER, the Greens reject any expansion of nuclear power in favour of clean technologies and alternative energies. They also support the dignity of all humans (including minorities), the self-expression of the young and the active participation of women, while they oppose corruption, the waste of natural resources and unrestricted global capitalism. In contrast to the Czech Greens, there is a lack of centre-right themes. The Greens (SZ) are today an extraparliamentary party with a few hundred active members and sparse resources for modern campaigning; thus they must endeavour to form electoral coalitions in hopes of winning parliamentary seats without losing their profile as a 'counterweight to today's political parties and their [short-sighted] programs'.[5]

Environmentalists in Hungary founded the Danube Circle movement in 1984. It mobilised large-scale opposition to the Gabcikovo-Nagymaros project to construct two hydroelectric dams on the Danube. In 1989, Hungary's communist government bowed to public pressure and halted its part of the joint project with Czechoslovakia (Horak, 2002). Hungarian environmentalists were active in 1985 in the formation of Greenway, the network for East Central European environmentalists, which despite harassment by the state security services organised international conferences and grassroots workshops (Jordan, 1991). In November 1989, the Hungarian Green Party (*Magyarországi Zöld Párt* – MZP) was founded. Despite the role of environmental activism in the erosion of the communist regime, Hungarian Greens performed dismally, winning only 0.36 per cent of the votes in (free) parliamentary elections in 1990. Perhaps competing anticommunist parties had expressed sufficient environmental concern in their campaigns, or perhaps the MZP was not perceived as authentically 'Green'. In any case, turmoil followed the election with right-wing groups seizing control of the party organisation and shifting its policies in a national conservative direction while retaining the Green Party name. In 1993, expelled MZP members and environmental activists launched a new party, the Green Alternative (*Zöld Alternativa* – ZA). In the 1994 parliamentary elections, the ZA fielded only one candidate and won a tiny 0.02 per cent of the national vote; the MZP barely did any better, winning 0.2 per cent. In the local elections later in the year, ZA ended up with only 12 local council seats.

The ZA decided to run with an alliance of small parties in 1998, which won few votes and no parliamentary seats. The ZA renamed itself the Alliance of Green Democrats (*Zöld Demokraták Szövetsége* – ZDS) in 2000. The ZDS participated in a heterogeneous Centre alliance of small parties and independents in the 2002 parliamentary elections, which won 3.9 per cent and no seats. Internal conflicts ensued, and the ZDS was unable to field candidates in the 2004 European Parliament (EP) elections. In 2008, the party leader moved to rename the ZDS as the Green Left (*Zöld Baloldal* – ZB) and sought an alliance with a reformist-communist splinter party, provoking the exit of a number of activists. The ZB failed to qualify for the 2009 EP elections and fielded only a couple of district candidates in the 2010 parliamentary elections (Jordan, 2010, p. 55). The ZB retains its membership in the European Green Party but has been totally overshadowed in recent years by the LMP.

Politics Can Be Different (*Lehet Más a Politka* – LMP) was founded by an informal network of young activists from Green, human rights and social non-governmental organisations in February 2009. Its roots can be traced back to the 'Another World Is Possible' alter-globalisation movement. Its founders sought an entirely new party with a broad appeal across the left–right spectrum. In June 2009, the LMP ran a joint list of EP candidates with the Humanist Party (now disbanded). It received only 2.6 per cent of the votes and no seats, but the LMP's performance was noteworthy because it came out ahead of the Alliance of Free Democrats (SZDSZ), a liberal party that had played an important role in recent national governments. The collapse of the SZDSZ prior to the 2010 parliamentary election along with the unpopularity of the Socialist Party (MSZP) presented an opening on the centre-left for a young party with 'clean hands' and a positive message ('politics can change'). The LMP campaigned with little money, but much enthusiasm for transparency in politics, against corruption and for a free press. The LMP won 7.5 per cent of the votes in the April 2010 parliamentary elections and 16 seats. It ranked as the fourth largest parliamentary party, after Fidesz–Hungarian Civic Union (which formed the government), the Socialist Party and the right-wing Populist Jobbik Party. In the October 2010 local elections, the LMP won 54 council seats, running well in Budapest.

In clearing the 5 per cent threshold, the LMP had steered clear of alliances with established parties. While the Socialists had done poorly in the 2010 elections, Viktor Orbán's national conservative Fidesz Party (and its allies) had won a two-thirds majority in the parliament, which meant that they could not only change the electoral laws, but also the constitution. Despite the protests of the opposition and the concerns of the leaders of the European Union about Orbán's undermining of democracy, his government proceeded to push through parliament legal and institutional changes that strengthened its hold on power. Factional strife developed within the LMP parliamentary group over the best strategy to advance the party's goals in face of such developments. The 'fundis' favoured maintaining independence in order to bring about change of the system in the long run, while the 'realos' favoured cooperating with liberal and left forces to oppose Orbán's regime (Magyar, 2013). The leaders of the latter faction formed the 'Dialogue for Hungary' platform within the party to advocate joining the 'Together 2014' alliance led by former Prime Minister Gordon Bajnai. After the 'fundi' position prevailed at the January 2013 party conference, LMP's parliamentary group split with eight members becoming independents and a month later transforming the platform into a new party with the same name (Dialogue for Hungary or *Párbeszéd Magyarországért* – PM).

In the April 2014 parliamentary elections, the Fidesz–Hungarian Civil Union retained its two-thirds majority of seats, winning 44.5 per cent of party list votes. Despite the party split, the LMP managed to win 5.3 per cent of the list votes (−2.2) and five seats.[6] The Dialogue for Hungary was one of five parties running in the Unity centre-left alliance (which collectively won 25.7 per cent of the list votes); it received one of Unity's 28 list seats. The right-wing Jobbik Party finished third with 20.5 per cent and 20 seats. Jobbik was very popular with younger voters, as was the LMP though to a lesser extent than in 2014. LMP outperformed Jobbik in more affluent parts of Budapest. The demographic profile of the LMP electorate resembles that commonly found for West European Greens: young, educated, middle class, residing in large and/or university cities, with strong representation of women.

Participatory democracy is one of the LMP's four core values (the others are sustainability, social justice and nonviolence). The LMP is an 'antiparty' in the sense that it views the Hungarian political structure as 'corrupt, self-serving and obstructing the creation of a meaningful democracy' (Fábián, 2010, p. 1008). According to the party's website,[7] organisationally, politics can be different by 'minimizing the hierarchy' and developing the 'spirit of the participation'. Any LMP member can join regional workshops, working groups and project teams as well as participate at the party congress. The national board consists of 13 members: 6 from the regional organisations, 6 appointed by the congress and the parliamentary group leader. The board has co-chairs (one male, one female) and a secretary. The national policy council oversees the work of the party organs, promotes cooperation and participates in candidate selection. There are special committees for ethics and auditing. A special feature is the 'women's escalator', a program to make eco-politics more attractive for women and to advance gender equality. The party rejected gender quotas in favour of an understanding that the minority gender would be represented in the leadership proportional to its numbers in the overall membership. The LMP would like to apply its 'small-scale, internal model of reaching consensus' to problems beyond gender inequality

(Fábián, 2010, p. 1010). The LMP's 'shoestring budget' relies on funds from small contributors raised via creative uses of new communications technology. It has 'practiced and preached financial transparency'; the first parliamentary bill it introduced was to promote transparency regarding campaign revenues and expenditures (Fábián, 2010). Its MPs have engaged in street protests to raise public awareness of vital issues.

An analysis of the LMP's 2010 electoral manifesto found its top three policy concerns to be environmental quality, welfare state expansion and equality/social justice (Carter, 2013). According to Fábián's assessment (2010, p. 1007), 'The LMP has creatively linked environmental sustainability with Hungary's social, economic and political problems while emphasizing the global, economic and human rights dimensions of sustainability'. The LMP's programmatic thrust has been compared with that of Scandinavian Green parties (Sitter, 2011, p. 260): 'participatory democracy, sustainable development, social justice and soft Euroskepticism'. Its 2014 EP election program calls not for 'less or more Europe', but rather for 'Better Europe'.[8] However, the LMP tends to be centrist on taxing and spending issues.

By a fraction of a per cent, the LMP in 2014 cleared the 5 per cent threshold to win parliamentary seats a second consecutive time on its own, which differentiates it from the Polish, the Czech and the Slovakian Greens. This second victory occurred despite new electoral laws that further disadvantaged small parties and a party split over strategy in 2013. Furthermore, the Hungarian situation is unique in that the LMP and its splinter, the Dialogue for Hungary (PM), are now both represented in the national and the European parliaments. In view of Inglehart and Welzel's cultural values study (2005), one would not anticipate that Hungary with the lowest level of self-expressive values in East Central Europe would currently have the region's most successful Green party.

The Baltics

Environmental issues played an important role in the surge of public support for Baltic independence movements in the late 1980s (Agarin, 2009). Soviet economic development projects posed a dual threat: first, further degradation of the natural environment, and second, further erosion of national identity due to the influx of a workforce from outside the Baltics. As in East Central Europe, Green parties emerged during 1989–1990, were elected to national parliaments and took part in coalition governments in the early 1990s. By the mid-1990s, their electoral support had sharply declined, and they were struggling to survive as small independent parties. From the outset, Baltic Greens have shared the environmental concerns of WE Greens but not on other issues such as the rights of minorities, nor have they ever had qualms about working with centre-right parties.

It was the controversy over Soviet plans in Estonia for expanded phosphate mining that lead to the birth of the Estonian Green Movement (*Eestimaa Rahvaliit* – ERL) in 1987 (Spolitis, 2008). The ERL won eight seats in the (free) elections for the Estonian Supreme Soviet in 1990 and its chairperson became the minister of environment. Personal quarrels and left–right differences during 1989–1990 resulted in the creation of two Estonian Green parties. After two years of conflict, the Green Party (*Eesti Roheline Partei* – ERP) and the Estonian Green Party (*Eesti Roheline Erakond* – ERE) merged in 1991 to form the Estonian Greens (*Eesti Rohelised* – ER). However, the new party and its allies only won about 3 per cent of the list votes and one constituency seat in the September 1992 parliamentary elections (Bugajski, 2002). With Estonian independence achieved and Soviet-era industrial pollution reduced, the party began to fragment. Its sole MP joined the Coalition Party before the next election. Some Green activists returned to the Movement while others migrated to centre-right and centre-left parties. For the 1995 parliamentary election, the Estonian Greens formed an electoral alliance with the Royalists. This awkward alliance won only 0.8 per cent of the votes. Due to electoral law changes that prohibited electoral alliances, the Greens merged formally with the Centre Party in order to contest the 1999 elections. Not able to recruit 1,000 members (the old requirement had been 200), the Greens could not participate in the 2003 elections (Sikk and Andersen, 2009). Spolitis (2008) attributes the party's legal demise to the declining appeal of its ideology and new institutional obstacles faced by small parties but also to its lack of leadership.

The Greens continued as a nonprofit organisation until competitive circumstances in the early 2000s became more encouraging. The Estonian economy was rapidly growing, and a sizeable new middle class was emerging. There had been a series of oil and chemical spills in the Gulf of Finland that threatened coastal areas. Energy controversies over nuclear power development and over-dependency on Russia's oil and gas were also receiving headline coverage. Marek Strandberg, a prominent Green, tested the political waters by running as an independent in the 2004 EP elections. He won 2.3 per cent of the Estonian votes, which lead to the formation of the Green Party Initiative Group in 2005. In November 2006, the new Party of Estonian Greens (*Erakond Eestimaa Rohelised* – EER), having enrolled 1,203 members, staged its first general assembly (Sikk and Andersen, 2009). In the March 2007 parliamentary elections, the new Green Party won 7.1 per cent of the votes and gained six MPs. Survey data indicated that its supporters tended to be somewhat more urban (when ethnicity is controlled for) and more educated, especially among younger cohorts. The Greens drew support from some of those who had abstained in 2003, but most of their support was at the expense of other parties, especially the Moderates/Social Democrats (Sikk and Andersen, 2009). The Greens were invited to coalition talks by the Reform Party, which had emerged as the election's clear winner. While there was agreement on some policy proposals, the talks failed to resolve differences over ministerial positions (Spolitis, 2008). The Greens assumed the role of constructive opposition.

During 2009–2011, environmental issues were not so high on the policy agenda due to the financial and economic crisis, and the Greens did not benefit from the scandals involving other parties. In the 2009 EP elections, the Greens won only 2.7 per cent of Estonian votes. They ran 183 candidates in the 2009 local elections; only two were successful. These disappointing results stirred opposition to the leadership of Marek Strandberg. Insurgents got the votes at the party's November 2009 general assembly to take control of the party board. However, Strandberg's legal challenge of the election of the new board was successful. Twenty members of the opposition were expelled from the party. To regain lost ground, the Greens sought to run popular independents on their party list (Sikk, 2011a). In the 2011 parliamentary elections, the Greens received only 3.8 per cent of the votes and lost all their seats.

The EER embraces democracy, personal responsibility and decentralisation as organisational principles for society (EER Program 2014). Earlier the Greens operated with multiple spokespersons, but the EER departed from tradition and settled on a single chair in 2008. The board, including the chair, has eight members. There is no gender equality on the board or in other party organisations (although the list of 2014 EP candidates was balanced). The board manages everyday activities at the national level. The 25-member council meets quarterly and has the final say on matters between general assemblies. Council members include EER public office-holders, board members, representatives of constituency and regional party organisations and other members selected by the general assembly. Specialised bodies include the 'Court of Honour' (a judicial panel), the election committee and the auditing committee. Currently, the EER has 1,142 members, which makes them the second smallest registered party.[9] Regular membership dues are 120 euros/year. Since 2005, there has also been state financing for those extraparliamentary parties winning at least 1 per cent of the votes. The cost of campaigns has soared so the EER must seek out private contributors as well.

A comparative study (cited by Carter, 2013, p. 83) of Green party manifestos found that the Estonian Greens' placed a higher priority on welfare state expansion, environment and education than did the Czech Greens. Survey research indicates that Estonian Greens voters in 2007 tilted to the right of centre, but still a 'considerable proportion' identified as left of centre (Sikk and Andersen, 2009). The EER 2014 Program has much in common with the views of WE Greens about environmental and energy issues (except nuclear power) and direct democracy, but closer inspection also reveals the embrace of entrepreneurship, balanced budgets, military training and Estonian cultural values. The Greens' public statements have tended to be 'conservative' when it comes to soft drugs, gay rights and alcohol. The EER website declares its top themes for 2014 to be energy security, direct democracy and food production with sustainable agriculture. Postmaterialist and materialist values proposals coexist, but the former are more numerous.

During the mid-1980s, Latvia's environmentalists organised protest demonstrations against the construction of a new hydroelectric dam on the Daugava River. With support from the scientific community these led to the project's cancellation by the Union of Soviet Socialist Republics Council of Ministers in 1987. Environmentalists went on to form the Environmental Protection Club (VAK). VAK helped to found the Latvian People's Front (LTF). In January 1990, VAK and LTF activists launched the Latvian Green Party (*Latvijas Zaļā Partija* – LZP) with 123 charter members. In August 1991, Latvian independence was restored. According to Galbreath and Auers (2009, p. 337), '[T]hereafter environmental discourse was eclipsed by the debates over economic transformation, democratic transition and the large noncitizen, Russian-speaking community in Latvia'. The Green Party and allied environmental organisations won only 1.2 per cent of list votes and one constituency MP in the 1993 parliamentary elections. For the 1995 elections, the Greens formed an alliance with the Latvian National Independence Movement. It won 6.1 per cent of the votes and received eight seats (four went to the Greens). During 1993–1998, Indulis Emsis of the Greens served as Latvian minister of the environment. To contest the 1998 elections, the Greens (with only 279 members) formed an alliance with two other small parties, the Labour Party and the Christian Democratic Union. They won 2.3 per cent of votes and no seats.

Latvian Green Party leaders have demonstrated 'ideological flexibility' in their choice of partners. After coalescing with nationalists and then with the centre-left, they formed a tactical coalition with the Farmer's Union (LZS), an agrarian-nationalist party with reactionary social policies and ample campaign resources. Defence of the Latvian countryside and its family farmers provided common grounds for an effective Populist campaign. The Latvian Farmers and Greens Union (*Zaļo un Zemnieku Savienība* – ZZS) won 9.4 per cent of the votes and 12 seats (4 for the Greens) in 2002. The victory allowed the ZZS to become part of the governing coalition. For the 2006 elections, the ZZS was expanded to include the regionalist party lead by Aivars Lembergs, the veteran mayor of the oil transit port of Ventspils. The ZZS won 16.7 per cent of the votes and 18 seats (3 for the Greens) in 2006 and joined the governing coalition. Liepaja's regionalist party joined the ZZS–Ventspils alliance for the 2010 parliamentary campaign. The 'Green, brown and black' alliance (Galbreath and Auers, 2009, pp. 333–334) did even better in 2010 by winning 19.7 per cent of the votes and 22 seats (5 for the Greens), and it remained in government.

Issues of parliamentary corruption moved the president to call for a referendum to force an early election to remove the 'oligarchs' from parliament. The prime target was multi-millionaire Lembergs, who has been the ZZS's prime ministerial candidate though charged with money laundering and corruption (Auers, 2012). In the 2011 parliamentary elections, voters dealt the ZZS a setback: it won 12.2 per cent of the votes (−7.5) and 13 seats (−9), with 4 for the Greens (−1). The Latvian Greens were back in the opposition after serving nine years in government – two years longer than the Greens served in Germany. They earned a place in the history of Greens when, in 2004, LZP chairperson Indulis Emsis became Europe's first Green prime minister. His minority government was to endure almost a year. In 2006, Emsis was elected speaker of the parliament, but he was forced out a year later after a briefcase with 'an unaccounted $10,000 in cash' was linked to him (Auers, 2012, p. 526). In the June 2013 local elections, the ZZS won 145 of 1,618 city and municipality seats, which was the second largest number of seats won by a registered party or alliance.[10] In the 2014 EP elections, the ZZS won 8.3 per cent of Latvian votes (+4.6) and elected its first member of the European Parliament (MEP), who subsequently joined the liberal Alliance of Liberals and Democrats for Europe (ALDE) political group in the European Parliament.

According to the LZP's Statute (2010), the organisational structure is based on decentralisation of power, the initiative of members and internal democracy. Leadership is collegial with two co-chairs elected for four years by the Congress. The Board consists of five members elected by the Congress for two years to manage daily activities of the party and to represent the party externally. The Council consists of the co-chairs, the Board, department heads, parliamentary and municipal office-holders. It monitors party activities, considers complaints and makes recommendations regarding candidates and other important issues. The annual Congress has the power of decision on such things as appointments, programs, statute changes, special party bodies, participation in alliances and audit committee reports. There are 26 regional offices. According to the LZP's website, the party has about 600 members. As of 2012, there was a flexible membership fee, ranging from $24 to $400 per year depending on the member's income level. All Latvian parties have had to rely on large individual and corporate donations as the costs of modern media campaigning have soared (Galbreath and Auers, 2009). The Union of Greens and Farmers has enjoyed financial support from Aivars Lembergs, head of Latvia's wealthiest family[11] and de facto leader of the Ventspils group of oil transit-related companies.

The LZP program's cornerstone is sustainable development, which it sees as implementable only in a knowledge-based society. The party stands for 'freedom, democracy, the rule of law, [a] secure, social country [with] strong, national identity, language and cultural diversity, conservation, global competition, the capacity to act in the European Union'. The party professes support for common EU principles including 'tolerance and respect for diversity'. It stands for traditional family values and describes education as 'the most important priority in Latvia'. Furthermore, the program emphasises the importance of private property, entrepreneurship, the market, reduction of taxes, the integration of immigrants via learning of the Latvian language and the protection of the countryside. The ZZS program covers basically the same principles and policies.[12] However, Auers (2012, pp. 525–526) points to the lack of Green policy initiatives while the ZZS has held national public offices, and the 'reactionary, nationalist, Eurosceptic, and homophobic values' reflected in the public comments of ZZS and LZP leaders, and observes that there may be an opening for 'a more modern and "European" environmental party in Latvia'.

As in Estonia and Latvia, public opposition to Soviet economic development projects during the 1980s in Lithuania paved the way for the national independence movement. The focal point of environmentalists was the construction of the nuclear power plant in Ignalina. Protest demonstrations were followed in October 1988 by the formation of the Lithuanian Green Movement (Rinkevicius, 2000). The Lithuanian Green Party (*Lietuvos Žaliųjų Partija* – LZP) was founded in July 1989. The LZP became part of *Sajudis*, the umbrella movement for national independence, and won four seats in the 1990 elections for the Lithuanian Supreme Soviet, which was reconstituted as the *Seimas* after independence was declared on 11 March 1990. The Greens' postindependence agenda focussed on improving the quality of both the environment and human rights in Lithuania. Although the

LZP participated in government with its leader Zigmas Vaisvila as deputy prime minister during 1990–1992, the Greens won only 0.1 per cent of the votes (no seats) in the 1992 parliamentary elections. Leading members of the Green movement migrated to liberal and conservative parties while others refocussed on local environmental projects. There were no LZP candidates in the 1996 parliamentary elections. Although there were subsequently public actions by the ecology club *Zemya*, the old LZP was essentially 'comatose' (Dautartas, 2011).

A new Green party was launched on 20 March 2011 after months of negotiations and planning. The Greens did not fully participate in the October 2012 parliamentary elections. However, antinuclear activist and former chief advisor to President Grybauskaitė, Linas Balsys was elected as an independent, becoming the first Green MP in Lithuania since 1992. The Lithuanian Peasants Popular Union recently renamed as the Lithuanian Peasant and Greens Union (LVŽS), won 3.9 per cent of the list votes and elected one constituency MP. In November 2012, an extraordinary assembly of the new Green party elected Balsys as chair and changed the party's name officially from Lithuanian Green Movement to Lithuanian Green Party. In the 2014 EP elections, the new LZP won 3.5 per cent of Lithuanian votes. On the other hand, the LVŽS won 6.2 per cent and elected one MEP, who decided to join The Greens/European Free Alliance political group. According to the July 2014 poll by Vilmorus, the LVŽS is supported by 4.5 per cent of potential voters while 2.9 per cent favour the new LZP.

The organisational structure of the new LZP resembles that of the Estonian Greens. There are the chairman, the board, the council, various control commissions, the assembly and the membership. In Lithuania, a party must have 1,000 members to be legally registered. Parties whose membership falls below 1,000 cannot participate in elections and cannot receive financial support from the state; and, if reorganisation fails, they must be liquidated.

The new LZP's founders justified its existence because neither parties of the left nor the right have proven capable of responding to the threats that civilisation is facing from the wasteful use of natural resources and the poisoning of the environment. On the other hand, only the Greens are offering 'a new economical and social developmental model to Europe . . . grounded on the cohesion between nature and humanity' (European Green Party News, 15 April 2011). Their top priority is to get the government to honour the views of the majority of Lithuanians who voted against the nuclear power development in the consultative referendum of 2012. The Greens' members have participated in the transnational campaign seeking better protection for the Baltic Sea. According to Balsys (2012), the ideological foundation of the new LZP is 'a new, Green attitude towards economy and energy . . . which guarantees social justice and agricultural activity . . . [without leaving] for future generations either huge debts or damaged environment'.

Southeast Europe

Within the geographical region of the Balkans, liberalisation of politics and society was already underway in Slovenia in the mid-1980s (Mønnesland, 2011). Milan

Kučan, the young leader of the Slovene Communist Party, was open to dialogue and enjoyed popularity as a defender of Slovene national rights versus Belgrade, where Serbian hardliners held sway. An important component of an increasingly active civil society in Slovenia was environmental nongovernmental organisations, which staged antinuclear demonstrations in 1986 in the aftermath of the Chernobyl disaster. The Greens of Slovenia (*Zeleni Slovenije* – ZS) was founded in June 1989 and soon joined *Demokratična Opozicija Slovenije* (DEMOS), the broad anticommunist electoral alliance. In the April 1990 elections for the political chamber of the Slovenian republic, DEMOS won a majority of the seats with the Greens winning 8.8 per cent of the votes and eight seats. They received three ministerial positions in the government (Jordan, 2010). Fink-Hafners sees the early success of the Greens as contributing to 'the "Greening" of other parties in the party arena' (2006, p. 214), which soon diminished their appeal.

On 25 June 1991, Slovenia declared its independence. In the 1992 elections for the new national assembly, the Greens (ZS) won 3.7 per cent of the votes and five seats. They received two ministerial positions in the government.[13] However, the party splintered in 1993 over the question of its relations with other parliamentary parties. The Green parliamentary group cut its ties with the party and formed the Ecological Social Party (*Zeleni Ekološko Socialna Stranka* – ZESS); in early 1994, these MPs switched to the (leftist) Liberal Democrats. Antinuclear activists and left-oriented environmentalists formed the Green Alternative Party (*Zelena Alternativa* – ZA) in 1995. Neither party did well in the November 1996 parliamentary elections: the ZA won 0.6 per cent of the votes while the more conservative ZS won 1.6 per cent (Jordan, 1998). For the 2000 parliamentary elections, the two Green parties agreed upon a joint list of candidates, but it received less than 1 per cent of the votes, and 'mutual animosity resumed' (Hloušek and Kopeček, 2010, p. 79). The ZS have continued to run candidates in parliamentary elections, but they have won insignificant shares of the votes: 2004 (0.7 per cent), 2008 (0.5 per cent), 2011 (0.4 per cent) and 2014 (0.5 per cent). There have been attempts to overcome Green fragmentation. For example, the Green Party, a splinter off the Greens, sought to form the 'Green Coalition' with two or three minor Green (or environment-related) parties; they won only 0.21 per cent of the votes in 2008. The Statistical Office of Slovenia data for 2010 local elections reveal no Green candidates, but they may be hidden under other headings.

The rise of the Youth Party of Slovenia in 2000 shows the willingness of voters to give brand-new 'antiestablishment' parties a chance. The Youth Party (*Stranka mladih Slovenije* – SMS) was formed on 4 July 2000 to rejuvenate politics by increasing the engagement of the young generation. Its special concern was the social and economic needs of young people. The party won 4.3 per cent of the votes in the 2000 parliamentary elections and gained four seats. The SMS in opposition worked with the Liberal Democrats (Hloušek and Kopeček, 2010). Soon they broadened their program beyond the issues of the youth by assuming an ecological orientation. The SMS joined forces with the Greens (ZS) and won 2.3 per cent of Slovene votes (no seats) in the 2004 European Parliament elections. Running independently in the 2004 parliamentary elections, the SMS won 2.1 per cent of the votes (no seats). In 2007, its status was upgraded from observer to full member in the European Green Party (EGP); the Greens (ZS) have not been a member of the EGP. For the 2008 parliamentary elections, the SMS formed an alliance with the (Christian democratic) Slovenian People's Party, which won 5.2 per cent of the votes, but the SMS received no seats. In the 2009 EP elections, the SMS won 2 per cent of Slovene votes. In July 2009, the party officially changed its name to The Youth Party – European Greens (in short, SMS–Zeleni). According to official statistics, the SMS has won local council seats: 44 in 2006 and 41 in 2010. In the December 2011 parliamentary elections, it won 0.9 per cent of the votes. The State Election Commission of Slovenia reports no votes for SMS–Zeleni in the May 2014 EP elections or in the July 2014 (early) parliamentary elections.

The Statute (2009) of the SMS–Zeleni provides for a chair, executive committee, council, convention and congress. There are also a chief secretary, a program board, policy sections, a court of arbitration, a supervisory board and local committees. Beyond its formally organised associations, the party has recruited an informal body of individual supporters with special expertise called the 'Green Government'. While the party's webpage provides no membership figures, the fact that the party ran almost 650 candidates in the 2010 local elections suggests an even larger membership. Their program declares that the SMS–Zeleni is 'a party of people who do not owe anyone anything and have no godfathers'. Thus it encourages the financial support of small contributors.

The Statute (2012) of the Greens (ZS) describes the procedures and functions of the central organs of the party. At the national level, there is a chairperson, an executive board, an executive committee, a program board, a control commission, an arbitration commission, a secretary-general, a Green ombudsman, a personnel committee, an autonomous youth council and a number of special associations. There is no gender quota, but there is the requirement that collegial bodies at the national level include both men and women. The Statute emphasises that members who fail to pay membership dues on time or who act in ways incompatible with the program will be expelled, which suggests a history of internal conflicts. The ZS webpage provides no membership figures, but SMS–Zeleni is generally seen as the larger of the two parties.

SMS–Zeleni sees its program as 'bold, revolutionary, and so real. . . . Now is the time to redefine capitalism and politics'. The party embraces the EGP's Green New Deal, with its three pillars – social justice, environmental protection and open democracy – and presents a comprehensive list of specific policy changes. However, it is prepared to address a wide range of issues. For example, in April 2014 the SMS–Zeleni president, in response to the prime minister's effort to curb spending, proposed bold cost-saving measures, such as withdrawal from North Atlantic Treaty Organisation, overhaul of pension insurance and municipal government consolidation. The Greens (ZS) are less bold in rhetoric and more nostalgic about 'the values from the independence period, when Slovenes joined by common efforts for [a] better tomorrow'.[14] However, the programs of the two parties do have much in common, such as enthusiasm for sustainable development.

In October 2011, a new Party for Sustainable Development (*Stranke za Trajnostni Razvoj Slovenije* – TRS) was founded as a vote of no confidence on the established parties. In the December 2011 parliamentary elections, the new TRS won 1.2 per cent of the votes, about as much as the combined share of the ZS and the SMS–Zeleni. In March 2014, the TRS joined the United Left alliance with the Democratic Labour Party (DSD) and the Initiative for Democratic Socialism (IDS). The United Left won 5.5 per cent of the Slovene votes (no seats) in the May 2014 EP elections, and then 6.0 per cent of the votes and eight seats in July 2014 parliamentary elections. Thus, the prospects for a comeback by the Greens in Slovenia do not appear very good in view of a policy agenda dominated by economic crisis, their fragmentation and the appropriation of classic Green themes by other parties.

During the 1980s, Croatia endured more political repression than Slovenia. But, 'heavily influenced by the cataclysmic events in late 1989 in East-Central Europe' (Mønnesland, 2011, p. 195), Croatian authorities moved to allow the registration of noncommunist parties. Environmentalists had not played an active role in regime change as they had in Slovenia. In the April 1990 (free) parliamentary elections, only 1 of 23 Green candidates on the ballot was elected, thanks to a coalition with ex-communists (Bugajski, 2002). Not until 1996 were the Croatian Green Party (*Hrvatska Stranka Zelenih* – HSZ) and the Green Party (*Zelena Stranka* – ZS), which stressed that it was not just an environmental party, officially founded. Neither of these parties won any seats in the parliamentary elections of 1996, 2000 or 2003. The Green 'high' point occurred in 2003 when the Green Party (ZS) and the Greens of Croatia (*Zeleni Hrvatske*), founded in 2001, each won 0.6 per cent of the national votes (Čular and Henjak, 2014). In the early twenty-first century, there have been simultaneously at least seven different Green or environment-related parties in Croatian politics. The situation has been made even more confusing by the tendency of parties to change their names and their electoral coalitions.

The Green List (*Zelena Lista* – ZL) has been the most successful of these small parties, although, in the 2011 parliamentary elections, it won only 0.36 per cent of the votes. The Green List was originally formed in 2004 to contest the Zagreb assembly elections. In 2007, the European Green Party granted the ZL observer status in its organisation. In the 2009 local elections, the Green List won 2.8 per cent of the votes in Zagreb, not enough to enter the city assembly, but enough to be represented in 11 of 17 districts (Jordan, 2010) and 5 other localities. In the May 2013 local elections, there were three competing Green electoral coalitions. The Green List with two coalition partners won 11.1 per cent of Zagreb's votes, narrowly missing a mandate in the city assembly. Their coalition won eight seats in lower municipalities and, running on their own received 3.5 per cent of votes in Dubarava. As a step toward the unification of Greens, the ZL's general assembly of members voted unanimously on 14 December 2013 to join the Croatian Sustainable Development Party (*Održivi Razvoj Hrvatske* – ORaH) and to disband as a party.

ORaH (the acronym means 'walnut' in the Croatian language) had been formed during October 2013. Its founding mother was Mirela Holy, the former Social Democratic minister for the environment (2011–2012), who after being forced out of office by a scandal had remained in the parliament as an independent MP. ORaH's Statute (2013) calls for 'parity democracy' in the selection of all party officials (except the party president and the president of the central programming forum) and in the nomination of candidate lists for public offices. Central leadership is provided by the president (elected by the membership), the vice-president and the deputy vice-president (elected by the assembly) and the presidency, which meets at least monthly and includes the three top officers plus eight members who represent the party's four regions. In addition, there is the president of the central programming forum, the secretary-general, the business director, the international secretary and four regional commissioners. The central leadership currently consists of ten women and nine men.

The other central bodies are the general board, the special programming forums, the supervisory board and the general assembly. The general board functions as the highest decision-making body between assemblies. There are currently three special programming forums on, respectively, environmental policy, economic policy and human rights, which are to develop concrete programs and are open to sympathisers as well as members. The supervisory board deals with statutory interpretations, financial oversight and disciplinary matters. The assembly of member parties has the final say in annual regular meetings, electoral meetings (every four years) and extraordinary meetings. The Statute provides detailed guidelines for the organisation of municipal, city and regional parties and of parliamentary and council groups of elected ORaH representatives. Membership fees depend on the income level of individuals. In addition to membership fees and levies on public office holders' salaries, the sources of party revenues may include the state budget, donations, project grants from EU and international sources and promotional events.

ORaH describes itself as 'a progressive, democratic party that stands for sustainable, balanced growth of Croatia', that is located on the 'centre-left' of the party spectrum and that is not just a 'Green' party because it also deals with 'sustainable solutions of critical social problems'.[15] ORaH is applying for full membership in the European Green Party with which its program is closely aligned. In its 2014 European election campaign, ORaH appealed, not only to those disenchanted with the incumbent Social Democratic government, but also specifically to young people and women. Despite the fact that ORaH faced a competing Green coalition formed by the Greens of Croatia (Zeleni HR), the Green Party (ZS) and the Alliance of Young Democrats (AMD), ORaH won 9.4 per cent of Croatian votes in the EP election, a higher proportion than any other CEE Green party, and received one MEP seat.

During the communist era, Bulgaria was isolated from the West and had no experience with economic or political liberalisation. Dissidents were dealt with harshly by the Zhivkov regime (Fish and Brooks, 2000). However, in April 1989, inspired by developments elsewhere in the East Bloc, anticommunist activists formed the umbrella opposition movement Union of Democratic Forces (UDF). A major component of the UDF was the *Ecoglasnost* movement. Bulgarian environmental activism can be traced back to the town of Ruse, where citizen protests began in 1987 about being 'gassed' by a chemical plant across the Danube River (Krastanova, 2012). On 10 November 1989, the day after the fall of the Berlin Wall, Zhivkov was removed from power. In January 1990, the new communist leadership initiated talks with the opposition and renamed the party the Bulgarian Socialist Party (BSP). Also in early 1990, the 'left-wing' faction of *Ecoglasnost* formed Political Club (PC) *Ecoglasnost* (Krastanova, 2012). In the (free) parliamentary elections of June 1990, the BSP finished first with a majority of the seats (211) while the UDF movement finished second with 144 seats. PC *Ecoglasnost* and the Bulgarian Green Party (*Zelena Partija Bulgaria* – ZPB, founded in December 1989) ran within the UDF, with the former ending up with 16 seats and the latter with 17 seats (Jordan, 2010). Mass street demonstrations forced the BSP into a coalition with the UDF in December 1990. The Bulgarian Green Party received two of the UDF's cabinet positions (Rüdig, 2004).

The UDF won a majority of seats in the October 1991 parliamentary elections, with the BSP finishing second. Filip Dmitrov, who became prime minister, was from the ZPB faction that stayed within the UDF under the name 'Conservative and Ecological Party'. The rest of the ZPB joined the UDF–Liberals, who won 2.8 per cent of the votes (no seats). Another UDF prime minister (Ivan Kostov, 1997–2001) as well as several cabinet ministers also began their political careers in PC *Ecoglasnost* or the ZBP; however, they were soon to shed their Green identities and join larger political formations (Rüdig, 2004).

During 1992–2007, the ZPB sought out ideological diverse coalition partners in its pursuit of parliamentary seats. Only in 1997 with the Union of National Salvation did the strategy bear fruit with two seats in the National Assembly. PC *Ecoglasnost* won seats as part of BSP-led formations in 1995 and 1997 elections. However, the ZPB received no seats from its participation in the BSP-led Coalition for Bulgaria in the 2005 parliamentary election. Running independently in 2007, the party won 0.5 per cent of Bulgarian votes in the special election to fill the new EU member state's seats in the European Parliament. The ZPB merged with the Green Bulgaria Party in July 2008. The ZPB reportedly had 2,000 members in April 2009,[16] which was about where it stood in 1995. The ZPB did not run candidates in the 2009 parliamentary or European elections because of the 'misconduct of party leadership'.[17] In the 2011 local elections, running independently, the ZPB elected 15 public office-holders, more than the Party of the Greens, *Zelenite and* PC *Ecoglasnost*, but fewer than the number it won in 1995 (Jordan 1998).

The Greens (*Zelenite*) party was launched in May 2008; within a year, it had registered nearly 7,000 members. According to Petko Kovatchev, co-chair of the new party, 'the effectiveness of the NGOs has reached a ceiling. And we still have not made enough progress in shifting Bulgaria's development toward sustainability . . . a new tool was needed' (Ciobanu, 2008). In the June 2009 European Parliament elections, *Zelenite* received 0.7 per cent of Bulgarian votes. In the July

2009 parliamentary elections, it received 0.5 per cent of the votes. To the distress of the ZPB, which has been a full member of the European Green Party (and its predecessor) since 1993, the EGP committee rapidly moved to approve *Zelenite*'s observer-member status. In 2012, the ZPB National Council petitioned the EGP unsuccessfully to expel *Zelenite* because of its defamation of the ZPB and its hindrance of Green unity in Bulgaria. The ZPB emphasised its long history, expertise and cooperative efforts with other Green parties. *Zelenite*'s view is that it is the 'Authentic' Green party and 'the real opposition – [the] only political force created directly by citizens'.[18] After disappointing results in the local elections of 2011, *Zelenite* received 0.7 per cent of the votes in the May 2013 parliamentary elections. The Bulgarian Spring coalition, including the Party of the Greens, won 0.1 per cent; while the ZPB won less than 0.01 per cent of the votes.[19] *Zelenite* won 0.5 per cent of the votes in the May 2014 EP elections compared to 0.4 per cent for the ZPB and 0.2 per cent for the Party of the Greens.

Zelenite is organised according to its Statute of 2011. Membership is open to anyone with Bulgarian citizenship except those involved in 'extreme nationalist' activities; furthermore, former members of 'totalitarian and nationalist parties' have to be a member of *Zelenite* for two years before they may be considered for election to leadership positions. Members must not only pay dues but also participate in electoral campaigns and other party activities. The supreme body of the party is the annual national assembly. Between its meetings, the national council of 29 members has the final say. A supervisory board deals with party policies and strategies. The nine-member executive board consists of three coequal chairs, the organisational secretary, the treasurer and four additional members. Members of the executive board are elected for two-year terms. There is a control board to provide oversight of the implementation of the party program and budget. The Statute does not mention a quota system to ensure equal representation of women. Currently only three members of the executive board and nine members of the national council are women.

In contrast, the Statute (2012) of the ZPB embraces gender equality for all elective party bodies. The composition of its executive board and its national policy council does approach gender parity. Another difference is that the ZPB excludes from membership persons in extractive industries that operate in a way that destroys the natural environment, as well as those involved in the past state security services. The ZPB and *Zelenite* have a similar organisational design. A noteworthy contrast is that the ZPB has a single chairperson rather than three coequal chairs as *Zelenite* has. It was intraparty conflict over leadership election that resulted in the BGP being suspended from the ZPB in 2010. Ultimately Aleksandar Karakachanov – the founder of the ZPB, interim mayor of Sofia (1990–1991), former MP and chairman of the ZPB since 1989 – and his allies gave way, and Marina Dragomiretzkaya became the new chairperson in 2013. The ZPB is again an EGP member in good standing.

Zelenite declares that preservation of nature in Bulgaria is its 'primary cause'.[20] However, there is more to the party than environmentalism. Its 2013 election program begins with political changes to make Bulgaria a more direct and participatory democracy. Two-thirds of the program is devoted to political, economic, health and educational reforms. Only toward the end does its focus shift to conservation and sustainability. In recent years, *Zelenite* has campaigned for organic farm subsidies, for renewable energies, against oil shale development and against GMOs. The ZPB has criticised *Zelenite* for trying to take credit for actions initiated by other Green parties. *Zelenite* has charged the (pre-2013) ZPB with being soft on nuclear power. The ZPB's political program also covers a wide range of policy areas. It devotes more space to foreign policy and cultural policy, but otherwise the two parties' programmatic orientations generally appear to be similar.

Since the early 1990s, Bulgarian electoral campaigns have become more expensive and electoral laws have become more burdensome for small parties (Kolarov and Spirova, 2011). To survive the ZPB has sought alliances with other parties. *Zelenite*, on the other hand, has sought to maintain an independent profile but failed to score a breakthrough in the 2013 parliamentary elections. *Zelenite* appeared poised to join the Reformist Bloc, an alliance including the UDF and the Democrats for a Strong Bulgaria (DGB) for the May 2014 European elections. However, in late 2013, *Zelenite*'s national council decided not to go ahead with the Reformist Bloc due to its centre-right policy orientations.[21] Recently, the ZPB has allowed young people to rise to the top of the party and its affiliated youth organisation has been active in promoting participatory democracy. Therefore, it is now more possible to visualise the two parties working toward Green unity in the future (Kondarev, 2014).

The 1989 revolution in Romania differed from those in other CEE countries, not only because of its bloodiness, but also because the rebels included elements of the Communist Party elite as well as thousands of average citizens, embittered by human rights abuses and economic hardships under the neo-Stalinist rule of Nicolae Ceausescu (Michta, 1994). The army played the pivotal role. The new government came under the control of Ion Iliescu and other anti-Ceausescu communists. In the May 1990 (free) parliamentary elections, Iliescu's National Salvation Front (later the Democratic *Frontul Salvării Naţionale* – FSN) received a two-thirds majority of the seats. The Romanian Ecologist Movement (*Miscarea Ecologista din Romania* – MER), which claimed 60,000 members, finished fourth with 2.6 per cent of the votes, winning 12 seats in the Chamber of Deputies and one in the Senate. During 1991–1992, MER's vice-president Marcian Bleahu served as Romania's minister of the environment. For the 1992 parliamentary elections, the Romanian Ecological Party (*Partidul Ecologist Român* – PER) joined the opposition Democratic Convention of Romania (DCR) and won four chamber seats; MER won none.

As the decade progressed, critical observers recognised little that was especially 'Green' or ecological about either party. In 1996, a faction of MER moved over to the Green Alternative Party-Ecologist (which was to be absorbed by PER in 2003).[22] For the 1996 parliamentary elections, PER and the Romanian Ecologist Federation (*Federaţia Ecologistă Română* – FER) that emerged from MER ran candidates on the DCR list. PER won five chamber seats and one senate seat while FER won one seat in both chambers. Support for the DCR alliance collapsed with the effect that *no* Green party was represented in the Romanian parliament for over a decade.[23] In the 2000 elections, the Ecological Pole alliance, which consisted of PER (claiming about 2,000 members) and two smaller Green or Ecologist parties, won slightly less than 1 per cent of the votes in both parliamentary chambers (no seats). Nevertheless, Green parties continued to win a number of seats in local elections; for example, in 2008, PER won 3 mayoral posts and 180 local council seats compared to 40 local council seats for the new Green Party (*Partidul Verde* – PV).

The PV was officially registered in 2006. The PV ran candidates in the 2007 special elections to fill Romania's seats in the European Parliament, winning 0.4 per cent of the votes (no seats). In 2008, the PV and PER (under new leadership) formed the 'Green Ecological Party' alliance to contest the national parliamentary elections. The alliance managed to win 0.3 per cent of the chamber votes and 0.7 per cent of the senate votes. After this disappointing outcome, party leaders shelved merger plans. Neither the PV nor PER could collect enough signatures to contest the 2009 EP elections. The 2009 Green presidential campaign of controversial civic activist Remus Cernea, who received 0.6 per cent of the first round votes (the PER's presidential candidate received 0.2 per cent), generated a disproportionate amount of media attention. His perceived overemphasis on gay rights, separation of church and state and national minorities, however, alienated elements of the party. Cernea resigned from the PV and created a new party, the Green Movement (*Mişcarea Verzilor* – MV), which after absorbing the minor People's Agrarian Party took the name Green Movement – Agrarian Democrats (*Mişcarea Verzilor – Democraţi Agrarieni* – MVDA) in 2011.[24] To the applause of the EGP, the PV and the MVDA agreed to collaborate in the upcoming parliamentary elections. In December 2012, Cernea was one of two Greens who were elected on the Social Liberal Union's (USL) list, receiving an estimated 1 per cent of the votes.[25] He resigned (again) from the PV in late 2013 after intraparty disputes regarding strategy for the 2014 European elections, but he has remained active as an unattached MP. On 25 May 2014, the PV won 0.3 per cent of the votes for Bulgaria's MEPs – less than PER, which won 1.1 per cent.

The PV is structured by its Statute of 2013. PV membership is open to all Romanian citizens except those 'who promote sexism, racism, xenophobia, authoritarianism, religious fundamentalism, homophobia, violence . . . or deliberate corruption'. One of the party's objectives (Article 4) is equality of women and men, but there is no mention on the website of a quota system to ensure implementation of this goal regarding party offices or candidacies. The structure of the party is territorial with executives and committees at multiple levels from village to national. The Congress is the supreme organ, which meets every four years; between its sessions, the National Council makes necessary decisions. There is a quarterly meeting of the National Permanent Bureau (NPB) involving nearly 50 party officials and representatives. The weekly meetings of the Central Executive Bureau involve the president, the chief executive officer, the first vice-presidents, the secretary-general and elected representatives of the NPB. There are also an arbitration commission, an audit committee, a dozen policy departments and a youth organisation. The central structure of PER is similar in organisational design to the PV's.

The PV is proud of its status as the only Romanian Green or Ecologist Party that has been accepted as a full member by the EGP. The PV platform covers the full gamut of environmental issues, with climate change, water shortages and energy given special emphasis. Regarding the national controversy about a cyanide-releasing gold mining project at Rosa Montana, the PV sees itself as unambiguously against the project compared to other parties, including PER. The PV platform includes economic and social issues but devotes noticeably less attention to them. It does declare that 'property is sacred, and privatisation is essential [for the] evolution of a society'.[26] In its political manifesto, the PV describes itself as a 'centrist party'. PER declares itself a party with 'a modern, European-oriented centre-right orientation'. PER bases its political ecology[27] on the 'liberal principles' of freedom, private initiative, fair competition and property. PER seeks the gradual transformation of individual and institutional behaviour toward greater respect for nature and links its pursuit of sustainability to Romanian patriotism. PER tends to be more socially conservative than the PV on issues such as gay rights. In recent years, policy differences have not prevented talks about collaboration or even about a merger of the two parties. The PV's Statute (Article 1) commits the party to work toward the unification of all environmental parties and movements in Romania. The PV took a symbolic step when it chose Prof Dr Marcian Bleahu – who had not only served as Romania's minister of the environment but also as a leader of MER and later of FER in the 1990s – as its honorary president. It is likely that there will be renewed consideration of practical steps toward Green unification, but crossing the threshold of relevance will require a long-range strategy in Romania.

Implications

CEE Green parties emerged during a historic period of regime change. Their general pattern of development was early success in winning parliamentary seats, followed by a rapid loss of popular support as nationalism and economics dominated the policy agenda, and then marginalisation, if not dissolution, by the end of the decade. The development of the Latvian Green Party, however, does not follow this pattern. Latvian Greens did not elect their first MP until 1993. They participated in government during 1993–1998 and then lost their MPs. However, they staged a comeback in 2002 thanks to a tactical alliance with an agrarian-nationalist party that had right-wing policies and deep pockets. Latvian Greens have remained in parliament and local councils ever since. They held cabinet positions in government during 2002–2011 (longer than the German Greens) and even occupied the prime minister's office in 2004. While other CEE Greens have faced internal strife over coalition strategy, the Latvian Greens held together and worked alongside politicians who enjoyed support from conservative rural voters and regionalist oligarchs. According to Bolleyer's (2013) study of new parties, after its breakthrough, a new party must be re-elected to parliament twice to 'reach the minimum threshold for national sustainability'. The Latvian Greens are the only CEE Green party active today that has 'sustainable' standing. Thus, they are the exceptional case, but also an inconvenient case with critics casting doubt on the authenticity of their 'Greenness' (Auers, 2012, pp. 525–526).

Despite their early formation, none of the Green parties of East Central Europe entered government until the Slovak Greens did in 1998–2002. They lost all their MPs in the 2002 elections and have not returned. Belatedly the Czech Greens surged in the 2006 elections, winning seats for the first time and joining the centre-right government. However, a sizeable portion of the party's activists were not pleased by the majority's coalition strategy, and some SZ ministers came off as not experienced enough to cope with governing. They lost all their seats in 2010 and have not (yet) staged a comeback though in recent years they have elected a senator and a number of local councillors. The SZ has survived as an extraparliamentary party before and cannot be counted out in the future because they have a 'postmaterialist' base that is likely to expand in more prosperous times.

In Southeast Europe, the early 1990s elections were essentially 'anticommunist plebiscites'. New Green parties (or better said 'protoparties') were elected to parliaments and participated in governing coalitions mainly because of their role in getting rid of communist regimes, not because of their policy positions. According to Inglehart and Welzel (2005), in the values surveys of the 1990s, Slovenes and Croatians resembled Czechs in having (moderately) 'self-expressive' values (indicative of postmaterialism) while Bulgaria and Romanians resembled Ukrainians in having (highly) 'survivalist values' (indicative of materialism). Over the last ten years, Slovene and Croatian Greens have performed only marginally better in national elections than Bulgarian and Romanian Greens. Obviously, there are many intervening variables between values and votes.

Since 2004, new Green parties have been founded in Poland, Hungary, Estonia, Lithuania, Slovenia, Croatia, Bulgaria and Romania. This second Green wave has coincided with the accession of CEE countries into the EU. In comparison with the parties of the first Green wave, the newcomers have benefited from the encouragement of international foundations and transnational political groups, as well as some WE Green parties. The new generation of activists has tended to be critical of the old CEE Green parties. As Krastanova (2012) puts it, too many Green parties have sought (top-down) to become integrated within the system to gain access to public office and resources; instead they should have been (bottom-up) more oriented to activities that would engage the young and educated professionals in urban areas. To date, the Hungarian LMP has been electorally the most successful of the new Green parties by winning a significant number of seats in the 2010 and 2014 parliamentary elections without environmental issues being prominent in the campaigns. Although it had suffered an intraparty split over strategy, the LMP (narrowly) cleared the 5 per cent threshold in 2014. The Estonian Greens rank as the second most successful of the new Green parties by winning six parliamentary seats in the 2007 elections with environmental issues high on the policy agenda. It slipped back to 3.8 per cent of the votes in the 2011 elections when environmental issues were not so prominent. There are recent individual cases of new Green party members being elected by running as an independent or as a candidate on the list of another party. However, so far, except for the LMP, the new CEE Green parties do not appear significantly more successful than the older Green parties in national parliamentary elections (or in local elections).

Today's new and old CEE Green parties are characterised by small memberships and limited resources. With the exception of the LMP, Green parties have sought to compensate for organisational weaknesses by making pre-election coalition agreements with other parties at the risk of obscuring their own profiles. Reliable recent membership figures are hard to come by for several CEE Green parties.[28] Among the parties covered in this chapter, *Zelenite* in Bulgaria has the highest reported membership, 7,000 (as of 2009), while the Latvian Greens have the smallest, 600 (2012). Once over 3,000 each (2008–2009), the Polish and Czech Greens have declined in recent years. Lithuanian and Estonian parties must have at least 1,000 registered members to participate in national elections. The average size of CEE Green party membership appears to be around 2,000 in recent years. Some Green parties explicitly disallow membership and/or candidacies to former communist operatives, extreme nationalists, those who advocate racism or sexism and (in the case of the Bulgarian Green Party) those associated with extractive enterprises that degrade the environment.

As small party organisations with small budgets, the CEE Greens have had to rely heavily on volunteers. Since the early 1990s, few of these parties have been able to draw upon the resources provide by the state for an extended period. Twenty-five years after the first wave of Green party formation, these parties still share some of the characteristics of the 'amateur-activist' model of party organisation (Lucardie and Rihoux, 2008). In contrast to WE Green parties, they have not had much opportunity to become professionalised. Compared to the WE Greens, the working relationships between movement groups and CEE Green parties became more tenuous and competitive in regards to recruiting volunteers and mobilising resources. A new generation of movement activists has tended to view leaders of old Green parties as office-seeking opportunists. New Green parties, like *Zelenite* and the LMP, have sought to reactivate party–movement linkages and to go into the streets when necessary.

One of the characteristics of the 'amateur-activist model' is collective leadership, which correlates with the Green principles of democracy. Twenty-five years after the first wave of CEE Green parties, they vary regarding the configuration of top leadership. One party, *Zelenite* (Bulgaria) is headed by three coequal chairs, which reflects the collective ethos of social movement leadership. Four parties have two co-chairs with Poland's *Zieloni*, the LMP and Croatian Green List specifying a male co-chair and a female co-chair, and the Latvian Greens not requiring gender parity. The other nine parties have a chair (or a president) as the head of the central organisation. In the case of Croatian ORaH, beyond the president, all party bodies and candidate lists are required to represent men and women equally. The Bulgarian Green Party requires equal representation of women on all collegial bodies. The Romanian Greens commit to gender equality but with no mention of a quota system. The Slovenian Greens require representation of women in the national bodies of the party organisation. Corporate terminology turns up in the statutes of some Green parties. For example, ORaH has a business director position, and the Romanian Greens and Romanian Ecologists parties each have a president of the board, a CEO and first vice-presidents.

Despite the conventional wisdom that Green parties are (too) narrowly focussed on environmental policy, CEE Green party programs range over a wide field of policy issues. The new Green parties are aligned with the EGP's 'Green New Deal' combining economic growth, renewable energies and climate protection. All advocate seeking a sustainable balance between economic development and environmental preservation. The popularity of sustainable development extends beyond the Greens. The Slovak Greens, ORaH and *Zelenite* are explicitly centre-left in their identities. Although not prepared to work with the Socialist Party, the LMP's program is centre-left, except on taxes and spending. The Estonian Greens' program includes both centre-right and centre-left themes. The Latvian Greens' platform takes centre-right positions on social and economic issues. The Lithu-anian Greens and the Romanian Greens present themselves as centrist parties. The Czech Greens' program is aligned with that of the EGP but, in 2010, prioritised economic goals. Polish and Czech Greens stand up for minority rights while the Latvian and Estonian Greens with large Russian minorities in their countries are cautious. Romania's Ecologist Party presents itself as an environmentally con-scious modern centre-right party. Despite their specific differences, CEE Green parties do constitute a 'family' of parties with overlapping views in sufficient areas; however, they have been a small family in terms of electoral support during the late twentieth and early twenty-first centuries.

Conclusion

What are the prospects for the future? Let us revisit the list of seven factors cited by Jordan (1998) to explain the decline of the CEE Green parties during the 1990s. First, the predominance of economic questions: this situation continues today with voters not seeing Green parties as having economic policy competence. The Green New Deal can serve as a foundation for further development of specific policies. Second, the absence of postmaterialist values: there is reason to believe that the portion of the electorate with postmaterialist values is growing in urban areas but elsewhere remains small. The Green parties will need to address the concerns of young centre-right voters while holding on to postmaterialists. Third, the rise of postindependence nationalism: public concern has been refocussed on immigra-tion, which threatens national culture and welfare, and on the loss of national sovereignty to the EU. A space for an alternative party that is unambiguously prohuman rights and pro-Europe may be opening. Fourth, the appropriation of environmental themes by other parties: Greens need to demonstrate competence on the implementation of sustainable development and expose the 'sloganeer-ing' of other parties. Fifth, Western material support was provided to Christian democratic, social democratic and liberal parties, not to Green parties: Greens need to expand networking with international foundations, transnational party organisations and Western parties. Sixth, electoral hurdles forced the Greens into awkward alliances: despite a package of electoral reforms enacted by the Orbán regime after 2010 to hamper small parties, the LMP was re-elected to parliament on its own. Other Green parties need to study this case. Seventh, intraparty splits and interest conflicts: still a perennial problem for Green parties, but also for larger CEE parties. The changing competitive circumstances of small parties and the ability of their leaders to respond quickly are obviously important. The collapse of support for the Freedom Union in the Czech Republic opened a centre-right space that the Czech Greens' campaign successfully targeted in the 2006 elections. The collapse of the Alliance of Social Democrats and the unpopularity of the Hungarian Socialist Party opened a centre-left space for the LMP's successful campaign in the 2010 elections.

What has been the significance of the May 2014 EP elections? For the first time CEE Greens have won seats in the European Parliament. Their MEPs will have access to new institutional resources, attract more media coverage and develop further substantive and procedural expertise. The new ORaH party won 9.42 per cent of the Croatian votes and one MEP. The appeal of 'the project of newness' (Sikk, 2011b), especially in a second order election, worked in favour of ORaH in 2014.[29] It will be interesting to see whether ORaH's high level of support endures in the next national elections. The now not-so-new LMP managed to win one MEP seat with 5.0 per cent of the votes despite its recent party split.

Twenty-five years after the collapse of communist party states in Central and Eastern Europe, party systems are still in flux and electorates volatile. Many things have changed since the early 1990s, but Green parties remain small and mostly marginalised in national politics. The 2014 EP election results in CEE countries hardly indicate a general Green 'breakthrough', but instead, some Green 'beachheads' in the long-term struggle to put Central and Eastern European countries on the path toward sustainable development, human rights and democratic renewal.

Notes

1 The focus here is on the CEE countries that are members of the European Union as of 2014: Bulgaria, Croatia, Czech Republic, Estonia, Hungary, Latvia, Lithuania, Poland, Slovakia, Slovenia and Romania.

2 Gawlik was to serve later as co-chair of the new *Zieloni* (Greens) 2004 party during 2011–2013.

3 The SZA merged with the Slovak Nationalist Party (SNS) in 1998 and had little impact thereafter.

4 Furthermore, there were 6 mayors and 43 councilors elected by local coalitions supported by the Green Party (SZ). See <http://europeangreens.eu/news/historical-success-slovakian-greens-muncipal-elections> (Accessed 2 December 2010)

5 See the party's website <http://www.stranazelenychpuchov.sk> (Accessed 8 June 2014).

6   The overall size of the parliament had been reduced from 386 to 199 seats in 2012. Ninety-three of the 199 were list seats. In the 2010 election, 210 seats were regional or national list seats. With a similar scheme in 2014, the LMP would have received around 11 seats.

7   <http://lehetmas.hu/szervezet>.

8   <http://lehetmas.hu/ep-valasztasi-program-2014>.

9   For membership in Estonian political parties, see <https//ariregister.rik.ee>.

10   Central Electoral Commission, Local Elections 2013 <http://cvk.lv/pub/public/30491. html>.

11   'The Lembergs still Latvia's wealthiest family in 2013', *The Baltic Course*, 14 November 2013 <http://www.baltic-course.com/eng/analytics/?doc=83681&ins_print>.

12   The LZP program can be found at <http://www.zp.lv/lv/par-mums/programma/>. The ZZS program can be found at <http://www.zzs.lv/11saeimas-velesanas/4000-zimju-programma>.

13   Bozidar Voljc, the Greens' minister for health, family and social affairs served 1992–1997 even though his party left government in 1994 (Rüdig, 2004).

14   <http://www.zeleni.si/greens-of-slovenia/>.

15   ORaH, 'Frequently asked questions and answers', 14 November 2013 <http://www.orah.hr>.

16   'Bulgaria "Green Votes" Predicted to Scatter at Coming Elections', *Sofia News Agency* <http://noinvite.com/articles/102812/Bulgaria>.

17   Green Party History <http://greenparty.bg/index.php/2010-05-10-21-27-04>.

18   The Greens (*Zelenite*) webpage, 'Who we Greens are' <http://zelenite.bg/greens>.

19   European Green Party internal party document, 7 November 2013.

20   Political platform of the Greens in the EP elections 2014 <http://izbori.zelenite.bg/plaforma_2014>.

21   'Bulgaria's Greens: Reformist Bloc Won't Win MEPs at EU Elections', 5 January 2014 <http://www.novinite.com/newsletter/print.php?id=156979>.

22   'About the Party: History', Romanian Green Party website <www.per.ro/despre-partid-2.html>.

23   See 'A Brief History of the Greens and Ecologist Parties in Romania – I', 17 August 2011 <http://blog.cavsplace.com/?p=833>.

24   'A Brief History of Green and Ecologist Parties in Romania – II', 23 August 2011 <http:/blog.cavspace.com/?p=836>.

25   European Green Party, internal party document, 7 November 2013.

26   Green Party (PV) website <http://www.partidulverde.ro/partidul/platforma-program/>.

27   'The political program of the Romania Ecologist Party', 2014 <http://www.per.ro/prima-pagina-1.html>.

28   Membership data are vulnerable to inflation to give parties more democratic legitimacy. In any case, the EGP does not factor membership into the formula used to allocate conference delegates to member parties. The EGP staff would (or could) not provide this author with information on CEE Green party memberships. Approximate figures are occasionally available on party websites and in the media. Useful academic sources include Bakke, 2011, and van Biezen, et al., 2012. In the case of Estonia, the names of members are reported by (registered) parties to the state officials and made available on the Internet!

29   ORAH's share of Croatian votes (9.42 per cent) in the 2014 EP elections exceeds the 6.4 per cent of the votes for the German Greens within the eastern territory of the former East Germany.

References

Agarin, T., 2009. Where have all the environmentalists gone? Baltic Greens in mid-1990s. *Journal of Baltic Studies*, 40(3), pp. 285–305.

Auers, D., 2012. The curious case of the Latvian Greens. *Environmental Politics*, 21(3), pp. 522–527.

Bakke, E., 2011. The Czech Party System 20 Years After the Velvet Revolution. In: E. Bakke and I. Peters, eds, *20 Years Since the Fall of the Berlin Wall*. Berlin: BMV– Berliner Wissenschafts–Verlag. pp. 221–248.

Balsys, L., 2012. Quoted by editor of the Lithuania tribune. Available at: <http://www. lithuaniatribune.com/19533/lithuanias-greens-changed-the-name-elected-l-balsys-as-chairperson-201219533/>.

Blum, M., 2004. Ein Kessel Buntes in Osteuropa. In: Heinrich Böll Stiftung, ed., *Die Grünen in Europa: Ein Handbuch*. Münster: Heinrich Böll Stiftung, pp. 131–137.

Bolleyer, N., 2013. *New Parties in Old Party Systems: Persistence and Decline in Seventeen Democracies*. Oxford: Oxford University Press.

Bugajski, J., 2002. *Political Parties of Eastern Europe: A Guide to Politics in the Post-Communist Era*. Armonk, NY: M. E. Sharpe.

Carter, N., 2013. Greening the mainstream: Party politics and the environment. *Environmental Politics*, 22(1), pp. 73–94.

Ciobanu, C., 2008. Q&A: Bulgarian Greens go political. *Sofia News Agency*, 4 June. Available at: <http://www.noinvite.com/newsletter/print.php?id=93796>.

Cisar, O., 2011. The Green party in the Czech Republic: Where they are now. *Agenda: Heinrich Böll Stiftung Magazine for South-Eastern Europe*, 6, pp. 7–8.

Čular, G., and Henjak, A., 2014. Croatia. *European Journal of Political Research Data Yearbook*, 53(1), pp. 66–77.

Dautartas, J., 2011. Interview by L. Jegelvicius. *The Baltic Times*, 6 April. Available at: <http://www.baltic times.com/tools/print_article/28422/>.

Deets, S., and Kouba, K., 2008. The Czech Greens revived. *Environmental Politics*, 17(5), pp. 815–821.

Fábián, K., 2010. Can politics be different? The Hungarian Green party's entry into parliament in 2010. *Environmental Politics*, 19(6), pp. 1006–1011.

Ferry, M., 2002. The polish Green movement ten years after the fall of communism. *Environmental Politics*, 11(1), pp. 172–177.

Fink-Hafners, D., 2006. Slovenia: Between Bipolarity and Broad Coalition-Building. In: S. Jungerstam-Mulders, ed., *Post-communist EU Member States: Parties and Party Systems*. Aldershot and Burlington: Ashgate. pp. 203–231.

Fish, S. M., and Brooks, R. S., 2000. Bulgarian democracy's organisational weapon. *East European Constitutional Review*, 9(3), pp. 63–71.

Frankland, E. G., 2002. East and Central European Greens. In: J. Barry and E. G. Frankland, eds, *International Encyclopedia of Environmental Politics*. London and New York: Routledge. pp. 137–140.

Galbreath, D. J., and Auers, D., 2009. Green, Black and Brown: Uncovering Latvia's Environmental Politics. *Journal of Baltic Studies*, 40(3), pp. 333–348.

Grzybek, A., and Szwed, D., 2008. Zieloni 2004 – Scenes from a Long March. In: P. Sadura, ed., *Polish Shades of Green: Green Ideas and Political Powers in Poland*. Brussels and Warsaw: Green European Foundation. pp. 22–26.

Hloušek, V., and Kopeček, L., 2010. *Origin, Ideology and Transformation of Political Parties: East-Central and Western Europe Compared*. Farnham: Ashgate Publishing.

Horak, M., 2002. Danube Circle. In: J. Barry and E. G. Frankland, eds, *International Encyclopedia of Environmental Politics*. London and New York: Routledge. pp. 115–116.

Inglehart, R., and Welzel, C., 2005. *Modernization, Cultural Change, and Democracy: The Human Development Sequence*. Cambridge: Cambridge University Press.

Jehlička, P., and Kostelecký, T., 1992.The development of the Czechoslovak Green party since the 1990 election. *Environmental Politics*, 1(1), pp. 72–94.

Jehlička, P., and Kostelecký, T., 2003. 'Czech Greens in the 2002 general election: A new lease of life? *Environmental Politics*, 12(2), pp. 133–138.

Jehlička, P., Kostelecký, T., and Kunštát, D., 2011. Czech Green politics after two decades: The May 2010 general election. *Environmental Politics*, 20(3), pp. 418–425.

Jordan, C., 1991. Greenway 1989–90, The Foundation of the East European Green Parties. In: S. Parkin, ed., *Green Light on Europe*. London: Heretic Books. pp. 76–83.

Jordan, G., 1998. The Greens in Eastern Europe. *Labour Focus on Eastern Europe*, 61. Available at: <http://labourfocus.gn.apc.org/GreensLF61.html>.

Jordan, G., 2010. Grüne in Mittel- und Osteuropa – ein wechselvoller Weg. In: Heinrich Böll Stiftung, ed., *Grünes Gedächtnis 2010*. Berlin: Heinrich Böll Stiftung. pp. 45–58.

Kolarov, R., and Spirova, M., 2011. Bulgaria. *European Journal of Political Research*, 50, pp. 922–928.

Kondarev, G., 2014. Bulgaria's Green political space could unite in time. *Sofia New Agency*, 25 April.

Kopeček, L., 2009. The Slovak Greens: A complex story of a small party. *Communist and Post-Communist Studies*, 42(1), pp. 115–140.

Kozek, B., 2013. The polish Green party and the upcoming elections – An interview with Barttomieji Kozek – European integration. *Heinrich Böll Stiftung*. Available at: <https://www.boell.de/en/democracy/political-parties-hungary-eco-politics-split-green-party-16858.html>.

Krastanova, R., 2012. *The Green Movement and the Green Parties in Bulgaria: Between System Integration and System Change*. Berlin: Friedrich Ebert Foundation.

Lucardie, P., and Rihoux, B., 2008. From Amateur-Activist to Professional-Electoralist Parties? On the Organizational Transformation of Green Parties in Western Democracies. In: E. G. Frankland, P. Lucardie and B. Rihoux, eds, *Green Parties in Transition: The End of Grass-roots Democracy?* Farnham: Ashgate. pp. 3–16.

Magyar, K., 2013. Hungarian eco-politics at a crossroads: The challenges faced by LMP's successor parties. *Heinrich Böll Stiftung*. Available at: <https://www.boell.de/en/democracy/political-parties-hungary-eco-politics-split-green-party-16858.html>.

Michta, A. A., 1994. *The Government and Politics of Post-communist Europe*. Westport, CT: Praeger.

Mønnesland, S., 2011. The Fall of Communism and the Dissolution of Yugoslavia. In: E. Bakke and I. Peters, eds, *20 Years Since the Fall of the Berlin Wall*. Berlin: BMV–Berliner Wissenschafts–Verlag. pp. 179–202.

Ostolski, A., 2013. Interview: Ecology in Poland is a laborious business. Available at: <https://friedemannkohler.wordpress.com/2013/11/25/>.

Pedersen, M., 1982. Towards a new typology of party lifespan and minor parties. *Scandinavian Political Studies*, 5(1), pp. 1–16.

Rinkevicius, L., 2000. Ecological modernisation as cultural politics: Transformations of civic environmental activism in Lithuania. *Environmental Politics*, 9(1), pp. 171–200.

Rüdig, W., 2004. Zwischen Öktopia und Desillusionerung: Regierungsbeteilgungen grüner Parteien in Europa 1990–2004. In: Heinrich Böll Stiftung, ed., *Die Grünen in Europa: Ein Handbuch*. Münster: Verlag Westfälisches Dampfboot. pp. 146–193.

Rüdig, W., 2006. Is government good for Greens? Comparing the electoral effects of government participation in Western and East-Central Europe. *European Journal of Political Research*, 45, pp. 127–154.

Sikk, A., 2011a. Estonia. *European Journal of Political Research*, 50, pp. 960–964.

Sikk, A., 2011b. Newness as a winning formula for new political parties. *Party Politics,* 18(4), pp. 465–486.

Sikk, A., and Andersen, R. H., 2009. Without a Tinge of Red: The Fall and Rise of Estonian Greens. *Journal of Baltic Studies,* 40(3), pp. 349–373.

Sitter, N., 2011. Absolute Power? Hungary Twenty Years After the Fall of Communism. In: E. Bakke and I. Peters, eds, *20 Years Since the Fall of the Berlin Wall.* Berlin: BMV–Berliner Wissenschafts–Verlag. pp. 249–268.

Spolitis, V., 2008. Taking Root: The Growth of the Estonian Green Parties. In: *Green Identity in a Changing Europe.* Brussels: Heinrich Böll Stiftung. pp. 66–71.

van Biezen, I., Mair, P., and Poguntke, T., 2012. Going, going . . . gone? The decline of party membership in contemporary Europe. *European Journal of Political Research,* 51, pp. 24–56.

Waller, M., and Millard, F., 1992. Environmental politics in Eastern Europe. *Environmental Politics,* 1(2), pp. 159–185.

Záhumenská, A., 2004. *Slovakia Greens: Green Political Development in the Former East – A Case Study.* Available at: <http://www.greeninstitute.net/print/54>.

Zakowski, J., 2008. The Greens Without Ecology – Interview. In: P. Sadura, ed., *Polish Shades of Green: Green Ideas and Political Powers in Poland.* Brussels and Warsaw: Green European Foundation. pp. 41–43.

4   From the Greens to Europe Ecology – The Greens

Renaissance or more of the same?

Bruno Villalba

Introduction

Europe Ecology – The Greens (*Europe Écologie – Les Verts* – EELV) was founded on 13 November 2010, in Lyon, during its constituent conference. The Greens (*Les Verts*), established with difficulty during the 1980s, gave way to a formation derived from a coalition created for the 2009 European elections. From the very beginning, there was not only talk of a transformation, but also of a 'Renaissance' of political ecology in France. The purpose was to rebuild a combative ecology movement that would be a popular political force, independent of other political formations and in particular the Socialist Party (Villalba, 2011, 2012).

The party's reorganisation was also the result of the ecologist leaders' concern to address better the constraints of the electoral system. The aim was to provide the party with a stronger influence in decision-making bodies and thus a stronger position in electoral alliances. It was supposed to meet the demands of an electorate that shows concerns for environmental issues: climate change, loss of biodiversity, depletion of natural and nonrenewable resources and technology-related emergency risks (nuclear power, and so on). This transformation was supposed to enable ecologists to enter a more mature stage. Another objective was to clarify their ideological positioning, which had been for a long time reluctant to reconcile its political agenda with the demands of government.

Beyond these priorities, what does this new denomination express? An analysis of how the ecology movement is involved in the political game (with various organisational choices and electoral strategies) provides keys to understanding the ideological and programmatic mechanisms at work and to address the issue of its available activist and electoral resources.

Origin and development: Unifying political ecology, over and over again

The project of political ecology in France has always been about enabling the convergence of ecologists towards a unique centre, while at the same time maintaining the diversity of approaches to political ecology (Sainteny, 2000; Lecœur,

2011). EELV comes as a new form of synthesis enabling the creation of a new alliance through the reform of the movement's statutes.

Maintaining diversity, while ensuring unity

From its inception, French political ecology has been characterised by a diversity of theoretical influences and made up of a multitude of more or less politicised actors. René Dumont's campaign for the 1974 presidential election, which was the first in which ecologists put forward their own candidate, was characterised by this concern to work as a coalition of social movements, environmental organisations and other structures, while strictly maintaining the independence of each coalition member. Since then, French ecologists have always tried to coordinate this diversity by associating movements within an open, flexible, decentralised and self-managed organisation. However, they have progressively realised that a perennial formation would be electorally more successful. Following long, heated debates, The Greens were founded on 28–29 January 1984 in Clichy-la-Garenne and established as an organisation that results from the merger of two major currents of political ecology. The first, the Ecologist Party (*Parti écologiste*), was more concerned with the establishment of an efficient political organisation; the other, the Ecologist Confederation (*Confédération écologiste*), was more concerned with maintaining the independence of the components of the ecology movement and rejected the development of a permanent centralised organisation. Yet they did not represent the whole spectrum of the ecology movement, which included other political formations close to The Greens or stemming from them (Table 4.1).

The Greens have had to deal with incessant dissidence, divisions and splits within their own ranks, especially in 1990 and 1995, with the law on the public funding of political parties making it easier to create small ones (Sainteny, 2000). They have also had to cope with the electoral competition from various organisations, which participated in creating a confused image among voters.

In the mid-1990s, The Greens followed a strategy targeted at the reunification of the ecological tendencies of the left (Federal Assembly of Le Mans, 10–12 November 1995). This common platform strengthened the position of The Greens as the dominant force of political ecology in France. Nonetheless, The Greens did not manage to bring together the whole ecology movement. Some groups have been reticent at the idea of forming alliances, not because of deep differences, but rather because of The Greens' strategic options. The members of the diverse degrowth movement (Semal and Szuba, 2009; Bayon, et al., 2010) remain dubious about The Greens' capacity to reform the current political system. They prefer to build a cultural alternative and press for significant changes in social practices on ecological matters (Ariès, 2010). However, their influence is far from being marginal, including within The Greens (Cochet, 2009). While alter-globalisation movements progressively incorporate environmental issues (Mouvements, 2010), they mainly remain outside of the electoral game and averse to making ecology a central element of their ideological offer (George, 2010).

Table 4.1 Ecology outside of the Greens

Generation Ecology (*Génération Écologie* – GE) was created by Brice Lalonde, Jean-Louis Borloo and Corinne Lepage with the support of the Socialist Party on 11 May 1990. GE was a very centralised organisation. GE was in favour of sustained industrial development and growth. Its realist political strategy consisted in 'Greening' all political tendencies. GE proved to be the main rival to The Greens before forming an alliance with them for the March 1993 legislative election. Lalonde progressively gave GE a centre-right orientation that went hand-in-hand with the decline of the organisation.

Independent Ecology Movement (*Mouvement écologiste indépendant* – MEI). Antoine Waechter, a former leader of The Greens, created a new ecology party in September 1994, aiming to reaffirm the political independence of ecology. However, MEI's membership and electoral impact remained low. The 2010 regional elections came as an opportunity for a new association within EE.

Citizenship, Action, Participation for the 21st Century (*Citoyenneté, action, participation pour le XXIe siècle* – Cap 21) was first a club and then a political party led by Corinne Lepage. She advocates pragmatism and realism with a focus on environmental issues and positions herself to the right of the Socialist Party. Lepage was Minister of the Environment in Prime Minister Alain Juppé's cabinet from 1995 to 1997. She built ties with the MoDem Party (F. Bayrou) and refused to join the process that led to the creation of EELV. Consequently, there is a high risk that Cap 21 (2,500 official members and 150 elected officials) will become marginalised.

Nicolas Hulot. The popular TV host entered politics during the 2007 presidential election. His *Ecological Pact* (*Pour un pacte écologique*, Calmann-Lévy, 2006) was a platform of commitments for the following presidential term that brought forward the notion of ecological emergency. Hulot's Pact was signed by the major presidential candidates and by more than 700,000 citizens. In January 2007, he withdrew his candidacy and did not give his support to any candidate. Hulot claims to have influenced the extension of the Ministry of the Environment to Sustainable Development and Planning in May 2007 and to have had a hand in the organisation of the 'Grenelle Environment Round Table'. He lost the EELV primary for the 2012 presidential election (41.3 per cent of the votes).

Europe Ecology: Expanding the electoral base of the Greens

In the summer of 2007, the idea emerged to transform the structures of political ecology. The preparation of the 2009 and 2010 elections was an opportunity to establish a political organisation with a reformed structure and a renovated ideology. This resulted in the creation of the Europe Ecology (EE) coalition on 20 October 2008 (Lecœur, 2011). EE was constituted around a few flagship proposals. The first was to revive the idea of doing politics differently through transformation of the 'party form'. With Europe Ecology, ecologists were making yet another attempt at creating an open formation that established new relations between the structure and its partisans – ranging from the actual members to occasional supporters. It was no longer necessary to become a paying member to engage in political action with the party. The second was more strategy-oriented, since the objective was to expand the electoral base of The Greens through an informal electoral alliance based on a minimum common platform and the selection of candidates for the 2009 European elections. This resulted in the ecologist contract for Europe: Europe Ecology's platform (*Contrat écologiste pour l'Europe, programme d'Europe Écologie*). Conscious of the failure of their recent electoral campaigns and the potential competition from Nicolas Hulot, The Greens intended to reposition themselves as the key players in French political ecology. EE's third objective was to pursue the effort to unite the ecologists, this time from the left to the centre-right. This was a renewed opportunity to bring together different components of activist ecology: political parties (The Greens), trades unions (*Confédération paysanne*, a farmers' trade union), civil society organisations (the Commission for Independent Research and Information about Radiation, CRII-RAD) – amongst others, as well as former leaders of the Nicolas Hulot Foundation and Greenpeace France), regionalists and so on. From an ideological point of view, beyond the traditional themes of political ecology, the main originality was the importance given to the theme of environmental urgency (EELV, 2012).[1]

The will to build an independent, decentralised and flexible ecology movement, connected to activist networks, is a constant feature of political ecology in France. There have been frequent attempts to merge its various schools of thought and small groups, either by takeover or by organising federalist unions. Nonetheless, The Greens, despite their position as the dominant electoral force, never managed this aggregation. That was the reason why EE adopted an open strategy of cooperation, in an attempt to maintain the independence of each member while trying to gain votes beyond their usual circles.

Table 4.2 Chronology of the main developments of political ecology in France

Year	Main development
1973	First candidates in a legislative election in the Alsace region, under the Ecology and Survival (*Écologie et Survie*) banner (led by A. Waechter and Solange Fernex).
1974	René Dumont, an agricultural engineer, is the first ecologist candidate to run for president in France.
1974–1983	Green movements (Friends of the Earth led by Brice Lalonde) rally against civilian nuclear energy (from Fessenheim in 1971 to Plogoff in 1981), military nuclear developments, maritime pollution (*Amoco Cadiz*) and large-scale development projects (the Rhone-Rhine canal). Ecology Movement (*Mouvement écologique*) is created in June 1974 and dissolved at the end of 1978. In November 1979, the Movement for Political Ecology (*Mouvement d'écologie politique* – MEP) is created at the initiative of Philippe Lebreton. The movement exists until 1982. Ecology activists are divided at the various elections and obtain a very limited number of votes at the national level.
1981	Lalonde is designated as candidate for the presidential election after a heated primary against Lebreton. Lebreton is more political, and Lalonde's approach favours lobbying while asserting the independence and political pragmatism of the ecology movement. The Ecologist Confederation (*Confédération écologiste* – CE) is set up in July 1981.
1982	The MEP becomes The Greens-Ecology Party (*Les Verts-Parti écologiste* – PE).

(Continued)

Table 4.2 (Continued)

Year	Main development
1984	Creation of The Greens (*Les Verts*) by merging PE and CE, on 28–29 January. Environmentalist movements distance themselves from this political approach. Lalonde and other moderates create Democratic Convergence (*Convergences démocratiques*) to represent a more 'liberal-libertarian' approach.
1986	The Greens adopt a strategy of independence (A. Waechter: 'Ecology is not to be married. . . . It is neither right, nor left'.)
1988	Waechter runs for president; Pierre Juquin, representing the alternative left, is a competitor in the field of ecology. Lalonde supports French President F. Mitterrand in his re-election and is appointed to various ministerial positions (Secretary of State, then Minister of the Environment) between 1988 and 1992.
1989	Foundation of Red and Green Alternative (*Alternative rouge et verte* – Arev), a group that includes former members of the Greens, the Socialists, and former leftists. Positioned on the far left, the organisation is dissolved in 1998 to make way for The Alternatives (*Les Alternatifs*), an organisation with close ties to the antiglobalisation network and that advocates a self-managed, Eurosceptic and feminist ecology movement.
1990	In May, Lalonde creates Generation Ecology (*Génération Écologie* – GE), a political party that positions itself on the left until 1994.
1992–1993	GE and The Greens form an alliance (*L'Entente des écologistes*) for the 1993 legislative elections.
1993	In November, D. Voynet and G. Onesta's movement (*Les Verts au Pluriel*) wins the majority at The Greens' congress, and The Greens position themselves on the left. Waechter quits the party. GE undergoes important divisions: the creation of Convergence Ecology Solidarity (*Convergence écologie solidarité* – CES) by N. Mamère and Blue Ecology (*Écologie bleue*), among others.
1994	The Greens change their statutes. In September, Waechter creates the Independent Ecology Movement (*Mouvement écologiste indépendant*), to defend an ecology movement independent of traditional political divides.
1995	The Greens adopt a strategy of alliances with the left. In April, Voynet is the only ecologist candidate for the presidential election; The Greens initiate a strategy to absorb all the 'left wing Green activists' (such as CES and Arev).
1995–1997	Lepage's appointment as Minister of the Environment in Juppé's cabinet legitimises the idea of centre-right ecology. GE slides into irreversible decline following Lalonde's change of positioning, first to the centre, then to the right.
1996	Emergence of the plural left (*gauche plurielle*) concept. The Greens definitively turn to the strategy of electoral alliances with the parliamentary left. Lepage creates a club, named *Cap 21*, which will become a political party in 2000.
1997	Seven Green candidates are elected to the Parliament (through an alliance with the Socialist Party); Voynet, G. Hascoët, and later on Y. Cochet, are appointed to Jospin's cabinet.
1998	Mamère joins The Greens in January.
1999	European elections (Cohn-Bendit), 9.7% of votes.
2002	Mamère replaces the winner of The Greens' primary, Alain Lipietz, as candidate for the presidential election and wins 5.3% of the votes. Lepage is also candidate (1.8% of the votes). In November, Voynet and Mamère lose the majority in The Greens. Once again, the party hesitates on the electoral strategy and tries to redefine its ideological positions.

Year	Main development
2003	G. Lemaire is elected as the new national secretary of The Greens in January, following an alliance of diverse tendencies.
2004	In the March regional elections, in an alliance with the Socialist Party in most regions, The Greens benefit from the momentum of the left. However, they win only 7.4% of the vote at the European elections in June and six seats in the European Parliament.
2005	In January, in a context of heated internal debates, The Greens elect Y. Wehrling as their new national secretary.
2006	C. Duflot is elected national secretary of The Greens on 16 December.
2007	Voynet is The Greens' candidate in the presidential election, after winning the primary against Y. Cochet.
2008	20 October: launch of Europe Ecology (*Europe Écologie* – EE); 16 November: a decentralised general assembly is held, with a focus on environmental urgency, degrowth and social ecology; C. Duflot is re-elected as national secretary.
2009	On 8 July, Green deputy M. Billard quits the party. She considers that the Green alliance moves the party toward the centre, away from her traditional positioning on the radical left. She joins the Left Party.
2010	4–11 July: A. Poursinoff is elected to the French parliament (in a special legislative election). November 13: birth of *Europe Écologie – Les Verts* (EELV). December: P. Meirieu becomes the first president of EELV's Federal council.
2011	On 12 July, Joly is chosen to run in the presidential election by EELV's members and cooperators. In the first round of the primary, Joly comes first with 49.8% of the vote against 40.2% for Hulot, 5% for Stoll and 4.4% for Lhomme. In the second round, on 12 July, Joly confirms her lead (13,223 votes; 58.2%) over Hulot (9,399 votes; 41.3%).
2012	On 16 May, two Green ministers are appointed to Ayrault's cabinet: Cécile Duflot (Minister of Territorial Equality and Housing) and Pascal Canfin (Minister Delegate attached to the Minister of Foreign Affairs, with responsibility for development). June 2012: Duflot leaves her position as national secretary of EELV.

Source: Author's own compilation.

Electoral fluctuations

The electoral results of the ecology movement have undergone rapid and significant changes (Table 4.3). However, apart from a few exceptions, these results have been relatively low, outside of the periods of electoral alliances.

Throughout their electoral history, ecologists have tried to adapt to the constraints related to the electoral system. The uninominal method of voting in national elections (both presidential and legislative) often forces them to restrain their ambitions. The distribution of constituencies in the framework of alliances between Green parties (1993), or with their partners of the Plural Left (1997–2002, 2012), does not make up for their lack of local strongholds and locally established personalities. The low results obtained at presidential elections are also a sign of the party's lack of credibility to assume the highest office (Boy, 2010a). Cantonal

Table 4.3 Electoral results of the ecology movement, 1974–2012 (% votes)

Year	Elections	% Votes	Notes
1974	Presidential	1.4	Candidate: René Dumont (various Green)
1978	Legislative	2.2	4.4% where there are candidates
1979	European	4.5	Solange Fernex
1981	Presidential	3.9	Candidate: Brice Lalonde
1981	Legislative	1.1	3.3% where there are candidates
1984	European	3.4	Didier Anger (The Greens); 3.4% Lalonde
1985	Cantonal		4.1% where there are candidates
1986	Legislative	1.2	2.4% where there are candidates
1986	Regional	2.4	3.4% where there are candidates
1988	Presidential	3.8	Candidate: Waechter (no voting instructions for the second round of the election)
1988	Legislative	0.4	Boycotted by The Greens
1988	Cantonal	1.6	300 candidates, 6,8% where they run; no seats
1989	European	10.6	Waechter (7 Green MPs + 2 seats for members of civil society)
1992	Regional	6.8	110 seats for The Greens; 7.1% Génération Écologie
1992	Cantonal		The Greens: 8% where there are candidates; 70 candidates present in the 2nd round, one seat; GE: 2% where there are candidates, no seats
1993	Legislative	7.6	Green coalition (The Greens + GE); 3% for other Green parties
1994	Cantonal	3.5	7.7% where there are candidates; 2 seats
1994	European	2.9	Marie-Anne Isler-Béguin; Lalonde (2%)
1995	Presidential	3.3	Candidate: Dominique Voynet
1997	Legislative	4.1	7 Green MPs (455 candidates; 5.1% where there are candidates. 29 reserved constituencies); GE: 1.7%; MEI: 0.7%; other Greens: 0.3%
1998	Cantonal		7.6% (where there are candidates, in 718 'cantons')
1998	Regional	5.6	37 independent lists (54 common platforms *Majorité plurielle* – Plural majority); 74 seats for The Greens
1999	European	9.7	Daniel Cohn-Bendit (9 seats); MEI: 1.5%
2001	Cantonal		11.3% where there are candidates
2002	Presidential	5.2	Candidate: Noël Mamère; other candidate: Corinne Lepage (Cap 21): 1.9%
2002	Legislative	4.4	3 seats (57 reserved constituencies); other Green: 1.2%
2004	Regional	2.2	10 independent lists; 14 alliance lists with the left; 168 seats
2004	Cantonal		4.1% where there are candidates
2004	European	7.4	6 seats
2007	Presidential	1.57	Candidate: Dominique Voynet; other candidate: José Bové, 1.3%

Year	Elections	% Votes	Notes
2007	Legislative	3.2	4 Green MPs: Martine Billard and Yves Cochet in Paris, Noël Mamère in the South-West and François de Rugy in western France
2008	Cantonal		+/− 20 seats (4.2% in the first round, 1.5% in the second round)
2009	European	16.3	14 seats; 3.6% for the Independent ecologist alliance (*Alliance écologiste indépendante* – MEI, GE, La France en Action), no seats
2010	Regional	12.2	Europe Écologie: 262 regional councillors – 5 senators, 4 MPs and 8 European MPs. 6 of the 14 MPs elected from the list of Europe Écologie are not members of The Greens, but are affiliated to the 'The Greens-European Free Alliance' group in the European Parliament
2011	Cantonal	8.2	1,155 candidates; 46 EELV or affiliated regional councillors.
2011	Senate		10 seats (5 men and 5 women)
2012	Presidential	2.3	Candidate: Eva Joly
2012	Legislative	5.5	EELV endorses candidates in almost all districts. An electoral agreement is signed with the Socialist Party, with 60 'more or less' reserved constituencies for the Greens nationwide. 16 MPs are elected. Creation of a parliamentary group

Source: Author's own compilation.

elections are not more favourable to ecologists. However, the 2011 cantonal elections appear as a relative success that could be interpreted as a sign of an increased Green foothold (the number of candidates is indeed a good indicator, although the number of seats obtained remains low). Other elections, such as supranational elections (European elections, with proportional representation) and local elections (municipal, regional, with an increased focus on local issues), appear more favourable to ecologists. Still, results remain low, with strong geographic and temporal variations that can be explained by the irregular presence of Green candidates in municipal elections.[2]

The strategies followed by ecologists also have an impact on their electoral results. They obtain their best scores when running in the framework of alliances, either with other Green parties or with partners on the progressive left (Faucher, 2004; Boy, 2010b). Unity clarifies their electoral offer and prevents the dispersion of votes, which is often a big issue for a party for which every vote counts. Still, results remain weak at the national level, even in case of alliances with the Socialist Party (low number of reserved constituencies). However, such alliances enable The Greens to get a few seats at the national level and to hold a few ministerial positions (in the Jospin and Ayrault cabinets). Nevertheless, it also creates

a situation of dependency that is sometimes detrimental to their desire for autonomy. For example, in 2010, The Greens had to make compromises on emblematic
environment-related issues such as the Notre-Dame-des-Landes airport project
in the Pays de la Loire region, the ITER (International Thermonuclear Experimental Reactor) project in the Provence-Alpes-Côte d'Azur region and others. In
the ten regional administrations where they enjoy a blocking majority, they have
never used it to block decisions; yet reasons for dispute subsist in most regional
executives (on transport policy, moralisation of politics, sports infrastructures and
so on).[3]

Electoral results also depend on public perception of the party's unity. Internal divisions have adverse effects on electoral results (1974–1988, 1994–1997).
However, the clarification of the organisation and a relative facade of unity have
proven beneficial in terms of electoral momentum (1993, 2009–2012).

Green politicians have less control over the extreme volatility of their electorate.
As such, it is worth examining to what extent the vote for ecologist candidates is
motivated by environmental issues. For example, votes for The Greens were not
significantly impacted by the terrible consequences of the Chernobyl accident in
1986. The same is true for recurring issues related to socio-technological risks
(nuclear energy, mad cow disease, genetically modified crops and so on). Widespread media focus on environmental issues between 2006 and 2009 (movies by Al
Gore, Yann-Arthus Bertrand and Nicolas Hulot; the Grenelle Environment Round
Table organised by the French government; international climate conferences and
so on) have not significantly impacted Green electoral results. Neither did the
Fukushima nuclear disaster have a significant effect on the 2011 cantonal elections.
Other motives may explain the Green vote. For example, success in the 2009 European elections could be partly explained by the prevalent anti-Sarkozy mood and
by the fact that the Socialist Party did not manage to appear as a clear alternative.

Finally, these results are also the consequence of an obvious professionalisation
of the Green elites. Over the years, The Greens have become more professional
in electoral campaigning (management of funds, training of candidates, campaign leadership and so on). They sometimes have difficulties in developing clear
electoral platforms (Bozonnet, 2002), but they have become more comfortable
with developing campaigning expertise such as political communication, use
of information and communication technology. Public funding received from
1988 onwards has greatly enhanced their organisational capacity. EELV won
1,418,141 votes in the first round of the 2012 legislative elections, representing (at
€1.68 per vote) public funding to the tune of €2,382,476.88 per year, as opposed to
€1.3 million previously. The second part of public funding depends on the number
of elected officials. EELV's 27 seats yield €2.38 million for the party. The recent
network/party strategy adopted by EELV has participated in this process of professionalisation. The 2009 European elections enabled the Greens/EE alliance to
have credible candidates and high-profile front-runners in all constituencies. As
elected officials, The Greens have established a culture of management, and they
have accumulated a certain negotiation expertise, which now they bring into play
more offensively with their partners.

Structure and organisation

In France and in Europe, political ecology structured itself around the issue of grassroots democracy as an alternative to traditional politics (Richardson and Rootes, 1994; Vialatte, 1996), both in its organisational dimension (modes of party-building, management of the professionalisation of the ruling elites and so on) and in its political expression (importance given to the participatory dimension) (Deschouwer, 1995; Rihoux, 2001).

Defining party statutes in accordance with political objectives

Throughout their history, French ecology movements, in particular The Greens and then EELV, have never ceased to express the will to define party statutes that reflect their political ideals and that enable grassroots democracy. They have tried to promote collective leadership, insisting on the collective development of party statements. They have also advocated regional independence, collegiality in their decision-making bodies (the Interregional National Council, the Executive Board), direct democracy (a yearly General Assembly, internal referendum) and gender equality (Serne, 2004). Priority is given to the involvement of grassroots members and regional decision-making processes. They have tried to prevent professionalisation of their leadership, and the statutes formally guarantee equality for all members whatever position they may hold in the movement. The objective of such democratic formalism is also to protect The Greens against any form of oligarchic drift. They have also established a principle of rotation in the exercise of office (for example, at mid-term, the elected official resigns in order to be replaced by their running mate), as well as restrictions against holding multiple internal and external mandates. Finally, The Greens were among the first parties to establish gender equality as a rule.

Since 1984, The Greens have made many amendments to their statutes and some major reorganisations, for example in 1994. These changes have two, sometimes contradictory, objectives: to improve the membership's involvement in the party and to be more competitive in elections. In 1994, The Greens adopted the principle of a Federal Assembly organised every two years with elected delegates from the regions. The history of the statutes reflects the will to maintain the fragile balance between theory and practice. To achieve this, the Greens relied on their statutory council and measures such as external audits and thematic workshops during their summer party conference. However, these basic rules (rotation, nonprofessionalisation and so on) were progressively rethought and only gender equality is still applied.

The different successive statutes of The Greens constitute a meaningful sequencing of the party's development. The repeated rewritings are an illustration of the necessary adaptations that were made to keep their identity, while adapting to the membership's claims as well as to the hopes of voters and the demands of partners. Despite these changes, The Greens did not succeed in overcoming a form of isolation. Paradoxically, the search for internal democratic integrity could be perceived as a form of exclusion for the uninitiated or, for others, as an excessive obsession.

Creating party statutes adapted to political constraints

The presence of Green activists at the local, national and European levels facilitates the professionalisation of the Green leadership, even if few are appointed to positions of responsibility. Elected officials, numbering approximately 2,000 in 2008, have a strong influence in the organisation. Being elected offers an opportunity to acquire a culture of the exercise of power, as well as the material capacity (money, time, networks and resources) to get involved in the internal debates of the party. It also enhances their capacity to capitalise activist knowledge into political skills. This party elite has the possibility to represent the political discourse of the movement internally and externally and thus to influence the ideological platform. The influence of advisors of elected officials should also be noted. Often, availability, knowledge and effective presence enable advisors to become key players in the organisation of the party's activities. Finally, professionalisation is also enhanced by the new profile of party members, who increasingly come to politics after specialised training in environmental issues.

Professionalisation is also a result of the lack of commitment of new members who do not get involved in the party's daily management. The Greens have regularly wondered how to contain the relentless competition for posts. The amendment of statutes and the adoption of rules for multiple offices are attempts to address the issue.

Lastly, professionalisation increases with public funding. Between 1984 and 1989, membership fees were the main financial resource for The Greens. After 1989, the contribution of elected officials, who pay back a portion of their remuneration to the party, improved the budgetary situation and increased the influence of elected representatives within the party. Like all other political parties in France, The Greens also benefit from public funding for electoral campaigns.[4] The implementation of the law on the public funding of political parties in 1988 also had an influence on management practices. In 2009, The Greens' budget was €6.6 million (14 per cent from membership fees, 28 per cent from the contribution of elected officials, 3 per cent from donations from individuals, 28 per cent from public funding and 27 per cent from various other sources).[5] To fund its activities, the party must constantly pay great attention to its resources, a fact that can have an influence on the nomination of candidates and alliance strategies.

From cooperative network (Europe Ecology) to 'new' party (EELV)

The setting up of Europe Ecology (EE) appeared as an attempt to address the latent professionalisation of the Green party. Under the influence of some leaders, such as D. Cohn-Bendit and J. Bové, a process was initiated with the aim of renewing the party. In his 'March 22 [2010] Appeal', Cohn-Bendit suggested creating a 'political cooperative', in the form of a very flexible network that would bring together members of the 'citizen left', the Communist Party, the environmental pole of the Socialist Party, the Independent Ecology Movement and the MoDem (Centre Party led by François Bayrou). The objective of such a structure would be to go beyond the usual electoral activities of a political party, by getting involved in popular education or training activities, and to create a pole of reflection. Upon its creation, EE adopted an extremely flexible organisation (until November 2010, the movement only had two full-time employees and relied mainly on the work of volunteers), meant to embody cooperative ideals.[6] The stated objective was to enable the coproduction of decisions in order to support them through consensus, as well as to improve the involvement of both partners and ordinary citizens. The organisation was based on local committees (510 at the end of 2009), coordinated by regional leadership and steering committees. The national level included a leadership and steering committee, as well as an executive board. At first, EE's main activity consisted in the organisation of electoral campaigns, in partnership with The Greens. The success of the approach rapidly led the main leaders to wonder whether this type of dual organisation for political ecology might be carried on.

After a long period of negotiations (January–October 2010), the statutes of *Europe Écologie – Les Verts* were adopted by a large majority.[7] EELV wanted to revive the original ideals of political ecology. The main idea was to build a party-movement by resetting the limits that define the party. A network of cooperators was set up around EELV, in order to join resources with EELV without imposing the constraints related to party membership itself. Cooperators participate in party activities on a more flexible and ad hoc basis. They agree with a charter of values, but the status of cooperator does not give access to all the rights available to actual party members. Cooperators may participate in debates and actions of local committees, vote on electoral platforms and apply to be candidates in an election. However, they do not directly take part in the selection process of candidates or in the development of the electoral strategy (except for the presidential election). They are not eligible for certain internal positions, and they do not have the right to participate in votes related to the party structures. Participatory culture was also reaffirmed with the production of various statuses for members, to offer opportunities to move from an occasional involvement in politics to positions with significant responsibilities. The aim was to offer an alternative to professional politics and to stimulate the continuous participation of all (random draw of members of the 'Agora', which is in charge of the development of EE's platform and strategy). The principles of gender equality, incompatibilities, differentiated federalism, budget transparency and political independence were reaffirmed; however, the principle of rotation was abandoned.

Would these statutes be sufficient to manage the 'overwhelming faith of new converts in the face of members with several decades of activism'?[8] Another challenge was to reconcile the political experience of The Greens and the utopian and sometimes libertarian inclinations of EE. Would cooperators be able to commit durably within a structure with loose boundaries? It would be their task to define their own prerogatives more precisely, in order to have an influence on the organisation and the orientation of the political party without giving up their ideal of self-management. Finally, EELV had to face the material difficulties related to the different structures of the two partners. How could a coalition be maintained, since *Europe Écologie* did not have a stable party organisation? How could funding issues be resolved?

Party membership and voters

The first striking observation is the low party membership (Figure 4.1). The maximum number of party members reached in the first decade of this century – 10,000 – is a sign of the difficulties of The Greens to attract their own electorate.

The weakness of Green party membership results in part from the general crisis of activism, but it is also enhanced by difficulties that are specific to this party. First, The Greens are highly dependent on electoral variations. Good results provide momentum that leads to increased membership (1989). Electoral setbacks have the opposite effect (decrease in 1994–1996). However, it seems that the positive electoral momentum of the 2009–2010 period did not lead to the expected increase of membership. The introduction of the 'cooperator' member status has not significantly influenced the membership curve. Upon its creation in November 2010, EELV claimed to have between 13,000 and 15,000 members, many of whom arrived in the euphoria that followed the European and regional elections. On the eve of 5 June 2011 congress, EELV claimed to have 10,700 members and between 1,500 and 3,000 cooperators. Those figures were later challenged by EELV's National Secretary P. Durand, explaining that there were actually only

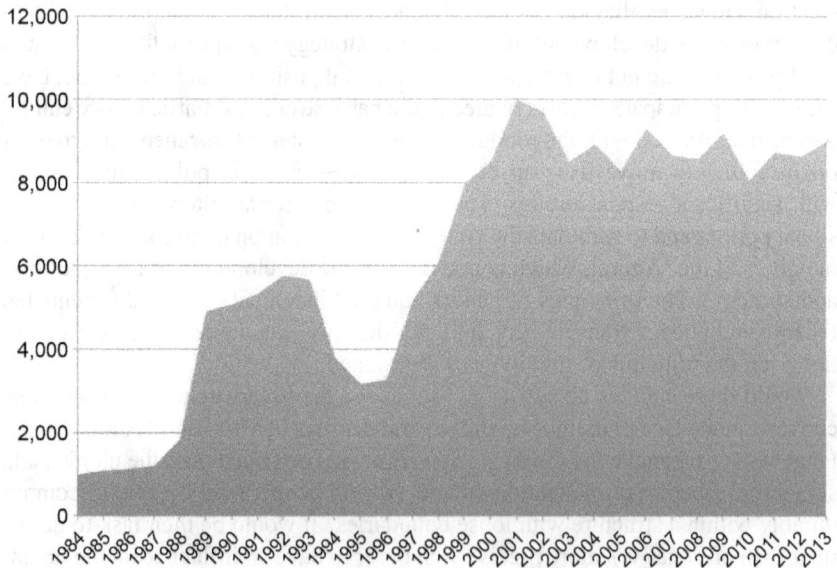

Figure 4.1 Party members, France (1984–2013)

Source: Author's own compilation based on data from The Greens, EE and EELV.

9,000 members at the time (*Le Monde*, 5 March 2013, see Figure 4.1). EELV's leadership now claims to have a little over 10,000 members.

In addition, periods when The Greens offered a clear vision of their political project seem to correspond to periods of positive membership development: between 1987 and 1993 (principle of political independence), in 1995 (positioning on the left) or with the strategy of unity with EE. Finally, in situations of low membership, internal divisions and organisational difficulties do not facilitate recruitment or membership renewals. In 1994, the resignation of Waechter resulted in a 31 per cent decrease in membership. Finally, The Greens suffered from significant membership turnover, accounting for 30 to 35 per cent of total membership over the 1984–1998 period.[9] Preliminary discussions to prepare the foundation of EELV often stressed this difficulty in retaining party members.

It is difficult to put together a profile of the typical Green party member, both for methodological reasons (lack of recent sociological work) and because of membership turnover. In addition, it should be noted that members originating from EE and The Greens have different activist and political backgrounds. In terms of sociological composition, The Greens and EE have had a stable gender composition, with women representing 30.4 per cent of members in 1998 for The Greens and 31 per cent for EE.[10] Membership is ageing, with the average age of members climbing from 39 to 47 over a period of 10 years (1992–2002). Over 49 per cent of EE members and sympathisers are over 50. People in their forties are still highly represented (31 per cent of EE members are aged between 35 and 49), while young people are under-represented (20 per cent of members under 34) (Boy, et al., 2003). The Greens and EE party-movement has always been more attractive to white-collar and intellectual workers (42 per cent in EE). The party member's average education is higher than the national average (in 1998, 22.7 per cent of members had a master's-level degree). Finally, low-income occupations have long been absent (1 per cent of blue-collar workers and 1 per cent of farmers in EE), while associate professionals are relatively well represented (13 per cent of associate professionals and 10 per cent of employees in EE).

The profile of voters is comparable to that of party members (for the composition of voters in the late 1990s, see Boy, et al., 2003, pp. 20–23). The disproportionate representation of white-collar and intellectual workers and professionals is a constant feature (32 per cent), with a relatively strong presence of associate professionals (24 per cent). People with higher education are thus very well represented (23 per cent) (Deloy, et al., 2009, pp. 34–35). Less-qualified occupations (such as blue-collar workers, farmers and employees) are much less represented. There tend to be more women and young people among voters than among party members (Boy and Chiche, 2010, pp. 623–635). Very few unemployed or retired people vote Green. The sociological composition of voters is thus built around a core of average-to high-income, highly educated and associate professionals. It includes very few small entrepreneurs or farmers. The party is therefore attractive 'not so much to 'bobos' (bohemian-bourgeois) as it is to 'petty bobos'' (Alain Lipietz).

The Green electorate tends to be positioned on the left, but it is characterised by a diversity of origins. According to a 2010 opinion survey (carried out by OpinionWay for *Le Nouvel Observateur*, 14 March 2010), three out of five EE voters claim to be on the left. EE thus finds itself in the position of an actual 'electoral magnet' at the heart of the centre and the left: 26 per cent of people who voted for Socialist Party candidate Ségolène Royal in the first round of the 2007 presidential election, 20 per cent of those who voted for the centrist François Bayrou and 20 per cent of those who voted for far-left candidate Olivier Besancenot voted *Europe Écologie* in 2010. The image of an outsider ('neither left, nor right'), difficult to categorise, still subsists. Could EE represent 'alternative centrism' for centre-right voters, facing a crisis of confidence in the MoDem party? (Perrineau, 2010, pp. 10–15).

The Green electorate tends to be urban. In the 2009 European elections, the Cohn-Bendit list received nearly 21 per cent of the votes in the Paris region. Elsewhere, the correlation is manifest in the electoral results: 18.3 per cent in the Southeast election constituency, 16.6 per cent in the West constituency, 15.8 per cent in the Southwest, 14.3 per cent in the East, 13.6 per cent in the Centre and 12.1 per cent in the Northwest. Urban areas with strong potential for managers contrast with more working-class or rural regions. Green parties generally have low electoral success in the countryside (in the 2010 regional elections, results were below 8 per cent in some rural *départements* such as Somme, Haute-Savoie, Cantal or Landes). There are a few exceptions, mainly in mountainous regions and/or the southern part of France, which can probably be explained by the influence of people who move from the city to those areas. The 2009 European elections show a certain permanence of votes in the regions where Green parties get good results: Alsace (16.8 per cent), Rhône-Alpes (19.6 per cent), Île-de-France (20.9 per cent), Brittany (17.9 per cent) and Pays de la Loire (16.4 per cent). It is also the case in some *départements* of the Midi-Pyrénées region, where the list led by Gérard Onesta received a significant number of votes (13.5 per cent).

Green voters tend to make their decisions rather late (61 per cent decided during the last week before the election, as against 45 per cent on average for all voters). This is an indication of the instability of Green voters. Many of them have supported other parties before (in particular the MoDem or the Socialist Party), have abstained (Boy, 2007, pp. 54–57) or claim to come from the (mainly moderate) right or to be 'neither right, nor left' (about 15 per cent in 2010, mainly among young voters – Pingaud, 2010, p. 22). Cementing the loyalty of these voters is a key issue that conditions EELV's capacity to influence durably the electoral game.

The political eclecticism of Green voters also manifests itself in their opinions on major issues. They tend to be in favour of maintaining or even strengthening the role of the state, while advocating the idea that public debt should be reduced, something that could be done by reducing the number of public servants. They are united by an anti-Sarkozy feeling, as well as by the support for the general, generous values put forward by Europe Ecology, namely a certain ethical position, the transition to a Greener economy and a new way of doing politics. On the other hand, voters are more averse to follow ecologists in their antinuclear struggle (51 per cent openly declare to be against this idea), as well as to ideas of degrowth (Pingaud, 2010, pp. 30–32). The results of the 2011 cantonal elections tend to confirm this gap, as the nuclear accidents in Japan did not lead to a significant breakthrough for Green candidates.

Ideology and policy positions: Towards ideological pragmatism

The general principle of political ecology involves a radical questioning of the socioeconomic order of the industrial and technological era. It plays a part in awareness of the incompatibility of current production and consumption modes, which come with a model of society based on individualism and accumulation, with the limits of the planet (Lipietz, 1999; Barry and Frankland, 2001). There have been different versions of this project over time, influenced by historical events and the constraints of the electoral calendar (Frémion, 2007). These developments can also be explained by the absence of a common, consistent culture within The Greens. Stemming from a variety of political traditions, and concerned with respect for individuality, The Greens have come together around a few common elements, even if they have not succeeded in establishing shared priorities. Through endless debates, The Greens do not cease to articulate their political platform based on a *corpus* of theory with no clear limits. Their liberal positions are more clearly asserted on cultural issues, in defence of social permissiveness and individual freedom.

Their founding manifesto[11] revives the desire to build a cultural majority in favour of political ecology (such an objective was already put forward by The Greens in 1986 and 1993). The objective is to create a credible alternative to 'old right-left divisions' (Duflot, 2010a), by transforming the cultural and political references of voters. The political offer is also more pragmatic. The manifesto benefits from The Greens' political experience. It takes on the strategy of reconciling the two principles of establishing electoral alliances and taking responsibility for public office (as The Greens have done since 1995). Accounting for the constraints of public policy has led to moderate ideological positioning (as shown by the participation in government from 1997 to 2002).[12] By accessing positions of responsibility, The Greens have been confronted with a typical challenge: to build a culture of government while maintaining a sufficiently differentiated political offer (Villalba, 2008, pp. 43–60). The manifesto specifies that no alliance should be made with right-wing forces, and the party may form alliances with left-wing forces, 'without this being an objective in itself' (Duflot, 2010b). Despite unresolved issues (the European nuclear Pressurised Reactor [EPR], Notre-Dame des Landes airport and so on), an agreement was signed between the Socialist Party and EELV on 15 November 2011,[13] leading to the appointment of EELV ministers to government.

The manifesto also takes into account international developments. The early 2000s have been characterised by intensified international mobilisation on environmental issues, which has led to a stronger institutional offer. EE's Ecologist Contract for Europe (*Contrat écologiste pour l'Europe*) intends to contribute to the establishment of public policies that are up to the severity of the social, economic and environmental crisis. EE has a project that is

> very concrete in order to organise the transition to a Green economy, which is the only solution for coming out of the financial slump and to implement policies at a European level that are more socially just and less damaging for the planet.
>
> (Canfin, 2009)

The political platform is articulated around long-held claims, such as the end of the nuclear sector and the moralisation of democratic life, and other more short-term demands, such as implementation of the measures of the Grenelle Environment Round Table and the implementation of a carbon tax. It also takes into account some of the major trends in society, in particular the increase in social inequality, in calling for a reduction of the difference between the highest and lowest salaries, the implementation of a maximum salary and heavy taxation for people with a yearly income over half a million Euros.

The Greens' transmutation has enabled political ecology to have a stronger presence in positions of power in the Fifth Republic. Still, the overall results of this proximity with centres of power is far from being globally positive, even in the opinion of the party executives and activists themselves. The ecologists did not obtain the phase-out of nuclear power even though the electoral agreement includes a significant reduction objective, nor the interruption of the EPR power plant in Flamanville (a third-generation reactor that is supposed to become a showcase of French industry in this sector). In the field of energy, the ecologists obtained, on paper, the commitment to close 24 nuclear reactors by 2025, not to build new nuclear power plants during the term of office, to give up retreatment and mixed oxides (MO – EPR's fuel), to establish a nuclear decommissioning sector and to adopt an overall energy transition strategy based on energy efficiency and the development of renewables. The issue of military nuclear power was not on the agenda. This shows a certain pragmatic approach compared to historical demands, which were challenging and complicated to support politically, in the media and above all electorally. In the end, EELV has adapted to a society that does not question a political vision based on technological innovation, giving up a deeper reflection on the ways to achieve energy sobriety with equity. This platform perpetuates the vision of a growthist societal project, with a stronger focus on a quality approach (source of produced energy and modes of usage) and redistribution. With this platform, political ecology departs even more from an ecocentric vision, which is best suited to building an effectively sustainable framework for reconciling the human and the nonhuman (Eckersley, 1992). In the end, this platform approves a vision of political ecology that poses fewer and fewer questions about the management of consequences and increasingly addresses the management of possibilities. Utopia now seems like a long-forgotten horizon.

Notes

1 Europe Ecology's manifesto includes the following warning: 'We have now reached a key moment, which could turn into a tipping point. . . . It is urgent for us to come together and make that happen. Not tomorrow, not maybe. But resolutely now!' (Europe Écologie, October 2008).

2 March 1989 municipal elections: 9% of the votes cast (8.1% in cities with a population over 9,000) and 1,369 seats; 1995 municipal elections: 6.5% of votes cast where there are candidates; 2001 municipal elections: 11.8% (there are Green candidates in 600 cities with a population of over 3,500, showing the increased Green foothold, mainly in urban areas). For the 160 independent lists in the municipal elections, results

are approximately 12% of votes cast and 33 mayors affiliated to the Greens; 2008 municipal elections, 8.7% (83 independent lists, 41 Green mayors).

3   This concurs with the conclusions from the first experiences of participation in regional executives (Boy, et al., 1995). In August 2010 in Nantes, one of the main themes of the party's summer conference was 'Ecology taking the test of power'.

4   Campaign budgets have increased from €900,000 for the 1989 European elections to €2 million in 1999 and €4 million in 2004.

5   French National Commission on Election Funding, *Journal officiel*, 29 December 2010.

6   See the founding texts, <http://www.europe-ecologie.fr/wp-content/uploads/2010/05/dossier-8mai_.pdf> (Accessed on 9 December 2010).

7   85.1% of members of The Greens (participation rate was less than 50%, with 3,900 votes), 10.3% voted against and 4.6% blank votes (statutes adopted on 13 November 2010). See <http://www.eelv.fr/le-rassemblement/5266-les-statuts/>.

8   Michèle Rivasi, <http://www.rue89.com/michele-rivasi/2010/11/12/europe-ecologie-a-mi-chemin-entre-la-cooperative-et-le-mouvement-politique> (Accessed on 7 January 2011).

9   Source: Surveys by Daniel Boy (Cevipof), Agnès Roche (University of Clermont-Ferrand) and Bruno Villalba (Ceraps) in 1998, in collaboration with The Greens (1,361 responses, representing a 68% return rate).

10 See EE internal survey carried out from 30 June to 26 July 2010, <http://www.europe-ecologie.fr/wp-content/uploads/2010/08/EuropeEcologie1908.pdf> (Accessed 19 December 2010).

11 <http://www.europe-ecologie.fr/2010/09/20/manifeste-pour-un-nouveau-cours-ecologique-et-social/> (Accessed on 7 January 2011).

12 Voynet's account of this participation (2003) is extremely interesting, as it reveals the lack of institutional culture of the Green political establishment and the attempt to assess the results of her ministerial experience. It also contributes to strengthening the ideological offer on the left around ecological issues (Löwy and Harribey, 2003).

13 <http://eelv.fr/wp-content/uploads/2011/11/texte_complet_daccord_EELV-PS1.pdf>.

References

Ariès, P., 2010. *La simplicité volontaire contre le mythe de l'abondance*. Paris: La Découverte.

Barry, J., and Frankland, E. G., eds, 2001. *International Encyclopedia of Environmental Politics*. London and New York: Routledge.

Bayon, D., Flipo, F., and Schneider, F., 2010. *La décroissance: Dix questions pour comprendre et en débattre*. Paris: La Découverte.

Boy, D., 2007. Les Verts: entre dissensions internes et électoral volage. In: P. Perrineau, ed., *Atlas électoral 2007: qui vote quoi, où, comment?* Paris: Presses de Sciences Po. pp. 54–57.

Boy, D., 2010a. Europe Écologie: la nouvelle opposition? In: O. Duhamel and B. Teinturier, eds, *L'État de l'opinion 2010*. Paris: TNS/SOFRES/Seuil. pp. 57–72.

Boy, D., 2010b. La situation politique du mouvement écologique aujourd'hui. *La revue socialiste,* 40, pp. 89–94.

Boy, D., and Chiche, J., 2010. Une vague Verte? *Revue internationale de politique comparée*, 16(4), pp. 623–635.Boy, D., Jacques Le Seigneur, V., and Roche, A., 1995. *L'écologie au pouvoir*. Paris: Presses de la Fondation nationale de sciences politiques.

Boy, D., Platone, F., Rey, H., Subileau, F., and Ysmal, C., 2003. *C'était la gauche plurielle*. Paris: Presses de Sciences Po.

Bozonnet, J.-P., 2002. Les Verts aux présidentielles et législatives 2002: échec et résistance. *Revue politique et parlementaire*, 1020–1021, pp. 150–161.

Canfin, P., 2009. *Le contrat écologique pour l'Europe*. Paris: Les Petits matins.

Cochet, Y., 2009. *Antimanuel d'écologie*. Rosny-sous-Bois: Bréal.

Deloy, C., Reynié, D., and Perrineau, P., 2009. *Élections Européennes 2009: Analyse des résultats en Europe et en France* (Fondapol note). [online] Paris: Fondapol (Published September 2009). Available at: <http://www.fondapol.org/etude/1548> [Accessed 14 March 2011].

Deschouwer, K., 1995. The Decline of Consociationalism and the Reluctant Modernisation of Belgian Mass Parties. In: R. S. Katz and P. Mair, eds, *How Parties Organize: Change and Adaptation in Party Organisations in Western Democracies*. London: Sage. pp. 80–108.

Duflot, C., 2010a. *Apartés: Entretien avec Guy Sitbon*. Paris: Les Petits matins.

Duflot, C. 2010b. *Le Monde*, 11 November 2010.

Eckersley, R., 1992. *Environmentalism and Political Theory: Toward an Ecocentric Approach*. Albany, NY: State University of New York Press.

EELV, 2012. *Vivre mieux: Vers une société écologique, projet d'EELV pour les élections de 2012*. Paris: Les Petits matins.

Faucher, F., 2004. The Greens 2002: Coming Down to Earth. In: J. Gaffney, ed., *The French Presidential and Legislative Elections of 2002*. Farnham: Ashgate. pp. 185–199.

Frémion, Y., 2007. *Histoire de la révolution écologiste*. Paris: Hoëbeke.

George, S., 2010. *Leurs crises, nos solutions*. Paris: Albin Michel.

Le Monde, 5 March 2013.

Le Nouvel Observateur, 14 March 2010.

Lecœur, E., 2011. *Des écologistes en politique*. Paris: Lignes de repères.

Lipietz, A., 1999. *Qu'est-ce que l'écologie politique ? La Grande Transformation du XXIe siècle*. Paris: La Découverte.

Löwy, M., and Harribey, J.-M., eds, 2003. *Capital contre nature*. Paris: PUF.

Mouvements, 2010. Altermondialisme saison 2: De Seattle à Cochabamba. *Mouvements*, 63(Autumn Issue), pp. 1–176.

Perrineau, P., 2010. *Régionales 2010: que sont les électeurs devenus?* (Fondapol note) [online] Paris: Fondapol (Published May 2010). Available at: <http://www.fondapol.org/etude/1799> [Accessed 12 March 2011].

Pingaud, D., 2010. *Europe Écologie: électorat volage, électorat stratège*. Paris: Fondation Jean Jaurès.

Richardson, D., and Rootes, C., eds, 1994. *The Green Challenge: The Development of Green Parties in Europe*. London: Routledge.

Rihoux, B., 2001. *Les partis politiques: organisations en changement: Le test des écologistes*. Paris: L'Harmattan.

Sainteny, G., 2000. *L'introuvable écologisme Français?* Paris: PUF.

Semal, L., and Szuba, M., 2009. Les transition towns: résilience, relocalisation et catastrophisme éclairé. *Entropia*, 7, pp. 178–188.

Serne, P., 2004. *Les Verts ont 20 ans: petite histoire de l'écologie politique en France*. Paris: Les Verts édition.

Vialatte, J., 1996. *Les partis Verts en Europe occidentale*. Paris: Economica.

Villalba, B., 2008. The French Greens: Changes in Activist Culture and Practices in a Constraining Environment. In: G. E. Frankland, P. Lucardie and B. Rihoux, eds, *Green Parties in Transition: The End of Grass-Roots Democracy?* Farnham and Burlington, VT: Ashgate. pp. 109–128.

Villalba, B., 2011. La transmutation d'Europe Écologie-Les Verts. In: P. Bréchon, ed., *Les partis politiques Français. Nouvelle édition.* Paris: La documentation Française. pp. 129–154.

Villalba, B., 2012. Que faire et comment faire (encore) de l'écologie politique? *Mouvements*, 69, pp. 93–100.

Voynet, D., 2003. *Voix off.* Paris: Stock.

5 The Green Party in Germany

Sebastian Bukow

Introduction

The German Green Party (Alliance 90/The Greens) has been the most success-ful novation in the German party system within the last 50 years. In December 2013, they count more than 60,000 party members and 324 Members of Parliament (MPs) at the European, Federal and *Land* levels (12.5 per cent of all German MPs). In January 2014, the Greens are participating in 7 of 16 *Land* governments, leading one of them. The German Greens, once an alternative movement and 'antiparty party', are now an important, completely incorporated part of the German political system and closely linked to civil society. Based on this account, the story of the German Greens seems to be a flawless success story; however, this success is not self-evident. There are specific reasons for this success, and there are ups and downs in the party history. The development of the German Greens – established in the late 1970s as a revolutionary societal movement and nowadays comfortably settled in the heart of society – is the subject of this article.

Origins and development

Due to the German unification process, today's German Green Party has two main roots. The West German party The Greens (*Die Grünen*), which itself is the party-organisational follow-up of the so-called New Social Movements (NSM) and the East German citizens movement, especially the group Alliance 90 (*Bündnis 90*), that emerged in the East German Peaceful Revolution. Up to now, the West German tradition is the more important one within the party organisation.

The West German Greens until 1990

In West Germany, the story begins in the 1970s (Frankland and Schoonmaker, 1992; Müller-Rommel and Poguntke, 1992; Poguntke, 1993; Raschke, 1993; Markovits and Gorski, 1997; Mende, 2011). In the aftermath of the student movement and the already weakening extra parliamentary opposition (*Außerparlamentarische Opposition* – APO), the NSM came into vogue. Several new issues were addressed, and action groups were formed (ecological, antinuclear, peace/nonproliferation, human rights, feminist and one-world movement groups; Probst, 2007, 2012b). Especially the report of the Club of Rome in 1972 was an initial point for eco-activisms. Ecological issues came on the agenda and protest actions against nuclear power plants, nuclear reprocessing and final disposal took place (in the early 1970s especially in southern Germany and in the late 1970s especially in Lower Saxony, for example Gorleben, Brokdorf). These two issues were most important for the emerging Greens. The established parties ignored these new issues.[1] Only very few conservative politicians like MP Herbert Gruhl (Christian Democratic Union – CDU) picked up the ecological question. As a reaction to this nonresponsiveness, the movements started to form their own electoral lists on the local and *Land* levels in the late 1970s. In these early beginnings, there were several conflicts between conservative ecologists (Green lists) and leftist alternative groups (open/alternative lists). One aspect among others in these conflicts was the question of the extent to which former communist groups should be integrated. In addition, not all leftist groups supported the idea of parliamentary representation. Nevertheless, the newly formed groups were electorally successful. First mandates were gained at the local level, especially in Lower Saxony as a core area of antinuclear protests.

At the federal level, the first attempts towards more coordination started a year before the 1979 European Parliament election (Müller-Rommel and Poguntke, 1992). This election was a starting point for the Green and alternative movements on their way towards a more formal organisation. Due to electoral law, a more formal cooperation was necessary. At a movement's convention in Frankfurt (17–18 March 1979), it was decided to form the Alternative Political Alliance The Greens (*Sonstige Politische Vereinigung/Die Grünen* – SPV/Die Grünen). This was a semiformal, but legally sufficient, organisational frame. With this electoral list, the Green movements received 3.2 per cent of the votes (900,000 votes, candidates such as Petra Kelly and Joseph Beuys). They did not pass the threshold, but they were entitled to state party funding and received about DM 4.5 million (€2.3m) in campaign cost reimbursement. This success accelerated the founding of Green-alternative lists at the local level and in party organisations at the *Land* level (for example Baden-Württemberg, 30 September 1979; North Rhine-Westphalia, 16 December 1979). The first Green MPs at the *Land* level were elected in Bremen in 1979 (7 October 1979, 5.1 per cent, 4 MPs). Due to the federal system in Germany, the Greens passed the thresholds of declaration, authorisation and representation (Pedersen, 1982) at the *Land* and European levels – including party funding at the federal level – even before the founding of a formal party organisation at the federal level took place.

In late 1979, another convention of the *SPV/Die Grünen* decided to found a formal party organisation, due to two reasons: a formal party organisation was mandatory to select list candidates for the 1980s federal election, and only reorganisation (contrary to a new party) would allow keeping the state funding.[2] Consequently, the founding of the Green Party can be seen as a state-driven process (Klein and Falter, 2003). Thereupon in January 1980, the first formal steps towards party founding were undertaken at a convention in Karlsruhe. The Greens (*Die Grünen*) were launched as a national party. The name of the party was intended to promote the ecological core issue. In a follow-up convention, the delegates undertook further steps towards a formal organisation, especially by electing party speakers and deciding upon a party basic programme.

Although the Greens were now organised according to German party law and thus were a formal party organisation, they denied being a 'real' party (and their opponents did as well). They claimed to be an 'antiparty party', as Petra Kelly pointed out (Frankland and Schoonmaker, 1992). Nevertheless, the party organisation institutionalised itself. Several branches of the party were founded. Existing Green/alternative lists and *Land* parties were integrated in the federal party organisation. Although the Greens failed to pass the threshold of representation at the federal election 1980 (1.5 per cent, see Table 5.1), and at a few *Land*-level elections, they were successful in several *Land*-level elections such as in Baden-Württemberg, Berlin, Hesse, Hamburg and Lower Saxony. These early electoral successes went hand in hand with the rise of civil-societal protest. Beside the antinuclear issue and in the wake of North Atlantic Treaty Organisation's (NATO) dual-track decision, the peace movement became more important in the early 1980s. The peace movement's protest walks became popular. The protests cumulated in 1983, when the new Christian-Democratic Chancellor Helmut Kohl supported NATO's dual-track decision. The Greens were strongly interlinked to protest groups and the peace movement, and that was most important for the Greens' organisational growth and electoral success. The power of the civil-societal movements brought the early Greens into parliament (Probst, 2012b), and the party organisation originates directly from these social movements and protest groups.

In the 1983 federal election, the Greens passed the threshold of representation at the federal level for the first time (5.6 per cent), only three years after the party's formal declaration and authorisation (Table 5.1). Twenty-seven federal MPs of the Greens (and one of [West-]Berlin Alternative List) started to change the parliamentary system, and the system started to change the Greens as well. The federal party in public office quickly gained in importance due to the possibility of allocating policy experts (Frankland and Schoonmaker, 1992). The party had matured, at least in terms of representation, but was not accepted as coalition partner by the established parties yet (Poguntke, 1993).

In spite of this electoral and organisational growth, intraparty conflicts between leftist and pragmatic groups (*Fundis* vs. *Realos*) continued. Intraparty policy positions ranged from the far left to conservative. In 1982, conservatives around Herbert Gruhl left the party and founded the Ecological Democratic Party (*Ökologisch-Demokratische Partei* – ÖDP), which has remained a small regional party. Finally, the Greens established themselves as a left-wing party, but intraparty conflicts remained. Furthermore, the discussion concerning the party's role within the political system became relevant. It was discussed if the party should participate in power or not. Some Green politicians even claimed complete abolishment of representative parliamentarianism. Relevant intraparty factions

Table 5.1 Electoral results of the Greens, *Bundestag* (federal elections), 1980–2013

	Greens		B90/Greens (East)		B90/Greens	
	% Votes	Seats	% Votes	Seats	% Votes	Seats
1980	1.5	0				
1983	5.6	27 + 1*				
1987	8.3	42				
1990	3.8	0	1.2	8		
1994					7.3	49
1998					6.7	47
2002					8.6	55 (1)**
2005					8.1	51 (1)**
2009					10.7	68 (1)**
2013					8.4	63 (1)**

Notes: Greens: *Die Grünen* (West Germany); B90/Greens: *Bündnis 90/Die Grünen – BürgerInnenbewegung* (East Germany); B90/Greens: *Bündnis 90/Die Grünen* (Germany); 1990: nation-wide calculation; Greens electorate west: 4.8%; B90/Greens electorate east: 6.0%; * 1 MP from the 'Alternative List for Democracy and Environmental Protection' (AL; Berlin); ** 1 MP elected directly in constituency; all others: *Land*-level list candidates.

Source: Federal Returning Officers, <https://www.bundeswahlleiter.de/en/>.

preferred alternative structures, like a strict separation of the party in public office and central office. They emphasised the movement quality of the party and policy seeking as a primary goal.

In the German party system, new coalition formats are tested at the *Land* level first. Accordingly, for the Greens this was the main area for new developments toward governmental maturation (Switek, 2012). If at all in these early years, coalitions with the Social Democrats (SDP) were most likely (Table 5.2). In 1982, the first coalition negotiations were carried on in Hamburg but were abandoned; Hesse was more successful. In the wake of the 1982 elections, Social Democrats tried to stay in government using the Greens' support (without a formal coalition). This strategy failed, and early elections took place in 1983. Still no decisive majority was reached, but after controversial intraparty discussions, the Greens decided to tolerate the SPD government without participating directly. In June 1984, Holger Börner (SPD) was elected prime minister. In December 1985, the SPD and the Greens even agreed on a formal coalition. Joschka Fischer was elected as first Green *Land*-level minister in German history (minister for the environment). The *Ausgrenzung* (keeping them out) of the Greens was suspended (Poguntke, 1993). However, at the federal level, government participation was not at all considered in these years. Intraparty conflicts predominated within the party (Poguntke, 1998; Probst, 2007). Nevertheless, the Greens matured in parliament and were successfully re-elected in 1987 (8.3 per cent, 42 MPs).

Table 5.2 German Greens in Parliament and government, 1978–2013

	1978	1979	1980	1981	1982	1983	1984	1985	1986	1987	1988	1989	1990	1991	1992	1993	1994	1995	1996	1997	1998	1999	2000	2001	2002	2003	2004	2005	2006	2007	2008	2009	2010	2011	2012	2013
European level																																				
Federal level							B 90/Greens																	g											g	
Baden-Württembg.																																				G
Bavaria																																				
Berlin												g												g												
Brandenburg															g*																	g				g
Bremen																g**																g+				
Hamburg																						g														g
Hesse									g																			+++							g	
Lower Saxony																	g																		g	
Mecklbg.-Vorp.																																				
North Rine-Westph.																							g									g				
Rhineland-Palatin.																																			g	
Saarland																																	g++	g		
Saxony																																				
Saxony-Anhalt																																				
Schleswig-Holstein																					g			g												g***
Thuringia																																				

Note: White: Greens did not run for election; Grey: Greens did not pass threshold; Black: Greens in parliament; g: Greens in government (SPD/Greens); *SPD/Greens; *SPD/Bündnis 90/FDP; **SPD/FDP/Greens; ***SPD/Greens/Südschleswigscher Wählerverband (SSW); +CDU/Greens; ++CDU/FDP/Greens; +++CDU/Greens (coalition agreement 12/2013, appointment 01/2014); G: Greens in government (Greens/SPD; Green Prime Minister).

Source: Author's own data, based on data from Federal and Land-level Returning Officers and government/party websites.

The Greens and the German unification process 1989–1990

Due to Greens' tradition of state-criticism and the party's origin in the leftist alternative society the party had trouble handling the 'German Question' 1989–1990. In fact, the Greens did not share the idea of unification and were afraid of a 'new Germany' as a powerful, nation-centred player in Europe. Consequently, within the first all-German electoral campaign 1990, the Greens emphasised their core issues and somehow ignored the dominating unification issue. They claimed, 'Everyone is talking about Germany; we're talking about the weather'. In fact, their 'campaign was strangely out of sync with the concerns and priorities of the German electorate' (Blühdorn, 2009). This strategy of an issue-ownership-based campaign failed. Greens did not pass the 5 per cent threshold and were expelled from parliament (4.8 per cent, electorate west). The party that had benefited so much from other parties' nonresponsiveness now failed due to its own nonresponsiveness. Luckily for them, within the East German Peaceful Revolution, an East German Green Party had formed in the German Democratic Republic (GDR) on 24 November 1989. This East German Green Party was formally founded on 9 February 1990, as a necessity for the upcoming election. Unlike the other established parties, East and West German Greens decided not to merge before the election but on the day after the first all-German election (Poguntke, 1998). This was a political decision to show mutual respect. Afraid of the 5 per cent threshold and due to uncertainty concerning some electoral regulations,[3] the East German Green Party finally decided to join an electoral list with several East German civil rights groups (especially *Neues Forum, Demokratie Jetzt, Initiative Frieden und Menschenrechte*). This electoral list (Alliance 90/The Greens – Civil Movement) passed the threshold for the East German electorate (6.0 per cent, electorate east). With eight MPs, two of them members of the East German Green Party, they remained a small parliamentary group. Nevertheless, this success was most important for the West German Greens. Only due to this was the newly merged all-German Green Party present in parliament during that legislature with at least two 'Green' MPs.

The Greens after 1990

External shocks are most important for party change (Harmel and Janda, 1994). Accordingly, the Greens reorganised themselves after the unexpected electoral defeat of 1990. All West German Greens' MPs were voted out of office and the parliamentary apparatus was lost. It was uncertain if the Greens would survive at all (Raschke, 1993), but finally a new phase of party development took place. The electoral setback was discussed at a party convention in 1991, and especially the leftist *Fundis* were blamed for the electoral defeat. The *Realos* dominated the convention. Finally, the Greens claimed to be no longer an antisystem or antiparty party. They admitted to parliamentary democracy and decided to professionalise their party structure. Within the next few years, several leading leftist politicians resigned.

In addition to this, the Greens realised that being an all-German party would be pivotal for survival. An exclusively West German party would have problems in passing the federal threshold. Participating in power, more and more an accepted (but still controversial) goal of the party would be inaccessible. Even though West- and East-German Greens had merged their parties on 3 December 1990, this was not sufficient. The East German Greens were only a small party in the eastern electorate. Quite similar was the political assessment of the situation in East Germany. The civil rights movements suffered from the success of the traditional West German parties and were afraid of a further decrease of influence (Poguntke, 1996). Due to that, the Greens and the East German Alliance 90[4] decided to merge in 1993, after lengthy negotiations (Probst, 2007). The party Alliance 90/The Greens was established, but it quickly turned out to be an unequal merger. The political cultures of both organisations were fundamentally different. The East German branches dissolved quickly. Several former members of Alliance 90 left the party (for example Matthias Platzeck, later chair of the Social Democrats Germany and prime minister of Brandenburg). The Greens' attempt to become an electorally and organisationally successful all-German party failed. In the mid-1990s, the Greens were no longer present in several East German parliaments. The East German branches were in a 'precariously weak organisational state' (Poguntke, 1998).

During this period, Joschka Fischer gained in importance. He functioned as informal party leader until 2005, although he never held a relevant intraparty office. As informal leader of the *Realos*, he pushed the Greens towards 'normalisation'. The Greens managed their comeback in the federal election of 1994 (7.3 per cent, 49 MPs). Back in parliament, they took their leave of being a one-issue party. Economics, social policy and other issues were addressed (Probst, 2013b). The Greens prepared themselves for federal government by modernising their policies and organisational structures (Poguntke, 1999; Bukow and Rammelt, 2003). The Greens transformed into an increasingly successful office-seeking organisation as well (Poguntke, 2003; Probst, 2011, 2013a).

In 1998, this goal was reached at the federal level, even though they performed badly in the election (6.7 per cent, 47 MPs). An SPD/Greens coalition was installed and even labelled as the 'red-green project' (Egle, et al., 2003). Joschka Fischer was appointed minister of foreign affairs and vice-chancellor (1998–2005). Further ministers were Jürgen Trittin (environment, 1998–2005; frontrunner for the federal election of 2013) and Andrea Fischer (health; renounced in 2001; followed by Renate Künast, consumer protection and agriculture, 2001–2005). After 15 years in parliament, the Greens passed the last threshold in a parties' life (Pedersen, 1982), the threshold of relevance in terms of 'participating in power' (Tables 5.2 and 5.3). Therefore, they can be classified as the 'professional type' of Green parties (Müller-Rommel, 2002) and as an established part of the German political system (Probst, 2013b).

Although the Greens were in government, they had limited powers. The 'red-green project' stood on shaky programmatic ground (Blühdorn, 2009), and the

Table 5.3 Policy areas of German Green ministers

	1985	1986	1987	1988	1989	1990	1991	1992	1993	1994	1995	1996	1997	1998	1999	2000	2001	2002	2003	2004	2005	2006	2007	2008	2009	2010	2011	2012
Foreign Affairs														X	X	X	X	X	X	X	X							
Environment														X	X	X	X	X	X	X	X							
Health														X	X	X	X											
Agriculture																X	X	X	X	X	X							
Prime Minister																											X	X
Environment	X	X	X X		X	X X	X X X	X X X	X X X	X X X X	X X X X X	X X X X	X X X X X	X X X X X	X X X	X X X X	X X X	X X	X	X	X		X	X X	X X X	X X X X	X X X X X X	X X X X X X X
Education					X	X X	X	X	X	X														X	X X	X X X	X X	X X X
Justice											X	X	X	X	X	X	X X	X X	X	X	X			X	X	X		
Social & Labour Affairs																	X	X									X X	X X

(Continued)

Table 5.3 (Continued)

	1985	1986	1987	1988	1989	1990	1991	1992	1993	1994	1995	1996	1997	1998	1999	2000	2001	2002	2003	2004	2005	2006	2007	2008	2009	2010	2011	2012
Agriculture																											X	X
Finance													X										X	X	X	X	X X	X X
Science & Research								X	X	X			X	X	X	X	X X	X									X	X
Health							X	X	X	X	X															X	X	X X
Other					X	X X X	X X	X X X	X X	X X X	X X	X X	X X X	X X X	X X	X X X	X X	X									X X	X X

Note: X stands for one minister in a cabinet; each cabinet is listed separately (even if a person remains in office).

Source: Author's own data based on data from government/party websites.

Greens were shocked by governmental praxis and demands (Raschke, 2001). Hardly in office, they had to decide about joining NATO's military action in Kosovo. This decision almost split the party in 1999. Formerly important linkages to the (meanwhile less powerful) peace movement were lost. One of the Green's core principles – nonviolence – had to be redefined. Finally, the party followed Foreign Minister Fischer and accepted the new policy of military intervention abroad.[5] Government participation went hand in hand with decisions that were more troublesome. The party had to accept compromises, necessary for remaining in government (Poguntke, 2003). The most important decision was to shut down nuclear power plants. Therewith, the Greens achieved a primary goal, but the nuclear shutdown turned out to be a mid-range process. Several antinuclear activists were disappointed, and several members left the party. From 1999 on, the Greens had to experience a long string of electoral losses at the *Land* and local levels. Being in government did not bring an electoral payback. Nevertheless, due to a unique situation during the campaign, particularly the possible Iraq War and the flood of the river Elbe in East Germany (Blühdorn, 2009), in 2002, the Greens managed a turnaround. The Greens achieved an unexpected result in the federal election (8.6 per cent, 55 MPs), and the 'red-green project' was prolonged (Fuchs and Rohrschneider, 2005).

The Greens were more successful in the next legislature. There are internal and external reasons for this success. Most important within the party was the ability to organise comprehensive cooperation instead of intraparty rivalry and distrust. Even though the party leaders in central and public office and the Green ministers were politically heterogeneous, they managed to cooperate. This well-balanced diversion of power was decisive. The Greens showed coherent policy management in public, not quarrelling chaos like before (Probst, 2011). An important external reason was (unintentionally) Chancellor Schröder's policy. His labour market reform (Agenda 2010) weakened the SPD (Jun, 2010) and worked to the Greens' advantage. However, the Social Democrats' low electoral performance weakened red-green coalitions at the *Land* level. In 2005, the last red-green government at the *Land* level was dropped (North Rhine-Westphalia). Thereupon Chancellor Schröder surprised the public (and the Greens) by declaring an inability of further governing. Early federal elections took place in 2005, and the Greens lost. They were expelled from government (even though their electoral result was quite stable: 8.1 per cent, 51 MPs) and came out as the smallest party group in parliament (as in 2009 and 2013). It was argued that their *raison d'être* had disappeared, that they were no longer needed and that they had passed a 'threshold of irrelevance' (Blühdorn, 2009). Joschka Fischer, the most important and most popular Green politician so far, retired. All in all, the 2005 election was an inflection comparable to 1990. Intraparty equilibrium, painfully arranged and quite stable in the years 2002–2005, disrupted. Intraparty conflicts flamed up. Interestingly, these conflicts were no longer conflicts between the left and right wings of the party but conflicts between the party elite and the party on the ground (Probst, 2011).

Dealing with the war in Afghanistan in 2007, the party elite turned out to be unable to manage strategy and conflict (Probst, 2011). An exceptional party convention almost collapsed. This convention was an intraparty shock, and this shock enabled the Greens to organise a turnaround. Party elites realised the necessity of a new party management and arranged compromises. Party organisational reforms toward professionalisation and centralisation came into effect (Bukow, 2013). The party focussed on its (redefined) core identity (Blühdorn, 2009). Furthermore, the federal Grand Coalition strengthened the smaller parties (Bukow and Seemann, 2010; Hunsicker and Schroth, 2010). Thereby, the Greens managed a fast comeback. Since 2008, the party has grown electorally and organisationally (voters and members). Consequently, in 2009 the Greens had the best result in federal elections so far (10.7 per cent, 68 MPs). Nevertheless, they were disappointed: they were still the smallest parliamentary group. Politically and electorally possible coalitions were not available at the federal level. However, the Greens were successful in *Land*-level elections, and at the end of 2009, Greens were participating in several *Land* governments again, partially experimenting with new coalitions (for example in Hamburg from 2008–2010: CDU/Greens; in Saarland from 2009–2011: CDU/FDP/Greens; Switek, 2010).

The Greens had high-level results and several peaks in election polls. It was discussed if the Greens would become a new catch-all party (Probst, 2011). The year 2011 can be classified as the most successful year in the Greens' history so far: for the first time, the Greens were leading a *Land* government (Baden-Württemberg, Minister-President Winfried Kretschmann – Keil and Gabriel, 2012; Probst, 2012a) and were represented in all parliaments at the *Land*, federal and European levels at the same time. The Greens had managed to become a nation-wide party. The number of Green politicians in government increased, but this success was adulterated. In summer 2013, a few weeks before the federal election, opinion polls reckoned with a 15 per cent share of the vote. However, the numbers then collapsed, and finally the Greens received 8.4 per cent (63 MPs), much lower than expected. Internal and external reasons were accountable for this last-minute loss. The party elites did not act in a coherent way. This became visible in their inability of deciding on the frontrunners, a problem that was solved surprisingly well by conducting intraparty primaries. Blinded by poll numbers, they made strategic mistakes. The Greens ignored the structure of the German oligopolistic party competition and vote-maximising strategies (Franzmann, 2014). They tried to occupy issues of social justice and financial policy, issues owned by Greens' designated coalition partner SPD. This strategy failed. Another problem was a partly grubby debate on the Greens' policy position concerning paedophilia in the early 1980s. This debate, fuelled by media, academics and political opponents, culminated only days before the election took place. It caught the Greens at an unpropitious moment and boosted their electoral loss. Another problem was their ambiguity towards coalitions – they ran half-heartedly for a red-green coalition, but a majority for that coalition was increasingly unlikely (Jesse, 2013). Once again, they had no clear track to government, and consequently, they had difficulties in mobilising voters. Overall, the Greens were shocked by their electoral result. Intraparty conflicts between the factions flared up, and the Greens started a moderate process of leadership renewal in central and public office. Furthermore,

Table 5.4 Chronology of the main developments of the Greens in Germany

Date	Development
1977	Green/open lists are initiated for local- and Land-level elections; isolated electoral success on the local level.
November 1977	The ecological party *Umweltschutzpartei Niedersachsen* (USP) (Environmental Protection Party of Lower Saxony, founded in may 1977) declares to be the first *Land* branch of a later federal Green Party (*Grüne Liste Umweltschutz* – GLU). The GLU is an ecological-conservative party.
1978	Herbert Gruhl (CDU, MP) leaves CDU and starts *Grüne Aktion Zukunft* (Green Action Future – GAZ), keeping his mandate. GAZ and the Green lists were up for elections in Hesse, Bavaria, Lower Saxony and Hamburg.
16–17 March 1979	Founding convention of the *SPV/Die Grüne*, a new electoral list for the European Parliament elections.
June 1979	The SPV achieves 3.2% at the European elections. No mandates but public party funding.
3–4 November 1979	Convention of the SPV. Decisions concerning formal party founding procedure and party name ('The Greens').
1979	First electoral success of the Greens at *Land*-level elections: 4 MPs (Bremer Green List).
12–13 January 1980	First regular party convention of The Greens (Karlsruhe; 1,004 delegates). Formal decision about party founding: 875 yes, 53 no, 12 abstentions.
21–23 March 1980	Second party convention; election of party speakers and decision on basic programme.
5 October 1980	Federal election: 1.5% (0 MPs).
6 March 1983	Federal election: 5.6% (27 MPs and 1 MP of the Alternative List Berlin).
1985	First SPD/Greens coalition on the Land level (Hesse); first Green Land-level minister (Joschka Fischer).
25 January 1987	Federal election: 8.3% (42 MPs).
2 December 1990	Federal election (separated thresholds for electorate west/east): West German Greens 4.8% (electorate west; 0 MPs); East German Alliance 90/Greens 6.0% (electorate east; 8 MPs).
3 December 1990	Merger of West and East German Greens.
1993	Merger of Greens and Alliance 90 (Alliance 90/The Greens); basic programme update.
1994	First CDU/Greens coalition on the local level (Mülheim/Ruhr).
16 October 1994	Federal election: 7.3% (49 MPs).
1996	First Green lord mayor of a major city (Horst Frank, Konstanz).
27 September 1998	Federal election: 6.7% (47 MPs).

(Continued)

Table 5.4 (Continued)

Date	Development
27 October 1998	First SPD/Greens coalition on federal level; Green Vice-Chancellor (Joschka Fischer).
1999	Greens decide to support NATO's military action in Kosovo.
1999	First CDU/Greens/FDP coalition on the local level (Bad Dürkheim, Rhineland-Palatinate).
2001	'Green Youth' becomes the official youth organisation of the party, now formally integrated in party structures (founded 1994 as 'Green-Alternative Youth Association').
2002	New basic programme.
22 September 2002	Federal election: 8.6% (55 MPs; one of them elected directly in constituency).
21 April 2004	Founding of the European Green Party (EGP).
28 August 2004	Founding of the intraparty group 'Elderly Greens'.
18 September 2005	Federal election: 8.1% (51 MPs; one of them elected directly in constituency).
21 November 2005	Angela Merkel (CDU) elected chancellor; SPD/Green coalition ends.
2008	First CDU/Greens coalition on the Land level (Hamburg).
27 September 2005	Federal election: 10.7% (68 MPs; one of them elected directly in constituency)
2011	First Greens/SPD coalition on the *Land* level (Baden-Württemberg); Green Minster-President (Winfried Kretschmann)
2011	Greens represented in all *Land*, federal and European parliaments at the same time.
10 November 2012	Reinhard Bütikofer (chair of German Greens 2002–2008) elected as EGP chair (with Monica Frassoni).
22 September 2013	Federal election: 8.4% (63 MPs; one of them elected directly in constituency).

Notes: Bold: Federal Greens pass life-cycle thresholds (Pedersen, 1982; Müller-Rommel, 2002; Blühdorn, 2009): declaration (1980), authorisation (1980), representation (1983), relevance (participation in government; 1998); irrelevance (2005).

Source: Author's own compilation.

the executive committee decided to appoint a working group in order to present ideas for the party's organisational renewal, preparing party structures for the electoral campaign 2017 (Alliance 90/The Greens, 2014). Independently, the Greens succeeded in *Land*-level elections 2013. After the 2013 Hesse election, the Greens and the CDU agreed on a coalition. This is the first CDU/Greens coalition in a nonurban *Land* and another important step towards new coalition options for Greens in Germany.

Ideology and policy positions: Programmatic developments

The Greens never were a real single-issue party; in fact, they quickly broadened their programme representing issues subsumed as 'new politics' (Müller-Rommel and Poguntke, 1992). One slogan was 'neither left nor right but out in front' (Mende, 2011; Markovits and Klaver, 2013), but in fact, the Greens connected environmental policy and nature conservancy to leftist positions. Nevertheless, the Greens remained heterogeneous. Intraparty conflicts were common and often accompanied by power shifts between *Fundis* and *Realos*. Several aspects were discussed intensively, for example parties' positions concerning representative democracy, the state's monopoly of power, foreign policy (Probst, 2013a) or government participation (subsequently, new coalitions) and foreign military assignments (especially Kosovo, 1999).

The Greens decided upon basic programmes only twice (1980, 2002). In 1980, they defined four points of reference: environmental, social, grassroots democratic, nonviolent. However, the Greens never formed a stable ideological framework or a 'Green' ideology (Bukow, 2008). In the new basic programme, they even emphasised:

> We are united by a set of basic principles, not an ideology. . . . Our basic position reads: We combine ecology, self-determination, expanded equitability and a vibrant democracy. With the same intensity, we are committed to nonviolence and human rights.

Further basic principles were no longer mentioned explicitly (for example grassroots democracy) or fundamentally redefined (for example nonviolence). In this new programme, the Greens especially addressed the sustainable renewal of industrial society (based on regulatory policies and market instruments) and the principle of equitability (inventing an extended concept of equitability, especially generation equitability). Notably, it was formally adopted more than 20 years after the first basic programme. It clearly is a reaction to electoral defeats (1999 et seq.), depletion by government and fundamental changes of parties' environment: the agenda of 'new politics' that had once been their original project has meanwhile become largely exhausted, and the profound transformation of societal structures, value preferences and party political competition necessitates a comprehensive reinvention of the Green politics' (Blühdorn, 2009). Within this context, the basic programme was at least an 'attempt to update the party's original foundation programme of 1980'. However, as Blühdorn criticises,

> [I]t was more suited to coming to terms – from the perspective of government incumbency – with the party's heritage of the social movement culture, grassroots democracy, the stance of the 'antiparty party' and radical opposition to the system of consumer capitalism than to formulating a programmatically concise and electorally appealing outlook for the future.
>
> (Blühdorn, 2009)

Election manifestos are perhaps more important than basic programmes and are used by parties to express their policy preferences. For each election, the central office prepares a draft manifesto (in cooperation with the party in public office). This draft is circulated among the party, and finally a party congress passes the manifesto. Draft manifestos are intensively discussed within the party, for example in 2013 about 2,500 change applications were filed (especially by party members and Standing Groups; Ernst and Westermayer, 2013). Meanwhile, the central office manages these applications in an experienced way and processes them quickly at the convention.

The Comparative Manifestos Project (CMP) data (Budge, et al., 2001; Volkens, et al., 2013) confirm that the Greens have started as a leftist party and are now centre-left (RiLe, Table 5.2), even though they moved slightly left again in 2013 (like all German parties). A more detailed picture is drawn in Figure 5.1, differentiating economic and noneconomic dimensions (Spies and Franzmann, 2011), whereby the poles of the latter dimension can be described in the composite terms 'Green/alternative/libertarian' and 'traditionalism/authority/nationalism' as well (Gal vs. Tan; Marks, et al., 2006). The Greens remain a left-wing party in both dimensions, but on some issues, the Greens are much more centre-positioned than the graph shows. It is argued that the Greens' continued left position 'may be especially due to the fact that environmental protection . . . as a left position issue has been a major component of its election programs' (Franzmann and Kaiser, 2006).

The Greens changed their position fundamentally on several aspects. They are no longer antimilitaristic or harsh critics of representative democracy; they are clearly pro-European and argue for a moderate renewal of European Union, including aspects of direct democracy; they combine the idea of a powerful state (to enforce 'Green' ideas) with arguments for a lean state in other dimensions. These changes are related to changes of saliency as well (Table 5.5). At first glance, environmentalism seems to become less important. In fact, in the mid-2000s, the Greens re-emphasised 'environmentalism' as their core policy, but they redefined it and interlinked it with economy, finance policy and social justice, developing the idea of a 'Green New Deal': 'Whilst the German Greens had once been the proto-typical ecology party, radically critical of the capitalist consumer economy, they were now talking of new economy growth' (Blühdorn, 2010). This is a core element of the Greens' concept of a new sustainable economy and a new social contract. The Greens, in their early years arguing for economic contraction and sceptical towards technology, have changed their position fundamentally, but this new concept is now compatible with the centre-left part of society (for the Greens' voters: Rüdig, 2012).

> [The] New Deal is geared to a middle-class clientele who are fully aware of the unsustainability of present arrangements but at the same time regard their established lifestyles and patterns of self-realisation as largely nonnegotiable. It acknowledges the necessity of a radical change but is designed to stabilise and perpetuate the established structures.
>
> (Blühdorn, 2010)

With these changes, the Greens are – overall – electorally quite successful.

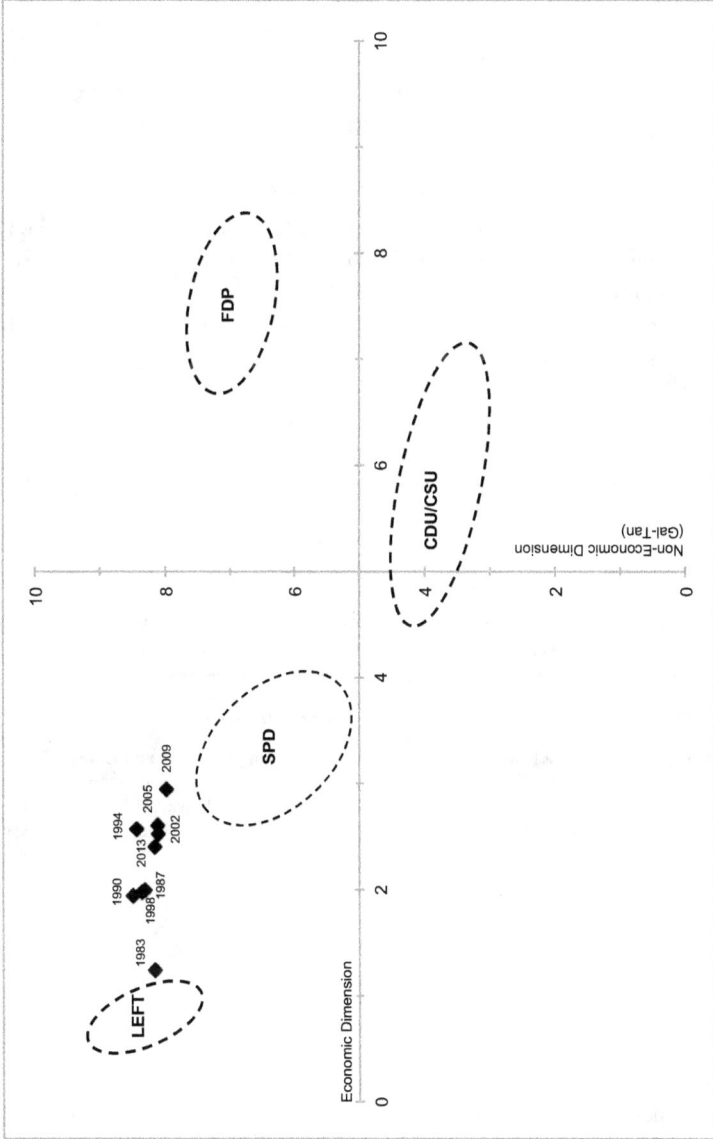

Figure 5.1 The Greens in the German political space

Note: Years indicate the policy position of the Greens (federal manifesto); dashed ellipses indicate the typical positioning of the other relevant parties (1983/1990–2013). Economic Dimension: All categories related to economic policy, economic ideas, redistribution and economic groups (0: market regulation to 10: market freedom); Noneconomic Dimension (Gal-Tan): All remaining, noneconomic categories (0: traditionalism/authority/nationalism to 10: Green/alternative/libertarian).

Source: Spies and Franzmann (2011), Franzmann and Kaiser (2006), Marks, et al. (2006).

Table 5.5 Position (left–right) and saliency of the Greens – Germany, 1983–2013

	1983	1987	1990	1994	1998	2002	2005	2009	2013
L-R (Laver/Budge)	3.8	3.9	4.2	4.0	4.0	3.8	4.4	4.3	4.0
L-R (Franzmann/Kaiser)	1.7	1.7	1.6	1.8	1.7	2.1	2.2	2.3	2.2
Economic dimension	1.2	2.0	1.9	2.6	2.0	2.5	2.6	2.9	2.4
Noneconomic Dimension	1.8	1.7	1.5	1.6	1.6	1.9	1.9	2.0	1.8
Green voters (L-R)	4.6	3.5	2.2	2.4	4.7	4.6	4.6	4.9	3.5
Environmental protection	15.9	16.1	17.4	18.9	14.0	14.0	9.1	10.7	10.5
Market regulation	0.6	0.2	4.2	3.5	0.0	3.5	5.2	6.7	6.2
Free enterprise	0.0	0.2	0.7	0.0	0.0	0.6	0.6	0.2	0.6
Social justice	6.7	5.9	2.1	6.7	5.0	4.2	10.5	12.1	11.3
Welfare state expansion	1.8	8.1	4.2	6.4	5.5	7.1	6.2	3.1	6.5
Welfare state limitation	0.6	0.0	0.0	0.0	0.0	0.0	0.1	0.1	0.1
Education expansion	0.0	0.0	0.7	2.3	5.5	4.6	3.3	4.0	3.3
Education limitation	0.0	0.0	0.0	0.0	0.0	0.0	0.0	0.0	0.0
Military: positive	0.0	0.0	0.0	0.0	0.0	0.4	0.1	0.1	0.2
Military: negative	12.2	5.3	11.8	3.8	8.0	1.6	1.6	1.3	1.1
Law and order	0.0	1.0	0.0	2.1	0.5	1.5	1.7	1.0	0.9
Freedom and human rights	4.9	4.7	8.3	3.7	1.0	4.2	6.4	7.2	5.1
Democracy	4.9	4.3	4.2	4.1	1.5	3.9	3.0	4.3	6.9
Multiculturalism: positive	0.0	0.0	0.7	1.0	0.0	0.6	1.8	1.0	0.8
Multiculturalism: negative	0.0	0.0	0.0	0.0	0.0	0.0	0.0	0.0	0.0
European Union: positive	0.0	0.0	0.7	1.0	8.5	5.9	4.0	2.6	2.7
European Union: negative	0.0	0.0	0.0	0.0	0.0	0.0	0.4	0.2	0.1

Note:
Parties: 1983, 1987: The Greens; 1990: Greens/B90; 1994–2009: B90/Greens

Source: Policy-positions: L-R (0: left to 10: right) calculated according to Laver and Budge (1992) (transformation: (L-R + 100) / 20) and Franzmann and Kaiser (2006); Economic/Noneconomic Dimension cp. Graph 1; GreenVoters: 1982; 1982–2009: Politbarometer (ZA2391; weight by Repräsentativgewicht); 2013: GLES Pre-Election Study 2013 (ZA5700; cp. GESIS Data Catalogue, www.gesis.org).

Saliency: MRG/CMP/MARPOR (Volkens, et al., 2013).

Structure and organisation

Main party structures

German parties operate in a legalistic culture (Poguntke, 1994). Several sources of law constrain parties' organisational freedom (especially the Basic Law, party law and electoral laws). These laws are very restrictive in terms of candidate selection procedures but much less authoritative in terms of party structures (Bukow, 2013).

In their early years, the Greens made use of this freedom extensively. Starting as a grassroots organisation, 'normal' party structures were a worst-case scenario, and grassroots democracy dominated. Afraid of Michels's 'iron law of oligarchy' (Michels, 1989), the Greens promoted a model of permanent bottom-up control of all office holders and all institutions, limited power of leaders, a stance against hierarchy, nonprofessionalisation, transparency and openness for nonmembers (1980 party program, early party statutes and decisions of the Sindelfinger Convention 1983). To ensure this, the Greens implemented several formal instruments (Müller-Rommel and Poguntke, 1992; Probst, 2012b).[6] However, all efforts to prevent the Greens from becoming a normal party failed. Accelerated by electoral success, the party in public office gained in importance and politics as a vocation became common. Nevertheless, until the 1990s, party activists often preferred the idea of an 'antiparty party' in political and organisational terms (Raschke, 1993).

Because of intraparty conflicts and maturation, the Greens undertook several organisational reforms. Some aspects were changed quite quickly (for example the rotation principle, repealed in 1991), others not that easily (for example incompatibility of central and public office). These reforms cannot be analysed in depth here, but it is evident that contemporary Greens reflect only a few aspects of early party life (Probst, 2012b). In fact, the organisational convergence with other parties was bidirectional: the Greens reorganised their formal structure towards normalisation, and the other parties adopted some of Greens organisational ideas (for example quota for women). Overall, the Greens started their organisational life as a movement, founded a new type of party (Poguntke, 1987) and ended up as a normal party organisation (Bukow, 2013; Bukow and Poguntke, 2013). Nowadays, their intraparty structure is based on representative democracy mainly (Bukow, 2013; Switek, 2015). Grassroots elements are fixed in their statutes but not used very often (Bukow and Poguntke, 2013; Detterbeck, 2013).

The formal organisation of the Greens is described best by the 'three faces' concept (Katz and Mair, 1993); however, like all German parties, the Greens do not only have three faces at the federal level but also in all 16 *Land* branches (Figure 5.2). The budget of the federal party was €8 million in 2012 (Greens' total budget in 2012, €39 million; Deutscher Bundestag, 2014).

The party on the ground counts more than 60,000 members (local organisation: *Kreis-/Ortsverband*). For the last few years, the Greens have been the only growing established party, even though there have been large fluctuations (Table 5.6).

The party members derive from the (new) middle class and are, compared to the other German parties, more highly educated and younger, but members' average age rises as well. In 1998, 81 per cent of Greens' members were younger than 50 years old; in 2009, only 48 per cent. The 50–64 age group is the largest within the party now. Although Greens promote gender equality, 62 per cent of their members are male – which is a good ratio compared to other German parties (all parties: 73 per cent male; society: 46 per cent; Klein, 2011).

The most important party body at the federal level is the party congress (*Bundesversammlung,* called *Bundesdelegiertenkonferenz*), a congress of local-level delegates.[7] The number of delegates depends on the number of local members (approximately 820 delegates, including 110 East German delegates). The congress meets a least once a year and is the highest body of the party. It decides on

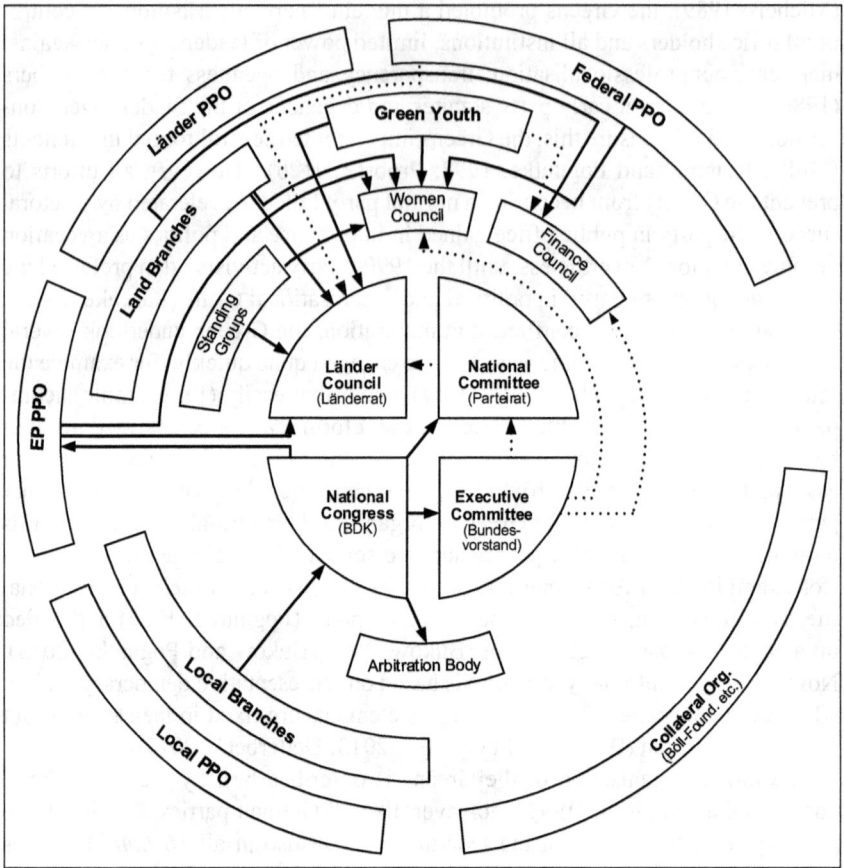

Figure 5.2 The Green Party organisation in Germany (simplified)

Notes: Solid line: delegation/election (partially bound to specific bodies/offices); Dotted line: ex officio membership (partially only specific body members).

Source: Author's own graph.

party programmes and elects the party leaders. For a long time, the congress was a bottom-up, hardly steerable meeting, but this has changed. In 1991, the Greens established the *Länder* council (*Länderrat*) as a small party congress, interlinking *Land*-level delegates and party council members. Meanwhile modified, the *Länder* council had to coordinate the federal and *Land* levels as well as the several party faces. It is the highest body of the party between the regular party congresses. A typical body of Green parties is the women's council (*Frauenrat*). This council decides on women's policies and coordinates these policies within the party. Additionally, there are further bodies (especially the arbitrating body, the finance council) and several groups and collateral/sub-organisations (for example

Table 5.6 Party members, the Greens in Germany (1980–2012)

Year	Members (M)	Ratio M/E (%)
1980	18,320	0.04
1981	15,352	0.04
1982	25,000	0.06
1983	25,222	0.06
1984	31,078	0.07
1985	37,024	0.08
1986	38,170	0.08
1987	42,419	0.09
1988	41,070	0.09
1989	37,956	0.08
1990	41,316	0.07
1991	38,873	0.06
1992	36,320	0.06
1993	39,761	0.07
1994	43,899	0.07
1995	46,410	0.08
1996	48,034	0.08
1997	48,980	0.08
1998	51,812	0.09
1999	49,488	0.08
2000	46,631	0.08
2001	44,053	0.07
2002	43,881	0.07
2003	44,052	0.07
2004	44,322	0.07
2005	45,105	0.07
2006	44,677	0.07
2007	44,320	0.07
2008	45,089	0.07
2009	48,171	0.08
2010	52,991	0.09
2011	59,074	0.09
2012	59,653	0.10

Note: Greens (including Alternative List Berlin); all figures are from the end of the year (exceptions: 1980 (June), 1981 (May); 1982: estimate; 1983: without AL Berlin).

Source: 1980–1989: Boll and Poguntke (1992); 1990–2012: Niedermayer (2013).

Green Youth, Elderly Greens, Federal Standing Groups on Policies [*Bundesarbeitsgemeinschaften*], Green Immigrants, Green Entrepreneurs, Green Unionists, Green Municipal Politicians), that function as linkages to several societal groups (Poguntke, 1994, 2000). In addition, like all established German parties, the Greens have a publically funded political foundation (€48 million; Heinrich-Böll-Stiftung, 2013).

The party central office consists of two parts. First, there is the federal office (*Bundesgeschäftsstelle*). This is small in total numbers (ca. 50 employees in 2012) but, proportionally to members, larger than in other parties (Bukow, 2013). In the beginning, it was a weak institution, short on money and merely tolerated as the head of a decentralised party. This has partly changed within the last years. Professionalisation took place, and the Greens' centralised their party management, for example by inventing trainee-programs, a database of all members and an intranet for (top-down) communication, direct mailings and so on (Bukow and Rammelt, 2003; Bukow, 2013). Nowadays, the *Bundesgeschäftsstelle* is a campaign- and service-oriented apparatus that tries to steer and develop the organisation.

The second part of the party central office is the national executive committee (*Bundesvorstand*). It was once a large body that was based on collective and unsalaried leadership, but it is now much smaller and professionalised. There are two chairpersons (at least one woman), a political general-secretary, a treasurer and two further members. All hold salaried positions. They are elected every second year by the party congress and run the party's day-to-day business (Table 5.7). The former limitation of legislatures was skipped in 1991; in 2003, the incompatibility of central and public office was resolved by members' ballot (after several attempts). Once a short-time job with a high drop-out quota, the Greens' 'speakers' are now 'chairpersons' and normally serve for longer than one legislature in office. Nevertheless, due to the double-double leadership (two party leaders and two leaders of the parliamentary group), personalised leadership within the Greens is still not that easy.

As a reaction to the lack of coordination during government, Greens invented an additional national committee (*Parteirat*) in the late 1990s. It was reformed meanwhile as well. The *Parteirat* is constituted of up to 16 members, including ex-officio the two party chairpersons and the political general-secretary. For this body, no rules of incompatibility are given – it is explicitly demanded that there are high-rank politicians of all party levels in the body. The *Parteirat* serves as a consulting body for the party executive committee and has to coordinate multi-level and multi-faces politics.

The party in public office must not be fully integrated in the formal party structure (permitted by law), but there are several linkages. Candidate selection is predominantly a member-exclusive decision that takes place at the federal (European MPs, selectorate: party congress) or *Land* level (federal MPs, selectorate: delegates or members).[8] Furthermore, MPs and party professionals are involved in several intraparty groups, are often delegates and so on. Due to this and due to its comprehensive resources (68 MPs, approximately 550 employees of the parliamentary fraction and MPs in 2010), the party in public office is the dominant face of the party organisation.

Table 5.7 Party leaders (The Greens; since 1993: Alliance 90/The Greens)

Date	Party leaders
March 1979	Herbert Gruhl (elected); August Haußleiter (elected); Helmut Neddermeyer (elected) (SPV/The Greens)
January 1980	Herbert Gruhl (re-elected); August Haußleiter (re-elected); Helmut Neddermeyer (re-elected)
March 1980	August Haußleiter (re-elected); Petra Kelly (elected); Norbert Mann (elected)
June 1980	After Haußleiter's resignation: election of Dieter Burgmann
October 1981	Dieter Burgmann (re-elected); Petra Kelly (re-elected); Manon Maren-Grisebach (elected)
November 1982	Manon Maren-Grisebach (re-elected); Wilhelm Knabe (elected); Rainer Trampert (elected)
November 1983	Wilhelm Knabe (re-elected); Rainer Trampert (re-elected); Rebekka Schmidt (elected)
December 1984	Rainer Trampert (re-elected); Lukas Beckmann (elected); Jutta Ditfurth (elected)
December 1985	Lukas Beckmann (re-elected); Jutta Ditfurth (re-elected); Rainer Trampert (re-elected)
May 1987	Jutta Ditfurth (re-elected); Regine Michalik (elected); Christian Schmidt (elected)
March 1988	Jutta Ditfurth (re-elected); Regine Michalik (re-elected); Christian Schmidt (re-elected)
December 1988	Resignation of executive committee; *Bundeshauptausschuss* as interim committee
March 1989	Ralf Fücks (elected); Ruth Hammerbacher (elected); Verena Krieger (elected)
June 1990	Renate Damus (elected); Heide Rühle (elected); Hans-Christian Ströbele (elected)
April 1991	Christine Weiske (elected); Ludger Volmer (elected)
May 1993	Marianne Birthler (elected); Ludger Volmer (re-elected)
December 1994	Krista Sager (elected); Jürgen Trittin (elected)
March 1996	Krista Sager (re-elected); Jürgen Trittin (re-elected)
November 1996	Gunda Röstel (elected); Jürgen Trittin (re-elected)
December 1998	Gunda Röstel (re-elected); Antje Radcke (elected)
June 2000	Renate Künast (elected); Fritz Kuhn (elected)
March 2001	Claudia Roth (elected); Fritz Kuhn (re-elected)
December 2002	Angelika Beer (elected); Reinhard Bütikofer (elected)
October 2004	Claudia Roth (elected); Reinhard Bütikofer (re-elected)
December 2006	Claudia Roth (re-elected); Reinhard Bütikofer (re-elected)
November 2008	Claudia Roth (re-elected); Cem Özdemir (elected)
November 2010	Claudia Roth (re-elected); Cem Özdemir (re-elected)
November 2012	Claudia Roth (re-elected); Cem Özdemir (re-elected)
October 2013	Simone Peter (elected); Cem Özdemir (re-elected)

Source: Author's own data partially based on data from Probst (2013).

Relation to society and social movements

In the first years, the Greens' rise was strongly connected to the New Social Movements. Activists were party members as well; their work overlapped in several ways. This was never an exclusive relationship: NSM were connected to other parties as well (Müller-Rommel and Poguntke, 1992). With the Greens' electoral success, the party in public office gained in importance, and party organisation and movement groups diverged, as societal movements and parliamentary parties complied with different logics. The idea of a 'movement party' became more and more a myth. Social movements changed as well. Some issues and groups shrunk in importance while other groups became institutionalised. Overall, the development of the German Greens is a typical case that shows how former civil societal actors are incorporated in the political system and how linkages between party and society change (Probst, 2012b). Nevertheless, up to now, Greens are still (or again) linked to the former NSM. Their relationship has normalised: the movements are no longer the Greens' most important organisational basis, but the Greens are still the most important party for those groups, and Green politicians regularly participate in protest activities.

In fact, the Greens are no longer a 'movement party'; they are much more like a 'professionalised member-party' (Bukow, 2013). Greens are an important, incorporated part of the German political system and closely linked to the several societal groups in different ways, even though they never had formal linkages to extraparty organisations (Poguntke, 2000). The collateral organisations play a vital part, but there are several personal linkages as well. Green politicians for example hold top positions in the Catholic and Protestant churches, in ecologic and consumer protection organisations, in trade unions as well as in economic enterprises. At the same time, the Greens try to bring the movement back in by adding leading activists on electoral lists (for example the 2009 European Parliament: Sven Giegold, co-founder of Attac Germany, and Barbara Lochbihler, former secretary general of Amnesty International Germany).

Main challenges for the future

The German Greens are now in their mid-30s and at the zenith of their career so far: more than 60,000 party members; government participation in 7 of 16 *Länder* (including one President-Minister); overall the third-strongest party in Germany (324 MPs at the European, federal and *Land* levels, that is, 12.5 per cent of all German MPs) and the only nation-wide party beside the two catch-all-parties (the CDU/CSU and the SPD). There is no doubt that the German Green Party has been the most successful innovation in the German party system since the 1950s. The Greens passed all thresholds of party life. Unsurprisingly, 30 years in parliament have left their mark. Derived from nonparliamentary societal protest groups, the Greens matured. They are an established parliamentary-professional, centre-left party. The revolutionary period is history, and today the Greens are above all a party of the well-established and upper middle-class. Along with that process of transformation, Greens survived several pivotal crises.

However, there are challenges for the party in the near future. These challenges are related to internal and external developments and became obvious in the federal election of 2013. One of the most important challenges is the ageing of the organisation and its members. Even though the Greens are not the project of a specific generation, the party has to push for generational renewal. The first steps have been successfully taken in several *Land* branches, but generational change at the federal level has merely started. The party's growth generated a need for organisational renewal and enhanced intraparty coordination of party levels and party faces. Consequently, the national committee appointed a working group to compile suggestions for reorganising party structures in preparation for the 2017 election (Alliance 90/The Greens, 2014). The electoral defeat of 2013 brought up another challenge: programmatic and strategic renewal. In 2005, 2009 and 2013, the Greens did not obtain an electoral majority for a red-green coalition. As a reaction, and in the new and fluid German party system, the Greens recently re-emphasised their course of independence (Alliance 90/The Greens, 2013). The party congress passed a resolution and pointed out that the party would be open for other coalitions than red-green. It shows that Greens have redefined themselves as an office-seeking and functional party, open for coalitions on both 'sides' of the German party system. This course is already practised at the *Land* level. It remains to be seen if the Greens can successfully manage these varieties of coalitions – or if this new flexibility will weaken their political identity.

Notes

1 In the 1970s, two major parties (Christian Democrats, Social Democrats) and one small party (Liberals) were represented in federal parliament and accumulated more than 99 per cent of all votes (1972, 1976).

2 In 1980, the Greens received almost 70 per cent of their revenues from the state (Bukow, 2008). At the federal level, they were almost completely financed by the state (Müller-Rommel and Poguntke, 1992).

3 Driven by electoral law, the Greens decided, after lengthy negotiations, to form an all-German electoral list with West German Greens, East German Greens and several civil rights groups (Alliance 90/Greens-Bündnis 90 – Citizens Movement). At the same time, the Greens filed a claim before the Federal Constitutional Court against the nation-wide 5 per cent threshold. The court decided that the two electorates (West/East) were to be considered separately and confirmed the Greens' doubt. Due to this, the Greens finally decided on separate East and West German lists. Consequently, the West German Greens missed their re-election, although they would have reached 5.1 per cent with a nation-wide calculation.

4 The Alliance 90 had its origins in the GDR peace and civil-rights groups. Established in 1990 as electoral lists of several civil rights movements, they organised themselves as a formal party in 1991.

5 Further problems concerning foreign policy followed, for example after 9/11 when Chancellor Schröder forced the Greens in parliament to support 'boundless solidarity with the USA'. In 2002, the Greens named this dilemma: 'Joschka Fischer – outside minister, inside Green'.

6 Instruments: a general 50 per cent quota for women; principle of collective leadership and incompatibility of central and public office; principle of rotation (MPs should retire after two years); limitation of legislatures; limitation of pay and benefits (limited to a craftsman's wage); imperative mandate (not enforced, illegal in Germany).

7 At the *Land* level, there are, in a few cases, member assemblies instead of delegate conventions. *Land* and local parties are autonomous but must not disagree with the basic federal principles and statutes.
8 In Germany, there are *Land* lists and local constituency candidates for federal elections (299 constituencies; selectorate usually all local members). The Greens' federal MPs are normally elected as list candidates. Yet, only Hans-Christian Ströbele (Berlin) won a constituency directly.

References

Alliance 90/The Greens, 2013. *Gemeinsam und solidarisch für eine starke grüne Zukunft: Resolution, 36th National Congress.* Berlin.

Alliance 90/The Greens, 2014. *Beschluss des Bundesvorstands von Bündnis 90/Die Grünen zur Einsetzung einer Strukturkommission.* Berlin.

Blühdorn, I., 2009. Reinventing Green politics: On the strategic repositioning of the German Green party. *German Politics,* 18(1), pp. 36–54.

Blühdorn, I., 2010. Green new deal and new social contract. Alliance 90/The Greens – An avant garde of what?, *36th IASGP Conference.* London, 24–25 May.

Budge, I., Klingemann, H.-D., Volkens, A., Bara, J., and Tanenbaum, E., 2001. *Mapping Policy Preferences: Estimates for Parties, Electors, and Governments 1945–1998.* Oxford: Oxford University Press.

Bukow, S., 2008. Green Politics. In: J. B. Callicott and R. Frodeman, eds, *Encyclopedia of Environmental Ethics and Philosophy.* Detroit: Gale. pp. 471–473.

Bukow, S., 2013. *Die professionalisierte Mitgliederpartei: Politische Parteien zwischen institutionellen Erwartungen und organisationaler Wirklichkeit.* Wiesbaden: Springer VS Verlag.

Bukow, S., and Poguntke, T., 2013. Innerparteiliche Organisation und Willensbildung. In: O. Niedermayer, ed., *Handbuch Parteienforschung.* Wiesbaden: Springer VS Verlag. pp. 179–209.

Bukow, S., and Rammelt, S., 2003. *Parteimanagement vor neuen Herausforderungen: Die Notwendigkeit strategischer Steuerung sowie Anforderungen an parteiinterne Organisation und externe Kommunikation für moderne (Regierungs-)Parteien am Beispiel der Grünen.* Münster: Lit Verlag.

Bukow, S., and Seemann, W., eds, 2010. *Die Große Koalition: Regierung – Politik – Parteien 2005–2009.* Wiesbaden: VS Verlag für Sozialwissenschaften.

Detterbeck, K., 2013. The rare event of choice: Party primaries in German land parties. *German Politics,* 22(3), pp. 270–287.

Deutscher Bundestag, 2014. *Bekanntmachung von Rechenschaftsberichten politischer Parteien für das Kalenderjahr 2012 (1. Teil – Bundestagsparteien): Unterrichtung durch den Präsidenten des Deutschen Bundestages. BT-Drs. 18/400.* Berlin: Deutscher Bundestag.

Egle, C., Ostheim, T., and Zohlnhöfer, R., eds, 2003. *Das rot-grüne Projekt: eine Bilanz der Regierung Schröder 1998–2002.* Wiesbaden: Westdeutscher Verlag.

Ernst, M., and Westermayer, T., 2013. *Regieren nach Zahlen: Was auf der BDK 2013 ansteht (Update),* [blog] 24 April. Available at: <http://blog.till-westermayer.de/index.php/2013/04/24/regieren-nach-zahlen-was-auf-der-bdk-2013-ansteht> [Accessed 3 November 2013].

Frankland, E. G., and Schoonmaker, D., 1992. *Between Protest and Power: The Green Party in Germany.* Boulder, CO: Westview Press.

Franzmann, S., 2014. The Failed Struggle for Office Instead of Votes: The Greens, Die Linke and the FDP. In: G. d'Ottavio and Th. Saalfeld, eds, *Germany After the 2013 Elections*. Farnham: Ashgate. pp. 155–180.

Franzmann, S., and Kaiser, A., 2006. Locating political parties in policy space: A reanalysis of party manifesto data. *Party Politics*, 12(2), pp. 163–188.

Fuchs, D., and Rohrschneider, R., 2005. War es dieses Mal nicht die Ökonomie? Der Einfluss von Sachfragenorientierungen auf die Wählerentscheidung bei der Bundestagswahl 2002. In: J. W. Falter, O. W. Gabriel and B. Weßels, eds, *Wahlen und Wähler: Analysen aus Anlass der Bundestagswahl 2002*. Wiesbaden: VS Verlag für Sozialwissenschaften. pp. 339–356.

Harmel, R., and Janda, K., 1994. An integrated theory of party goals and party change. *Journal of Theoretical Politics*, 6(3), pp. 259–287.

Heinrich-Böll-Stiftung, 2013. *Jahresbericht 2013*. Berlin: HBS.

Hunsicker, S., and Schroth, Y., 2010. Die Große Koalition aus der Sicht des Wählers. In: S. Bukow and W. Seemann, eds, *Die Große Koalition: Regierung – Politik – Parteien 2005–2009*. Wiesbaden: VS Verlag für Sozialwissenschaften. pp. 336–356.

Jesse, E., 2013. Nach allen Seiten offen? Der Ausgang der Bundestagswahl 2013 und mögliche Folgen für das Parteiensystem und das Koalitionsgefüge. *Zeitschrift für Politik*, 60(4), pp. 374–392.

Jun, U., 2010. Die SPD in der Großen Koalition: Selbstverschuldeter Niedergang oder zwanghafte Anpassung an veränderte Ausgangsbedingungen der Politik? In: S. Bukow and W. Seemann, eds, *Die Große Koalition: Regierung – Politik – Parteien 2005–2009*. Wiesbaden: VS Verlag für Sozialwissenschaften. pp. 299–318.

Katz, R. S., and Mair, P., 1993. The evolution of party organizations in Europe: The three faces of party organization. *The American Review of Politics*, 14, pp. 593–617.

Keil, S., and Gabriel, O. W., 2012. The Baden-Württemberg state election of 2011: A political landslide. *German Politics*, 21(2), pp. 239–246.

Klein, M., 2011. Was wissen wir über die Mitglieder der Parteien? In: T. Spier, M. Klein, U. von Alemann, H. Hoffmann, A. Laux, A. Nonnenmacher and K. Rohrbach, eds, *Parteimitglieder in Deutschland*. Wiesbaden: VS Verlag für Sozialwissenschaften. pp. 31–38.

Klein, M., and Falter, J. W., 2003. *Der lange Weg der Grünen: eine Partei zwischen Protest und Regierung*. München: Beck Verlag.

Laver, M., and Budge, I., 1992. Measuring Policy Distances and Modeling Coalition Formation. In: M. Laver and I. Budge, eds, *Party Policy and Government Coalitions*. New York: St. Martin's Press. pp. 15–40.

Markovits, A. S., and Gorski, P. S., 1997. *Grün schlägt rot: Die deutsche Linke nach 1945*. Berlin: Rotbuch Verlag.

Markovits, A. S., and Klaver, J., 2013. *Dreißig Jahre im Bundestag: Der Einfluss der Grünen auf die politische Kultur und das öffentliche Leben der Bundesrepublik*. Berlin: Heinrich-Böll-Stiftung.

Marks, G., Hooghe, L., Nelson, M., and Edwards, E., 2006. Party competition and European integration in the East and West. Different structure, same causality. *Comparative Political Studies*, 39(2), pp. 155–177.

Mende, S., 2011. *'Nicht rechts, nicht links, sondern vorn': Eine Geschichte der Gründungsgrünen*. München: Oldenbourg Wissenschaftsverlag.

Michels, R., 1989 [1911]. *Zur Soziologie des Parteiwesens in der modernen Demokratie: Untersuchungen über die oligarchischen Tendenzen des Gruppenlebens*. Stuttgart: Alfred Kröner Verlag.

Müller-Rommel, F., 2002. The Lifespan and the Political Performance of Green Parties in Western Europe. In: F. Müller-Rommel and T. Poguntke, eds, *Green Parties in National Governments*. London: Routledge. pp. 1–16.

Müller-Rommel, F., and Poguntke, T., 1992. Die Grünen. In: A. Mintzel and H. Oberreuter, eds, *Parteien in der Bundesrepublik Deutschland*. Opladen: Leske+Budrich. pp. 319–361.

Pedersen, M. N., 1982. Towards a new typology of party lifespans and minor parties. *Scandinavian Political Studies*, 5(1), pp. 1–16.

Poguntke, T., 1987. The organization of a participatory party – The German Greens. *European Journal of Political Research*, 15(6), pp. 609–633.

Poguntke, T., 1993. *Alternative Politics – The German Green Party*. Edinburgh: Edinburgh University Press.

Poguntke, T., 1994. Basisdemokratie and Political Realities: The German Green Party. In: K. Lawson, ed., *How Political Parties Work: Perspectives from Within*. Westport: Praeger. pp. 3–22.

Poguntke, T., 1996. Antiparty sentiment – Conceptual thoughts and empirical evidence: Explorations into a minefield. *European Journal of Political Research*, 29(3), pp. 319–344.

Poguntke, T., 1998. Alliance 90/The Greens in East Germany. From vanguard to insignificance? *Party Politics*, 4(1), pp. 33–55.

Poguntke, T., 1999. Die Bündnisgrünen in der babylonischen Gefangenschaft der SPD? In: O. Niedermayer, ed., *Die Parteien nach der Bundestagswahl 1998*. Opladen: Leske+Budrich. pp. 83–101.

Poguntke, T., 2000. *Parteiorganisation im Wandel: Gesellschaftliche Verankerung und organisatorische Anpassung im Europäischen Vergleich*. Wiesbaden: Westdeutscher Verlag.

Poguntke, T., ed., 2003. *Die Bündnisgrünen nach der Bundestagswahl 2002: Auf dem Weg zur linken Funktionspartei?* Opladen: Leske+Budrich.

Probst, L., 2007. Bündnis 90/Die Grünen (Grüne). In: F. Decker and V. Neu, eds, *Handbuch der deutschen Parteien*. Wiesbaden: VS Verlag für Sozialwissenschaften. pp. 173–188.

Probst, L., 2011. Bündnis 90/Die Grünen auf dem Weg zur 'Volkspartei'? Eine Analyse der Entwicklung der Grünen seit der Bundestagswahl 2005. In: O. Niedermayer, ed., *Die Parteien nach der Bundestagswahl 2009*. Wiesbaden: VS Verlag für Sozialwissenschaften. pp. 131–156.

Probst, L., 2012a. Aufbruch zu neuen Ufern? Perspektiven der Grünen. In: E. Jesse and R. Sturm, eds, *'Superwahljahr' 2011 und die Folgen*. Baden-Baden: Nomos. pp. 109–131.

Probst, L., 2012b. Übergänge von der Zivilgesellschaft zur politischen Institution: Der Parteiwerdungsprozess der Grünen. In: C. Fraune and K. Schubert, eds, *Grenzen der Zivilgesellschaft: Empirische Befunde und analytische Perspektiven*. Münster: Waxmann. pp. 75–92.

Probst, L., 2013a. Bündnis 90/Die Grünen (Grüne). In: F. Decker and V. Neu, eds, *Handbuch der deutschen Parteien*. Wiesbaden: Springer VS. pp. 166–179.

Probst, L., 2013b. Bündnis 90/Die Grünen (Grüne). In: O. Niedermayer, ed., *Handbuch Parteienforschung*. Wiesbaden: Springer VS. pp. 509–540.

Raschke, J., 1993. *Die Grünen: Wie sie wurden, was sie sind*. Frankfurt am Main: Büchergilde Gutenberg.

Raschke, J., 2001. *Die Zukunft der Grünen: 'So kann man nicht regieren'*. Frankfurt am Main: Campus.

Rüdig, W., 2012. The perennial success of the German Greens. *Environmental Politics,* 21(1), pp. 108–130.

Spies, D., and Franzmann, S., 2011. A two-dimensional approach to the political opportunity structure of extreme right parties in Western Europe. *West European Politics,* 34(5), pp. 1044–1069.

Switek, N., 2010. Neue Regierungsbündnisse braucht das Land!. *Zeitschrift für Politikberatung,* 3(2), pp. 177–196.

Switek, N., 2012. Bündis 90/Die Grünen: Zur Entscheidungsmacht grüner Parteitage. In: Korte, K.-R., and Treibel, J. (eds), *Wie entscheiden Parteien? Prozesse innerparteilicher Willensbildung in Deutschland.* Baden-Baden: Nomos. pp. 211–231.

Switek, N., 2015. *Bündnis 90/Die Grünen: Innerparteiliche Entscheidungsprozesse und neue Koalitionsoptionen auf Länderebene.* Baden-Baden: Nomos.

Volkens, A., Lehmann, P., Merz, N., Regel, S., and Werner, A., 2013. *The Manifesto Data Collection: Manifesto Project (MRG/CMP/MARPOR).* Version 2013a. Berlin: Wissenschaftszentrum Berlin für Sozialforschung (WZB).

6 *GroenLinks* in the Netherlands: No longer a protest party, not yet a coalition partner

Gerrit Voerman and Paul Lucardie

Introduction

In 1990, *GroenLinks* (Green Left; since 1 October 1992, written as *GroenLinks*, without the space) was founded. Contrary to most other Green parties in Western Europe, *GroenLinks* did not descend directly from new social movements: it was the outcome of a rapprochement, under a Green label, of four initially very different parties. In its name and in its party platform, *GroenLinks* professed itself to be both a Green party and a left-wing party. In this way, it differed from most other Green parties, which claimed (at least in their early years) to transcend the 'old-fashioned' left–right scheme. Nonetheless, *GroenLinks* was accepted by the European Federation of Green Parties as the official Green party in the Netherlands and began to behave like a 'normal' Green party. Yet in some ways – for example in its organisational structure and party culture – *GroenLinks* has retained unique characteristics resulting from its peculiar genesis, which made it quite exceptional compared with other Green parties in Europe (Rüdig, 2010).

In this chapter, we focus on the ideology and organisation of *GroenLinks* as it has developed through time. Before doing that, we present a brief survey of the genesis and evolution of this party.[1]

Origins and development

The 'party lifespan approach' of the Danish political scientist Pedersen (1982) is not fully applicable to *GroenLinks* (Rüdig, 2010, p. 214) (see Table 6.1). *GroenLinks* started in 1989 as an electoral federation of four small left-wing parties that all had been represented in the Second Chamber of the Dutch Parliament and consequently had passed the threshold of representation: the Communist Party of the Netherlands (*Communistische Partij van Nederland* – CPN), from 1918 until 1986; the Pacifist-Socialist Party (*Pacifistisch-Socialistische Partij* – PSP), from 1959 until 1989; the Political Party of Radicals (*Politieke Partij Radicalen* – PPR), from 1971 until 1989, which was founded by Christians but would become libertarian and ecologist; and the progressive Christian Evangelical People's Party (*Evangelische Volkspartij* – EVP), from 1982 until 1986. Despite their variety, cooperation between the CPN, PSP and PPR started in the late 1970s (the EVP

Table 6.1 Chronology of the main developments of *GroenLinks*, 1989–2014

Year	Developments
1989	Electoral cooperation among the CPN, PSP, PPR and EVP, under the name of *GroenLinks*
1990	Foundation *GroenLinks* as a political party
1991	Dissolution of the CPN, PSP, PPR and EVP
1994	Rosenmöller becomes party leader
1999	*GroenLinks* wins 11.8% of the vote at the European elections
2002	Halsema succeeds Rosenmöller as party leader
2006	For the first time in its history, *GroenLinks* is invited to take part in coalition negotiations; Halsema refuses for strategic reasons
2010	Serious participation in coalition negotiations; *GroenLinks* remains in opposition
2010	Sap succeeds Halsema as party leader
2012	Severe electoral defeat
2012	Van Oijk succeeds Sap as party leader

Source: Authors' own compilation.

only got involved in the merger at the very last minute), stimulated by the introduction of New Left ideas and the rise of the new social movements, combined with the declining electoral fortunes of the parties themselves. In the course of its transformation, the CPN lost its rigid Stalinist traits, while the PPR shed its Christian heritage and shifted towards the left, and the PSP became less reluctant to work together with the other parties. The result was growing electoral cooperation in the 1980s at the municipal, provincial and European levels, culminating in a common platform and list of candidates at the national elections of 1989, together with the EVP (Voerman, 1995; Lucardie, et al., 1999; Lucardie and Voerman, 2003). At that time, however, only two of the four, namely the PPR and the PSP, were still represented in the Second Chamber. The CPN and the EVP had dropped below the threshold of representation in 1986, which certainly has stimulated their readiness to cooperate and eventually to merge with the PPR and the PSP.

In 1990, *GroenLinks* was founded as a new political formation; subsequently, the four parties dissolved, most of their members having joined the new party. Opponents of the merger tried to resurrect the Communist Party and the Pacifist-Socialist Party in 1992 but met with very little electoral success (Lucardie, et al., 1995). Later, some *GroenLinks* members would join the Socialist Party (SP), which became a serious competitor when it entered the Dutch Parliament in 1994. At nearly every subsequent election, the SP expanded its electorate, and since 2003, it has won more seats than *GroenLinks*.

In 1989, the *GroenLinks* electoral federation won 4.1 per cent of the popular vote and six seats in the Second Chamber (Table 6.2): more than the four predecessors had acquired in the previous elections but not as much as had been expected.

Table 6.2 Election results for *GroenLinks* in the Netherlands (Second Chamber), 1989–2012

Year	% votes	N seats	N votes
1989	4.1	6	361,274
1994	3.5	5	311,033
1998	7.3	11	625,968
2002	7.0	10	660,692
2003	5.1	8	495,802
2006	4.6	7	453,054
2010	6.7	10	628,096
2012	2.3	4	219,896

Source: 1989–2010: Lucardie and Voerman, 2010, 2012: www.verkiezingsuitslagen.nl (Accessed on 5 March 2014).

The 'pure' Green rival, *De Groenen*, obtained only 0.4 per cent, not enough for a seat; they would never pass Pedersen's threshold of representation. *GroenLinks* suffered a mild setback in 1994, losing one of its six seats. As a consequence, party leader Ina Brouwer resigned because she felt responsible for the defeat.

Yet within a few years, the tide would turn. A new leader, Paul Rosenmöller, a former trade-union leader with a Maoist past, attracted new voters, no doubt with his charming personality and lively debating style. In 1998, the party won 7.3 per cent of the vote, enough for 11 seats in parliament. At the 1999 European elections, it increased its share of the vote to almost 12 per cent. The popularity of the party continued to rise until 2001, when the polls predicted 16 seats for the party. Participation in government appeared within reach. The Christian Democrats had signalled their willingness to consider a cabinet with *GroenLinks* and the Labour Party after the 2002 elections. In anticipation of such talks, the party refrained from very radical demands in its election platforms (see "Ideology and policy positions" section).

However, since 2002, when *GroenLinks* lost one seat at the parliamentary elections, fortune no longer smiles on the party. Pim Fortuyn, a charismatic and articulate maverick politician, mobilised latent discontent with multiculturalism and immigration very effectively. A few days before the parliamentary elections in May 2002, he was assassinated by an animal rights activist who sympathised with *GroenLinks*. The List Pim Fortuyn (LPF) he had founded, disintegrated rapidly after his death, but his ideology – a mixture of cultural nationalism, economic liberalism and democratic populism – did not die. The assassination of filmmaker Theo van Gogh by an Islamic extremist in 2004 seemed to confirm Fortuyn's direst predictions with respect to the failure of multiculturalism in the eyes of many native Dutchmen. Geert Wilders, who left the Liberal Party in 2004 and founded his own Freedom Party (PVV) two years later, would take over the role of Fortuyn. Rosenmöller, who had disposed of Fortuyn as a 'rightwing extremist', received so many threats that he resigned the party leadership in November 2002. Femke Halsema, a young social scientist who previously had been member of the Labour Party, was elected party leader.

Though Halsema was an eloquent debater, she could not stop the electoral decline. At the parliamentary elections of 2003, *GroenLinks* lost two seats. At the 2004 European elections, it lost two of its four seats, and at the 2006 parliamentary elections, it lost another seat. Nevertheless, in 2006, the party was asked for the first time in its history to take part in the formation of a cabinet (together with Christian Democrats and the Labour Party), but it refused for strategic reasons. Only in 2010 did Halsema lead the party to victory – back to ten seats –, and for the first time, serious participation in coalition negotiations, about a 'purple-green' coalition together with right- and left-wing Liberals and Social Democrats. However, the negotiations failed. A few months later, Halsema resigned and was succeeded by Jolande Sap, an economist. She tried to continue Halsema's strategy and negotiated about support for certain policies with the right-wing minority government, which was to some extent officially supported by Wilders's PVV. Voters may not have appreciated this and deserted the party in massive numbers at the anticipated elections of 2012, leaving it with only four seats – the lowest number in its electoral history so far. Sap stepped back as party leader after the party executive had withdrawn its confidence. She was replaced by Bram van Ojik, who had been chair of the PPR in 1988–1990 and MP for *GroenLinks* in 1993–1994.

In 2014, *GroenLinks* was further away from crossing the threshold of relevance as ever since its foundation. The party has frequently participated in local governments, including some of the largest cities like Amsterdam, Rotterdam and Utrecht. After the 1990 municipal elections, the party got 15 aldermen, 0.8 per cent of the total number. In 1994, its share was 1.4 per cent; in 1998, 2.2 per cent; in 2002, 2.9 per cent; in 2006, 4.0 per cent and in 2010, 3.8 per cent. Occasionally since 1999, *GroenLinks* also took part in a few of the 12 provincial governments. However, it has never taken part in the national government, although its strategy is definitely aimed at reaching this goal. Initially, *GroenLinks* regarded itself as a radical reformist party, which wanted to combine parliamentary and extraparliamentary action in coalition with 'other progressive forces', hoping to realise 'fundamental social change'. In its manifesto of 2008, however, *GroenLinks* placed even greater emphasis on parliamentary politics and the need to make compromises in order to secure 'concrete results' (GroenLinks, 1992, pp. 14–16; GroenLinks, 2009, p. 10). In order to qualify as a reliable governmental partner, the party also adapted its platform regarding several issues (see "Ideology and policy positions" section). The strategic and programmatic adjustments were to little avail. There were three moments when *GroenLinks* was really close, as already mentioned above: around 2000 (in a period in which Green parties in Germany and Belgium made their governmental debuts), in 2006 and in 2010. Every time, *GroenLinks* missed the boat.

Ideology and policy positions

The ideology of *GroenLinks* is a mixture of different elements, as might be expected from a party that brought together communists, Christian and democratic radicals, pacifists and libertarian as well as ecological socialists and a few others. Some ideological convergence had taken place between the merging parties, but significant differences had survived (Lucardie, et. al., 1995; Voerman, 1995; Lucardie and Pennings, 2010). The differences were reconciled with obvious difficulty in a party manifesto, approved after protracted discussions in December 1991. The main ideals of the party were defined in the manifesto as democracy, respect for nature and the environment, social justice and international solidarity (GroenLinks, 1992, p. 5).

Democratic principles should prevail not only in the political realm, but also in business corporations and other organisations. *GroenLinks*, however, did not call for workers' self-management any more (quite popular with PSP and PPR in the 1970s, but losing popularity in the 1980s), only for more power for works councils and trade unions. Parliamentary democracy was taken for granted; the government should guarantee political freedom as well as other social rights and freedoms. The government should be active but not dominant in society. These ideas seem typical of what one could describe as democratic radicalism: a not fully developed ideology shared by the PPR, to some extent by the PSP and even by the CPN in its last years (Lucardie, 2014, pp. 29, 93).

An active government was needed especially to turn the growth-oriented economy into a sustainable economy. This may require global planning of production and consumption. Yet internalisation of ecological costs through environmental taxes ('ecotaxes') might often be as efficient as a legal ban on a product. The manifesto clearly reflects a compromise between the socialist and liberal tendencies within *GroenLinks* – members from the CPN and PSP versus those from the PPR. On the one hand, it is stated: 'the capitalist mode of production is reaching its [ecological] limits' and 'the present capitalist market economy is at odds with the economic order which *GroenLinks* aspires to'; on the other hand, 'a centralised planning economy is unthinkable', and 'the market is indispensable for fine-tuning production and consumption' (GroenLinks, 1992, pp. 4, 9, 10). However, this was a compromise between eco-socialists and eco-liberals: both wings of *GroenLinks* agreed on the need for ecological limits to growth.

Social justice means social equality: a more equal distribution of power, income, work, knowledge and property. Naturally, the government has a role to play here too. *GroenLinks* had obviously embraced the social welfare state, without too much debate.

GroenLinks found it difficult to come to an agreement about foreign affairs. International solidarity was an ideal accepted by all parties. The PSP and the EVP, however, had known strong pacifist tendencies, rejecting the use of any violence. When discussing the new manifesto, the issue was postponed. In October 1992, *GroenLinks* added a chapter to the manifesto on peace and security, calling for 'nonviolent solutions to conflicts' and 'total disarmament' as well as the dissolution of the North Atlantic Treaty Organisation (NATO) and the Western European Union (WEU) (GroenLinks, 1992, pp. 16–19). Throughout its history, international armed conflicts would lead to tempestuous debates within the party.

The manifesto of the early 1990s contained a few elements that came down from the communist tradition, but overall, it reflected more the ideological influence of the PPR and, to a lesser extent, of the PSP. Despite clear shifts in emphasis, if this text is compared with the party manifesto adopted some 6 years later, in November 2008, the similarities are more striking than the differences. Ecological sustainability, the first plank mentioned in 2008, was given even greater prominence than in 1991. People's wellbeing and happiness and environmental concerns took precedence over economic growth. The 'respectful treatment of animals' made its first appearance, prompted perhaps by the rise of the Party for the Animals, which entered the Second Chamber in 2006 (GroenLinks, 2009, p. 6). Freedom and self-fulfilment also ranked high on the list in 2008, alongside social justice and international solidarity. Radical democratisation was no longer a stated objective; it was replaced by an 'equal say for all' and 'citizen participation' (GroenLinks, 2009, p. 9). *GroenLinks* still sought to change the economic order and steer the market through the 'democratic involvement of government, employees, employers and consumers' (GroenLinks, 2009, p. 7). Privatisation and competition were deemed appropriate, however, including in the state sector (healthcare, public utilities, public housing and public transport). This is a marked shift vis-à-vis 1991, despite the proviso that privatisation could not be an end in itself. In addition, *GroenLinks* continued to advocate global solidarity, openness and a generous admission policy for refugees (GroenLinks, 2009, pp. 8, 11). Overall, we see a cautious shift towards the political centre, although *GroenLinks* continued to adopt a radical stance on the environment, economic growth and global solidarity.

The same can be said of the election platforms of *GroenLinks*. Though there is a remarkable continuity in the platforms until the early 2000s, significant socialist or communist elements declined in importance. In 1989, the party called for 'socialisation of the economy', socio-economic planning and parliamentary control of banks and other financial institutions (GroenLinks, 1989, pp. 18–20). All land should be owned by the state, while citizens or companies could rent it for an indefinite period. In 1994, the demand for planning is more abstract and less specific, while land ownership does not seem an issue at all. Since then, planning socialism has disappeared from the platform. *GroenLinks* gradually felt more sympathy for the market economy. In every platform, the party claimed a redistribution of power, income, wealth and labour, but its demands became gradually less radical. It wanted to increase welfare and minimum wages for example and called for additional taxation of higher incomes. The demand for a basic income (in the past advocated by the PPR), did not figure prominently in any election platform but was somewhat hidden. Later *GroenLinks* proposed a plan for a negative income tax, which might possibly result in a basic income.

Under the leadership of Halsema, the party began to look at social equality from a different perspective. The cleavage between rich and poor or between capital and labour was perceived as less important than the one between insiders and outsiders. Insiders could be managers or workers with a secure full-time job, whereas outsiders were unemployed, temporarily employed or freelance workers without much security. Immigrants, women and youngsters were over-represented among the outsiders. The government should facilitate their participation in society (Halsema and Van Gent, 2005).

In the 1990s, ecological, sustainable policies gained weight and specificity in the election platforms. *GroenLinks* called for (more) ecotaxes on energy, especially fuel and petrol (gas), pesticides, water, waste, air travel and even the consumption of (nonorganic) meat. Moreover, the party called for closing down nuclear power stations (almost done in the Netherlands); reducing car use and improving public transport; restricting hunting and fishing; and reducing factory farming and encouraging organic agriculture. Genetic modification of food should be banned altogether, as long as the safety of man and nature is not guaranteed. *GroenLinks* remained ambivalent towards economic growth. In 2010, it introduced a new term – 'Gross National Happiness' instead of Gross National Product – to put the economic growth-oriented discussion in another context (GroenLinks, 2010, pp. 5–6).

Democratic radicalism has been present in all election platforms, as indicated by demands for a referendum and people's initiative, and in the elections of burgomasters (mayors), provincial governors and the head of state. Society should become more democratic as well. Hence, more power to patients and workers in healthcare, teachers and students in schools and universities, tenants in housing projects and workers in industry. In 2010, *GroenLinks* proposed that the Second Chamber of Dutch parliament should elect the prime minister.

International solidarity has remained an important theme in all platforms. Foreign aid should be increased, although the aid *GroenLinks* advocated dropped from 2 per cent of the gross national product in 1989 to 'at least' 0.8 per cent in 2012. Immigration policy had to be liberalised. In 2002, *GroenLinks* was the only party that called explicitly for the admission of labour immigrants (at least under certain conditions) and legalisation of illegal immigrants. Moreover, it wanted to facilitate dual citizenship and to grant even immigrants without Dutch citizenship the right to vote at all levels (municipal, provincial and national). Thereafter, *GroenLinks* became somewhat more cautious in its admissions policy.

'Multiculturalism', an explicitly stated ideal in 1998, made way for 'liberalism' in a cultural sense and an 'open culture' or 'open society' (GroenLinks, 1998, p. 5; GroenLinks, 2010, pp. 35–36). In 1994, *GroenLinks* wanted ethnic minorities to be able to 'maintain a living connection with their own language and culture', and in 1998, it was still calling for 'sufficient resources to make education in minority languages part of the curriculum if this is what parents want' (Groen-Links, 1994, p. 61; GroenLinks, 1998, p. 12). This demand was dropped from the 2002 platform, and greater emphasis was placed on integration, 'a two-way process' requiring efforts from both ethnic minorities and native Dutch (GroenLinks, 2002, p. 38). Educational segregation ('black' and 'white' schools) now emerged as a major problem. *GroenLinks* continued, however, to be positively disposed towards the multicultural society, also calling for 'room for difference' in 2010. Migrants were nevertheless still expected to integrate, to learn Dutch and to either work or undergo training or education. Among marriage migrants in particular, the government needed to promote emancipation (GroenLinks, 2010, p. 28). Thus, for *GroenLinks*, multiculturalism did not extend so far as to respect patriarchal cultures where women's emancipation was a taboo.

From the outset, *GroenLinks* accepted the European Community (or European Union after 1993), despite reservations about its lack of openness and democratic procedures and about the refugee policy enshrined in the Schengen Agreement. *GroenLinks* began to adopt a more positive view of the European Union in the course of the 1990s. In 1994, it described itself as a 'critical supporter of further European integration' and opted unequivocally for 'federal rather than intergovernmental development'. The main criticism related to the 'democratic deficit' in the European Union and neglect by 'Brussels' of social and environmental policy (GroenLinks, 1994, p. 19). This led to *GroenLinks* opposing the European Monetary Union in 1998, while at the same time striving for a European constitution. The party did eventually accept the euro, but continued to work towards a more social Europe and called for a fiscal union. In 2005, *GroenLinks* campaigned for the European constitution, and in 2006, it argued for a European convention to draw up a new constitution that would once again be submitted to citizens in a referendum. Although generally a supporter of a strong Europe, the party now also demanded safeguards for national control in matters such as soft drugs, euthanasia and gay marriage. Turkey could become a member if it would meet the normal admission criteria. In 2010, *GroenLinks* paid relatively little attention to the European Union, but the party did advocate greater democracy and cross-border electoral lists for the European Parliament – which would undoubtedly promote integration. In its 2012 platform, *GroenLinks* demanded stronger European regulation and supervision of the financial market.

Regarding foreign policy, *GroenLinks* gradually accepted NATO and the use of military force to guarantee human rights. Dutch armed forces should become a peace force, preferably with a United Nations' mandate and no longer tied to NATO but to the Organisation for Security and Cooperation in Europe (OSCE). Initially, *GroenLinks* found that NATO had to be disbanded. Nevertheless, in the platform for the 2002 elections, the party was more cautious and ambiguous. On the one hand, it should be replaced (in the long run) by a regional peace force of the United Nations; on the other hand, it might help develop a European reaction force; after all, it did contribute to peace in the Balkan area. In 2012, *GroenLinks* advocated a European security policy, including the formation of a European army. For the time being, it wanted to reform NATO into 'a broader military executive body of like-minded countries in support of the protection of civilians and respect for international law' (GroenLinks, 2012, p. 35). Nuclear weapons should still be removed from the Netherlands, however.

Thus one might conclude that the influence of communist and Marxist ideology was never very strong within *GroenLinks* (undoubtedly also because the CPN was hardly communist any longer when it merged into *GroenLinks*). This influence declined with time after 1989 – for obvious reasons, which can be summarised with the German word *Zeitgeist* or, in other words, the increasing dominance of liberal ideology and the collapse of the Soviet system.

Since its foundation in 1990, *GroenLinks* has adapted its ideals here and there to the spirit of the times but has never entirely surrendered. With regard to international politics, the party accepted NATO, but without abandoning its ideal of another security policy under the auspices of the United Nations. After some initial reservations, it adopted a more enthusiastic approach to the European Union. Its focus on the Third World also remained a constant. *GroenLinks* retained its radical ecological vision, but there was a shift in emphasis in the measures needed to bring this about – away from 'hard' prohibitions and towards 'softer' Green taxes, subsidies and levies. In relative terms, the shift was greatest in the socio-economic sphere – from planning socialism to acceptance of the market economy, with an active, regulatory role for the state. It was the job of the state to distribute work, income and capital more equitably. While the government no longer needed to impose a shorter working week (as *GroenLinks* had demanded in the 1990s), it had to enforce participation of all citizens in either paid work, training or voluntary work. The democratisation of state and society stayed on the agenda, but here too the demands were somewhat more cautious and less radical. *GroenLinks* continued to defend the multicultural society, but from 2002, the party spoke more about a 'liberal [in a cultural sense] and open society', which seems to indicate a subtle but more than purely symbolic shift.

This analysis of *GroenLinks*' election platforms thus largely confirms the picture that emerged when we compared the 1991 and 2008 party manifestos. The same ideals were articulated in different ways – in particular, they were less emphatic and more restrained. This is reflected in a diminishing aversion to measures designed to stimulate economic growth and in greater acceptance of the free market economy. As a result, *GroenLinks* moved slightly towards the established centre parties (which could be seen also in the negotiations about possible government participation in 2010, see "Origins and development" section). This confirms the evolution of the party's platform: the party started off as a green-red party and gradually diluted the socialist component of its profile by incorporating more liberal elements.

How is this transformation to be explained? Apart from the wish to govern, the key drivers could be electoral competition and – in connection – adaptation to the *Zeitgeist*. After all, political parties usually seek to maintain, and preferably expand, their electoral support. Because most voters occupy the political middle ground, parties tend to shift towards the centre unless this renders them virtually indistinguishable from their rivals. This is more likely to happen if the party's ideology and organisation are more flexible. Although *GroenLinks* had a flexible ideology from the outset, this was less true of its organisation. Party activists can use the party council and party congress to block or slow down changes to its platform, something that has in fact happened on occasions. This could explain why *GroenLinks* has made gradual, not too drastic, modifications to its platform.

Structure and organisation

Main party structures

As *GroenLinks* was the result of a merger, it may have inherited organisational characteristics from some of its predecessors (Lucardie and Voerman, 2003;

Lucardie and Voerman, 2008). The first congress of the new party adopted a constitution and by-laws, which seemed inspired by its left-libertarian predecessors the PSP and PPR, rather than the more centralised CPN. The congress was open to all members, who also had the right to vote, but it approved a constitution that limited the right to vote in the future to delegates from local branches. In the middle of the 1990s, this was changed again: Local branches were allowed complete freedom to decide the number of delegates (with voting rights). The interpretation of this change remained contested; yet by 2002 congresses were open to all members who had registered in time.

The party congress occupies a pivotal position within the *GroenLinks* party organisation. It makes all the important decisions: adopts party manifestoes, platforms and by-laws; elects the party executive and nominates candidates for parliament. However, the rank-and-file could correct the decisions of the congress by a membership vote or referendum (by mail), under certain conditions. Until 1997, they would elect the political leader of the party – number one on the list of candidates, who becomes usually the leader of the parliamentary group in the Dutch system – also by a membership vote. The membership vote was abolished after negative experiences in 1994, but reintroduced in 2006 (see "Structure and organisation: Party leadership" section).

Nomination of candidates for parliament as well as for the party executive would be prepared by an advisory 'candidate committee'. The members of the party executive would serve a term of two years and could be re-elected two times. Members of parliament could also serve three terms – but those terms were normally twice as long: four years each, twelve years altogether. Dispensation was possible, however, party leaders Rosenmöller and Halsema were allowed to serve a fourth term. Rotation was never discussed, but recall was possible – at least in theory. Members of parliament could not hold a party function at the national level, not even membership of the *GroenLinks* Council, in 1995 replaced by a party council. From then on, this body was elected mainly by local branches and would supervise the party executive, appoint candidate committees and chairpersons for the party congress and approve the party budget. Political issues were discussed in the *GroenLinks* Forum, which was introduced in 1995. The Forum was open to anyone, both members and nonmembers.

In 1996, the Strategy Committee was founded in which the chairs of the party and the national and European parliamentary caucus were represented, together with the campaign leader and several others. In the course of time, this semiformal organ became quite powerful. Since 2004, it could decide on the campaign budget, direct the campaign team and determine the political line and strategy of the party. From a democratic point of view, this was a questionable development. The Strategy Committee was not an elected organ and was not accountable to the party congress, for instance. In 2008, the Committee lost its formal competences, due to opposition within the party against its dominant position.

Apart from this vertical structure, the party constitution also recognised 'categorical groups', which would be allowed to propose motions and nominate candidates – functions similar to those of local branches. In the course of the

1990s, seven such 'categories' organised themselves: women in the Feminist Network, gays and lesbians in 'Pink Left', immigrants in the Progressive Immigrant Bloc, youth in *Dwars* (Intractable), as well as handicapped and chronically ill and people over 50 years old. Christians, mainly but not only former members of the EVP, organised a Platform for Gospel and Politics, which held regular meetings and published a journal but which hardly acted as a faction in the decision-making process.

Left Forum had more characteristics of a faction (founded in September 1989 and named after a similar grouping in the German Greens), though it did not focus only on the party *GroenLinks* but was open to other leftists as well. Yet even the Left Forum seemed more interested in organising debates than in lobbying within *GroenLinks*. In 1994, it decided to disband due to lack of active members. Factions were in fact neither forbidden nor allowed in *GroenLinks* but simply ignored in the constitution and by-laws. In February 2007, Critical *GroenLinks* (*Kritisch GroenLinks*) was founded, organising party members who were opposed to Halsema's 'neo-liberal agenda'. The group advocated a more left-wing position of *GroenLinks* and more internal democracy (it blamed for instance the powerful position of the Strategy Committee). After the party adopted a new manifesto in 2008, the group faded away.

Quotas for women were heatedly debated but rejected by the first party congresses in the early 1990s. Yet the party constitution and by-laws prescribed 'equal participation of women and men in all functions'. This rule was applied fairly consistently. Women and men alternated on most lists of candidates, and as a result, they were almost equally represented in parliaments and local councils. Immigrants should be represented in proportion to their share in the population (GroenLinks, 1990, pp. 7–20). There was no such rule for representation of members from constituent parties. The first parliamentary caucus, however, had represented the three main constituents more or less in proportion of membership.

Party leadership

In 1989, PPR leader Ria Beckers became the leading candidate of *GroenLinks* at the national elections (see Table 6.3). After the elections, she became chair of the parliamentary caucus and consequently, after the foundation of *GroenLinks* as a party one year later, its first party leader. She resigned in April 1993. MP Peter Lankhorst succeeded her as chair only temporarily, for he was not interested in qualifying as the first candidate at the elections of 1994. Seven others did, two of whom had indicated they would only share the leadership with another candidate. As in a membership vote no candidate won a majority, and a second one was held, which resulted in a narrow victory for Ina Brouwer, a Communist lawyer and MP in 1981–1986 and from 1989 onwards, who was going to share the leadership with Mohammed Rabbae, a former director of an immigrant organisation. The relatively fierce competition between the candidates – which was covered extensively by the press – was later perceived as a major cause for the electoral loss in

Table 6.3 Party leaders, *GroenLinks*, 1989–2014

Year	Candidates	Selection Method	Results	Length in office (months)	Reason for resigning
September 1989	Ria Beckers	Congress delegates PPR*	By acclamation	44	Private reasons
April 1993	Peter Lankhorst	Appointed by parliamentary caucus		10	Private reasons
February 1994	Ina Brouwer	Membership vote (organised in two rounds)	51% majority in second round (turnout 70%)	2	Electoral defeat
May 1994	Paul Rosenmöller	Appointed by parliamentary caucus		102	
February 1998	Paul Rosenmöller	Membership congress	'Nearly all members'		
February 2002	Paul Rosenmöller	Membership congress	85%		Private reasons, electoral defeat
November 2002	Femke Halsema	Membership congress	97.6%	98	
October 2006	Femke Halsema	Membership congress	90%		
April 2010	Femke Halsema	Membership congress	92%		Failure to participate in govern-ment
December 2010	Jolande Sap	Appointed by parliamentary caucus		21	
June 2012	Jolande Sap	Membership vote	84% (turnout 56%)		Electoral defeat
October 2012	Bram van Ojik	Appointed by parliamentary caucus			

Note: * In the negotiations prior to the electoral alliance of *GroenLinks*, it was agreed that the largest of the participating parties would appoint the first candidate.

Source: Authors' own compilation.

1994. After this defeat, Brouwer resigned. She was succeeded by her main rival, MP Paul Rosenmöller. In 1998, no one opposed his leading position on the list of candidates at the parliamentary elections. Moreover, the party had decided in 1997 to abolish the membership vote and leave the nomination of parliamentary candidates entirely in the hands of the party congress: the argument was that party members were not informed enough to make a balanced judgement.

Because of the growing popularity and prestige of party leader Rosenmöller, *GroenLinks* decided in 2000 to adjust the rule by which members of parliament could only serve a maximum of three terms. This cleared the road for Rosenmöller to lead the party again at the elections of May 2002. After the loss of one seat and – more important probably – having received serious threats in the wake of the assassination of Fortuyn, Rosenmöller resigned in November 2002. He put forward MP Halsema as his successor as party leader. She stepped down in December 2010. She had not been able to lead *GroenLinks* into a government coalition and was no longer motivated to lead the party. As her successor, she cleared the way for MP Jolande Sap, who in 2012 was challenged for the first place on the party list by fellow MP Tofik Dibi. The national executive had not anticipated a challenger, and only two weeks after Dibi's candidacy had become public, it decided to organise a membership vote, which Sap won with 85 per cent of the vote. After the severe electoral defeat in 2012, however, Sap resigned and was succeeded by MP Bram van Ojik as party leader.

In the evaluation of the electoral defeat, it was explicitly stated that the parliamentary group had become too dominant vis-à-vis the party organisation, notably in terms of policy making (Halsema's revaluation of the party's social policy) and the selection of the party leader (Halsema choosing Sap). Another criticism was that the focus in the campaign had been too much on government participation (Commissie Van Dijk, 2012). The position of the party executive with respect to the parliamentary group had to be strengthened.

GroenLinks has never had leaders without parliamentary experience: All of them have been MP for a number of years before they became leader of *Groen-Links*. Up until now the party has had 3 female leaders, who have been leading the party for nearly 14 out of 24 years – more than half of the party's history. In this sense, *GroenLinks* distinguishes itself strongly from the other Dutch parties, which generally are led by men. As we have seen, the way in which the leader is selected varies. In 1994 and 2012, the membership as a whole could appoint the party leader; in the years in between, it was the membership congress. However, two times the leaving party leader has put forward his or her successor: Rosenmöller chose Halsema, and Halsema chose Sap, even if their nominations had to be approved by the congress or the membership.

Party membership

Like most Dutch parties, *GroenLinks* lost members during the 1990s, declining from 16,000 in 1990 to less than 12,000 in 1996. Subsequently membership started to grow continuously – not always in parallel to its electoral development – to 23,500 by the end of 2007. It peaked at 27,500 in 2011 and declined to 22,500 in 2014 (Table 6.4). The penetration of *GroenLinks* within the electorate is relatively weak. The ratio of the number of party members to the electorate as a whole varied between 0.1 per cent and 0.2 per cent.

As in most parties, a majority of members did not take part in any party activity, as has become clear from membership surveys in 1992, 2002 and 2010 (Lucardie

Table 6.4 Party members, *GroenLinks*, 1990–2014

Year	Members (M)	Number of voters	M/E ratio (%)
1990	15,900		
1991	14,971		
1992	13,548		
1993	12,500		
1994	12,500	11,455,924	0.11
1995	12,000		
1996	11,700		
1997	11,873		
1998	13,821	11,755,132	0.12
1999	13,855		
2000	14,314		
2001	15,037		
2002	15,037	12,035,935	0.13
2003	18,469	12,076,711	0.15
2004	20,503		
2005	20,709		
2006	21,383	12,264,503	0.17
2007	23,490		
2008	21,410		
2009	20,324		
2010	20,961	12,524,152	0.17
2011	27,477		
2012	26,505	12,689,810	0.21
2013	22,953		
2014	22,435		

Source: www.dnpp.nl (Accessed on 5 March 2014).

and Van Schuur, 2010). Even so, a relatively large proportion (32 per cent in 1992, 42 per cent in 2010), claimed to devote at least an hour or more a month to *GroenLinks*, and 7 to 10 per cent spent more than 20 hours a month in the political arena. Most of these activities took place at the local level.

The significant growth of the membership of *GroenLinks* was accompanied by a rejuvenation of the rank-and-file, yet without reversing the steady rise in the average age: this increased from 43 to 47. In 1992, only 25 per cent of the *GroenLinks* members were older than 50; by 2002, this percentage has increased to 40 and in 2010 to 47. In fact, since the early 1990s, *GroenLinks* has been grey-ing, but less quickly than the Dutch population as a whole. The baby boomers still dominated the party in 2002 but no longer in 2010. The number of members with experience in one of the predecessor parties (CPN, EVP, PPR or PSP) had declined from 80 per cent in 1992 to 26 per cent by 2010. The share of women has increased little since 1992: from 34 per cent to 37 per cent in 2002 to 40 per cent in 2010. Most members in 2010 (almost 80 per cent) could be considered secular.

Education levels were quite high, as might be expected. More than half of the members held a university degree; one-third had completed tertiary education in a vocational college. Most respondents held a full-time job (54 per cent), few were part-timers (16 per cent) and hardly anyone was full-time housewife or home-maker. Most jobs are found in the public service and nonprofit sector; 40 per cent worked in healthcare, social services or education, only 8 per cent in the produc-tion industry and the same number in a commercial service. The type of work can be classified as 'professional and highly technical' (48 per cent) or 'managerial' (23 per cent).

The members may not much have changed in either socio-demographic or ideo-logical respect since the 1990s, but in one way, they have. In 1992, they regarded *GroenLinks* primarily as an opposition party, which tried to change society and the state in collaboration with social movements and through extraparliamentary action – which was completely in line with the PSP, PPR and CPN before the foundation of *GroenLinks*. In 2010, only a small minority still stuck to this strat-egy; a large majority, however, was in favour of taking part in government. The ideals of *GroenLinks* have remained largely (but not quite) the same, but they have to be realised through parliamentary action and sometimes by governmental participation, and no longer by extraparliamentary activity and opposition 'against the system'.

Relations with social movements

GroenLinks maintained informal but friendly relations with the new social move-ments, especially the environmental movement – which survived the 1980s better than the peace movement and the women's movement (Van der Heijden, 1992). At national elections, large environmental organisations like *Milieudefensie* (Defense of the Environment: the Dutch Friends of the Earth) and to a lesser extent Nature and Environment (*Natuur en Milieu*) tended to support *GroenLinks*, although not directly. Ties between *GroenLinks* and some environmental organisations were quite close. Marijke Vos, who was the first party chair (1990–1994) and would later become MP, had been a staff member of the Dutch Friends of the Earth. This organisation elected in 1995 as president a former *GroenLinks* MP, van Ojik (who would become party leader in 2012). Wynand Duyvendak was director of Nature and Environment before he became MP in 2002. The first party leader Beckers was elected president of Nature and Environment in 1994. In 2010, Liesbeth van Tongeren became MP, after having been director of the Dutch section of Green-peace in 2003–2010. Britta Böhler, senator from 2007 until 2011, was respectively secretary and chair of this section from 1994 until 2003.

Although most *GroenLinks* members seem to think positively of the trade unions, relations are not very close – yet within the parliamentary group, there always have been one or two members with roots in the trade unions. While the largest trade union federations in the Netherlands, the Federation of Dutch Trade Unions (*Federatie Nederlandse Vakbeweging* – FNV) and the National Christian Federation of Trade Unions (*Christelijk Nationaal Vakverbond* – CNV) try to stay aloof from party politics, their leaders and activists tend to show more sympathy for the Labour Party and the Christian Democrats (respectively) than for the smaller parties on the left.

Main challenges and opportunities for the future

In his comparison of *GroenLinks* with other European Green parties, Rüdig refers to Dutch 'Green exceptionalism' (2010, pp. 212–214). In most countries, the foundation of a Green party was part of a wider transition process from a social movement into a political party. Green parties were founded as so-called 'movement parties'. These parties retained for a long time many characteristics of a social movement, such as the emphasis on extraparliamentary activism, even when they had passed the threshold of representation. However, the history of *GroenLinks* was entirely different: the party did not originate in the social movements – although they certainly influenced its foundation – but was the result of a merger of four existing parties. As a result, the identity of *GroenLinks* was less determined by the social movements; from the outset, it was essentially a 'normal' party. This was visible in its organisational structure: grassroots democratic principles as the rotation of MPs, hard quotas for women and immigrants or collective leadership – usually present in the Green movement parties – were not implemented in *GroenLinks*. Building on the tradition of especially the CPN and the PPR, *GroenLinks* from the beginning took part in local government and from 1999 in provincial government. In the late 1990s, *GroenLinks* prepared itself for participation in the national government.

It is a paradox that *GroenLinks*, given its origins, was never able to pass the threshold of relevance, while other Green parties evolving from social movement did, like in Germany and Belgium. Participation in a coalition, however, depends on the configuration of the party system. Given the fragmentation of the Dutch party system, sometimes a relatively small party can play an important role in coalition formation. *GroenLinks* was not able to reach that far, even when the party got 10 or 11 seats in 1998, 2002 and 2010 and programmatically had moved to the political centre. This can be explained by the fact that there has consistently been a right-wing majority within the Dutch political system. After all, *GroenLinks* remains a radical party, which despite its increasingly moderate attitude is positioned left of the political centre and left of the Labour Party in the perception of the voters.

After the devastating electoral defeat in 2012, *GroenLinks* is further away from government participation as ever before in its history. In the opinion polls in spring 2014, the party is somewhat improving its position (six seats) but hardly benefiting from the present electoral collapse of the Labour Party, which is governing in a coalition together with the right-wing liberals. A European comparison shows that Green parties usually flourish when they do not have to deal with postmaterialistic and libertarian competitors of social-democratic, left-liberal or left-socialistic origin around them. An 'old-fashioned' materialist social democracy, which focuses on the workers, and a likewise materialist right-wing liberal party, supported by the old middle class, offers a Green party more opportunities to recruit new voters from a postmaterialist new middle class (Kitschelt, 1988). In the Netherlands, however, such left-liberal and left-socialist competitors do exist, and social democracy is no longer solidly materialist and working class. There is even a Party for the Animals (*Partij voor de Dieren*) represented in Dutch Parliament (two seats), which advocates animal rights. This implies that the opportunities for *GroenLinks* to expand electorally are rather limited. Seen from this perspective, it is likely that the 10 or 11 seats *GroenLinks* obtained in the past should be considered upside outliers, just as the 4 seats in 2012 are to be regarded as a downside outlier. Within the present competitive conditions on the left side of the Dutch party system, six or seven seats might be the 'natural' support of *GroenLinks*. This would mean that the party need not worry about falling below the level of representation and might even pass the threshold of relevance, at a certain point, given the volatility and fragmentation of the Dutch party system.

Note

1 The authors would like to thank Simon Otjes for his useful comments.

References

Commissie Van Dijk, 2012. *Terug naar de toekomst*. Utrecht: GroenLinks.
GroenLinks, 1989. *Verder kijken: Het verkiezingsprogramma van Groen Links*. Amsterdam: GroenLinks.
GroenLinks, 1990. *Statuten en huishoudelijk reglement Groen Links*. Amsterdam: GroenLinks.
GroenLinks, 1992. *Uitgangspunten van GroenLinkse politiek*. Amsterdam: GroenLinks.
GroenLinks, 1994. *Verkiezingsprogramma voor de Tweede Kamer en Europees Parlement 1994–1998*. Amsterdam: GroenLinks.
GroenLinks, 1998. *Verkiezingsprogramma 1998–2002*. Utrecht: GroenLinks.
GroenLinks, 2002. *Overvloed en onbehagen: Verkiezingsprogramma 2002–2006*. Utrecht: GroenLinks.
GroenLinks, 2009. *GroenLinks, partij van de toekomst*. Utrecht: GroenLinks.
GroenLinks, 2010. *Klaar voor de toekomst: Verkiezingsprogramma 2010*. Utrecht: GroenLinks.
GroenLinks, 2012. *Groene kansen voor Nederland: Verkiezingsprogramma 2012*. Utrecht: GroenLinks.
Halsema, F., and Van Gent, I., 2005. *Vrijheid eerlijk delen: Vrijzinnige voorstellen voor sociale politiek*. Utrecht: GroenLinks.
Kitschelt, H., 1988. Left-libertarian parties. Explaining innovation in competitive party systems. *World Politics*, 40, pp. 194–234.

Lucardie, P., 2014. *Democratic Extremism in Theory and Practice: All Power to the People*. London and New York: Routledge.

Lucardie, P., and Pennings, P., 2010. Van groen en rood naar groen en paars? De programmatische ontwikkeling van GroenLinks'. In: P. Lucardie and G. Voerman, eds, *Van de straat naar de staat? GroenLinks 1990–2010*. Amsterdam: Boom. pp. 149–162.

Lucardie, P., Van der Knoop, J., Voerman, G., and Van Schuur, W. H., 1995. Greening the Reds or Reddening the Greens? The Case of Green Left in the Netherlands. In: W. Rüdig, ed., *Green Politics Three*. Edinburgh: University of Edinburgh Press. pp. 90–111.

Lucardie, P., and Van Schuur, W. H., 2010. Meer vertrouwen in de staat dan in de straat? Een vergelijkende analyse van de opvattingen en achtergronden van de leden van GroenLinks in 1992, 2002 en 2010. In: P. Lucardie and G. Voerman, eds, *Van de straat naar de staat?* Amsterdam: Boom. pp. 163–175.

Lucardie, P., Van Schuur, W. H., and Voerman, G., 1999. *Verloren illusie, geslaagde fusie? GroenLinks in historisch en politicologisch perspectief*. Leiden: DSWO Press.

Lucardie, P., and Voerman, G., 2003. The Organizational and Ideological Development of Green Left. In: J. Botella and L. Ramiro, eds, *The Crisis of Communism and Party Change: The Evolution of West European Communist and Post-Communist Parties*. Barcelona: ICPS (Institut de Ciències Polítiques i Socials). pp. 155–175.

Lucardie, P., and Voerman, G., 2008. Amateurs and Professional Activists: De Groenen and GroenLinks in the Netherlands. In: E. G. Frankland, P. Lucardie and B. Rihoux, eds, *Green Parties in Transition: The End of Grass-Roots Democracy?* Farnham and Burlington, VT: Ashgate. pp. 157–174.

Lucardie, P., and Voerman, G., 2010. The Netherlands. *European Journal for Political Research*, 49(7–8), pp. 1095–1101.

Lucardie, P., and Voerman, G., 2012. The Netherlands. *European Journal for Political Research*, 51(1), pp. 215–220.

Pedersen, M.N., 1982. Towards a new typology of party life spans and minor parties. *Scandinavian Political Studies*, 5(1), pp. 1–16.

Rüdig, W., 2010. Verschillend sinds de geboorte. De leden van GroenLinks vergeleken met leden van andere groene partijen in Europa. In: P. Lucardie and G. Voerman, eds, *Van de straat naar de staat?* Amsterdam: Boom. pp. 163–175.

Van der Heijden, H. A., 1992. Van kleinschalig utopisme naar postgiro-activisme? De milieubeweging 1970–1990. In: J. W. Duyvendak, H. A. Van de Heijden, R. Koopmans and L. Wijmans, eds, *Tussen verbeelding en macht: 25 jaar nieuwe sociale bewegingen in Nederland*. Amsterdam: SUA (Socialistische Uitgeverij Amsterdam). pp. 77–98.

Voerman, G., 1995. The Netherlands: Losing Colours, Turning Green. In: D. Richardson and Chr. Rootes, eds, *The Green Challenge: The Development of Green Parties in Europe*. London and New York: Routledge. pp. 109–127.

7 Green parties in Finland and Sweden
Successful cases of the North?[1]

Niklas Bolin

Introduction

According to Inglehart (1997), value preferences among citizens in industrialised countries have shifted towards more postmaterialist values. Although issues as gender equality and abortion rights often are regarded as examples of important postmaterial concerns, perhaps environmental protection is the most politicised postmaterial issue. Given that the Scandinavian countries generally are characterised as being relatively postmaterialistic, we can regard them to be most-likely cases for Green party success. The empirical record, however, shows mixed results. While the Green wave in the 1970s and 1980s was manifested in parliamentary entrance in both Finland and Sweden, their Danish and Norwegian counterparts have failed to reach the same levels of success.

The relative failures of the Green parties in Denmark and Norway have been suggested to be a consequence of how established parties have managed to adjust to new demands from the electorate and, therefore, have successfully gained ownership over the environmental issue. In Denmark, new left parties, especially the Socialist People's Party, profited from the emerging salience of new politics issues (Schüttemeyer, 1989). At the same time, people within the Green movement had a hard time deciding whether or not to form a party. While the Danish Greens (*De Grønne*) was formed in 1983, they did not take part in elections until 1987. By then, other parties had adopted their core issues (O'Neill, 1997, pp. 371–372). In a similar manner, one could ascribe the relative lack of success for the Norwegian Greens (*Miljøpartiet de Grønne*) with how both the Socialist Left Party and the Liberal Party accommodated the environmental issue into their programmes, while a pure Green party did not materialise until as late as 1988 (Andersen, 1988; Aardal, 1990; O'Neill, 1997; Wörlund, 2005; Arter, 2012). It was not until the election of 2013 that the Norwegian Greens finally made it into the national parliament.

Both in Finland and in Sweden, Green parties managed to pass the threshold of representation by the 1980s. However, while the Finnish and Swedish Greens have many things in common, there are also important differences. Most apparently, while the Finnish Green League (*Vihreä liitto*, hereafter VL)[2] on several different occasions has been a part of the political executive, its Swedish counterpart, the

Green Party (*Miljöpartiet de Gröna*, hereafter MP) has up to now, despite a number of serious attempts, failed to enter the government.

In this chapter, I will follow the development of the VL and the MP, leaving their less successful Scandinavian sisters aside. The chapter is divided into four sections. First, I will present some information on their origins and development. Second, programmatic developments will be discussed. Third, some aspects of the organisational characteristics of the parties will be presented. In a final section, I conclude by discussing some of the main findings of the chapter. Here I discuss why the VL to some extent has been more successful than the MP. The section ends with some words on the parties' main challenges for the future.

Origins and development

Already in the 1970s, Green candidates were standing for election at the local level in both Finland and Sweden (Paastela, 2008, p. 64; Bolin, 2012, p. 106). However, it was not until the 1980s that party formation took place at the national level (see Table 7.3 at the end of this section). In Sweden, the MP was formed in 1981 whereas its Finnish sister, the VL, did not turn into a formal party until as late as 1988. Despite the VL's later appearance, it seems fair to say that it has been more successful than its Swedish counterpart. Both electorally and in terms of government experience, the VL outperforms the MP.

Although the environmental issue had gained in importance in Sweden since the 1960s, it was not until the nuclear energy issue was given priority at the end of the 1970s that a party embryo evolved. At the local level, Green parties had competed in elections since 1973. Many of these would subsequently join the MP as local branches. At the national level, the environmental issue was initially advocated the strongest by the Centre Party, but also to some extent by the Left Party. Two events, however, paved the way for the formation of a Green national party. First, while leading the first postwar government without the Social Democrats, the Centre Party failed to live up to its promise about not giving permission to load new nuclear power reactors. Despite the fact that the party had taken a pre-electoral, nonnegotiable, antinuclear stance, it found itself compromising on the issue with its coalition partners, the two nuclear power-positive parties, the Liberals and the Moderates.[3] This failure made the Centre Party less environmentally trustworthy in the eyes of the electorate.

Second, in the aftermath of the nuclear power plant accident on Three Mile Island in 1979, the Social Democrats accepted demands from the Centre Party and the Left Party to initiate a referendum on the future of nuclear power energy in Sweden. Essentially, the referendum asked the voters how fast nuclear power should be phased out. The result was disappointing for the antinuclear side, as their alternative was defeated with a very small margin. Moreover, the way the referendum had been designed was a source of frustration within the Green movement. Above all, the fact that the pronuclear side could not agree on how their vote choice should be formulated and consequently presented two different alternatives caused the environmentalists to raise objections. It was argued that now they had to fight not just one, but two sides (Vedung, 1991). However, while the referendum caused a lot of discontent, it also showed that there were many nuclear sceptics in Sweden. Furthermore, the actions taken by the established parties had made them less attractive.[4] This, together with the failures of the Centre Party, gave rise to a favourable political opportunity structure. In short, there was a demand for a Green party. As demand not does automatically turn to supply, someone needed to capitalise on the situation. Former liberal Member of Parliament Per Gahrton was the driving force behind this. Despite Gahrton's pronounced wishes to create a party where individuals were secondary, he inevitably became the undisputed frontperson. In its early years, the media even sometimes labelled it the Garthon Party.

The VL´s formative years differ somewhat from those of the MP. Green activism, as was the case also in Sweden, more and more became apparent in Finland during the 1970s. As early as 1976, an independent Green list was presented in the municipal election of Helsinki (Zilliacus, 2001). While there were many different social movements, some argue that a dispute between the landowners and Green activists over whether the lake of Koijärvi should be dried out or not can be seen as a formative moment for the Finnish Green movement (Konttinen, 2000; Paastela, 2008). Although the event did not turn out according to the wishes of the protesters, and even ended with legal sanctions for several Green activists, it showed that the fragmented Green movement could act collectively.

Since the quarrels over the lake persisted for over a year, it also gave the Green movement a lot of publicity (Paastela, 2008). However, partly because of restrictive rules regarding party formation and partly because of a widespread scepticism toward the party organisational form within the Green movement, it did not transform into a political party. Instead, the Green movement made use of the possibility stipulated by the Election Act to form a voters' association (Sundberg and Wilhelmsson, 2008). As such, it managed in the 1983 election to seat the first two Green parliamentarians. Still not competing as a formal party the success continued in the 1987 election (Table 7.1). With 4 per cent of the votes, they gained another two seats. By then, however, opinion within the Green movement somewhat had shifted toward a more positive view of party formation. Some important drawbacks of not being a party had been acknowledged. Without a formal party organisation, such things as selecting who should represent the party in debates and electoral campaigning was difficult (Paastela, 2008, p. 64). Perhaps even more importantly, only formal political parties are entitled to receive public subsidies in Finland (Sundberg and Wilhelmsson, 2008).

Given these circumstances, the Green movement finally decided to establish the Green League in 1987. However, it was not until a year later that the decision was taken to also register as a formal party.[5] Ever since, the party has consistently polled over 6.5 per cent in the parliamentary elections. The electoral success also has resulted in a rather strong blackmail position towards the other parties. After the 1991 election (the first after the creation of the party), the VL was invited by the Centre Party to discuss participation in the government (Table 7.2). However,

Table 7.1 Electoral results in Finland and Sweden (% votes and N seats)

Green League (Finland)			Green Party (Sweden)		
Year	Votes	Seats (share)	Year	Votes	Seats (share)
1983	*1.5*	*2 (1.0)*	1982	1.7	0 (0)
1987	*4.0*	*4 (2.0)*	1985	1.5	0 (0)
1991	6.8	10 (5.0)	1988	5.5	20 (5.7)
1995	6.5	9 (4.5)	1991	3.4	0 (0)
1999	7.3	11 (5.5)	1994	5.0	18 (5.2)
2003	8.0	14 (7.0)	1998	4.5	16 (4.6)
2007	8.5	15 (7.5)	2002	4.6	17 (4.9)
2011	7.3	10 (5.0)	2006	5.2	19 (5.4)
			2010	7.3	25 (7.2)

Note: Numbers in italics indicate the results of independent Green candidates.

Source: Author's own compilation.

Table 7.2 Government experience of the Green League in Finland

Year	Parties in government	VL portfolios
1995–1999	Social Democrats, National Coalition Party, Swedish People's Party, Left Wing Alliance	1 (environmental policy)
1999–2002	Social Democrats, National Coalition Party, Swedish People's Party, Left Wing Alliance	1.5 (environmental policy, health)
2007–2011	Centre Party, National Coalition Party, Swedish People's Party	2 (justice, labour)
2011–	National Coalition Party, Social Democrats, Left Wing Alliance, Swedish People's Party, Christian Democrats	2 (environmental policy, international development)

Source: Author's own compilation.

this time, they raised their demands a bit too high, and their offer was turned down. The VL was more successful after the 1995 election. Together with the Social Democrats, the National Coalition Party, the Swedish People's Party and the Left Wing Alliance, the VL entered the government as part of the so-called Rainbow Coalition. This was the first time the conservative National Coalition Party and a former communist party, the Left Wing Alliance, joined the same executive. Moreover, it was also the first time ever that a Green party made its way into national government (Jungar, 2000). As the first Green minister, party chairperson Pekka Haavisto was appointed the portfolio of environmental policy.

Entering government is not only associated with advantages. First, incumbency, more often than the opposite, costs votes (Strøm, 1990; Rüdig, 2006; Bolleyer,

2008). Second, coalition governance entails compromises. This potentially can bring internal disputes, typically between party leadership and grassroots, that are intrinsically policy seeking. In the case of VL, the decision to enter government was not undisputed. While Haavisto's fears were mostly directed towards being firmly associated with the left side, others were sceptic about the idea of sharing executive responsibility. Finally, it was decided to join the executive after a joint vote by the party council and the parliamentary group. A rather large majority voted in favour of governmental participation (31 'yes' votes against 6 'no' votes (Jungar, 2000, p. 279).

The electoral success of the VL continued in the 1999 election. Contrary to conventional wisdom, the party's vote share increased despite being in government. Therefore, the VL was invited to be a part of a second executive. This time, however, the party left the government after a dispute over nuclear energy (Sundberg and Wilhelmsson, 2008). Electorally, the party still polled well and gained a couple of new seats in the 2003 election. Yet, the party did not manage to get into government. However, after both the 2007 and the 2011 elections, the VL has been a part of the executive coalition (Sundberg, 2012). In 2007, the VL joined a government led by the Centre Party leader Matti Vanhanen while the 2011 election led up to the formation of the so called 'six-pack' government led by Prime Minister Jyrki Katainen of the National Coalition Party.

The Swedish Greens first ran for election in 1982 (Table 7.1). Although winning a fair amount of sub-national seats, the result was disappointing. Despite scoring above the national electoral threshold of 4 per cent in a couple of opinion polls, the MP only managed to win 1.7 per cent of the votes in its first election (Bolin, 2012, p. 109). The story repeated itself in 1985. However, in the 1988 'environmental election', the MP finally managed to make its national breakthrough (Bennulf, 1995). With 5.5 per cent of the popular votes, it gained its first 20 parliamentary seats. Due to the parliamentary situation, this result had very little impact. The Social Democrats, the postwar hegemonic party of Swedish politics, with the tacit support of the Left Party, held a parliamentary majority. The MP did not manage to gain any influence, even when the Left Party withdrew its support in 1990 and the MP was invited for negotiations with the Social Democrats. After demanding too much, the Social Democrats turned down their offer and once again relied on the support from the Left Party (Bale and Blomgren, 2008, p. 89).

After losing its parliamentary status in the 1991 election, the MP regained it in 1994 and has since then continuously kept it. Despite more than 20 years of parliamentary experience and a favourable position in the middle of the party system, the MP still lacks formal governmental experience. Apart from the above-mentioned discussion in 1990, the party has been involved in negotiations on two different occasions. After the 1998 election, the Social Democrats sought support to secure a majority. It had relied on the support of the Centre Party between 1995 and 1997, but after both of these parties had suffered electoral losses in 1998, the seats of the Centre Party would no longer be enough to ensure a majority. Moreover, a party leader shift to the right had made the Centre Party a less likely coalition partner. The Social Democrats initiated negotiations with the two most adjacent parties, the Left Party and the MP. While no portfolios were offered, a formal written agreement was struck that included cooperation in five specific policy areas: economy, employment, distributive justice, gender equality and the environment.

The story almost repeated itself in 2002. However, this time, the Greens publicly announced its aspirations of becoming a member of the executive. In the end, however, the party once again had to settle a deal without ministerial portfolios. This time, the three parties agreed on a far-reaching policy deal, a '121-point programme' but also an innovative semiexecutive arrangement. Inspired by the deal that the Social Democrats had with the Centre Party between 1995 and 1997, both the Left Party and the MP were allowed to position a number of political advisors within government offices (Bolin, 2004; Bale and Bergman, 2006).

It is surprising that the MP did not manage to get into government given that the party held the median legislator position both in 1998 and in 2002. However, as Aylott and Bergman (2011) have shown, intraparty politics weakened the bargaining position of the MP. Although the party leadership openly declared its wishes of being part of the government and had initial negotiations with the centre-right parties, they could not make it credible that they would enter a non-Social Democratic coalition. The rank-and-file had clearly shifted to the left during the last year and would not have supported a centre-right government.

Developments on the other side of the political spectrum prior to the 2006 election indirectly gave the Greens new hopes. With the emergence and electoral success of the 'Alliance for Sweden', a centre-right pre-electoral coalition consisting of the Moderates, the Liberals, the Centre Party and the Christian Democrats, the political landscape was rearranged (Aylott and Bolin, 2007). The long-lasting cooperation problems within the centre-right that had kept the MP out of government for many years, were now resolved. Instead, the left bloc now appeared fragmented. This caused the Social Democratic Party lead by Mona Sahlin to seal a pre-electoral agreement to enter a coalition with the MP and the Left Party once winning a majority. However, things did not turn out according to plan. Although the Alliance lost its parliamentary majority, the so-called red-green coalition did not manage to oust them from government (Widfeldt, 2011). Instead, a new parliamentary party, the anti-immigration Sweden Democrats, managed to get a hold of the important 'balance-of-power' position. However, this opened up new avenues for the MP since the Alliance needed parliamentary support from at least one opposition party. With pledges from both the governmental parties and the parties to the left not to engage in any cooperation with the Sweden Democrats, the Alliance sought to strike deals on a more or less day-to-day basis with some of the other opposition parties. In one area, immigration policy, the Alliance and the MP formalised a deal to circumvent the Sweden Democrats and deprive them from any actual impact (Dagens Nyheter, 2011a).

It could be argued that the VL has been more electorally successful. On average, the VL has attracted a significantly bigger share of the vote than its Swedish counterpart (6.2 per cent compared to 4.3 per cent). However, if we look at the seat distribution, the difference is lower. This is due to the more proportional electoral

Table 7.3 Chronology of the main developments of the Green parties in Finland and Sweden

Green League (Finland)		Green Party (Sweden)	
Year	Event	Year	Event
1983	First seats won in Eduskunta/ Riksdag	1981	Party formation
1987	Green League (VL) established	1982	Competed in first national elections
1988	VL reorganises into a formal political party	1984	Office of party spokespersons introduced
1991	Failure of coalition discussions with the Centre Party	1988	First seats won in Riksdag
		1991	Lost its seats in the Riksdag
1993	Party executive introduced	1992	Large organisational reform
1995	Entering the Rainbow coalition government	1994	Re-enters the Riksdag
		1998	Formal deal with the Social Democrats and the Left Party
1999	Rainbow coalition is prolonged		
2002	VL withdraws from government after dispute over nuclear power energy	2002	Deal renewed and expanded
		2007	Agreement with the Social Democrats and the Left Party to form a pre-electoral coalition
2007	VL returns to government		
2011	VL once again into government	2011	Formal agreement with the centre-right coalition government on immigration policy
2012	Haavisto gets through to the second round of the presidential election		

Source: Author's own compilation.

system in Sweden (Aylott, et al., 2013, p. 89). In Finland, the district magnitude differs rather substantially between constituencies, and the seat distribution for small parties is dependent not only on their overall electoral support but also on how votes are geographically spread (Paastela, 2002). Therefore, small parties with evenly distributed electoral support are underrepresented in the Finnish parliament at least compared to Sweden. Even though the VL's support is stronger in big cities its support still is rather evenly distributed, which is detrimental for their seat distribution.

However, the VL managed to obtain minister portfolios on several occasions while the MP has repeatedly fallen short of government participation. It may be due to the different cooperation traditions in the two countries. Swedish politics has, at least in the past, been dominated by one party, the Social Democrats. The party has always opted for governing alone even in a minority configuration, preferably with the tacit support from the Left Party (Aylott, et al., 2013).

In Finland, government is shared among the 'big three' (Paastela, 2008), the Social Democrats, the Centre Party and the National Coalition Party. In fact, two of these parties have been in each government since the mid-1970s. Most governments are not only majoritarian but also surplus governments (Raunio, 2011). In the past, this could be explained by the requirements of a qualified majority in some decision-making areas. However, this practice was shifted out in 1992. Jungar (2000) suggests that the VL's participation in the 1995 Rainbow Coalition could be understood partly from the willingness of the Social Democrats to include them in order to force the VL to share the responsibility of government and partly through the intraorganisational discussions of the VL. Although government participation was not uniformly supported within the VL, the decision was taken with a rather large majority.

While traditions and institutions frame the contextual, we cannot ignore the role of individual politicians. The VL leadership has been instrumental in governmental negotiations whereas the MP leadership has been less successful. At the same time, one should not underestimate the importance of the formalised deals between the Social Democrats, the Left Party and the MP. Despite not formally being part of the executive, these comprehensive written agreements surely gave the MP (and the Left Party) a real impact on everyday politics, especially after the 2002 election. Therefore, even if the MP fell short of its aim of executive representation, it came at least halfway.

Apart from national elections, both the VL and the MP have competed in a number of other elections. In European elections, both parties have been rather successful and have scored significantly better than in national elections. Finland held its first election to the European Parliament in 1996. The VL won 7.6 per cent of the votes, that is slightly more votes than in the national election two years earlier. This share was enough to win one seat. In the 1999 election, the party achieved its best electoral result up to date. With 13.4 per cent of the votes, the VL managed to get two seats. The party did not get as many votes in 2004 (10.4 per cent, one seat) or in 2009 (12.4 per cent, two seats). However, it was still comparatively more successful in European elections than in national ones.

This pattern also holds for the MP, with the exception of the 2004 election where the MP won 6 per cent of the votes and only one seat. In 1995, the party was the third largest party and won 17.2 per cent of the votes and four seats. In 1999, the party lost half of its seats after attracting 9.5 per cent of the votes. Finally, the MP managed to win two seats after polling 11 per cent of the votes in 2009. These results seem to fit nicely with the second-order election thesis according to which elections to the European Parliament are less important to both voters and media (Reif and Schmitt, 1980). This results in lower turnouts and an electorate more prone to vote for parties outside the mainstream. The position of the parties on European integration is also part of their success in European elections (see below).

In Finland, there are also direct presidential elections. Although this official position has lost in power since the new constitution of 2000, it still is an important political position (Raunio, 2011). In the 1994 election, the VL did not present a candidate. However, both in 1999 and 2004, former party chairperson Heidi

Hautala ran for the presidency, albeit with rather modest results ranging between 3 and 4 per cent of the votes. The 2012 presidential election present a complete different pattern. The VL candidate Pekka Haavisto, another former party chairperson, attracted almost 19 per cent of the votes in the first round and knocked out the candidates from the Centre Party and the Social Democrats. Although Haavisto's 37 per cent in the second round was far from the 63 per cent of Niinistö, the candidate for the National Coalition Party, it can still be regarded as a major success.

Ideology and policy positions

The VL and the MP have much in common when it comes to their political programmes. This comes as no surprise given the fact that they were born out of the same societal conflicts during the same period. At the very beginning, both parties were eager to position themselves beside conventional politics. Catchwords such as 'neither right, nor left' illustrated their position. This could be seen as a logical standpoint as many of those involved in the VL and the MP lacked prior political experience. Furthermore, among those who were prior party members, there was no clear dominance of former leftist such as in the case of the German Greens (Paastela, 2008, p. 63). However, different factors have made it hard to successfully defend this position.

In a comparative perspective, Swedish politics have been described as rather one-dimensional (Bergman and Bolin, 2011). For a long period, party politics was structured almost exclusively by the traditional economic left–right cleavage.[6] The advent of the MP can be regarded to some extent as a sign that this one-dimensional polity has ended. However, the left–right dimension is still by far the most important dimension, and it is hard for a party not to take a position on this dimension. Moreover, the media and other political parties position the MP in the 'left camp' because of their alliance with the Social Democrats and the Left Party on several different occasions. Available data also suggest that the MP leans towards the left. According to manifesto data (Volkens, et al., 2012), the party consistently placed to the left of all the centre-right parties.[7] Moreover, in three consecutive elections (1994, 1998 and 2002), the party also positioned itself to the left of the Social Democrats. Another way to estimate party position is to ask voters. According to the Swedish election studies, the MP, in the eyes of the voters, has slowly but steadily moved from the centre to the left. In the last election, the MP for the first time was considered to be to the left of the Social Democrats (Oscarsson and Holmberg, 2013, pp. 225–226).

Due to somewhat different traditions, the Finnish party system is less bipolar. The left–right dimension has also traditionally been the strongest, but other dimensions have now come into play. In addition, the tradition of large surplus majority governments has made cooperation between left and right less odd. Some observers characterise Finnish politics as pragmatic and consensual, at least more so than Sweden (Aylott, et al., 2013). Manifesto data support the idea that the Finnish party system is less bipolar than the Swedish one with less distance between parties. On average, the Left Wing Alliance and the Social Democrats are to the left of the centre-right parties. Similarly to the MP, the VL is positioned somewhat to the left.

Next to socio-economic issues, the issue of environmental policy and especially of nuclear energy, has been at the forefront of both the VL and the MP programmes. While the MP was created on the nuclear energy issue, the VL has had to deal with the nuclear issue in government on several occasions. Promises of no further nuclear power developments was crucial to accepting the governmental invitation in 1995; the decision in 2002 to build a fifth nuclear power plant made the VL withdraw from the executive. The parties' emphasis on environmental issues is also highly visible in their election manifestos. According to the manifesto data, this issue is by far the most salient issue. In 1983, the Greens of Finland (still not formally a party) devoted about 40 per cent of their manifesto to environmental issues.[8] The corresponding figure for the MP in 1988 was 38 per cent. Since then, both parties have significantly reduced the share of statements related to environmental issues. In the 2011 manifesto, the VL dedicated 14 per cent and the MP 23 per cent of their manifesto to environmental issues. However, the issue is still the most salient issue in their respective manifestos, and they are the party emphasising this issue the most in their respective countries.

The analysis of their election manifestos reveals other important similarities. Besides the environmental issue, the two most emphasised issues are those of welfare state expansion and social justice. However, contrary to the environmental issue, these issues are shared with other parties, predominately of the left. While the evidence here is not clear-cut, this further fuels an assessment of the Green parties in Finland and Sweden as being predominately left leaning.

Finally, the VL and the MP differ on at least one issue: the EU. The MP was from the beginning anti-EU, whereas the VL has been more ambivalent. Many within the VL were initially sceptical to join the EU, but the party decided that it should abide by the results of the 1994 referendum on EU accession. Furthermore, the VL also formally stood by the decision to join the third stage of the European Monetary Union as its party council and parliamentary group jointly decided to vote for this in the parliament (Jungar, 2000, p. 260). The MP, on the other hand, advocated for a long time for Sweden to withdraw from membership (Elander, 2000). However, in 2008, the party decided to change its position after a party referendum was held (Rosén Sundström, 2011). Nevertheless, the party is still composed of many EU sceptics. Moreover, the EU succession demand was not officially removed from the party programme until the adoption of a new programme at the 2013 party congress (Miljöpartiet, 2013).

Structure and organisation

Most Green parties have roots in social movements and frequent individual links, but formal ties are rare (Pogunktke, 2006). This seems to be the case for the VL and the MP. Social movements were important sources for both personnel and ideas in their formative years. Nevertheless, there is no formal link to organised interests as there is no mention of them in party statues or programmes.

Both the VL and the MP have made profound changes in their party organisation since they started as alternative organisations in the 1980s. While the MP was formed in 1981, the VL only formally became a party in 1988 when its congress decided to collect the signatures needed to register as a party according to Finnish law (Paastela, 2008, p. 65). Despite its later genesis, it seems fair to say that the VL more rapidly evolved into an ordinary party organisation. Both parties have kept some (but not all) of their alternative character.

Green parties do not only have new ideas about policies; most often their organisations have also been guided by scepticism towards how politics is made within the established parties. Above all, there is often an intrinsic aversion against hierarchy and power concentration. Although this manifested itself differently in the VL and the MP, there are also important commonalities.

The VL introduced unorthodox organisational structures, but the MP initially stretched power dispersion even further. Like in most other parties, the highest body of the VL and the MP is the congress. Between congresses, which are held annually, the VL and the MP had different ways of running their organisation. The highest decision-making body in the MP was the Party Council. Oddly enough, this body was not elected by the congress but consisted of delegates elected by the regional branches. However, the MP also had no less than four different committees elected by the congress, parallel to the Council. These bodies were formally preparatory bodies; in reality, they handled the day-to-day activities of the MP. Among these, the Political Committee became important, as it was responsible for both developments of political programmes and the media contacts. The principle of power dispersion also guided the MP in their conception of party leadership. When the MP was formed in 1981, a decision was taken that the party should not have a party leader. Instead, daily responsibilities were circulated among individuals in the different committees. In the Political Committee, a convener was selected for a period of three months.

The VL initially also had a Party Council beside the congress. This council was elected in an annual meeting and consisted of delegates from the basic units of the party, which reflected the decentralised character of the organisation.[9] A declaration voted by the congress in 1988 stated that elected candidates were primarily responsible, not to the party, but to their own 'understanding and conscience' (Paastela, 2008, p. 65). Hence, in practice, power within both the VL and the MP was thoroughly dispersed.

Initially both parties also had noticeable restrictions on mandates (incompatibilities and rotation). The first principle manifested itself through a clear separation of the central party and the parliamentary party. In the VL, there was an informal rule that the chairman could not be a member of parliament (Paastela, 2008). Likewise, the MP had a clear separation between the parliamentary group and the two party spokespersons that were introduced in 1984.

These principles did not work very well with the realities of politics. Without a leader, the MP instantly experienced difficulties in attracting attention from the media. The resistance toward leadership was still strong within the party. As a compromise, the Political Committee in 1984 chose to introduce quasi-leadership when they decided that the party should have two spokespersons, one woman and one man. These persons should not lead the party but only communicate its message. It is also indicative that the introduction of spokespersons was not codified in the party statues until 1992 (Miljöpartiet, 1992; Bolin, 2012, pp. 115–116).

Later, parliamentary entrance made the parties aware of the inherent difficulties of power dispersion. This was amplified by the incompatibility rules that prohibited MPs to hold positions of trust within the party. Problems appeared when representatives of the parliamentary branch and the central party organisation expressed different opinions. Since day-to-day politics takes place in parliament, it was hard for leaders of the central party organisation to be fully informed about the latest events. In addition, they were not always in agreement with the opinions expressed by the parliamentarians. Hence, during the MP's first period in parliament, many raised demands for organisational change. The loss of parliamentary status in 1991 was a catalyst. In 1992, the party decided on new statues and introduced more of an ordinary party organisation. The four-committee system was abandoned, and a party executive was introduced (15–19 members). In the new statutes, the Party Council was also demoted and was no longer the second body of the party. Instead, it should 'provide support' for both the party executive and the parliamentary group. Moreover, some of the party's more rigid prohibitions, such as the incompatibility rules, were shifted out (Miljöpartiet, 1992; Burchell, 2008).

The VL also made changes to its organisation after parliamentary experience. In 1993, a new body, the party executive, was introduced. This body initially consisted of eight persons, the party chairperson included. Today there are 12 members elected for 2-year periods by the congress. The informal practice of disqualifying MPs from party chair has also been abolished when MP Pekka Haavisto was elected chairperson in 1993 (Paastela, 2008; Vihreä liitto, 2012).

However, some initial restrictions are still valid. In both the VL and the MP, there are still restrictions regarding being in more than one of the central party bodies at the same time. In the VL, one could not be member of both the executive and the council. Furthermore, the same person cannot be a member of the executive for more than two consecutive terms. This holds also for the party chair (Vihreä liitto, 2012). Similar rules are stipulated in the MP statues. It is forbidden to hold a seat in any of the party's national bodies for more than nine consecutive years. Limits also apply to nonparty offices such as ministers (12 years), MPs (3 terms) and MEPs (2 terms) (Miljöpartiet, 2011). Finally, both parties have rules regarding gender equality. While the MP stipulates a general 60–40 rule, that is, there should be at least 40 per cent of each sex in all party bodies at the national level, the rules of the VL demand practically the same thing. In addition, the MP always elects one female and one male spokesperson.

To some extent, party leadership selection processes also show signs of an egalitarian party culture. The common practice in established parties, especially

Table 7.4 Party leaders of the Green parties in Finland and Sweden, 1984–2014

Green League (Finland)		Green Party (Sweden)		
Period	Party chair	Period	Female spokesperson	Male spokesperson
1987	Kalle Könkkölä	1984–1985	Ragnhild Pohanka	Per Gahrton
1987–1991	Heidi Hautala	1985–1986	Ragnhild Pohanka	Birger Schlaug
1991–1993	Pekka Sauri	1986–1988	Eva Goës	Birger Schlaug
1993–1995	Pekka Haavisto	1988–1990	Fiona Björling	Anders Nordin
1995–1997	Tuija Brax	1990–1991	Margareta Gisselberg	Jan Axelsson
1997–2001	Satu Hassi	1991–1992	*Vacant*	Jan Axelsson
2001–2005	Osmo Soininvaara	1992–1999	Marianne Samuelsson	Birger Schlaug
2005–2009	Tarja Cronberg	1999–2000	Lotta Nilsson Hedström	Birger Schlaug
2009–2011	Anni Sinnemäki	2000–2002	Lotta Nilsson Hedström	Matz Hammarström
2011–	Ville Niinistö	2002–2011	Maria Wetterstrand	Peter Eriksson
		2011–	Åsa Romson	Gustav Fridolin

Source: Author's own compilation.

in Sweden, is to select party leaders by consensual decisions. In the VL and the MP, party congresses are given several candidates to choose from. Furthermore, as illustrated by the recent leadership changes, the outcome of these contests is often hard to predict (Table 7.4). The 2011 vote for the VL chair gave Ville Niinistö a clear majority, but the competitive character of the selection could not be disputed as the incumbent competed and was beaten by no less than three candidates (Hufvudstadsbladet, 2011). In the selection of spokespersons for the MP the same year, the outcome of the vote for the female post was, until the very end, undecided. Even though the nomination committee had proposed the aspiring spokesperson Åsa Romson, a significant minority of the congress delegates voted for the parliamentary economic spokesperson (Svenska Dagbladet, 2011).

The VL and the MP have both had rather steady increases in their membership numbers, but they remain rather small (Table 7.5). Both parties have had a rather large influx of new members in recent years. In the Swedish case, it is evident that parties normally attract new members during election years. Hence, the MP set an all-time high in 2010 when the party counted more than 15,000 members for the first time. In the following years, the party lost some members, and today, it has less than twice as many members as its Finnish sister party, which reported more than 8,000 members at the end of 2012.

Table 7.5 Party membership of the Green parties in Finland and Sweden

Year	Green League (Finland)		Green Party (Sweden)	
	Members	*Members/electorate*	*Members*	*Members/electorate (per cent)*
1981			1,979	
1982			5,800	0.09
1983			2,500	
1984			3,000	
1985			4,000	0.06
1986			5,000	
1987			5,500	
1988			8,500	0.13
1989			8,000	
1990	875		7,600	
1991			6,900	0.11
1992	1,000		6,400	
1993	1,100		5,300	
1994	1,000		6,500	0.10
1995	1,158	0.03	5,600	
1996			6,950	
1997	1,140		7,500	
1998	1,081		7,900	0.12
1999	1,165	0.03	7,285	
2000	1,472		6,918	
2001	1,658		6,701	
2002	1,621		8,011	0.12
2003	1,728	0.04	7,483	
2004	2,193		7,178	
2005	2,393		7,249	
2006	2,713		9,543	0.14
2007	3,115	0.07	9,045	
2008	3,760		9,110	
2009	4,413		10,635	
2010	4,576		15,544	0.22
2011	7,400	0.17	14,600	
2012	8,034		13,400	

Note: Members per electorate are based on the numbers of registered voters according to the IDEA Voter turnout database.

Sources: VL membership: Mickelsson (2007) and Vihreä liito (1994–2012). MP membership: Bergman and Bolin (2011), *Dagens Samhälle* (2010), *Dagens Nyheter* (2011b), *Dagens Opinion* (2013).

Main challenges for the future

The Finnish and the Swedish Green parties have had non-negligible success both in terms of votes and influence. In a comparative perspective, they belong to the group of the most successful Green parties in Europe (see Chapter 11 in this volume). Furthermore, their prospects for the future look bright. As the environmental issue in general and the climate issue in particular are destined to be important questions in a foreseeable future, there are good reasons to expect that these parties can play important roles in their respective countries.

Although the VL and the MP look similar on most aspects, the MP has been surpassed by its younger, eastern neighbour the VL. It may only be a matter of time before the MP experiences government participation, but there will be some time before it gains the same experience as the VL. Being in government for the first time brings not only benefits but also potential challenges such as being held accountable for government decisions, increased media pressure and internal strife (Deschouwer, 2008). While the VL went through this and survived, the MP is only about to experience these challenges.

There also seem to be a well-grounded argument that a rookie hardly can make full use of its executive position the first time. At the same time, there are reasons not to exaggerate the importance of governmental participation. Especially in cases of broad executive alliances, like in the Finnish case, it might be hard for small junior partners to obtain any substantial influence. This is best illustrated by the fact that the VL, despite its inclusion in the executive, has been unsuccessful in its attempts to influence Finnish nuclear energy policy. In 2010, the parliament voted 'yes' to a proposition to permit the building of two new nuclear power plants despite VL's presence in the executive. Unlike in 2002, the party chose to stay in the executive this time (Ylä-Anttila, 2012). In this sense, perhaps the most important challenge for the VL is to make further inroads in the electoral market in order to become one of the leading parties in a system where there are more parties inside than outside government.

So what are the prospects for the MP to gain executive experience in the near future? One important aspect is the party's positioning towards the long-lasting bloc politics of Sweden. The MP has long been keen to emphasise its lack of affiliation. However, few would dispute that the party leans more to the left. The formalised cooperation with the Social Democrats and the Left Party from 1998 to 2006 made this evident.

After the failure of the 2010 pre-electoral coalition, the party has once again tried to fuel its maverick character. Former spokesperson Maria Wetterstrand, for instance, revealed in an interview how the MP aimed for the weakening of the once almighty Social Democrats (Nilsson, 2010). Furthermore, in 2011, the Greens struck a deal with the centre-right government over the country's immigration policies. Although this was primarily a deal to ostracise the anti-immigration party the Sweden Democrats, it also signalled a willingness to cooperate with parties on the right side of the political spectrum. Moderate Prime Minister Fredrik Reinfeldt has at least implicitly invited the Greens to cooperate on other topics on several occasions. The MP is closer to the centre-right in policy areas such as free schools and labour-market regulation. However, it still seems that a coalition with the Social Democrats would be the most likely pattern if the MP holds the balance of power. It remains open if such a governmental coalition would be a pure leftist coalition including the Left Party or a cross-bloc agreement with one or two of the minor parties of the centre-right. It seems fair to say that the MP is now more open to being part of a government. In this sense, we should maybe expect the MP to become a little bit more like the VL in terms of pragmatism.

Notes

1 The author would like to thank Nicholas Aylott, Torbjörn Bergman, Svante Ersson and Jan Sundberg for valuable comments on previous versions of the manuscript.
2 In the English version of the party's statutes, available at its website, the party name is only given in Finnish, Swedish and Sami. On the same site, an English version of the party programme is also available. The name of the document is 'The Greens of Finland's Statement of Principles'. In the English literature, the Finnish Green party has been given different names. While it occasionally, mostly in the early literature, has been referred to as the Green Association (for example Paastela, 1989; O'Neill, 1997), it seems as if the Green League is now the most commonly used translation of *Vihreä liitto*.
3 In a famous episode of Swedish politics, Torbjörn Fälldin, the Centre Party leader and aspiring prime minister, clarified the Centre Party's position on government participation and the nuclear power issue in a parliamentary debate a couple of months ahead of the 1976 election: 'No government portfolio can be so desirable that I am willing to compromise with my beliefs' [my translation].
4 With 38.7 per cent of the votes, the antinuclear alternative was distanced by less than 0.5 per cent to the winning alternative supported by the Social Democrats and the Liberals. The third option (actually option no. 1), put forward by the Moderates, received less than 19 per cent of the votes.
5 Actually, two different parties were registered. However, the Ecology Party never became a significant party as it only managed to win one seat in the national parliament in 1995 before it ceased to exist in 2003.
6 For a more explicit discussion of the content and development of this cleavage, see Bergman and Bolin (2011, p. 254).
7 Party positions on the traditional left-right scale is estimated using the RiLe formula in the CMP database, downloaded from <https://manifesto-project.wzb.eu/>.
8 That is the 'Environmental protection: positive' category of the CMP database.
9 Unlike many other parties, basic units are not necessarily equivalent with local branches. Instead, these could be local as well as nation-wide societies (Paastela, 2008, p. 66).

References

Aardal, B., 1990. Green politics: A Norwegian experience. *Scandinavian Political Studies*, 13(2), pp. 147–164.
Andersen, J. G., 1988. Miljøpolitiske skillelinjer i Danmark. *Politica*, 20(4), pp. 393–413.
Arter, D., 2012. 'Big Bang' elections and party system change in Scandinavia: Farewell to the 'enduring party System'? *Parliamentary Affairs*, 65(4), pp. 822–844.
Aylott, N., and Bergman, T., 2011. When Median-Legislator Theory Fails: The Swedish Greens in 1998 and 2002. In: R. W. Andeweg, L. De Winter and P. Dumont, eds, *Puzzles of Government Formation: Coalition Theory and Deviant Cases*. London: Routledge. pp. 44–64.

Aylott, N., Blomgren, M., and Bergman, T., 2013. *Political Parties in Multi-Level Polities. The Nordic Countries Compared*. Basingstoke: Palgrave Macmillan.

Aylott, N., and Bolin, N., 2007. Towards a two-party system? The Swedish parliamentary election of September 2006. *West European Politics*, 30(3), pp. 621–633.

Bale, T., and Bergman, T., 2006. A taste of honey is worse than none at all? Coping with the generic challenges of support party status in Sweden and New Zealand. *Party Politics*, 12(2), pp. 189–209.

Bale, T., and Blomgren, M., 2008. Close but no cigar? Newly governing and nearly governing parties in Sweden and New Zealand. In: K. Deschouwer, ed., *New Parties in Government: In Power for the First Time*. London: Routledge. pp. 85–103.

Bennulf, M., 1995. Sweden. The Rise and Fall of Miljöpartiet de Gröna. In: D. Richardson and C. Rootes, eds, *The Green Challenge: The Development of Green Parties in Europe*. London: Routledge. pp. 128–145.

Bergman, T., and Bolin, N., 2011. Swedish Democracy: Crumbling Political Parties, a Feeble Riksdag and Technocratic Power Holders? In: T. Bergman and K. Strøm, eds, *The Madisonian Turn: Political Parties and Parliamentary Democracy in Nordic Europe*. Ann Arbor: University of Michigan Press. pp. 251–293.

Bolin, N., 2004. *Samarbete, stöd eller opposition? Majoritetsbyggande i Skandinaviska parlament*. [unpublished] MA-thesis. Umeå universitet.

Bolin, N., 2012. *Målsättning riksdagen: Ett aktörsperspektiv på nya partiers inträde i det nationella parlamentet*. Ph.D. Umeå universitet.

Bolleyer, N., 2008. The Organizational Costs of Public Office. In: K. Deschouwer, ed., *New Parties in Government: In Power for the First Time*. London: Routledge. pp. 17–44.

Burchell, J., 2008. Sweden: Miljöpartiet de Gröna. In: E. G. Frankland, P. Lucardie and B. Rihoux, eds, *Green Parties in Transition: The End of Grass-Roots Democracy?* Farnham and Burlington, VT: Ashgate.

Dagens Nyheter, 2011a. Regeringen och MP i 'historisk överenskommelse'. *Dagens Nyheter*, 3 March 2011.

Dagens Nyheter (Fridolin, G., Wallner, A., Öberg, H.), 2011b. 250.000 svenskar ska ta fram Miljöpartiets politik. *Dagens Nyheter*, 30 October 2011.

Dagens Opinion (Ardalan Samini), 2013. 1200 medlemmar lämnar MP. *Dagens Nyheter*, 28 January 2013.

Dagens Samhälle, 2010. Partierna växer efter medlemsras. *Dagens Samhälle*, 20 February 2010.

Deschouwer, K., 2008. Comparing Newly Governing Parties. In: K. Deschouwer, ed., *New Parties in Government: In Power for the First Time*. London: Routledge. pp. 1–16.

Elander, I., 2000. Towards a Green welfare economy? The Green Party in Sweden since the 1998 parliamentary election. *Environmental Politics*, 9(3), pp. 137–144.

Hufvudstadsbladet, 2011. Brakseger för Ville Niinistö. *Hufvudstadsbladet*, 12 June 2011.

Inglehart, R., 1997. *Modernization and Postmodernization: Cultural, Economic, and Political Change in 43 Societies*. Princeton: Princeton University Press.

Jungar, A.-C., 2000. *Surplus Majority Government: A Comparative Study of Italy and Finland*. Uppsala: Acta Universitatis Upsaliensis.

Konttinen, A., 2000. From grassroots to the cabinet: The Green league of Finland. *Environmental Politics*, 9(4), pp. 129–134.

Mickelsson, R., 2007. *Suomen puolueet: Historia, muutos ja nykypäivä*. Tampere: Vastapaino.

Miljöpartiet de gröna, 1992. *Party Statutes*. Stockholm: Miljöpartiet de gröna.

Miljöpartiet de gröna, 2011. *Party Statutes*. Stockholm: Miljöpartiet de gröna.

Miljöpartiet de gröna, 2013. *Party Programme*. Stockholm: Miljöpartiet de gröna.

Nilsson, T., 2010. Den verkliga Wetterstrand. *Fokus*, 2010/11, 19 March 2010.

O'Neill, M., 1997. *Green Parties and Political Change in Contemporary Europe*. Farnham and Burlington, VT: Ashgate.

Oscarsson, H., and Holmberg, S., 2013. *Nya svenska väljare*. Stockholm: Norstedts.

Paastela, J., 1989. Finland: the 'Vihreät'. In: F. Müller-Rommel, ed., *New Politics in Western Europe: The Rise and Success of Green Parties and Alternative Lists*. Boulder, CO: Westview Press. pp. 81–86.

Paastela, J., 2002. Finland. *Environmental Politics*, 11(1), pp. 17–38.

Paastela, J., 2008. The Finnish Greens: From 'Alternative' Grass-Roots Movement(s) to Governmental Party. In: E. G. Frankland, P. Lucardie and B. Rihoux, eds, *Green Parties in Transition: The End of Grass-Roots Democracy?* Farnham and Burlington, VT: Ashgate.

Pogunktke, T., 2006. Political Parties and Other Organizations. In: R. S. Katz and W. Crotty, eds, *Handbook of Party Politics*. London: Sage. pp. 396–405.

Raunio, T., 2011. Finland: Moving in the opposite direction. In: T. Bergman and K. Strøm, eds, *The Madisonian Turn: Political Parties and Parliamentary Democracies in Nordic Europe*. Ann Arbor: University of Michigan Press. pp. 112–157.

Reif, K., and Schmitt, H., 1980. Nine second-order national elections – A conceptual framework for the analysis of European election results. *European Journal of Political Research*, 8(1), pp. 3–44.

Rosén Sundström, M., 2011. The Swedish Green party: From alternative movement to third biggest party. *Environmental Politics*, 20(6), pp. 938–944.

Rüdig, W., 2006. Is government good for Greens? Comparing the electoral effects of government participation in Western and East-Central Europe. *European Journal of Political Research*, 45(supplement 1), pp. S127–S154.

Schüttemeyer, S. S., 1989. Denmark: De Grønne. In: F. Müller-Rommel, ed., *New Politics in Western Europe: The Rise and Success of Green Parties and Alternative Lists*. Boulder, CO: Westview Press. pp. 55–60.

Strøm, K., 1990. A behavioral theory of competitive political parties. *American Journal of Political Science*, 34(2), pp. 565–598.

Sundberg, J., 2012. Finland. *EJPR Political Data Yearbook*, 51(1), pp. 96–102.

Sundberg, J., and Wilhelmsson, N., 2008. Moving from movement to government. The transformation of the Finnish Greens. In: K. Deschouwer, eds, *New Parties in Government: In Power for the First Time*. London: Routledge. pp. 121–136.*Svenska Dagbladet*, 2011. Maktskiftet klart i Miljöpartiet, 22 May 2011.

Vedung, E., 1991. The Formation of Green Parties, Environmentalism, State Response, and Political Entreprenurship. In: J. A. Hansen, ed., *Environmental Concerns: An Interdisciplinary Exercise*. London: Elsevier Applied Science. pp. 257–274.Vihreät liitto, 2012. *Party Constitution*. Helsinki: Vihreät liitto.

Volkens, A., Lacewell, O., Lehmann, P., Regel, S., Schultze, H., and Werner, A., 2012. *The Manifesto Data Collection: Manifesto Project (MRG/CMP/MARPOR)*. Berlin: Wissenschaftszentrum Berlin für Sozialforschung (WZB).

Widfeldt, A., 2011. The Swedish parliamentary election of 2010. *Electoral Studies*, 30(3), pp. 584–587.

Wörlund, I., 2005. Miljöpartier i Sverige och Norge. In: M. Demker and L. Svåsand, eds, *Partiernas århundrade: Fempartimodellens uppgång och fall i Norge och Sverige*. Stockholm: Santérus. pp. 253–278.

Ylä-Anttila, T., 2012. Does your child still vote for the Greens? The Green league and the environment in the Finnish parliamentary elections 2011. *Environmental Politics,* 21(1), pp. 153–158.

Zilliacus, K. O. K., 2001. 'New politics' in Finland: The Greens and the left wing in the 1990s. *West European politics*, 24(1), pp. 27–54.

8   Green parties in Southern Europe (Italy, Spain, Portugal, and Greece)

Roberto Biorcio

Introduction

The European elections of 2014 have highlighted and partly accentuated the problems of Green parties in Southern Europe. Discontent with the policies of national governments decided in line with the European Union has grown. The votes of the governing parties have fallen to levels not seen in recent years; protests against the traditional parties have developed, and votes for the Populist right parties has increased. Monica Frassoni, co-chair of the European Green Party, underlined that, 'while it is positive that the turnout in these elections has not fallen below the level of 2009 (and is now even a little bit higher), it is obviously worrisome that a number of political actors will enter this new parliament with an anti-European, antidemocratic agenda' (European Green Party, 2014). The lists of the left who seek to give representation to the protest movements have had good results. In Greece, the *Syriza* list headed by Tsipras prevailed with 27 per cent of the vote. In Spain, the 'We Can' list (*Podemos: Por la Democracia Social*), which seeks to give representation to the movement of the *indignados*, has reached 8 per cent of the votes. The *Izquierda Plural* list has also obtained a significant increase of the votes (10 per cent).

The Green parties, which had been founded in the 1980s in many European countries, were not simply institutional projections of the demand for environmental protection; rather, they were a more complex phenomena. In fact, they have not merely expressed widespread concerns about the environment, nature and animals; they have also sought to reaffirm demands put forward by the new movements described by Melucci (1996). A distinctive feature of the Greens in all countries has been their endeavour to present themselves as 'party-movements' (or 'nonparty parties') and to work for the renewal of politics and political representation.

In Southern European countries, several Green parties were founded in the 1980s; they have tried to build new forms of participation and political organisation from the experiences and values of the movements: 1982 in Portugal, 1984 in Spain, 1986 in Italy and 1989 in Greece.

The events affecting these parties highlighted, not only the opportunities, but also the problems and considerable difficulties encountered in their attempts to

construct new forms of participation and political organisation based on the experiences and values of the environmental movement.

In the recent elections of 2014, the Green parties of Southern Europe succeeded
only in a very limited extent to capture the widespread criticism of European
policies, of the choices in favour of austerity and of neoliberal globalisation.
Moreover, they have not been able to offer convincing alternatives with respect to
the political parties that govern their countries.

The difficulties of Green parties in Southern Europe

The factors behind the rise of Green parties in Southern Europe are analogous to
those that have fostered the spread of this 'family' of parties in other countries
since the 1980s. These factors are:

1)   the severity of the environmental crisis and its effects;
2)   changes in social values, with the growth of 'post materialist' values (Ingle-
     hart, 1977);
3)   the growing inability of party systems to channel social demands and to main-
     tain an adequate level of legitimation and
4)   the availability, after the social mobilisations of the 1960s and 1970s, of
     resources and organisational skills for political activism on issues that were
     previously marginal.

The Green parties of Southern Europe have encountered greater problems and difficulties than their counterparts in other countries and have remained in a situation
of relative political marginality.

Table 8.1 shows evidence of the difficulties for these parties in acquiring electoral support and their narrow share of seats obtained in the European elections
between 1984 and 2014. The percentages of votes for the Green parties have
invariably been very low in elections for which they presented independent lists.

Table 8.1 Electoral results, European elections 1984–2009 (% votes and N seats)

Country	1984		1989		1994		1999		2004		2009	
	%	N	%	N	%	N	%	N	%	N	%	N
Italy		0	3.8	3	3.1	3	1.8	2	2.5	2	3.1*	0
Spain	0.6	0	1.4	0	0.2	0	1.5	0	43.5*	2	2.5*	1
Portugal		0	14.9*	1	11.2*	0	10.3*	0	9.1*	0	10.6*	0
Greece		0	1.1	0	0.3	0		0	0.7	0	3.5	1
Total Seats		0		4		3		2		4		2

Note: * In coalition.

Source: Author's own compilation.

In addition, very few Green candidates have been elected to the European Parliament. However, the table shows marked differences in electoral results between the Italian Greens and the others. In the past ten years, however, the difficulties have increased for all the Green parties in Southern Europe. This chapter seeks explain why the Greens have found it so difficult to consolidate in this part of Europe.

There are three possible explanations for the difficulties encountered by the Green parties in Southern Europe. The first relates to the difference among countries in the importance given to environmental issues. The second – partly connected with the first – concerns the differences in the levels of involvement of citizens in environmental movements and associative networks. The third relates to the problems that Southern European countries have faced during the latest economic crisis and the austerity policies adopted by the European Union, which led to increased unemployment and affected the incomes of most households.

Identifying environmental issues as a priority for political action is an indirect indicator of the saliency of the issue in public opinion and therefore of the Green parties' chances of success. At the end of the 1980s, the environmental issue appeared less important in Southern European countries compared to other European countries (Table 8.2). Comparatively, Italy was the country in which more importance was given to environmental issues. Twenty years later, concern for environmental issues has on average decreased in Europe, partly because of the development of other economic and social problems (unemployment, inflation, crime, crisis of welfare systems, etc.). Nevertheless, the differences between southern and central-northern European countries are still significant. In 2013, environmental issues almost disappear of citizens' priorities in Southern Europe.

The same differences can be observed if we consider the levels of participation in associations committed to the objectives that characterise Green parties.

Table 8.2 Important issues: Environment protection (%)

Country	1989	2008	2011	2013
Netherlands	34.1	9.6	8.9	4.0
Germany*	17.6	5.6	10.7	14.1
United Kingdom	13.4	6.0	5.6	5.4
Belgium	13.0	5.8	7.7	5.3
France	4.6	7.7	9.1	4.7
Italy	11.5	2.4	5.2	0.9
Greece	6.3	6.4	2.7	0.2
Spain	3.9	1.5	1.1	0.7
Portugal	1.8	1.3	0.2	0.2

* West Germany until 1989; reunited Germany thereafter.

Source: Eurobarometer 1989, 2008, 2011, 2013.

Table 8.3 Participation in activities of environmental or peace organisation

Country	% participation
Belgium	5.8
Germany	3.9
United Kingdom	3.8
France	3.3
Netherlands	2.9
Italy	2.7
Spain	2.1
Greece	0.7

Source: European Social Survey 2002.

Participation in environmental and pacifist associations in Southern Europe is relatively lower than it is in central-northern Europe (Table 8.3).

The lesser importance given to the problem of the environment, and the lower participation in environmental associations, may partly explain the greater difficulties encountered by Green parties in gaining electoral success in Southern Europe. However, other explanations should also be considered, tied to the histories of political systems and the political polarisations that have characterised them. The relations between environmentalist objectives and the main political cleavages in different national contexts must also be considered. Accordingly, we analyse the specific histories of, and the problems encountered by, the Green parties in Italy, Spain, Portugal and Greece.

Italian Greens: Electoral performance and participation in power

The Italian Greens have followed the classic lifecycle of small parties arising from a single-issue social movement (Müller-Rommel, 2002). The new party originated from the environmental movement, enjoyed increasing support in the second half of the 1980s, took the institutional status of a party and sent representatives first to parliament and then to government (Biorcio, 1999, 2002).

Political ecology had emerged in Italy in the 1970s. The most important experience had been the antinuclear movement, which included groups and militants from the most varied backgrounds of mobilisation from the 1960s and 1970s (Diani, 1990). The first national assembly for the constitution of the Green Lists in Italy was organised in December 1984. The Green Lists were presented in 12 regions in the 1985 regional elections and obtained 648,832 votes. In November 1986, a national organisation of a federative type was formally set up, the Federation of the Green Lists (*Federazione delle Liste Verdi*), in which 70 local lists initially took part. In the 1987 general election, support increased to 2.5 per cent

Table 8.4 Electoral results of the Italian Greens, Lower Chamber, 1987–2013 (% votes and N seats)

Year	%	N	
1987	2.5	13	
1992	2.8	16	
1994	2.7	11	
1996	2.5	14	
2001	2.2	8	
2006	2.1	15	
2008	3.0*	0	*Sinistra Arcobaleno*
2013	1.8*	0	*Rivoluzione* Civile

Note: * In coalition.

Source: Author's own compilation.

at the national level (969,534 votes for the Lower House). Thirteen Green deputies and two senators entered parliament for the first time (Table 8.4).

In the second half of the 1980s, a context highly favourable to the strengthening of the Federation of the Green Lists and the institutionalisation of the new party arose in Italy. After the Chernobyl disaster, Italian public opinion considerably increased its concern with environmental issues: the programme to construct new nuclear power stations; the closure of polluting factories; the use of pesticides in agriculture; restrictions on urban traffic; the management of industrial and urban waste and hunting.

In order to mobilise citizens and to overcome the resistance raised by the main Italian political parties against binding decisions on environment protection, the Greens, together with environmental associations, promoted various referenda at both the national and local levels. The most important results were achieved with three referenda against the development of Italy's nuclear programme, which were approved by the majority of voters and led to the abandonment of the programme.[1] Both the Italian Greens and the environmental organisations consolidated in those years (Rhodes, 1995). In the same period, new Green Lists were created at the local level: those belonging to the National Federation amounted to 219 in 1988 and to 420 in 1990.

At the end of the 1980s, the possibility of creating a strong Green political actor also exerted a powerful attraction on the activists and members of other political movements. A number of parliamentary deputies elected in the lists of *Democrazia Proletaria* and the *Partito Radicale* left their respective parties and founded the Green Rainbow (*Verdi Arcobaleno*) political group.

Two competing Green lists stood for the 1989 European elections, and they both obtained good results. The *Federazione delle Liste Verdi* received 3.8 per cent of votes and the *Verdi Arcobaleno* almost 2.4 per cent. The overall result – 6.1 per cent of votes – represented the highest level of consensus hitherto attained in Italy. In December 1990, the *Verdi Arcobaleno* merged with the *Federazione delle Liste Verdi* to form the *Federazione dei Verdi*. New activists who were part of the institutions (parliament, regional, provincial and municipal councils) joined the Green Party and gave greater impetus to the party's institutionalisation by imposing better definition of its organisational rules and leadership.

During the 1980s, the Greens had seen their support increase further because of the crisis of public trust in the traditional Italian parties. However, the crisis of the Italian political system provoked during the 1990s by judicial investigations into corrupt practices by the political parties found the *Federazione* undergoing a phase of difficult political and organisational consolidation. It prevented stabilisation of the electoral scores obtained at the end of the 1980s. In the 1992 general elections – the last to be held with the proportional system – electoral support for the Greens fell to 2.8 per cent, less than half the level reached three years previously. In this phase, the political weight of environmental issues had greatly diminished, and other themes dominated the political agenda: the fight against corruption, institutional reforms, the state's budget deficit, unemployment, increased fiscal pressure and the problems caused by the growth of non-European Community immigration.

The new, largely majoritarian, electoral system introduced in 1993 for local and national elections induced the Greens to join the centre-left coalition. The *Federazione dei Verdi* was thus able to leave its position of relative extraneousness to the competition between right and left. A leader of the Italian Greens, Francesco Rutelli, was elected mayor of Rome in June 1993 with the support of a centre-left coalition.

Having allied with the centre-left parties, the *Federazione dei Verdi* could now compete for direct participation in local and national government. However, the 1994 elections were won by the centre-right coalition headed by Berlusconi. The Greens obtained only 2.7 per cent of the votes and were unable to overcome the 4 per cent threshold necessary to obtain seats in parliament. However, 18 Greens who had stood as candidates for the centre-left coalition were elected in as many constituencies. After the elections, the Greens actively participated in mobilisations promoted by the trade unions and the centre-left parties against the centre-right government. The Greens joined a new centre-left coalition (*l'Ulivo*) headed by Romano Prodi, which won the 1996 elections. The Greens entered the government with the minister of the environment, Ronchi, and three under-secretaries. Participation in the national government assumed a much stronger symbolic nature through inclusion of the *Verdi* in the existing political system. Their presence in the government ensured media visibility for all ministerial initiatives on environmental protection. However, the autonomous political role of the Greens diminished because they were unable to enlarge their electoral base.

The Greens were again allocated the ministry of the environment in the next centre-left government headed by D'Alema, which took office in 1998. Prodi founded a new party (the *Democratici*), which included both the mayor of Rome,

Rutelli and the president of *Lega Ambiente*, the largest Italian environmental association.

The alliance at the national and local levels with the centre-left coalition had greatly increased the party's presence in governance. Participation in the national government and numerous regional, provincial and municipal administrations enabled the distribution of numerous posts in the councils, committees, boards and institutions controlled by local governments. Internal struggles intensified when the Green lists were presented for elections. However, the *Federazione*'s political presence and visibility were diminished by its confinement within a heterogeneous and often quarrelsome coalition. In fact, the Greens were mandated to take initiative on only one issue – and over which they were no longer able to claim monopoly. New problems and difficulties were created for the Greens by Italy's participation in the North Atlantic Treaty Organisation (NATO) offensive against Serbia that begun on 24 March 1999: a group of activists launched a public appeal ('Greens against the War') and left the *Federazione*.

The results of the European elections of June 1999 represented a clear defeat for the Greens. Votes for the party, in fact, fell to the lowest level ever recorded (1.8 per cent). The Greens suffered particularly from the electoral competition raised by the *Partito Radicale* and the new formation of the *Democratici*, which had been supported by the *Lega Ambiente*. Moreover, the *Federazione* lost a great deal of support from voters active in environmental and pacifist movements and in associations for the defence of civil rights. The loss of votes was interpreted as a failure due to the policy pursued by *Federazione* as part of the government.

An extraordinary national assembly of the Greens reckoned the defeat and elected as federal president Grazia Francescato, a former spokesperson of the World Wide Fund for Nature (WWF) International. The electoral defeat, moreover, had reduced the power of the group of Green leaders that had originated from the new left.

In the new centre-left government headed by Amato, the Greens were allocated the ministry of agriculture and the ministry for community policies, but they lost the ministry of the environment. The decision aroused protests and divisions in the *Federazione dei Verdi*.

However, refounding the party did not increase the electoral support for the Greens, who obtained only 2.8 per cent of votes in the 2001 general elections, in which the centre-left lost to the centre-right coalition headed by Berlusconi. The Greens elected eight deputies and nine senators, and they returned to the opposition together with the *Ulivo* coalition.

In the 2004 European elections, the *Verdi* obtained 2.5 per cent of votes and elected two MEPs (one of whom was Monica Frassoni, chairperson of the parliamentary group of the European Greens).

The centre-left coalition renewed itself in February 2005. It took the name of *L'Unione* and once again selected Romano Prodi as its leader. The *Verdi* participated in the coalition as founding members. The Green Pecoraro Scanio stood in the primaries held to elect a candidate for the prime ministership: he came fifth with 2.2 per cent of the votes.

The electoral law was changed for the 2006 general elections and reinstated a proportional system with a majority bonus. The Greens, again in alliance with the centre-left, presented its own list for the Chamber of Deputies, which received 2.1 per cent of votes and elected 16 deputies. The centre-left won the elections and in the new government headed by Prodi, Pecoraro Scanio was appointed minister of the environment.

In the 2008 general elections, the Greens joined the Left Rainbow coalition (*Sinistra–l'Arcobaleno*) together with the parties of the left: *Rifondazione Comunista, Comunisti Italiani* and *Sinistra Democratico*. By obtaining only 3 per cent of votes, the coalition had no member of parliament elected.

For the 2009 European elections, the *Federazione dei Verdi* joined the *Sinistra e Libertà* list and obtained only 3.1 per cent of the votes. None of its candidates was elected to the European Parliament.

The *Federazione dei Verdi* participated in the 2013 Italian general elections within a new left coalition, called *Rivoluzione Civile*, which supported judge Antonio Ingroia's candidacy for the prime ministership. The coalition, which also included the *Federazione della Sinistra* and *Italia dei Valori* obtained only 2.2 per cent of the votes, and none of its candidates was elected to parliament.

The Italian Greens led by Bonelli participated in the European elections of 2014 as an independent party, gathering only 0.8 per cent of the vote. The majority of the voters who criticised the policies of the European Union and supported the objectives proposed by the environmental mobilisations supported the 5 Star Movement led by Beppe Grillo, who got more than 21 per cent of the vote.

Italian Greens: Organisation and programmatic developments

The formation of the Federation of the Green Lists in Italy had been supported by only a few ecologist associations but had obtained widespread support from several components of the environmentalist movement. The movement ensured the new political subject major symbolic resources, providing the electoral proposals with a connotation of a universalistic type. Commitment to the new political subject was motivated, not only by their ability to express the demand for environmental defence, but also by the proposal for a new style of political action (Biorcio, 1988). The image of the new political subject appeared both alternative and nonaggressive. It gained voters' approval and sympathy.

Commitment to the Green Lists' formation came from both activists from the environmentalist associations (often growing up in less politicised environmental organisations) and those who had already experimented (or at least supported with their votes) the attempt to construct new parties in the 1970s. Over half of the activists who had taken part in the foundation of the Green Lists had voted for the Radical Party or *Democrazia Proletaria* in previous years.

The large majority of the activists founding the Green Lists had previous experience in political and social activity within various movements and associations. Their commitment to the environmentalist movement and the Green Lists had been preceded by experience of militancy in various movements, associations and parties. In most cases, militant experiences had been multiple. Over half of the militants had been active in political parties or groups (52 per cent); almost two-thirds of them (63 per cent) had taken part in the activities of movements, groups and associations; a third (34 per cent) had had both experiences. In the initial phase of the formation of the Federation of the Green Lists, there were no great differences between motivation for taking part in the environmental movement and that for taking part in the new political formation. The new political formation was seen as part of a wider 'Green Archipelago'.

The institutionalisation process of Italian Greens – with the development of their own organisational model – was difficult and complex (Biorcio, 1999). The new political formation sought a way to organise and make decisions, which avoided the alternative of reproposing the traditional party model or getting lost in local problems and sectionalism (Farro, 1990, pp. 187–189). On the other hand, the Greens also had to deal with the problem of differentiating from other small parties, which were both allies and rivals: the Radical Party and *Democrazia Proletaria*.

Three phases may be distinguished in the institutionalisation of the Greens, from 1986 to 1999. In the first phase (1986–1989), the Green Lists essentially took on the task of representing environmentalist initiatives in the institutional setting (without however being exclusive representatives), as a service structure ('a technical tool') for the Green movement. In this phase, the real organised subjects of political initiative remained the environmentalist associations present at national level, which had multiplied initiatives at political level. The participation of the Green Federation was no different from that of the environmentalist movement. The incentives put forward by the Greens' informal leadership were exclusively of a collective nature (identity and pursuit of goals) (Panebianco, 1986). The Lists' principle of 'biodegradability' – together with that of a rotation of those elected – was also supposed to assure the environmentalist archipelago that they would not follow the classic development of political organisations with an increase in importance of material incentives and status (Panebianco, 1986). In this phase, both the Italian Greens and the environmental associations were strengthened.

In the second phase (1990–1995), there was a progressive growth and strengthening of an autonomous political-organisational structure of the Green Lists that – although linked to the environmentalist movement – sought to establish a direct relation with the entire community for the transmission of instances and demands not only of an environmentalist nature. Specific forms of participation emerged, with independent attitudes to membership of the Green Federation differentiated from, and sometimes competing with, the environmentalist associations.

In the third phase (1996–1999), the Green Federation tended to assume the traditional forms of a political party, with a widening of the range of policies chosen and a greater commitment to the themes of peace, minority rights and social inequalities. Much commitment was devoted to the organisational strengthening of the Green Federation, which had always been marked by fragile, uncertain structures, a lack of clarity in decision-making procedures and a lack of strong leadership. The forms of recruitment were transformed. Previously members had only joined local lists or regional units of the Greens, and no party membership campaigns were set up. In 1996, the national membership campaign for the Green Federation was started, with the promotion of specific campaigns assigning precise goals for regional federations. Membership rose from a few thousand to over 23,000 in 1999. The financial resources of the Green Federation also increased considerably, attributed in Italy in proportion to the number of representatives in Parliament. There were greater opportunities to distribute selective incentives (individual material advantages or status). There was, however, a decrease in the strength of collective incentives for the participation of Green activists (incentives linked to identity and the pursuit of shared values). This trend depended on the lesser identification of the Green Federation with the environmentalist movement and its ideal values.

In a context of a crisis of mass parties, the Italian Greens rediscovered some traditional forms of political organisation. Nevertheless, this strengthening was only apparent. While membership increased, active grassroots participation decreased. The Italian Greens tended increasingly to take on the physiognomy of a party of fellow travellers, with a few grassroots militants and reduced electoral support.

Nor did the Green Federation achieve wide consensus from the environmentalist movement. In the 1980s, the ecologist associations had promoted and largely supported the birth of the Green political subject, while in the 1990s they had frequently confirmed their difference and autonomy and established relations with various political interlocutors. Even fewer of those committed to pacifist associations, civil rights movements, consumer associations, youth centres and feminist groups voted for the Greens.

The defeat of the Green Federation in the 1999 European elections brought about a general questioning of the political identity, organisation structures and forms of participation. The Federal Council of the Greens took stock of the defeat and the serious political crisis. Their spokesperson Manconi resigned, and the Political Office was dissolved. The national and regional administrative organs of the *Federazione* were dissolved. The extraordinary Assembly of the Green Federation decided to set up the constituent process of a new political subject. Direction of the constituent process was entrusted to a promotional committee led by Grazia Francescato, the former spokesperson of the European WWF.

The Green leaders attempted to enact a radical refoundation of the *Federazione*, an attempt to return to a *statu quo ante*, with a return to a grassroots democratic model, a better relationship with environmental nongovernmental organisations (NGOs), more radicalism, a less conventional form of action and an ecological worldview as the main features of the party's identity. The mobilisation of the no-global movement (from Seattle to Genoa and Florence) was assumed as a reference for party initiatives, in the perspective of strengthening grassroots activism. Nevertheless, the return to a kind of *statu quo ante* was quite impossible. Since 1994, the survival of the Greens in parliament has been totally dependent on the possibility of joining the centre-left alliance. In addition, the experience of government at national, regional and local levels, had deeply transformed the goals, attitudes and preferences of Green leaders and cadres. Besides, the light electoral support for the *Federazione* had weakened its bargaining power within the coalition.

The *Federazione*'s refoundation process, and the bargaining for the distribution of single-member constituency seats for the general elections in 2001, provoked sharp conflicts and divisions among the Greens. A new faction took power in the party, formed by the opponents to Manconi's leadership (led by Pecoraro Scanio), by opponents to the Kosovo war (led by Cento) and by environmental NGO activists (led by Francescato). The group of historical leaders coming from the new left and the antinuclear movement did not support the party's and parliamentary roles.

In December 2001, the national assembly of the Greens elected a new president, the former minister Alfonso Pecoraro Scanio. Some of the historical leaders of the party (including Masconi, Ronchi, Mattioli and Scalia) left the *Federazione*. After the mobilisations against the military intervention in Iraq, the inscription 'For Peace' and the rainbow colours of the pacifist movement were included in the party's symbol. The Green Federation took part in the centre-left coalition, but in the last year, it has taken up positions that are often more radical and more left-wing. Pecoraro Scanio favoured a positioning on the political left, while various leaders and moderate sympathisers left the *Federazione* to join other centre-left parties. Even after its refoundation, the party was unable to regain broad consensus within the environmental movement.

The electoral failure in 2008 provoked Pecoraro Scanio's resignation from the chair of the Greens and the convening of an extraordinary party congress. Grazia Francescato was elected national spokesperson with 60 per cent of the votes, while a minority proposal calling for closer alliance with the Democratic Party (PD) was defeated.

After the defeat in the 2009 European elections, the national assembly of the *Federazione dei Verdi* elected Bonelli as its spokesperson, and he put an end to its involvement with the political project of *Sinistra Libertà*. However, a group of party members, including Francescato, formed a new environmental association and in 2010 took part in the foundation of *Sinistra Ecologia Libertà*, the political formation led by Vendola that participated in the centre-left coalition in national elections of 2013.

The Spanish Greens

The formation of a Green party in Spain was a long and complex process; they had to overcome numerous difficulties and conflicts. In Spain, the Green political movement has taken the form of diverse political parties often confined to only local or regional contexts (Cabal, 1996). A national party, The Greens (*Los Verdes*), was founded in November 1984.

The environmentalist movement began in Spain towards the end of the 1960s in the context of the strong mobilisation that had developed in the last phase of the Franco dictatorship. After Franco's death in 1975, numerous local and regional environmentalist groups were created. Although attempts to unify the Green movement were unsuccessful, the periodic meetings and assemblies favoured the drafting of manifestos that would steer the movement's future development (Fernández, 1999). During that period, environmentalists had high expectations that the Socialist Party (PSOE) would undertake a major reform of economic and social policies. However, when the PSOE took power in 1982, it set environmental concerns aside because they were in conflict with the need to promote economic development and to create employment.

Disappointed by the PSOE's policies, some sectors of the movement decided to form a Spanish Green party after the 1983 electoral success of the German *Grünen*. In May of that year, encouraged by the leader of the *Grünen* Petra Kelly, a group of environmentalists assembled in Tenerife signed a manifesto for the foundation of a Spanish Green Party able to pursue a joint strategy with the other European Green parties. There thus began a process that concluded in 1984 with foundation of the *Los Verdes* party and its enrolment on the register of political parties kept at the Ministry of the Interior.

The party was structured on the model of the German Greens, and it shared the principles and features of Green parties in other European countries. This new political actor wanted to be different from the other Spanish parties. It sought to advance participatory democracy, and it rejected the formation of a bureaucratic and hierarchical structure dominated by a leader (Espinoza, 1995, p. 120).

Los Verdes obtained recognition from the European Green Alliance. From June 1987 onwards, Spanish Greens were elected councillors in various cities and provinces and deputies in various regional parliaments. In the 1989 general elections, however, the Greens obtained the disappointing result of only 1.1 per cent of the votes. The electoral results were also highly unsatisfactory in subsequent years, especially in the general elections. The Spanish electoral system favours large parties and hinders the consolidation of new small ones.

In Catalonia, the Green Alternative (*Alternative Verda* – AV) had been in existence since 1983. It had initially subscribed to the creation of *Los Verdes* but immediately thereafter split off from the Spanish Green party. The new party, moreover, competed for votes with the other small parties operating in various regions that defined themselves as 'Green' or 'environmentalist' and that pursued programmes that combined social and environmental themes.

At the national level, the successful creation of a strong Green party was hampered by the presence of *Izquierda Unida*, a leftist political formation founded in 1986. The presence of two 'alternative left' parties created numerous difficulties and strong competition for electoral consensus (Richardson and Rootes, 1995).

The confusion of potential voters was heightened by the propensity of the Greens to change their name from one election to the next according to shifts in strategies or alliances. Further problems were caused by internal conflicts due to personal rivalries.

At the beginning of the 1990s, the Spanish environmentalist movement entered into profound crisis marked by numerous disputes and conflicts, which led to the creation of several Green parties in some regions. The executive officers of the *Los Verdes* party sought to counter the tendency towards fragmentation by turning *Los Verdes* into a confederation of regional parties. Consequently, at the 1995

Table 8.5 Electoral results of the Spanish Greens, Lower Chamber, 1996–2011 (% votes and N seats)

Year	%	N
1996	0.2	0
1989	0.8	0
1993	0.8	0
1996	0.3	0
2000	0.5	0
2004	42.6*	2
2008	0.2	0
2011	6.9*	0

Note: * in coalition with PSOE; ** in coalition with *Izquierda Unida*.

Source: Author's own compilation.

Congress of Granada, the *Confederación de los Verdes* was founded. However, the results obtained in the general elections were once again very modest (Table 8.5). The *Confederación de los Verdes* was one of the founding members the European Green Party at its Rome convention of 2004.

In 2004, the *Confederación de los Verdes* ran for election in coalition with the PSOE. It contributed to the latter's victory and had two candidates elected to the national parliament. In 2007, the agreement with the PSOE broke down, and the Confederation stood on its own account in the 2008 elections, but again with very disappointing results. Some members of the party, however, had formed alliances with other local political groups on the left. Moreover, *Izquierda Unida* had included some Green candidates on its lists, although they failed to gain election.

The main problem that has often weakened the Spanish Greens is a tendency to fragmentation due to irreconcilable differences in strategy and leadership styles. The differences have been exacerbated by disputes on alliances with the various parties on the left, and particularly with *Izquierda Unida*, the PSOE or the local lists of the alternative left (Larios, 2006). The Spanish Greens have always been aware of the necessity to unify the formations that relate to the environmentalist movement. However, the attempts made have not been successful.

In 2010, López de Uralde, president of Greenpeace, established, with the support of various environmentalist associations, a foundation – called *Equo* – which sought to create a new political party inclusive of all the Spanish Greens, but also for the alternative left at the local and regional levels. The new party aims in particular to obtain the support and commitment of the Spanish environmentalist movement.

The majority of the Green parties belonging to the Confederation (13 out of 16) decided to undertake another type of political project in September 2010. Together with other groups, they participated in founding the new *Equo* Party. Committed to policies on the environment but also social equity, the new Green party obtained

0.9 per cent of the votes in the general election of 2011. It succeeded in gaining one seat in parliament thanks to the *Compromís-Equo* coalition, which stood for election in Valencia. The Confederation and some party members ran for the 2011 elections in coalition with *Izquierda Unida*. The list obtained a considerable success, increasing its votes from 3.8 per cent in 2008 to 6.9 per cent, and it had 11 deputies elected. Nevertheless, no Green candidate was successful.

In May 2012, the European Green Party (EGP) decided that the *Confederación de los Verdes* could no longer be a member of the EGP because 'it does not meet the requirements in terms of internal democracy'. The decision was taken based on a formal request by 13 members of the Confederation, which had united with *Equo*.

The *Confederación de los Verdes* maintained its electoral alliance with *Izquierda Unida*. The latter, after having 11 deputies elected in the 2011 elections, achieved good results also in the 2012 regional elections held in Andalusia and Asturias.

In the elections for the European Parliament in 2014, Initiative for Catalonia Greens (*Iniciativa per Catalunya Verds* – ICV) ran on the *Izquierda Unida,* in the coalition with *Izquierda Plural*. One MEP, Raül Romeva, was elected from ICV and joined the Green Group in the European Parliament. Even the *Confederación de los Verdes* participated in the 2014 European elections on the *Izquierda Plural* list.

The environmental movement and the role of the left in Portugal

During the first years of democracy, a large number of protests based on environmental issues have developed in Portugal. After 1974, environmental problems have worsened because of economic development policies. Environmental protests decreased in the 1980s but have increased again since the beginning of the 1990s, with a more extensive involvement and participation of civil society. These fluctuations are closely associated to the process of consolidation of democracy (Mansinho and Schmidt, 1994).

The Green Party of Portugal – originally called *Movimento Ecologista Português – Partido 'Os Verdes'* – was founded in 1982 by a group of activists who wanted to foster the formation of an environmentalist movement. The foundation of the Green Party was supported by the Portuguese Communist Party and by some of its activists. Immediately after its foundation, the *Os Verdes* Party created regional groups that promoted actions on local problems in order to heighten public ecological awareness.

In recent decades, especially after Portugal joined the European Union (EU), the country has faced some major problems that could cause social conflicts between socio-economic development and environmental protection.

The attention of politicians and observers of the environmental movement has focussed on formal and organised groups, neglecting those spontaneous and informal, grassroots movements that are formed in the course of social conflicts on

Table 8.6 Electoral results of the Portugal Greens, Lower Chamber, 1987–2011 (% votes and N seats)

Year	%	N
1987	12.2*	2
1991	8.8*	2
1995	8.6*	2
1999	9.0*	2
2002	7.0*	2
2005	7.6*	2
2009	7.9*	2
2011	7.9*	2

Note: * In coalition with CDU.

Source: Author's own compilation.

environmental issues. These basic movements are forms of activism and of commitment to the environment beyond the traditional ways of protest, because they are much more radical in their demands and in their mode of action than formally organised movements. The basic movements are distinguished by their composition, the level of commitment of the participants and their duration (Kousis, 2001). The state (in its various levels) is the organ that is most often challenged during the protests, along with the interests of private industries. The nature of popular protests ('Nimby') reveals its geographical localism and focus on the protection of local interests.

Since its foundation, the *Os Verdes* Party has had a close relationship with the Portuguese Communist Party, and it has always participated in general elections as part of the same coalition, the Unitarian Democratic Coalition (CDU). The Portuguese Greens have systematically had two parliamentarians elected to the national assembly and numerous mandates in local assemblies (Table 8.6). In 1987, the *Os Verdes* Party joined the European Green Coordination and then became a member of the European Green Party.

Its close links with the Communist Party have aroused numerous criticisms because the Portuguese Greens have never stood on their own for elections. On some issues, the official position of the two parties diverge: the Portuguese Communist Party is in favour of the use of nuclear energy, while the Portuguese Greens are against it.

In the 1990s, the environment was regarded as one of the main problems of the country after problems like drugs, unemployment, health and poverty. In the current context of economic crisis, and due to the effects of austerity measures, concern for the environment seems to have almost disappeared for the Portuguese public opinion (Table 8.2). In the 2014 European elections, the Green Party of Portugal was still presented in a coalition with the party Communist who got 12.7 per cent of the votes, but the Greens did not get MEPs elected.

The Greens in Greece and the effects of the economic crisis

In Greece, environmentalist movements first developed during the decline of the authoritarian regime. The formation of Green parties came about only in subsequent years, and it encountered many problems and difficulties. Ecological groups emerged after 1974, when democracy was re-established in the country after the fall of the Ioannis Metaxas dictatorship. Various local groups, often of small size, which had fought against the dictatorship, continued their action on environmental issues. The emergence of the Socialist Party (*Pasok*) and its rapid ascent to power obstructed the organisation of the ecological movement and its engagement in politics. The Socialists absorbed a large number of activists, who were confident in the party's ability to promote policies to protect the environment. However, after 1982, when the *Pasok* headed the government, these expectations were disappointed. Various groups of activists formed to promote campaigns and initiatives on environmental issues. More structured groups were formed, as well as numerous informal ones that campaigned on issues of local interest, but without clear programmes and identity. Frequent proposals were made to establish alliances, and some groups ran in elections (Demertzis, 1995). At the end of 1980s, the Greek environmentalists participated for the first time in the European elections with the Federation of Ecologists Alternatives (FEA). The list managed to have a representative elected to the national parliament, obtaining 0.8 per cent of valid votes. In 1992, the FEA collapsed, and other small parties, which unsuccessfully ran in the European and national elections, took its place. The attempt in 1999 to create a political representation of the Greens by the Green Politics group (*Prassini Politiki*), which had been endorsed by the European Greens, was also unsuccessful. It is only in 2002 that a new political actor – the Green Ecologists (*Oikologoi Prasinoi*) – was created thanks to a merger of various environmentalist movements and groups (Botetzagias, 2003).

In the 2007 elections, the party obtained 1.1 per cent of the votes and 2.5 per cent in 2009 (Table 8.7). However, it failed to achieve the required 3 per cent threshold to have a deputy elected. In the 2009 European elections, the party obtained 3.5 per cent and for the first time won a seat in the European Parliament.

Table 8.7 Electoral results of the Greens in Greece, Lower Chamber, 1987–2013 (% votes and N seats)

Year	%	N
2007	1.1	0
2009	2.5	0
2012 (May)	2.9	0
2012 (June)	0.9	0

Source: Author's own compilation.

In recent years, the Greek Green party has actively encouraged popular mobilisation to oppose the austerity policies imposed on Greece by the EU. In the general elections of May 2012, *Oikologois Prasinoi* received 2.9 per cent of votes, although the percentage fell to 0.8 when the elections were repeated in the following month.

The European Union has put a great deal of pressure on Greece to make cuts, fiscal reforms and extensive privatisation to avoid defaulting on its repayments of loans. The Troika claims that the legislation is necessary for a loan to be given so that Greece can pay its debts. This risks to cause irreparable damage to social welfare if drastic cuts are pushed through. The people of Greece have responded angrily and *en masse* to this severe threat to the fabric of their society.

The Green Party of Greece calls for much more effective and fairer alternatives to austerity measures, including investment in the Green New Deal and meaningful financial reform. The Greens have developed a strong polemic against the two main parties in power. However, in the recent European elections, the Green Greeks have got only 0.9 per cent of the vote. Citizens' protests weakened the ruling parties but rewarded the *Syriza* list headed by Tsipras.

Conclusion

The construction of Green parties with an important role in the political system has encountered more difficulties in Southern European countries than in other countries. In Italy, Spain, Greece and Portugal, parties belonging to the European Green Party (EGP) have few members and occupy a marginal role in national politics.

The lesser importance given to environmental issues in Southern Europe is undoubtedly responsible for this situation, but other factors and processes have also impeded the construction of Green parties and the conquest of electoral support. Three factors seem to have been crucial:

(1) The weight and the forms of the left–right polarisation
(2) The relationship with environmental movements and associations
(3) The inability to capitalise on criticism toward the main political parties and austerity measures imposed by the European Union

The left–right polarisation has always been crucial in Southern European countries, albeit for different reasons. In Spain, Greece and Portugal, democracy was restored after the fall of right-wing authoritarian regimes. Consequently, the leftist mobilisations and political forces that fought for democracy had, and still have, great importance. In Italy, the left–right polarisation was very pronounced in the postwar period, and it largely expressed the opposition between *Democrazia Cristiana* and the *Partito Comunista*. After 1994, the same opposition continued between the centre-right coalition (formed by *Forza Italia*, *Lega Nord* and *Alleanza Nazionale*) and the coalition of the centre-left parties.

The Green parties in Southern Europe have put forward demands and values largely unconnected to the traditional cleavages, but they have had to deal with the left–right polarisation. In Italy, Spain, Greece and Portugal, the Green parties have been aligned and allied – in different ways – with the left (or with the centre-left). They have often assumed the role of the environmentalist component in these coalitions or alliances. The Green parties have thus more easily had representatives elected in the national and local political institutions. In Italy, they have also obtained ministers in the national government. However, they have scaled down the specificity and autonomy of their political profile ('neither right nor left'), thus greatly reducing their capacity to attract activists and voters regardless of their political affiliation. Moreover, their relationships with parties and coalitions on the left have also provoked internal divisions and often conflicts among leaders. Some components of the Green parties have privileged relationships with the radical or alternative left; others have instead established good relationships with the moderate left and centre-left. Splits have thus arisen within the Green parties, with numerous executives and several Green activists joining left or centre-left parties.

Environmentalist movements and associations have played an important role in the formation of Green parties in Southern Europe. However, divisions have also progressively emerged, with the relative competition to acquire resources, activists and recognition in public opinion. Numerous environmentalist associations and groups have preferred to support other left or centre-left parties. They have often sought to assume a direct role as interlocutors with the political institutions and engaged in lobbying with no mediation by the Green parties. Such separation from the environmentalist movement and associations has greatly weakened the parties that endeavour to relay their demands to the political institutions.

In recent years, the effects of the economic crises and the austerity policies decided by the European Union have heavily impacted on and impoverished the countries of Southern Europe. Protest movements (the *indignados*) have consequently developed in all countries, and the divisions on the left between the opponents and supporters of the austerity policies have widened. In this context, public concern with environmental degradation has diminished. The Greens in the countries of Southern Europe, together with the European Green Party, have criticised the neoliberal and austerity measures imposed by the European Union, but they find it difficult to redefine their political project so that they can assume an important and autonomous role in current conflicts.

Note

1   The three referenda in November 1987 against nuclear energy were approved by 79.7 per cent, 80.6 per cent and 71.9 per cent of the voters, respectively.

References

Biorcio, R., 1988. Ecologia politica e Liste verdi. In: R. Biorcio and G. Lodi, eds, *La sfida verde. Il movimento ecologista in Italia.* Padua: Liviana editrice. pp. 113–145.
Biorcio, R., 1999. Les Verts en Italie: marginalité et pouvoir. In: P. Delwit and J. M. De Waele, eds, *Le partis verts en Europe.* Brussels: Éditions Complexe. pp. 181–196.

Biorcio, R., 2002. Italy. In: F. Müller-Rommel and T. Poguntke, eds, *Green Parties in National Governments*. London: Frank Cass. pp. 39–62.

Botetzagias, I., 2003. The re-emergence of the Greek Greens. *Environmental Politics*, 12(4), pp. 127–132.

Cabal, E., 1996. *Historia de los Verdes*. Madrid: Mandala Ediciones.

Demertzis, N., 1995. Greece: Greens at the Periphery. In: D. Richardson and C. Rootes, eds, *The Green Challenge: The Development of Green Parties in Europe*. London: Routledge. pp. 193–207.

Diani, M., 1990. The Italian Ecology Movement: From Radicalism to Moderation. In: W. Rüdig, ed., *Green Politics One*. Edinburgh: Edinburgh University Press. pp. 153–176.

Espinoza, L. E., 1995. Izquierda Unida marco de referencia verde. *Ecología Política*, 10, pp. 119–120.

European Green Party, 2014. Green Result Is a Mandate for Change in Europe . Available at: <https://europeangreens.eu/news/green-result-mandate-change-europe>.

Farro, A., 1991. *La lente verde: Cultura, politica e azione collettiva ambientaliste*. Milano: Angeli.

Fernández, J., 1999. *El ecologismo Español*. Madrid: Alianza editorial.

Inglehart, R., 1977. *The Silent Revolution: Changing Values and Political Styles Among Western Publics*. Princeton: Princeton University Press.

Kousis, M., 2001. Competing Claims in Local Environmental Conflicts in Southern Europe. In: K. Eder and M. Kousis, eds, *Environmental Politics in Southern Europe – Actors, Institutions and Discourses in a Europeanizing Society*. Dordrecht: Kluwer Academic Publishers. pp. 129–150.

Larios, J., 2006. La experiencia andaluza de Los Verdes. In: A. Valencia Sáiz, ed., *La izquierda verde*. Barcelona: Icaria. pp. 273–300.

Mansinho, I., and Schmidt, L., 1994. A emergência do ambiente nas Ciências Sociais. *Análise Social*, 39(127), pp. 441–481.

Melucci, A., 1996. *Challenging Codes*. Cambridge: Cambridge University Press.

Müller-Rommel, F., 2002. The Lifespan and the Political Performances of Green Parties in Western Europe. In: F. Müller-Rommel and T. Poguntke, eds, *Green Parties in National Governments*. London: Frank Cass. pp. 1–16.

Panebianco, A., 1986. *Political Parties: Organization and Power*. Cambridge: Cambridge University Press.

Rhodes, M., 1995. Italy: Greens in an Overcrowded Political System. In: D. Richardson and C. Rootes, eds, *The Green Challenge: The Development of Green Parties in Europe*. London: Routledge. pp. 168–192.

9   Greens in the United Kingdom and Ireland

Weak but persistent

Lynn Bennie

Introduction

Greens in the United Kingdom (UK) and Ireland have a long history of participation in electoral politics, spanning over four decades. They have experienced highs and lows but have maintained a permanent presence in party politics. There are a number of Green parties operating in the UK and Ireland – the Green Party of England and Wales (GPEW), the Scottish Green Party, the Green Party in Ireland and the Greens of Northern Ireland.[1] Each has its own unique story, in the context of UK and Irish politics, from long-term but limited electoral impact (the Greens in Britain) to involvement in coalition government (the Irish Green Party). However, Greens across the islands of the UK and Ireland are characterised by durability and persistence, despite the relatively inhospitable political systems in which they operate. This chapter outlines the major developments in the evolution of Green party politics in the UK and Ireland. The discussion aims to document the electoral journey of the Greens, to investigate their ideological and policy character and to examine their organisational form. The radicalism of Green ideas has largely remained intact, but this can be interpreted as a sign of weakness, with Greens remaining outsiders in an unfavourable political environment.

Origins and development

The foundations of the UK Greens were laid more than 40 years ago (Table 9.1). The party began in 1973 with the name 'People'. It was Europe's first Green party, forming soon after the world's first national Green party in New Zealand in 1972. Narratives describing party formation emphasise the importance of a small number of highly motivated individuals (two solicitors, an estate agent and the estate agent's assistant) who were gravely concerned about ecological problems but who had little experience of party politics or of the wider environmental movement (Rüdig and Lowe, 1986; Parkin, 1989; Rootes, 1995). In many countries, Green parties emerged *from* environmental groups, but in the UK the relationship has been complex, based more on mutual respect than cooperation.

Table 9.1 Chronology of the main developments of the UK and Irish Greens

UK Greens		Irish Greens	
Year	*Important developments*	*Year*	*Important developments*
1973	Party formation, name of 'People'	1981	Party formation, Ecology Party of Ireland
1974	First participation in a national election	1982	First participation in a national election
1974	First national conference	1983	Change of name to Green Alliance
1975	Change of name, from 'People' to Ecology Party	1985	First seats won in local councils
		1987	Change of name to Green Party
1979	First national television election broadcast	1989	First seat in national parliament (the *Dáil*).
1985	Change of name, from Ecology Party to Green Party	2001	'Leader' of party created
		2002	Most successful national election performance to date, with six TDs (*Teachtaí Dála* – member of the lower house of the Irish Parliament)
1989	Party achieves 15% in European elections		
1999	First UK Green parliamentarians elected, to Scottish Parliament		
		2006	Northern Ireland party joins Irish party
2007	'Leader' of party created	2007	First member elected to Northern Ireland Assembly
2010	First seat in national parliament (House of Commons)	2007–2011	Part of coalition government (with Fianna Fáil and Progressive Democrats)
		2011	All six Green TDs lose seats in general election

Source: Author's own compilation.

The first Green candidates stood in February 1974, in five seats. A change of name took place in 1975, when 'People' became the Ecology Party, partly because the media regularly and incorrectly referred to the 'People's party'. The first significant presence of Greens in a general election was in 1979 when the fielding of more than 50 candidates led to a party political broadcast. In 1983, Green candidates exceeded 100, and in 1985 the party settled on its present name, the Green Party. Since that time, the Greens have gradually increased their presence in general elections (Table 9.2). However, it is only since 2001 that the party has enjoyed the thrill of 'saved deposits', when the level of support in some constituencies is sufficient to retain the electoral deposit required to stand as a candidate.[2] In 2005, the party saved 10 per cent of deposits. The party's greatest general election achievement was the election of its first Member of Parliament (MP) in 2010, 36 years after it took its first steps in national politics. Caroline Lucas became MP for the seat of Brighton Pavilion, a relatively affluent area in the southeast of England, achieving 31 per cent of the vote and gaining the seat from

Table 9.2 Electoral results of UK Greens: General elections, 1974–2010 (including Northern Ireland)

Election	Candidates (N)	Saved deposits (N)	Total votes	% National vote	% Vote in seats contested	Best individual result (%)	MPs elected
Feb 1974	5	0	4,576	0.01	1.8	3.9	0
Oct 1974	4	0	999	0.0	0.7	0.8	0
1979	53	0	39,918	0.1	1.5	2.8	0
1983	108	0	53,848	0.2	1.0	2.9	0
1987	133	0	89,753	0.3	1.3	1.3	0
1992	256	0	171,927	0.5	1.3	1.3	0
1997	95	0	63,991	0.2	1.4	4.3	0
2001	145	10	166,477	0.6	2.9	9.3	0
2005	203	24	283,414	1.0	3.4	22.0	0
2010	335	7	285,612	1.0	1.8	31.3	1

Sources: Rallings and Thrasher, 2012; http://news.bbc.co.uk/; http://www.politicsresources.net/area/uk/; http://www.electoralcommission.org.uk/; http://www.ukpolitical.info.

Labour. Nationally, support for the Greens declined, but the party benefited from the targeting of limited resources and a high-profile, well-liked candidate. Lucas's success has been a fillip for party followers.

The election of a single Green MP in nearly four decades demonstrates that UK politics is not fertile territory for Green activists. While the UK Greens surpassed the first two of Pedersen's (1982) thresholds (declaration and authorisation) in advance of many other European Green parties, electoral results have been poor, and the party has struggled to penetrate the national parliament (the threshold of representation). The final threshold of relevance, if defined as having coalition potential or governmental power, looks like an unachievable dream for UK Greens. However, this is explained not by any strategic errors on the part of the Greens, nor by a lack of receptiveness of voters. Rather, institutional and political system constraints impede the progress of the Greens. Single member constituencies and a simple plurality principle – or first-past-the-post – are used to elect MPs to the UK Parliament. This challenges small parties with limited resources and a lack of concentrated support. In the constituency competitions, small parties are squeezed out of the race by major party candidates, with votes for the Greens and others widely perceived as 'wasted'. The result is a party system dominated by two to three major parties.[3] Furthermore, the Greens – with no important source of funding beyond their members and supporters – must generate funds for electoral deposits. Nor do British political parties receive any significant state funding. The Greens have never presented a full list of candidates in a general election. The best achieved was in 2010, when 335 candidates stood in approximately half of all constituencies.[4] In all, these factors create a 'cold climate' for Green politics (Rootes, 1995).

A more optimistic picture emerges when attention is focussed on other electoral arenas. The European elections are known as 'second-order' elections, with low turnouts, high levels of experimental voting and, since 1999, a proportional electoral system. In these elections, UK Greens attract higher levels of support. The peak in support was 1989, when they achieved nearly 15 per cent of the national vote. This event was nothing short of an electoral phenomenon, taking pundits and party by surprise. A complex coming-together of factors explains the events of 1989 (Curtice, 1989; Rootes, 1995; Rüdig, et al., 1996). These include a series of environmental 'incidents', heightened media interest in the environment and the behaviour of mainstream parties' politicians, which raised the public's awareness of environmental issues. Ironically, because the electoral system remained first-past-the-post in 1989, no Greens surmounted the threshold of representation. Since the introduction of a party list system of proportional representation with large multi-member constituencies, British Greens have had a continuous presence in the European Parliament (Table 9.3).[5] The most recent test of electoral

Table 9.3 Electoral performance of Greens in Britain (excluding Northern Ireland) and Ireland, European Parliament elections, 1979–2014

Britain

Election	Total votes	% national vote	MEPs elected
1979	17,953	0.1	0
1984	70,853	0.5	0
1989	2,292,718	14.9	0
1994	494,561	3.2	0
1999	625,378	6.3	2
2004	1,028,283	6.1	2
2009	1,303,745	8.6	2
2014	1,255,573	7.9	3

Ireland

Election	Total votes	% national vote	MEPs elected
1984	5,242	0.5	0
1989	61,041	3.7	0
1994	90,046	7.9	2
1999	93,100	6.7	2
2004	76,917	4.3	0
2009	34,585	1.9	0
2014	82,458	4.9	0

Sources: http://www.bbc.co.uk/news/; http://www.results-elections2014.eu/en/country-results-ie-2014.html; http://www.electoralcommission.org.uk/; http://www.politicsresources.net/area/uk/eu.htm.

support was the 2014 European elections. The party attracted 8 per cent of the vote and three Green MEPs were elected, all from the South of England. The party finished ahead of the unpopular Liberal Democrats but the UK Independence Party (UKIP) 'won' this election, with 27 per cent of votes, scooping up antiestablishment protest votes coveted by the Greens.

The UK political system has experienced some decentralisation, presenting new opportunities for Greens. In Scotland and Wales, new legislative chambers were established in 1999, with a semiproportional Additional Member System (AMS) used to elect representatives. The Scottish Greens were immediately rewarded in 1999 when Robin Harper became the first ever Green parliamentarian in the UK (Harper, 2011) (Table 9.4). By 2003, the Scottish Greens had seven MSPs and enjoyed a high profile in what was referred to at the time as Scotland's 'rainbow parliament' (Bennie, 2004). Support for Scottish Greens has been most concentrated in and around the central belt of Scotland, in the big cities, especially the capital city of Edinburgh. As parliamentarians, the Greens claim credit for ambitious greenhouse gas reduction legislation and increased support for community-based sustainability initiatives (Harper, 2011, pp. 132–133). At times, Green support was necessary to pass governmental budgets (Harper, 2011, p. 130). The fortunes of the Scottish Greens were also improved at local government level by the introduction of the Single Transferable Vote (STV) (Bennie and Clark, 2008). Before these elections, there had been, briefly, one Green councillor in Scotland (elected in 1990); after, there are 14, mostly in Edinburgh and Glasgow.

The Greater London Assembly (GLA) was established in 2000 and contains 25 representatives elected using a form of AMS. Greens have made a notable contribution here too. In 2000, three Greens were elected, two in every election thereafter, and it is widely accepted that they have influenced assembly policies, such as the introduction of the London congestion charge. It is clear from these various experiences that electoral reform leads to enhanced influence for Greens. However, the Greens have not been as successful in Wales (Table 9.4), highlighting

Table 9.4 Electoral results of the Greens in elections to the Scottish Parliament and Welsh National Assembly

	Scottish Parliament					Welsh National Assembly				
	Constituency		Region		Seats	Constituency		Region		Seats
	Votes	%	Votes	%		Votes	%	Votes	%	
1999	–	–	84,024	3.6	1	1,002	0.1	25,858	2.5	0
2003	–	–	132,138	6.9	7	–	–	30,028	3.5	0
2007	2,971	0.2	82,584	4.0	2	–	–	33,803	3.5	0
2011	–	–	87,060	4.4	2	1,514	0.2	32,649	3.4	0

Sources: Author's own data; http://news.bbc.co.uk/; http://www.politicsresources.net/area/uk/.

that proportional representation does not substitute for lack of support. It is also of note that, against the odds, the Greens have a meaningful presence in local government in England, where voting systems are nonproportional. The party boasts over 160 councillors in England and Wales, and areas of electoral strength are emerging, such as Lancaster and Leeds in the North and Oxford and Brighton in the South. Together with Lucas's election, this suggests the party is now benefiting from some concentration of support. Nevertheless, first-past-the-post remains an impediment to Greens.

On the other side of the Irish Sea – in Éire – a different trajectory of Green politics is evident. While the UK Greens have made gradual, long-term progress, the Greens in Ireland have followed a bumpy path, experiencing a place in government, but followed by an acute decline. This has taken place in a political context that is very different from Britain's. Formally a free state since the 1920s, Ireland has its own unique political system and culture; for example constituencies are multi-member, and STV is used in elections to the main legislative body or lower house (the *Dáil*). Traditionally, Irish politics has been portrayed as a two-and-a-half party system, dominated by two large catch-all parties. However, in recent years, the party system has experienced some fragmentation. Since 1989, the system has moved from one where one centre-right nationalist party (*Fianna Fáil*) dominated, to one where multiple parties compete for a role in coalition (Taylor and Flynn, 2008; Gallagher and Marsh, 2011). The Greens have benefited from this 'more tactically flexible era' where coalition politics has become the norm (Taylor and Flynn, 2008, p. 97). Irish politics is also renowned for its localism, personality politics and a tradition of independents, as well as for its distinct nationalist discourse. In her 1989 review of world Green parties, Parkin (1989) noted that Irish politics was pragmatic, rather than obviously left and right, and revolved around leader personalities, which made it difficult for Greens to develop a profile.

The Irish Greens were founded in 1981 as the Ecology Party of Ireland by Dublin teacher and environmental campaigner Christopher Fettes, English by birth. Fettes moved to Ireland in 1958 and was active in the Green movement in the 1970s, in Friends of the Earth, various animal welfare groups and the Vegetarian Society. He claims the conception of the party took place during this decade (Boyle, 2006). By 1981, he was convinced that PR created 'room' for an ecology party in Ireland (Boyle, 2006, p. 45). In 1981, Fettes advertised, via the letters page of the *Irish Times*, for 'like-minded' people to form 'a branch of the UK Ecology Party in Ireland' (Boyle, 2006, p. 24). Eighty individuals responded by attending a meeting in a Dublin hotel, and forty agreed to become members (Boyle, 2006, p. 32; Bolleyer, 2010, p. 608). This was the first genuinely new party in Irish politics since the 1920s, and it had close associations with the Irish antinuclear movement of the late 1970s, which involved a successful public resistance to the building of a nuclear plant in 1979. The Greens in Northern Ireland were established a little later, in 1983.

The party first stood in a general election in November 1982, attracting 0.2 per cent of votes (Table 9.5). In 1983, the party became the Green Alliance, and in

Table 9.5 Electoral results of Irish Greens: *Dáil* elections, 1982–2011

Election	Candidates (N)	1st preference votes	% national vote (1st preference)	TDs elected
1982	2	3,716	0.2	0
1987	3	7,159	0.4	0
1989	11	24,827	1.5	1
1992	19	24,110	1.4	1
1997	26	49,323	2.8	2
2002	31	71,470	3.8	6
2007	44	96,936	4.7	6
2011	43	41,039	1.8	0

Sources: Gallagher and Sinnott, 1990; Gallagher, et al., 2003; Gallagher and Marsh, 2011; http://electionsireland.org; http://electionresources.org/.

1987 the Green Party (*Comhaontas Glas*). The first Green local councillor was elected in 1985, and by 1989 the party had won its first seat in the national parliament, in Dublin South. The Greens attracted sufficient levels of support to be represented at the local and European levels (Table 9.3) and gradually increased their parliamentary representation (two Dublin seats in 1997). The position of national leader was created in 2001, and a major breakthrough occurred in 2002, when six Green TDs were elected (with 4 per cent of the national vote). This has been described as a 'quantum leap' for the party, when the party moved to 'turning its attention to the considerations of governing, rather than eternally opposing' (McGee, 2006, p. 10). However, the party lost its two MEPs in 2004. The year 2006 saw the formal coming together of the Green parties in Ireland, making them an all-island party, and in 2007 a Green was elected to the Northern Irish Assembly. In the same year, the Greens retained six TDs, and this opened the door to coalition. The party entered the national government in 2007, in alliance with two other parties, *Fianna Fáil* and the Progressive Democrats. Two Green senior ministers were appointed, one for the Department of the Environment, Heritage and Local Government, the other for Communications, Energy and Natural Resources, along with a number of junior ministerial positions.

However, this was not the most fortuitous time for any party to gain power for the first time, due to major economic turmoil (Little, 2002; Marsh and Mikhaylov, 2014). The crisis that engulfed Ireland from 2008 is described by Little (2011, p. 1305) as 'unprecedented economic and financial decline'. A dramatic end to a property boom and the collapse of Ireland's banking system coincided with rapid decline in economic activity and rising unemployment. This culminated in a 'bailout' of 67.5 billion Euros from the European Union (EU) and other countries and led to deep spending cuts. To be part of the government at this time was ill fated for the Greens.

The Greens withdrew from government in January 2011, publically citing a 'breakdown of trust between the parties' (Little, 2011, p. 1307). The Greens went on to lose all six TDs in the 2011 election. The party's national vote share fell to below 2 per cent of first preference votes, which resulted in a major reduction in party income. In short, as the country faced economic catastrophe, the Green Party dealt with its own crisis. The Green leader of the day, John Gormley, claimed that being in government with an unpopular coalition partner at a time of economic crisis amounted to an 'insurmountable challenge' (Little, 2011, p. 1309). Thus, following the 2011 election, the Irish Greens entered a period of 'reduced circumstances' (McGee, *Irish Times,* 19 May 2012), with no TDs or senators, and a very small number of local councillors.

By 2014, the party base had been badly damaged. Like many Greens, those in Ireland have experienced dramatic highs and lows. In Pedersen's (1982) terms, the party has passed all four thresholds but appears to have retreated to a point somewhere just beneath the threshold of representation. As Pedersen (1982, p. 11) argues, parties can travel in both directions, that is 'in some cases parties will cross the various thresholds several times'. There may be signs of a recovery in Green politics in Ireland. Local and European elections took place at the same time. The Greens won 12 local government seats, an increase of 9, and 1.6 per cent of the total vote. In the European elections, the party won 5 per cent of the vote, an increase of 3 percentage points on 2009. However, the decline was so severe for this party that recovery is likely to take considerable time. In Northern Ireland, despite having one representative in the Assembly, the party remains weak. Following 2014 local elections in Northern Ireland, the Greens had only four councillors (from 462), and in the European elections they attracted less than 2 per cent of first preference votes.

Ideology and policy positions

The ideology and policy programmes of the Greens have become more comprehensive and taken on a distinct 'left of centre' flavour, certainly in Britain. Rüdig and Lowe (1986, p. 272) argue that the British Greens' early ideological position was confused and perceived as 'reactionary', influenced by the 'survivalist' Edward Goldsmith who advocated population and immigration control. Some thought the party to be authoritarian, and this damaged the relationship between the Greens and left groups (Rüdig and Lowe, 1986). The party was also subject to a 'factional divide' between electoralists and anarchists, but a more pragmatic approach emerged (Rüdig and Lowe, 1986). The Greens now promote a radical and coherent programme, challenging economic growth and the continued reliance on fossil fuels and promoting fundamental restructuring of society. The critique of ecological damage is widely understood, but their position on other issues less so. The party endorses interconnected values, including sustainability, equality and social justice, decentralisation of power and nonviolence. The Scottish Greens list ecology, equality, radical democracy, peace and nonviolence as their key principles (http://www.scottishgreens.org.uk/policy/). The GPEW states that 'we believe in the common good' (http://greenparty.org.uk/values/).

On socio-economic issues, the Greens in the UK are to the left. They advocate a number of redistributive policies, including a wealth tax on high earners, a living wage for low earners, investment in public services and 'renationalisation' of the railways. They are strong critics of the austerity programme in Britain, and they promote a citizens income, a 'benefit' for all, to encourage 'a more flexible approach to work' (http://policy.greenparty.org.uk/sw.html). The Greens are unmistakeably libertarian. They emphasise the 'social causes of crime' and promote religious freedom and the rights of all minority groups, including migrants and same-sex couples. As MP, Lucas campaigns for equal pension rights for same-sex couples. The Greens advocate 'radical democracy' for example Scottish independence. Like most Greens, they are in favour of European collaboration but argue that EU institutions require reform. They are against Britain joining the Euro on the grounds that 'monetarist policy should be sensitive to local economic needs' (Green Party, 2014). Belief in decentralisation of power led to the organisational separation of Green parties in the UK, but there is little disagreement in policy terms, although differences in emphasis reflect regional politics. In the 2014 Euro election manifestos, 'welcoming immigrants' was placed more prominently in the Scottish document (Scottish Green Party, 2014).

The UK Greens have confidently positioned themselves as left, libertarian *and* Green, achieved without major tension or debate within the party. Carter (2008, p. 234) charts this move from ecological party to a distinctly left-libertarian position, describing the Greens as 'actively embracing a social justice agenda'. This more distinctive strategy was partly made possible by the repositioning of the Labour Party in Britain. Following her election as MP in 2010, Lucas stated that 'we are a party of the left: as well as environmental policies, the issues we're standing on are fairness and social justice' (McDonald, 2010). Patrick Harvie (2013), co-convenor of the Scottish Greens and Member of the Scottish Parliament, argues that independence is 'an opportunity to close the chronic inequality gap in our country, and of course to make the shift to a Greener, more sustainable economy'. There is now no pretence that UK Greens are 'neither left nor right'.

The Irish Greens adopted seven ideological principles in 1982, namely conservation of resources, local decision-making, self-reliance, cooperation, the rights of future generations, peace and redistribution of the world's resources (Boyle, 2006, p. 37; Mullarney, 2006, p. 33). On Northern Ireland, the Greens advocated public consultation with a view to creating a 'community of regions' in Ireland and independence from Britain (Boyle, 2006, p. 38). Tensions have existed in the party, and there have been times when 'ideologues' came to the fore. For example in the 1980s, the movement was a loose alliance between radical Green groups (Bolleyer, 2012, p. 114; Farrell, 1989). A pragmatic approach has dominated since, but the core of the party's ideology is similar to the early principles. The party remains radical and progressive, particularly in the context of socially conformist Ireland where, for example, abortion is still severely restricted. Taylor and Flynn (2008, p. 95) describe the very liberal position of Greens in a 'small c' conservative country, supporting 'a modern secular state . . . social diversity and tolerance'. In the context of the Irish party system, however, the Irish Greens appear less 'left wing' than their counterparts in the UK. They exist in a system where significant parties are positioned to their left, namely Sinn Fein and Labour (Dalton, et al., 2013, p. 134).

The party has walked a difficult tightrope on the issue of Europe, in favour of international cooperation on environmental, peace and human rights policies, but sceptical of the undemocratic elitism of the European project (McGee, 2006). Taylor and Flynn (2008, p. 99) describe how the party was 'willing to ease its euro-sceptic stance to enhance its electoral prospects', partly because the Irish economy appeared to benefit from the European project in the 1990s. Taylor and Flynn (2008, p. 98) also argue that the British Greens have been more consistently critical of Europe. Today, the issue of Europe remains a point of contention. Many members are against the neoliberal principles contained in the Lisbon Treaty, although most support the measures designed to improve Ireland's economy.

The fragmentation of Ireland's party system meant that the Greens became potential coalition participants, and this shaped the Irish party in ways not evident in Britain. The party compromised on some of their more radical policies; their approach to tax policies became more moderate, both corporation tax and income tax, and the party abandoned their commitment to a basic income. The political system encouraged compromise. Opposition parties have relatively little influence in a centralised Irish system where government legislation dominates and the parliamentary committee system is weak. The incentive to be part of government was strong, in order to directly influence policy (Bolleyer, 2010, p. 615). However, the experience of government was unpleasant for the party, leading to loss of identity and an inability to prevent un-Green policies (Bolleyer, 2012, p. 124). The Greens were powerless to resist economic development such as new motorway construction and a waste incineration project in Dublin; and many Greens balked at the party's support of financial restructuring, including establishing the National Asset Management Agency (NAMA). Yet, the Greens point to concrete policy achievements in power: the setting up of a carbon levy and other tax reforms designed to improve energy efficiency; changes to planning regulations; local government reform; increases in renewable energy; a national home insulation scheme and the introduction of civic partnership legislation, enhancing the position of same-sex couples.[6] The Greens also demonstrated that they could perform competently as 'effective coalition partners' (Gallagher and Marsh, 2011, p. 13). Nevertheless, the 2011 election was an electoral annihilation for the party. As Bolleyer (2012, p. 125) argues, '[T]he price the Irish Green Party paid for government participation was exceptionally high compared to other Greens' experiences in government'.

Structure and organisation

Social movement roots and links

Rüdig (2008, p. 204) notes that the individuals responsible for the foundation of the British Greens 'had no background in radical or social movement politics'. Others have observed the lack of connection between party and groups when compared to environmental movements in other countries (Rüdig and Lowe, 1986; Rootes, 1995, 2003; Carter, 2008). These relationships, like many other features of the Green movement in the UK, have been moulded by the political system. In Britain, governmental decision-making was traditionally centralised and difficult to penetrate for Greens and other radical voices (Jordan and Richardson, 1987). Governments granted privileged status to respectable and professional groups, leaving ideologically and strategically radical organisations 'on the outside looking in'. Groups like Friends of the Earth were incentivised to be moderate and low profile, resulting in insider status and some degree of policy influence. In these circumstances, groups can be wary about working alongside a political party with a radical agenda, and this is a common interpretation of events in Britain. Parkin (1989, p. 219) refers to the 'coolness' of environmental and peace groups and how they 'kept their distance' from the party. Irish Greens appear to have had more involvement in antinuclear movement politics, but even here the party was 'far from an organised representative of any new social movement' (Taylor and Flynn, 2008, p. 94). Nowadays, the parties and groups maintain a respectful but distant relationship.

Organisation and leadership

Like other European Green parties, the Greens in the UK and Ireland were founded on highly participatory, decentralist principles, and significant efforts were made to ensure that party organisation reflected these beliefs (Rüdig, 2008, p. 215; Boyle, 2006, p. 49). However, Green parties experience phases of organisational development, which lead to increasing pressure to professionalise and centralise, to meet the demands of traditional electoral politics. The UK and Irish Greens are no exceptions to this trend.

The very early days of Green party development in Britain were in fact notable for the 'absence of debate on organisational matters' but over time the question of internal party democracy became the 'key internal divide', not values or party policy (Rüdig, 2008, pp. 203–204). Throughout the 1980s and 1990s, a central cleavage emerged on how the party should organise itself, commonly portrayed as a competition between 'anarchists' and 'electoralists', or 'decentralists' and 'centralists' (Rüdig, 2008, p. 206; Parkin, 1989, p. 222). These debates about professionalising and streamlining the party involved the role of party 'speakers' and whether conferences should be attended by delegates or open to all members and continued throughout the decades, with various initiatives (including Maingreen and Green, 2000) debated at length (Rüdig, 2008).

The initial constitutional structure of the British Greens reflected their participatory values. Decision-making power resided with the party conference, and the 'executive' consisted of a 25-member party council. All members were entitled to attend local and regional meetings and the national conference. The party resisted leadership through the rotation of key roles and group leadership, that is a team of party speakers and chairs, with individuals serving a maximum of three years. Changes to the party organisation occurred in two phases. The first took place in

1991, when the party created a new national executive to exist alongside a larger regional council, a party chair and two principal speakers. These reforms were the result of the 'Green 2000' initiative in which Jonathan Porritt and Sarah Parkin played prominent roles. The changes were accompanied by raucous, fractious debate, but the effective streamlining of the organisation remained intact even when many of the protagonists left the party and the 'decentralist wing subsequently held the ascendancy' (Carter, 2008, p. 233). In addition, rules on rotation and the length of time a person could serve as national office holders were relaxed. A second phase of reforms confirmed the professionalisation of party structures, but these were met with compliance, not resistance (Carter, 2008, pp. 233–234; Rüdig, 2008, p. 214). In 2007, three-quarters of members voted to reform the party leadership, moving away from a collective leadership to the adoption of a Leader and Deputy Leader. The first leader was Caroline Lucas, followed by Natalie Bennett, the incumbent (Table 9.6). The Scottish party has two Co-convenors but has always been tolerant of the use of the term 'leaders'.

The early days of the Irish Greens were also characterised by a loose, decentralised model of organisation. Accounts of decision-making by consensus in the Irish party reveal the hours of debate and 'patient discussion' involved; for example when the party adopted its programme of ideological principles in 1982 (Mullarney, 2006, p. 33). There have always been debates on whether participation

Table 9.6 Party leaders (2001–2014), Green Party of England and Wales (GPEW) and Irish Green Party

Year	Name	Method	Votes cast/ turnout (%)	1st pref votes (%)	Time in office	Reason for resigning
Green Party of England and Wales						
2008–2012	Caroline Lucas	Full Member Postal Vote	2,769/37.9	92.4	4 years	End of term and became MP
2012–present	Natalie Bennett	Full Member Postal Vote	3,111/25.1	42.2	2 Years	In post
Irish Green Party						
2001–2007	Trevor Sargent	Special convention	–	–	6 years	Due to party's decision to enter coalition
2007–2011	John Gormley	Full Member Postal Vote	478/35.0	65.0	5 years	Following poor election of 2011
2011–present	Eamon Ryan	Full Member Postal Vote	550/71.6	40.5	3 years	In post

Note: Caroline Lucas was re-elected in 2010 but unopposed (on a turnout of 25%). While the GPEW elects leaders every two years, the Irish party conducts this process less frequently, that is, it is tied to the cycle of national elections (Cross and Blais, 2012, p. 95).

Source: Author's own compilation; Cross and Blais, 2012.

in electoral politics is the best route to influence. In 1986, for example, GANG (the Green Action Now Group) parted company from those Greens committed to participation in conventional politics (Whiteman, 1990). Bolleyer (2010, 2012) documents the 'organisation-building' of the Irish Greens. The parallels with other European Green parties are striking. Pragmatists rather than ideologues have been in ascendancy at crucial times in the party's development, from the decision to participate in electoral politics through to the Greens' participation in government. In Ireland, at least three organisational compromises occurred. The first was a move away from consensus decision-making at the end of the 1980s; the second was the election of a fully fledged leader (and deputy) in 2001; and the third involved adjustment of party structures in the light of parliamentary and government experience, shifting the focus of power in the party towards the centre (Taylor and Flynn, 2008; Bolleyer, 2010, 2012). The party now has a national council, designed to meet a number of times a year and provide direction in-between conferences. The other key levels are a party national executive and the party's constituency or local groups. The party executive nominates candidates for the leadership, and the party's parliamentary group, should it exist, has the constitutional right to negotiate with potential coalition partners (Taylor and Flynn, 2008, pp. 100–101).

It is clear that the prospect of power 'incentivised' the rationalisation of party organisation. This is best demonstrated by the party's decision to create a national leader in 2001 (Table 9.6). Historically, leadership had been a tricky issue for the Greens in Ireland. Parkin (1989, p. 72) had commented on this, stating that the Green 'distaste' for leaders in the 'personality-strewn environment of Irish politics' created difficulties for the party. Trevor Sargent, elected as the party's first leader, had previously been forced to publicly apologise for referring to himself as 'head of the party'. However, media demands and the desire to compete on a level playing field with other parties by participating in important leadership debates pressurised the party to adopt a leader. In addition, a formal leader 'allowance' exists in Ireland.

In parliament and in government, a separation can occur between the party on the ground and the party in office. Elected representatives benefit from important resources – assistants, researchers and other support staff – and they are in demand from the media. This can lead to resentment amongst party members. With participation in government, these problems can intensify. The Irish Greens experienced a form of disconnect between the governmental arm of the party and the ordinary members, leading some to argue that the experience of government was not worth the costs to the Green movement. While the members were given a say on entering into the formal coalition in 2007 (with more than 80 per cent in favour), governmental status meant that power shifted further to the party elite (Bolleyer, 2012, p. 124). Due to the pressure to respond quickly in government, there were significant difficulties maintaining open communication between government ministers and ordinary members. Another consequence of governmental participation is the 'loss of activists to government roles', with Greens becoming 'absorbed by government business' and members become 'increasingly frustrated by the lack of consultation' (Bolleyer, 2010, pp. 607, 617). Additionally, the Irish Greens faced the problems of all small parties in coalitions, that is the dominance of major parties. Finally, Green parties can lose as well as gain governmental status, leading to major instability in party organisation. The funding and privileges the Irish Greens gained through governmental participation disappeared in 2011, forcing the organisation to rely on its grassroots again. Overall, the Irish Greens have succumbed to a process that looks like professionalisation combined with realism. Attempts to maintain collective leadership and highly participatory decision-making have been casualties of this process. In the UK, there have been organisational compromises but these have been less pronounced, principally due to limited electoral success.

Members

Despite the organisational reforms documented above, the parties being examined here are membership-focussed, democratic organisations, certainly when compared with conventional parties. An analysis of parties operating in Britain suggests that only the Greens offer members a meaningful say in the running of their party but with some limits (Bennie, 2015). Members and local parties are responsible for candidate selection, although the central party implements rules to ensure gender balance. Ordinary party members are entitled to attend and vote at the annual policy-making conference, but the constitution states that delegate conferences will be reinstated if membership exceeds 25,000. Undoubtedly, the Greens are the most 'consultative' on the question of who leads the party. Through an annual postal ballot, members select the party executive (50 per cent are elected each year), and the leader and deputy leader are elected every two years in the same way. The Greens encourage member participation but acknowledge that this is not always practical. For instance, in the event of coalition talks in Britain, consultation with members is not constitutionally guaranteed; the GPEW constitution refers to 'maximum consultation that is practical, given timescales and resources available' (Green Party, 2013).

In Ireland, *Fianna Fáil* and *Fine Gael* adopt elite-driven models of party organisation, with Labour more democratic but not to the same extent as the Greens. Irish Green party members elect the leaders through a national ballot, although this is subject to some constraint in that the party executive determines the precise details (Cross and Blais, 2012, p. 62). In effect, the executive nominates and presents the candidates. However, members can exert influence by threatening a vote of no confidence in the leader at the annual conference. Candidate selection lies in the hands of local party members, but the party executive does have some power to veto or modify selections (Taylor and Flynn, 2008, p. 100). All members can attend the annual conference, where they vote on motions submitted by constituency parties, and members are constitutionally enabled to vote on any coalition agreements negotiated by the party elite. Members are also invited to join internal policy groups. Thus, members are given a say on 'major decisions', from whether to join a coalition to the party's approach to Europe (the Lisbon Treaty); these require the support of two-thirds of the members. Even in Green parties, ordinary members are not all-powerful, but the parties do offer significant opportunities for members to influence intraparty decision-making.

Attracting and keeping members is crucial to the success of the Greens. However, membership patterns in the UK and Ireland are characterised by instability and fluctuation (Rüdig, et al., 1991; Rüdig, et al., 1996). Prior to 1990, membership data is unreliable and sporadically reported, but in 1984, there were approximately 5,000 members in Britain, and this rose to about 9,000 by 1989. In Ireland, membership in 1989 was reported to be a negligible 379 (Bolleyer, 2010, p. 616). Table 9.7 reports data from 1990 onwards. Membership patterns reflect periods of electoral success. The aftermath of the 1989 European elections saw British membership reach its peak and Irish membership spiked when the Greens

Table 9.7 Party membership in UK and Irish Green Parties since 1990

Year	England & Wales	Scotland	Ireland
1990	14,900	1,250	1,200
1991	18,500	–	1,200
1992	10,000	–	1,200
1993	6,500	300	1,200
1994	5,000	–	1,200
1995	–	300	1,000
1996	–	–	1,000
1997	–	300	1,000
1998	5,000	–	700
1999	–	400	–
2000	–	–	–
2001	–	400	–
2002	6,000	500	–
2003	5,000	700	–
2004	6,000	–	–
2005	7,000	–	900
2006	7,000	–	1,200
2007	7,000	–	2,100
2008	8,000	1,000	1,900
2009	10,000	1,100	–
2010	13,000	1,200	–
2011	15,000	1,300	800
2012	13,000	1,300	–
2013	14,000	1,200	–

Note: Figures are rounded.

Sources: Electoral Commission (electoralcommission.org.uk); media accounts; author's own data. Irish data from media accounts and Bolleyer (2010, p. 616).

entered coalition, soon to be followed by a decline. However, Green member-ship as a proportion of the total electorate is infinitesimally small; for example at the time of the last general election in 2010, Green Party membership in the UK amounted to 0.03 per cent of the total electorate (5 per cent of Green voters). Plainly, membership of these parties is very much a minority sport and pales into insignificance when compared to campaigning groups like Greenpeace, which attracts over 100,000 members. Nevertheless, in recent years, the Greens in Brit-ain have experienced a stabilising of membership, and in the past year, the party has seen a marked boost in numbers, pointing to a small but dependable grassroots base. It has been reported that the Young Greens saw a 70 per cent increase in members between March and August 2014.[7] In Ireland and Northern Ireland, the Greens continue to struggle to attract members; for example at the end of 2013, there were only 209 Green party members in Northern Ireland (Green Party of Northern Ireland Statement of Accounts 2013).[8]

Perhaps even more problematic for the Greens is the evidence that activists, members and voters derive from a narrow electoral pool. Green party members have quite distinctive social characteristics and attitudes. They tend to be male, middle class and middle aged, highly educated and professional, with a public sec-tor orientation and a left-of-centre, libertarian and postmaterial outlook, including strong opposition to nuclear power (Bennie, 2015). Moreover, this profile has not changed greatly since the 1990s (Rüdig, et al., 1991). Green voters are less radical in their beliefs but display rather similar characteristics. European Green voters in 1989 exhibited a combination of youth, high levels of education and environ-mental concern and, to some extent, were motivated by protest voting (Franklin and Rüdig, 1995; Rüdig, et al., 1996). However, studies revealed that support for the Greens depended on the context of the election, and Greens in the UK and Ireland at the time had 'not built up any sizeable core support' (Rüdig, et al., 1996, p. 14). By the late 2000s, Birch (2009, p. 59) demonstrated that Green party sup-port was by then indeed 'building up' in some areas of the UK, creating 'Green electoral oases' in university towns and urban areas, such as Brighton Pavilion. The evidence, then, suggests that Greens may be benefiting from the development of a core vote. This is reflected in the electoral strategy of the Greens. They have become more focussed and professional in their election campaigns, targeting areas where they are strong. Commentators on Irish politics note that this focusing of grassroots activity also helps explain the electoral success of the Irish Greens in 2002 and 2007 (Gallagher, et al., 2003; Bolleyer, 2010; Gallagher and Marsh, 2011).

Main challenges and opportunities for the future

Greens operating in the UK and Ireland continue to face significant challenges. Institutional barriers remain and, by and large, explain why Greens elsewhere have been more successful. Other challenges entail the wider political and economic environment and the ebb and flow of 'issue-attention cycles' (Downs, 1972). In times of recession, Greens struggle to maintain a profile, despite their fundamental critique of the dominant economic system that lead to recession in the first place. Especially unfortunate economic circumstances unfolded during the Irish Greens' period of government, leaving the party battered and bruised. Also critical has been the behaviour of other political parties, in government and in opposition. The main parties all claim to be Green now, offering policies on the environment and climate change, which may be sufficient to satisfy potential Green voters. Carter (2014) describes the journey of climate change politics, from 'low' to 'high' politics, which led to significant changes in energy policy. However, these issues have a lower profile during times of recession, and it is no coincidence that commitments from some parties have weakened. The Greens must also compete with 'other' parties for antiestablishment, antipolitics votes. As a recent party of government, the Irish Greens are not presently viewed as a vehicle for protest against the political establishment. In 2011, voters turned to small parties like the 'People Before Profit Alliance' and Independents to perform this role. In Britain, UKIP claims to challenge the old order of politics, crowding the party system and adding to the Greens' difficulty of mobilising support on a large scale. The potential to benefit from antipolitics sentiment remains however.

An additional problem for the Greens is that the media can be quick to portray them as 'barmy' and divided. In August 2013, it was widely reported and ridiculed that Green councillors in Brighton and Hove had used mediators to resolve party disputes. Some tensions do still exist amongst the Greens but probably no more so than in other parties, and Greens of course would argue that this is democracy in action. The problem for the Greens is that the media often perpetuates a negative, eccentric image, leading to the wrong kind of publicity. As a single MP, Lucas receives quite extensive media attention, recently by taking part in protests against fracking (*The Guardian,* 18 April 2014). In addition, in sub-national elections, Greens tend to enjoy more balanced coverage. Nevertheless, with some justification, the Greens complain that they receive limited and unfair media coverage. Nor are the Greens sufficiently well-off to generate or control media stories. Opposition parties do not have access to significant state funding, meaning the Greens rely heavily on a small number of members for financial support. The financial basis of the Greens compares poorly with major parties, and this has significant implications for spending on election campaigns. In Britain, the Greens are often excluded from national leadership debates, contributing to lack of exposure in national elections. For all these reasons, and despite the rise of social media, the Greens rely heavily on party activists on the ground, what the current leader in England and Wales – Natalie Bennett – refers to as 'shoe-leather and enthusiasm'.[9] Former Green TD Paul Gogarty, who lost his seat in 2011, refers to the importance of 'hard work and face to face contact' for Greens, an aspect of the campaign that was lacking in 2011 (Gallagher and Marsh, 2011, p. 133).[10]

When viewed over the long term, it is clear that new opportunities have gradually opened up for the Greens, and other opportunities have been created by the Greens themselves. Greens have been elected to all levels of representation in Irish and UK politics – local, sub-national, national and European. In the UK, the democratic reform programme of the last Labour government has opened up new routes to influence, and the party has made sensible strategic choices. The present leadership has reinforced the party's 'left' strategy, and this has coincided with some electoral success and a recent increase in membership, suggesting the Greens are correct to emphasise a broad left agenda. Finally, the Greens have managed to maintain their radical ideology. There has been less compromise/deradicalisation of policy, explained by a lack of governmental experience. Only the Irish Greens have faced the benefits and pitfalls of national government status, and some question whether the costs to the party outweigh the benefits. However, choosing not to enter government was never a viable option. Moreover, the party's record in government is not all bad. The Greens in Ireland proved they could be a viable party of government, and it could be argued that they made impressive contributions to political debate, presenting a coherent and consistent message on many issues, for example nuclear power, incineration planning issues and the Iraq War (McGee, 2006). Greens who have been elected in Ireland and the UK at a national level also tend to be well-respected and talented politicians. As a general rule, once they enter legislative chambers, they prove to be effective communicators, injecting colour and innovative policy ideas. McGee (2006, p. 10) observed that the Green TDs 'punch[ed] above their weight in terms of profile, integrity, and ability'.

Alongside their radical agenda, the Greens have accepted the need to professionalise. This process has been observed in many parties and has been given many labels, from the iron law of oligarchy (Michels, 1962) to electoral professionalism (Panebianco, 1988), and modern parties continuing to 'centralise' (Cross and Blais, 2012; Cross and Katz, 2013). For Greens, this has been described as the logic of electoral competition (Kitschelt, 1989) or the victory of electoral professionalism over amateur activism (Lucardie and Rihoux, 2008). The Greens in the UK and Ireland have not been immune to these pressures, best demonstrated by the lack of resistance to leadership. Effective media communicators like Lucas, Harvie and Ryan are relied on heavily to present the Green case. In this key respect, Greens appear more realistic or pragmatic than in the past. This can be explained by media demands imposed on parties in the modern era, but also by system characteristics; for example registration of parties requires the identification of a leader. Whatever the reason, leadership has proved to be an irresistible force. Rüdig (2008, p. 219) describes 'the loss of the taboo associated with the concept of a single-party leader that can be seen throughout the UK'.

Following 40 years of Green party politics in the UK and Ireland, how do we assess if the effort and toil of Green activists has been worth all the effort? In the four decades since the UK Greens entered stage, they have made significant progress but remain weak by comparison with other European Green parties. The explanations remain similar to those outlined by Rüdig and Lowe in 1986, not least the institutional barriers of British politics. The Irish Greens, meanwhile, have travelled further in the voyage of party development, functioning within an institutional environment that is slightly more favourable than Britain's. However, success meant that the Greens in Ireland had further to fall, and losing all representation in the national parliament was a severe blow to the Green movement. In the final analysis, the Greens in the UK and Ireland have endured. In the context of UK and Irish politics, maintaining a long-term and persistent presence has been no mean accomplishment. If we were to imagine a school-style report card for the UK and Irish Greens in the year 2014, an appropriate assessment would be that they have performed admirably under the circumstances.

Notes

1 The Greens in Wales have become increasingly autonomous but remain part of the 'national' organisation of GPEW. The Welsh Greens produce their own manifestos, have their own annual conference and have a 'leader in Wales'. They manage their own membership lists, but members join GPEW. Conversely, in 2006, the Greens in Northern Ireland voted to join with the Irish Greens, a demonstration of their belief in cross-community Irish politics, but they remain a separate organisational unit with their own leader, convention, manifestos and members.

2 At present, for each single candidate the deposit is £500.00, which is returned if the candidate achieves more than 5 per cent of the vote.

3 In the UK Parliament, Conservative and Labour MPs account for 87 per cent of all representatives, despite attracting only 65 per cent of the vote in 2010. The Liberal Democrats, presently in coalition with the Conservatives, gained 9 per cent of seats in 2010, with a 23 per cent vote share.

4 The 2010 general election cost the party £164,000 to field 335 candidates.

5 STV is used in Northern Ireland for European elections, but support for the Greens is lower in this part of the UK. In 2014, the party attracted 1.7 per cent of votes, down from 3.3 per cent in 2009.

6 Note, however, that the incoming *Fine Gael*-Labour government has since watered down many of these commitments, for example climate change legislation and local government reform.

7 <http://www.theguardian.com/politics/2014/aug/05/young-greens-growth-spurt>.

8 Electoral Commission UK (http://electoralcommission.org.uk).

9 Interview on the BBC's *Andrew Marr Show*, 27 April 20014.

10 He adds that social media 'had absolutely no impact on the campaign itself' (Gallagher and Marsh, 2011, p. 133).

References

Bennie, L., 2004. *Understanding Participation: Green Party Membership in Scotland.* Aldershot: Ashgate.

Bennie, L., and Clark, A., 2008. The transformation of local politics? STV and the 2007 Scottish local government elections. *Representation*, 44(3), pp. 225–238.

Bennie, L., 2015. A Minority Pursuit: Party Membership in Britain. In: E. van Haute and A. Gauja, eds, *Party Members and Activists*. Abingdon, Oxon: Routledge. pp. 169–185.

Birch, S., 2009. Real progress: Prospects for Green party support in Britain. *Parliamentary Affairs*, 62(1), pp. 53–71.

Bolleyer, N., 2010. The Irish Green party: From protest to mainstream party? *Irish Political Studies*, 25(4), pp. 603–623.

Bolleyer, N., 2012. The Rise and Decline of the Green Party. In: L. Weeks and A. Clark, eds, *Radical or Redundant? Minor Parties in Irish Politics*. Dublin: The History Press Ireland. pp. 110–125.

Boyle, D., 2006. *A Journey to Change: 25 Years of the Green Party in Irish Politics.* Dublin: Nonsuch.

Carter, N., 2008. The Green Party: Emerging from the political wilderness? *British Politics*, 3, pp. 223–240.

Carter, N., 2014. The politics of climate change in the UK. *WIRES Climate Change*, 5(3), pp. 423–433.

Cross, W., and Blais, A., 2012. *Politics at the Centre: The Selection and Removal of Party Leaders in the Anglo Parliamentary Democracies*. Oxford: Oxford University Press.

Cross, W., and Katz, R. S., 2013. *The Challenges of Intra-Party Democracy*. Oxford: Oxford University Press.

Curtice, J., 1989. The 1989 European election: Protest or Green tide? *Electoral Studies*, 8(3), pp. 217–230.

Dalton, R. J., Farrell, D., and McAllister, I., 2013. *Political Parties and Democratic Linkage: How Parties Organise Democracy*. Oxford: Oxford University Press.

Downs, A., 1972. Up and down with ecology – The issue-attention cycle. *Public Interest*, 28, pp. 38–50.

Farrell, D., 1989. Ireland: The Green Alliance. In: F. Müller-Rommel, ed., *New Parties in Western Europe: The Rise and Success of Green Parties and Alternative Lists*. Boulder, CO: Westview Press. p. 123–130.

Gallagher, M., and Marsh, M., 2011. *How Ireland Voted 2011: The Full Story of Ireland's Earthquake Election*. Houndmills and Basingstoke: Palgrave MacMillan.

Gallagher, M., Marsh, M., and Mitchell, P., 2003. *How Ireland Voted 2002*. Houndmills, Basingstoke: Palgrave MacMillan.

Gallagher, M., and Sinnott, R., 1990. *How Ireland Voted 1989*. Galway: PSAI Press.

Green Party, 2014. *Real Change: Manifesto for the European Parliament Elections 2014*. Available at: <http://greenparty.org.uk>.

Green Party of Northern Ireland Statement of Accounts, 2013. *Constitution of the Green Party*. London: Green Party.

Harper, R., 2011. *Dear Mr Harper: Britain's First Green Parliamentarian*. Edinburgh: Birlinn.

Harvie, P., 2013. Even the longest journey begins with a single step, *Scottish Green Party Blog*. Available at: <http://www.scottishgreens.org.uk/uncategorized/even-the-longest-journey-begins-with-a-single-step/> [Accessed Wednesday, 27 November 2013].

Jordan, A. G., and Richardson, J., 1987. *Government and Pressure Groups in Britain*. Oxford: Clarendon Press.

Kitschelt, H., 1989. *The Logics of Party Formation: Ecological Politics in Belgium and West Germany*. Ithaca, NY: Cornell University Press.

Little, C., 2012. Explaining the office attainment outcomes of Green parties in governing coalitions. Paper presented at the *European University Institute workshop on Political Parties and Institutions*, Florence.

Lucardie, P., and Rihoux, B., 2008. From Amateur-Activist to Professional-Electoral Parties? On the Organizational transformation of Green Parties in Western Democracies. In: G. Frankland, P. Lucardie and B. Rihoux, eds, *Green Parties in Transition: The End of Grass-Roots Democracy?* London: Ashgate. pp. 5–16.

Little, C., 2011. The general election of 2011 in the republic of Ireland: All changed utterly. *West European Politics*, 34(6), pp. 1304–1313.

Marsh, M., and Mikhaylov, S., 2014. A conservative revolution: The electoral response to economic crisis in Ireland. *Journal of Elections, Public Opinion and Parties*, 24(2), pp. 160–179.

McDonald, A., 2010. *The New Statesman*. Interview: Caroline Lucas. Available at: <http://www.newstatesman.com/environment/2010/05/interview-climate-european>.

McGee, H., 2006. Preface. In: D. Boyle, ed., *A Journey to Change: 25 Years of the Green Party in Irish Politics*. Dublin: Nonsuch. pp. 9–21.

McGee, H., 2012. *Irish Times blog*, 10/05/2012. Available at: <http://www.irishtimes.com/blogs/politics/2012/05/19/green-party-conference/>.

Michels, R., 1962. *Political Parties: A Sociological Study of the Oligarchical Tendencies of Modern Democracy*. New York: Collier Books.

Mullarney, M., 2006. Maire Mullarney, Dublin. In: D. Boyle, ed., *A Journey to Change: 25 Years of the Green Party in Irish Politics*. Dublin: Nonsuch. pp. 32–33.

Panebianco, A., 1988. *Political Parties: Organization and Power*. Oxford: Oxford University Press.

Parkin, S., 1989. *Green Parties: An International Guide*. London: Heretic Books.

Pedersen, M., 1982. Towards a new typology of party lifespans and minor parties. *Scandinavian Political Studies*, 5(1), pp. 1–16.

Rallings, C., and Thrasher, M., 2012. *British Electoral Facts 1832–2012*. London: Biteback Publishing.

Rootes, C., 1995. Britain: Greens in a Cold Climate. In: D. Richardson and C. Rootes, eds, *The Green Challenge: The Development of Green Parties in Europe*. London: Routledge. pp. 66–90.

Rootes, C., 2003. *Environmental Protest in Western Europe*. Oxford: Oxford University Press.

Rüdig, W., 2008. Green Party Organization in Britain: Change and Continuity. In: G. Frankland, P. Lucardie and B. Rihoux, eds, *Green Parties in Transition: The End of Grass-Roots Democracy?* London: Ashgate. pp. 199–223.

Rüdig, W., Bennie, L., and Franklin, M., 1991. *Green Party Members: A Profile*. Glasgow: Delta Publications.

Rüdig, W., Franklin, M., and Bennie, L., 1996. Up and down with the Greens: Ecology and politics in Britain 1989–1992. *Electoral Studies*, 15(11), pp. 1–20.

Rüdig, W., and Lowe, P., 1986, The withered 'Greening' of British politics: A study of the ecology party. *Political Studies*, 34, pp. 262–284.

Scottish Green Party, 2014. *For a Just and Welcoming Scotland: The Scottish Green Party European Manifesto 2014*. Available at: <http://www.scottishgreens.org.uk>.

Taylor, G., and Flynn, B., 2008. The Irish Greens. In: G. Frankland, P. Lucardie and B. Rihoux, eds, *Green Parties in Transition: The End of Grass-Roots Democracy?* London: Ashgate. pp. 93–105.

Whiteman, D., 1990. The progress and potential of the Green Party in Ireland. *Irish Political Studies*, 5, pp. 45–58.

10 The Greens in the European Parliament

Evolution and cohesion

Nathalie Brack and Camille Kelbel[1]

Introduction

The Greens are relatively new political actors, yet they have been at the heart of some renowned work in the last three decades (Kitschelt, 1988, 1989; Müller-Rommel, 1989; Rüdig, 1990; Doherty, 1992; Poguntke, 1993; Frankland, 1995; O'Neill, 1997; Bomberg, 1998; Delwit and De Waele, 1999; Frankland, et al., 2008). However, the participation of the Greens in the European Parliament (EP) has received rather limited attention so far.

Although Green parties have been quite successful in securing seats in the EP since 1984, the literature on the Greens at the supranational level remains rather sparse. There has been some research on the electoral fortunes of the Greens at the European Union (EU) level (Curtice, 1989; Bowler and Farrell, 1992; Carter, 1994, 2005) and on the development of European party federations (Hix, 1996; Delwit, et al., 2001). Dietz (2000) compared the European Greens to other trans-national party federations. He showed that, despite similarities, the Greens have not yet managed to establish a real European party given the relatively low degree of interaction between members of the federation. Other scholars focussed on the Europeanisation of the Greens, mostly understood as the adaptation of national political actors to European integration (Burchell, 2001; Bomberg, 2002). They showed that Europeanisation led to an ideological 'mellowing' among the Greens and a partial shift away from traditional Green issues by accelerating the professionalisation of Green party politics. Hines (2003) showed how EP rules produce incentives for Green parties to increase their cooperation, which in turn reduce their factionalism and promote their professionalisation.

By focusing mainly on the Europeanisation and its consequences for national actors, authors have left aside the organisation of the Green group in the EP, its cohesion and internal relations. If observers note that the group is highly cohesive and coherent, they often underline the absence of a pan-European Green ideology. Differences between and within Green national parties remain strong, notably on issues related to the EU.

In parallel, specialists of the EP have extensively studied parliamentary groups, as these groups 'make up the linkage between mass suffrage, parties and parliaments' (Heidar and Koole, 2000, p. 1). They found evidence that EP groups increasingly achieved a cohesive voting behaviour in plenary and that 'the cohesion of the political groups has increased over time as the main groups have gained in size and as the powers of the Parliament have increased' (Hix, et al., 2007, p. 104). However, most of these studies tend to focus on the major parliamentary groups that dominate the parliament, that is the Socialists (currently Socialists and Democrats – S&D), the Christian Democrats (European People's Party – EPP) and to a lesser extent, the Liberals (Alliance of Liberals and Democrats for Europe – ALDE) (Faas, 2003; Hix, et al., 2003; Hix, et al., 2005).

This chapter aims to contribute to a better understanding of the Greens at the supranational level. It focuses on the Greens/European Free Alliance (Greens/EFA) in the European Parliament in order to examine its organisation and cohesion. The first part explores the evolution of the Greens in the EP since 1979. The second part considers the cohesion of the group across time and issues. The third section analyses the factors behind the cohesiveness of the group and focuses on external and internal factors, including the group's characteristics and structure. In order to explain the high cohesiveness of the Greens/EFA, we stress the role of its organisational specificities, the relations between the Greens and the regionalists and the national delegations, as well as the role of the leadership. Concluding remarks are dedicated to the challenges and opportunities for the Greens in the EP.

Evolution of the Greens at the European level

In this section, we adopt an historical perspective to examine the evolution of the Greens within the EP. Party politics at the EU level has indeed largely been analysed through studies of the EP, whether focusing on the role of Europarties (Lord, 2002), Members of European Parliament's (MEPs) voting behaviours, including voting coalitions (Hix, et al., 2003; Kreppel and Hix, 2003), party groups and their cohesion (Kreppel, 2002) or the dimensions of the political space (nationalism–supranationalism and left–right) (Hix, 2001; Hix, et al., 2006). Our chapter subscribes to this approach. It focuses on voting behaviours although acknowledging that the Greens in the EP are also largely involved in nonvoting activities such as political campaigns, coordination with the European Green Party (EGP) and national parties, and so on, which will be touched upon. Although the specific case of the Greens could also call for accounting for the link between the group and civil society, in particular (environmental) nongovernmental organisations, which however falls out of the scope of this research. At the first European elections in 1979, the Greens did not succeed in gaining any seat (Bowler and Farrell, 1992) despite their attempt to develop transnational cooperation through the Coordination of European Green and Radical Parties. In view of the second EP elections in 1984, the Greens held a congress in Liège, which established a loose coordination (European Green Coordination) with a secretariat and a joint declaration. Twelve Green MEPs were elected in 1984 (seven from the German *Grünen*, two from the Dutch Greens, two Belgian Greens, and one from Italy). They formed the 'Green – Alternative Europe Link' (GRAEL), which took part in the Rainbow Group, together with regionalists and anti-EU Danish MEPs (Table 10.1; Rüdig,

Table 10.1 Chronology of the Greens in the EP (1979–2014)

EP legislatures	Political group	Number of MEPs of the group (Greens)	Ranking in the EP by group size
1979–1984			
1984–1989	Rainbow Group (RBW)	20 (12↑)	7th
1989–1994	Green Group in the European Parliament (GGEP)	30 (27↑)	5th
1994–1999	Green Group in the European Parliament (GGEP)	23 (22↓)	7th
1999–2004	Greens/EFA	48 (38↑)	4th
2004–2009	Greens/EFA	42 (35↓)	4th
2009–2014	Greens/EFA	58 (47↑)	4th
2014–2019	Greens/EFA	50 (36↓)	6th

Note: 1993: Creation of the European Federation of Green Parties; 2004: Creation of the European Green Party.

Source: Authors' own compilation.

1985; see also Table 10.6 at the end of this chapter). The Rainbow Group was the successor of the Technical Coordination and Defence of Independent Groups and Members. It was a technical rather than a political group that aimed at gaining access to rights and resources restricted to parliamentary groups. Joining this existing group arguably allowed the Greens to be socialised into the 'culture' of the EP and to benefit from the experience and expertise of their incumbent colleagues (Hines, 2003, p. 316).

The 1989 elections constituted a major turning point for the Greens in the EP, with a 'Green tide' that allowed 30 Greens representatives into the EP (Table 10.1). They could form a group on their own: the Green Group in the European Parliament (GGEP). It became the fifth largest of the (then) 11 parliamentary groups. It gathered MEPs from seven countries – Belgium, Germany, France, Italy, the Netherlands, Portugal and Spain – and was mainly dominated by the French and German delegations (nine and eight members, respectively) (Curtice, 1989; Corbett, et al., 2011). According to Bowler and Farrell (1992, p. 134), the group lacked a collective dimension as there were many national differences and individual members seemed 'unwilling or unable to adequately pool their strengths and resources as a group'. Since the mid-1980s, there had been an increased effort to develop a common electoral platform.

Nevertheless, it was only prior to the 1994 elections that an institutionalised form of cooperation emerged with the creation of the European Federation of Green Parties (established in June 1993)[2] and a strengthening of the ties between the Federation and the EP group. The 1994 elections, however, brought mixed fortunes: the French and British Greens failed to win any seats, while in Germany, Italy, Luxembourg and Ireland, the Greens were rather successful. The Greens managed to reconduct the GGEP and even gained new MEPs with the accession of Austria, Finland and Sweden to the EU in 1995 (Bomberg, 1996). With the domination of the pragmatic German MEPs and the absence of the (more fundamentalist at the time) French MEPs, the group became more cohesive but still highly individualistic (Hines, 2003). In fact, as Bomberg (1996, p. 327) noted, Green parliamentarians enjoyed considerable freedom in the group, and 'each member ha[d] his or her own projects or policy areas to which they devote[d] intense energy'. This individualism limited the ability of the group to act as a coherent whole. Despite having the reputation of being hard workers and despite their involvement in many parliamentary committees, Green MEPs still failed to develop a collective dimension within their EP group and to agree on common positions. They tended to use the group as a platform to play out internal battles and personal disputes, which was especially true of the German Greens (Bowler and Farrell, 1992; Bomberg, 1996).

In the 1999 election, the Greens won a record number of 38 seats in the EP (Table 10.1). They joined forces with ten MEPs from the European Free Alliance (regionalists) to form the Greens/EFA Group, the fourth largest EP group. While the German Greens suffered a loss of five seats, the leadership of Cohn-Bendit revitalised the French delegation that returned to the EP with nine seats. The two Belgian Green parties benefited in part from the dioxin scandal and won five seats, whereas the British Greens finally entered the EP (Corbett, et al., 2011). Despite these changes and the new alliance, the group displayed a high degree of cohesion under the fifth legislature (Hines, 2003). Prior to the 2004 elections, the Greens became a fully fledged European political party during their congress in Rome. They decided to fight the campaign in each country with a common manifesto and common slogans. They managed to consolidate their previous electoral results, as 35 Green MEPs were elected. They also renewed their alliance with the regionalists to form once again the fourth largest political group in the EP with 42 MEPs. Although some delegations did suffer some losses (notably the Belgian, French, Irish and Dutch delegations), others proved very successful (the German Greens), while some made their entry in Parliament (the Spanish Greens). It is however striking that the group benefited less electorally than any other from the Eastern enlargement. It did not succeed in gaining any seats from the ten acceding states in 2004. This can largely be attributed to the poor performance of Green parties in these member states and to the environment not being a visible issue in elections in the Central and Eastern European (CEE) countries (De Waele, 1999a; Carter, 2005).

In the 2009 election, the Greens did better than expected, especially in France where the list *Europe Écologie* secured 15 MEPs (Bressanelli, 2012). They also gained additional seats in Germany (14 MEPs), as well as in Belgium, Finland, Greece, the Netherlands and Sweden. They renewed their alliance with the regionalists and incorporated a few independents, thus remaining the fourth largest group in the EP with 59 members. Again, not a single Green was elected in the new member states, although two non-Green members of the group came from the Baltic States (an independent MEP from Estonia and a representative from the party 'Human Rights in United Latvia').

General patterns of cohesion of the Greens/EFA group

While the Rainbow Group had the lowest cohesion of the five EP groups, the subsequent Green parliamentary groups progressively increased their cohesion. By the fourth EP legislature, they became the most cohesive group in the EP. Party cohesion designates the behavioural observation according to which members of a party or group vote together (Bowler, 2000; Hazan, 2003; Bailer, et al., 2009). While Bomberg (2002) considers that the group's positions remain vague, the level of internal cohesion of the Greens/EFA is impressive, especially if one considers that most national Green parties face internal divisions, that the group actually contains two main sub-groups, and that EP groups do not have formal mechanisms for sanctioning disloyal members. If loyalty designates the behaviour of voting along a group's political line, cohesion levels represent aggregate (dis) loyalties.

Figure 10.1 portrays the progression of the Greens in terms of cohesion. Cohesion, or the unity of the group in voting situation, is calculated by VoteWatch Europe using a statistical method based on the arithmetical average of the scores of the Agreement Index, following the work of Hix, et al. (2005). Although there has been much criticism on the methodological bias related to roll-call votes (Carrubba and Gabel, 1999, 2004; De Waele, 1999b; Hug, 2006),[3] they remain a privileged source to assess cohesion in parliamentary voting behaviour (Raunio, 1999; Hix, 2006; Hix, et al., 2007). Figure 10.2 shows that the group increased its cohesiveness by almost 10 percentage points since 1989. In the last legislature, it has managed to be cohesive 95 per cent of the time during roll-call votes across policy areas. Figure 10.2 shows that, with the exception of internal EP

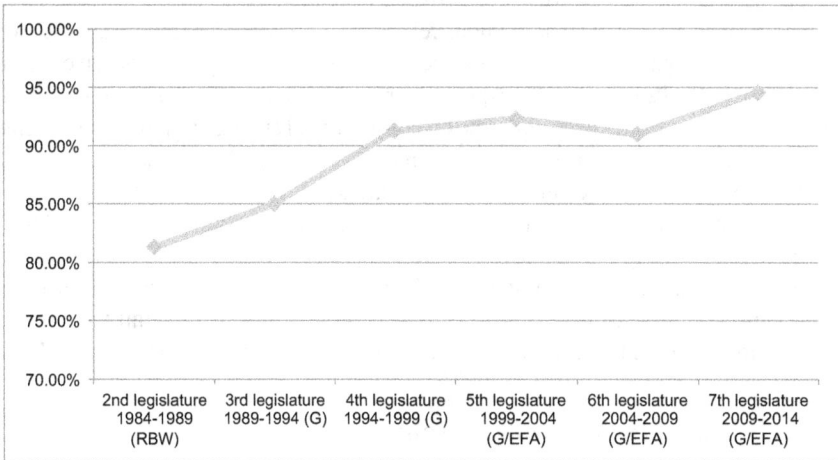

Figure 10.1 Cohesion of the Greens/EFA group in the EP, 1984–2014

Source: VoteWatch Europe.

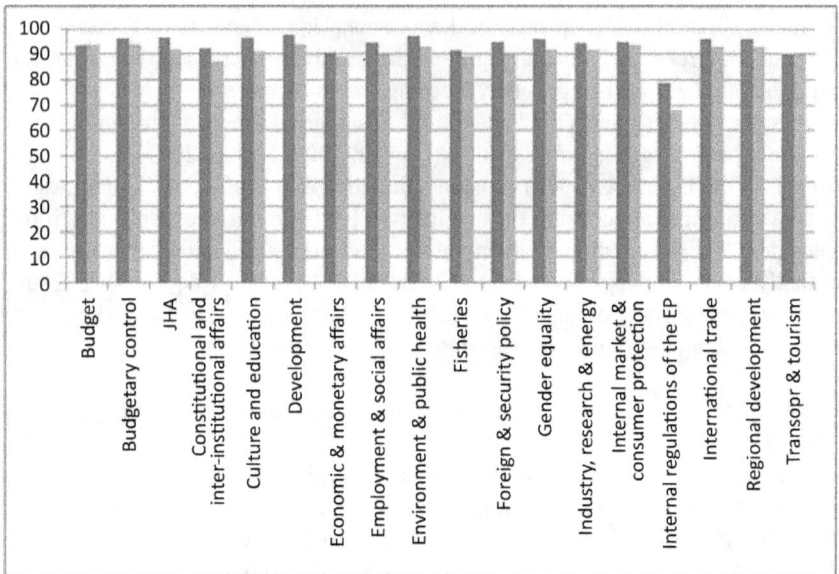

Figure 10.2 Cohesion by policy issue in the Sixth and Seventh Legislatures
Source: VoteWatch Europe.

regulation (that is, mainly the reforms of the rules of procedure), the cohesion of the Greens/EFA group remained high and stable across policy issues over the last two legislatures.

This does not mean however that there is no tension or disagreement among the group, be it among Green MEPs or between Green and other MEPs of the group. Indeed, Greens have had an ambiguous relation to European integration and the EU (Rüdig, 1996; Bomberg, 1998). If most members are nowadays pro-European or even 'European federalists', some still express strong criticism towards EU institutions and eventually defect from the group's line on constitutional and institutional issues. This is particularly the case for the Swedish Greens who originally campaigned against the membership of their country to the EU and are still very sceptical vis-à-vis the EU (Interviews, Brussels, 28 April 2009 and 10 May 2010). Similarly, tensions have emerged within the group on the position the EU should take in its relationship with China, as well as on the definition of notions such as growth or minimum income (Interview, Brussels, 24 February 2013). However, it seems that overall the Greens are able to overcome these tensions and to agree on common positions.

What is behind the Greens/EFA cohesion?

Focusing on the 2009–2014 legislature, we examine to what extent the structural characteristics and organisation of the group help explaining the remarkably high level of cohesion of the Greens/EFA group. The literature often distinguishes between two main dimensions for voting cohesion: the external dimension (the relation with the executive) and the internal dimension (incentives within the legislative arena) (Cicchi, 2011).

External dimension: The Greens/EFA EP group in the wider EU political system

The existing literature on the EP distinguishes specific forms of relations with the executive. First, political groups in the EP 'are not emanations from highly structured political parties having led a political campaign on a precise program or ensuring a voting discipline in order to back-up the executive' (Costa, 2005). Previous research has indeed largely underlined the underdevelopment of Europarties (Lord, 2002)[4] based on the observation that they do not fulfil most of the traditional functions of political parties, which often remain in the hands of their national member parties (Bardi, 2002; Kreppel, 2004). In other words, because of the disconnection of European parliamentary activities from campaigns and elections, groups are not necessarily defending a predetermined political line and do not fulfil the same function as in national parliaments. Furthermore, the increase of power and competences of the EP bear unclear consequences as to the group cohesion.

> On the one hand, it may be hypothesised that the growing significance of the EP has provided party groups with further incentives to coordinate and monitor their members' activities. On the other hand, it may be claimed that the widened scope of EU legislation has fostered the intervention of national principals, thus rendering voting behaviour less coherent.
>
> (Bailer, et al., 2009, p. 362)

This latter point is intrinsically linked to the relations with the executive, since the strengthening of the EP is to be understood in relative terms: a bigger 'share' for the EP is synonymous of relatively less power to the Council and the Commission (the two executive powers within the institutional triangle). The increasing use of the codecision procedure – now referred to as the ordinary legislative procedure – illustrates this view. As such, this argument does not offer a satisfactory explanation of the Greens/EFA cohesion, mainly because of the specific relationship between the executive and the legislative that prevails at the EU level.

The percentage of MEPs from parties in national government is also often considered as a variable leading to higher levels of cohesion (Faas, 2003). Indeed, parties represented in the Council are more likely to put pressure on their MEPs to ensure that the legislative proposal that was adopted by the Council passes the hurdle of the EP (Faas, 2003; Hix, et al., 2007). In the 2009–2014 legislature, 32.2 per cent of the Green MEPs (19 out of 59) came from parties in national governments, which could enhance the cohesion of the group. Most of these MEPs (15 out of 19) belong to the French *Europe-Écologie*. A number of MEPs come from parties in regional governments. However, in the case of the Greens, there is little evidence of a link between governmental participation and Greens' EP positions (Interview

Table 10.2 Frequency of contact (%)

	At least once a week	At least once a month	At least every 3 months	At least once a year	Less often	No contact	Total (N)
Members of my national party executive							
EPP	25.0	51.6	15.6	1.6	3.1	3.1	100 (64)
S&D	23.7	52.7	14.5	5.5	1.8	1.8	100 (55)
ALDE	30.0	53.3	6.7	6.7	3.3	0.0	100 (30)
Greens/EFA	26.7	26.6	40.0	6.7	0.0	0.0	100 (15)
Others	33.3	45.9	12.5	8.3	0.0	0.0	100 (24)
Leaders of my European political group							
EPP	52.3	32.3	9.2	1.5	1.5	3.2	100 (65)
S&D	52.7	27.3	18.2	1.8	0.0	0.0	100 (55)
ALDE	50.0	30.0	13.3	0.0	6.7	0.0	100 (30)
Greens/EFA	66.7	26.7	6.6	0.0	0.0	0.0	100 (15)
Others	41.7	58.3	0.0	0.0	0.0	0.0	100 (24)
Members of my national political party							
EPP	54.7	35.9	3.1	1.6	3,1	1.6	100 (64)
S&D	44.4	50.0	5.6	0.0	0	0.0	100 (54)
ALDE	51.7	38.0	10.3	0.0	0.0	0.0	100 (29)
Greens/EFA	46.7	33.2	6.7	6.7	6,7	0.0	100 (15)
Others	52.2	39.1	8.7	0.0	0	0.0	100 (23)
Ministers from my national government							
EPP	6.2	51.6	32.8	3.1	1.6	4.7	100 (64)
S&D	7.3	23.6	27.3	20.0	16.3	5.5	100 (55)
ALDE	13.8	31.0	20.7	6.9	13.8	13.8	100 (29)
Greens/EFA	0.0	6.6	26.7	26.7	33.3	6.7	100 (15)
Others	20.8	16.7	33.3	8.3	16.7	4.2	100 (8)

Note: Others = ECR, EUL/NGL, EFD.

Source: EPRG 2010 MEP Survey.

with a Green/EFA MEP, Brussels, 7 March 2013). There seems to be little contact between Green MEPs and ministers. More than 65 per cent of the Green MEPs report to have contact with ministers from their national governments once a year or less (Table 10.2).

Internal dimension: The key role of the organisation of the group

Internally, voting cohesion is generally attributed to some form of discipline mechanisms and/or similar preferences (Bowler, 2000; Hazan, 2003; Carrubba and Gabel, 2004). Regarding the incentives for Greens/EFA MEPs, the literature points out several key determinants. Contextually, the characteristics of particular votes are considered as key short-run determinants. Structurally, the general characteristics displayed by the group and its organisation matter. It appears that the cohesiveness revealed by the data on roll-call votes is at least partially explained by structural discipline mechanisms. Such discipline, however, does not echo the group's general characteristics but rather its organisational specificities.

Characteristics of the group

Some authors associate the cohesiveness of a European political group with considerations regarding its size and diversity (Heidar and Koole, 2000; Noury, 2004; Hix, et al., 2007). Hix, et al. (2005) demonstrated that size matters for the cohesion of the group, an increase in party group size leading to more cohesion. Although the number of MEPs increases the coordination and monitoring costs as well as the probability of diverging views, larger groups are more cohesive. Such groups receive more staff and resources, but more importantly, they worry more about their cohesion as they have much at stake during the votes. Indeed, due to their position, they have the power to influence or even determine the legislative outcomes and are interested in increasing the credibility of the EP in the inter-institutional negotiations (Heidar and Koole, 2000; Hix, et al., 2007). They are thus more likely to put discipline mechanisms in place such as whips to ensure cohesion, and have a larger array of sanction mechanisms and incentives for compliance (Bailer, et al., 2009). The major groups in the EP control most of the institutional positions, have more power in the rapporteurship allocations and more resources at their disposal (Raunio, 2000; Hix, et al., 2005). In the case of the Greens, these elements only offer a partial explanation of the high cohesion of the group. It does not qualify as a large group, with (only) 59 members.[5] Although the group manages to be more influential on some policies than its size would suggest (for example on environment or data protection), it still is not able to play a similar role as the EPP or S&D. The group is not in a position to influence strongly the legislative outcomes on most issues as the EP tends to be dominated by a '2 + 1 coalition' (EPP and S&D + ALDE). In addition, it does not have many 'sticks and carrots' to reward or punish its members in case of defection, as the group does not control the main power positions in the parliament.

Highly diverse groups are often associated with lower cohesion levels: '[W]ith high fragmentation, say with many small national delegations from all member states, there will be more free-riding and bargaining to reach an agreement will be tougher' (Hix, et al., 2007, p. 97). On the contrary, the higher the ideological homogeneity of a party group, the fewer measures needed by the group to ensure discipline (Bowler, et al., 1999). Yet, if policy compatibility is the main factor behind group membership and political groups are aggregations of like-minded parties (McElroy and Benoit, 2010; Bressanelli, 2012), it does not mean that groups are ideologically homogeneous. The internal diversity of the Greens/EFA group is rather high. First, as mentioned previously, the group contains members from two European political parties – the Greens and the regionalists from the European Free Alliance – that negotiate a political agreement on a yearly basis. Second, the group contains MEPs from 15 member states and 21 different national parties, as well as two independent members. This internal diversity may be moderated by the clear domination of the two main delegations, that is the French and the German Greens, which represent half of the group. Yet, this high fragmentation may be problematic for the cohesiveness of the group. Third, the Greens/EFA group is relatively ideologically diverse. Whitaker and Lynch (2014) measured the ideological diversity of EP groups on the left–right and the pro-/anti-EU scales. They noted that the Greens/EFA is the second most heterogeneous group on the left–right axis (after ALDE) and the third most diverse group on the 'EU dimension', after the Europe of Freedom and Democracy (EFD) and the European United Left–Nordic Green Left (EUL-NGL) groups.

In sum, the factors related to the characteristics of the group cannot explain the high level of cohesion in the group. Being a rather small group with high internal diversity, it faces many obstacles to cohesiveness, yet paradoxically still achieves to be the most cohesive group in the EP.

Internal organisation of the Green group in the EP

The literature on the EP highlights the role of the intragroup organisational structure in fostering cohesion. Political groups in the parliament display different degrees of institutionalisation (McElroy and Benoit, 2010). Most groups play a key role in aggregating the position of their members through internal deliberative processes. As noted by Costa and Saint Martin (2009), bigger groups form 'assemblies within the assembly', holding preparatory meetings and thematic working groups and determining the position of the group on individual texts. Although the Greens/EFA group cannot be considered as one of the major groups, its organisation is very similar and plays an important role in terms of the cohesiveness of the group.

First, Costa (2001) underlines the similar structures adopted by the groups, namely a bureau, a treasurer, a secretariat (which plays a fundamental role in the day-to-day functioning of the group) and a president. For the Greens/EFA group, the secretariat seems indeed to act as a broker of interest and primary information relay (Interview, Brussels, 24 February 2013). While the secretary general belongs to the Green party family, there are two deputy secretaries general: one from the Greens and one from EFA. They maintain permanent contacts with MEPs, policy experts, the president of the group and external actors. They attach great importance to the cohesion of the group (Interview, Brussels, 26 February 2013). Moreover, the Greens/EFA group has a structure similar to that of the larger EP groups: it has a large network of policy experts on a wide range of issues. Group meetings and thematic working groups contribute to define the common line. But the most important body is the bureau. It is composed of the presidents, vice-presidents, the secretary general and deputy secretaries general (plus the head of the press office). The bureau takes the main political decisions, in particular when a position needs to be defined. It plays a key role in defining a 'common language when the position of the group is not self-evident' (Interview, Brussels, 24 February 2013).

Second, the Greens have adopted a copresidency system, the position being held jointly by a French-elected MEP (Daniel Cohn-Bendit) and a German MEP (Rebecca Harms). The leadership plays a crucial role in ensuring the political unity of the group. In their study of EP groups, Bailer, et al. (2009) underline the link between group cohesion and leadership. They note that group leaders participate to the hallmark of the party by appraising and bringing together the positions of the MEPs. Leaders can exercise control over the group by several means and can be more or less strict in terms of voting discipline (Müller, 2000). For the Greens/EFA group in particular, these means are however limited. In the 2010 MEP survey of the European Parliament Research Group (EPRG), almost 43 per cent of the Greens/EFA respondents expressed a mitigated opinion on the use of far-reaching means by the leader to ensure unity, while over a third of the participants did not respond.[6] Only 21.4 per cent of the Greens/EFA respondents agreed to some degree, compared to over 30 per cent in the three larger groups.

Leaders can also use other softer internal processes. The analysis of the frequency of contact (Table 10.2) shows that Greens/EFA MEPs indicate a higher contact frequency with their group leaders than with national ministers, members of their national political party or members of their national party's executive. Besides, Greens/EFA MEPs also indicate a higher contact frequency with their group leader than MEPs from any other political group.

The patterns in terms of voting recommendation reinforce this idea (Table 10.3). Group leaders dispense voting recommendations on specific policy issues. Greens/EFA MEPs indicate that they received voting recommendations from the group leadership more frequently than from other sources (national government, national party leadership, national party delegation of MEPs or EP committee leadership).[7] The frequency of voting recommendations from the group leadership is higher among Greens/EFA MEPs than in any other political group.

Some characteristics of the party group leader(s) also have an impact on the group voting cohesion: these characteristics include experience (noticeably within the EP and in particular as head of a committee), not being a senior member of the EP, as well as a relative 'extremism' (Bailer, et al., 2009). Although such findings would need further empirical research, they might be of some relevance to understand the role of leadership in the Greens/EFA group. Neither of the two co-chairmen has headed an EP committee, although Cohn-Bendit acted as Delegation Chairman for the EU – Turkey Joint Parliamentary Committee from 1999 to 2002. Both co-chairmen would fall in the more senior category of MEPs (the average age of MEPs being 55 as of 2012). However, in terms of 'extremism', Cohn-Bendit is still largely associated with his participation in the social movements of 1968 and his political activism.

Third, the role of national delegations is often pointed out as a key determinant for the cohesion of a group. National delegations are quintessential of the EP political

Table 10.3 Frequency of voting recommendation (%)

	1 – Never	2	3	4	5 – On almost every vote	Total (N)
From national party leadership						
EPP	25.8	40.9	13.6	13.6	6.1	100 (66)
S&D	22.6	45.3	22.6	5.7	3.8	100 (53)
ALDE	25.8	38.7	25.8	9.7	0	100 (31)
Greens/EFA	33.3	53.3	6.7	6.7	0	100 (15)
Others	34.8	26.1	34.8	4.3	0	100 (23)
From European political group leadership						
EPP	3.0	6.1	12.1	13.6	65.2	100 (66)
S&D	3.8	5.7	15.1	22.6	52.8	100 (53)
ALDE	3.2	9.7	3.2	29	54.8	100 (31)
Greens/EFA	0	0	26.7	40	33.3	100 (15)
Others	8.7	17.4	17.4	13.0	43.5	100 (23)
From national party delegation of MEPs						
EPP	4.5	7.6	30.3	27.3	30.3	100 (66)
S&D	3.8	11.3	18.9	34.0	32.1	100 (53)
ALDE	13.3	6.7	20.0	23.3	36.7	100 (31)
Greens/EFA	26.7	6.7	40.0	20.0	6.7	100 (15)
Others	8.7	4.3	4.3	30.5	52.2	100 (23)

Note: Others = European Conservatives and Reformists (ECR), European United Left–Nordic Green Left (EUL/NGL), European United Left–Nordic Green Left = EFD.

Source: EPRG 2010 MEP Survey.

groups. They maintain links with the national party, national leaders or national governments, and Kreppel (2004) even defines EP groups as conglomerations of national parties. Therefore, national delegations may be seen as an obstacle to the cohesion of the group, essentially because the national party constitutes another 'principal' for the individual MEP (Miller, 2005). Hix (2006) sees national party positions as the strongest predictor of the voting behaviour of the MEPs. After all, national parties establish lists for EP elections and dominate the subsequent campaigns (Delwit, et al., 2004). They have the power to decide the electoral future of an MEP, and MEPs are thus likely to vote against the EP group in case of disagreement between the group and the national party (Faas, 2002).

Although the Greens are the only transnational party group with a genuine common platform for European elections (run by the European Green Party), the Greens/EFA group is nonetheless not fully remote from the influence of national delegations. However, this influence is arguably lower than in other groups. As indicated in Table 10.4, most Greens/EFA MEPs would follow their own judgment first, and then the EP group in case of conflict. Their national party and the national party

Table 10.4 Choices in case of conflicting views between the 'principals' (%)

	1st choice	2nd choice	3rd choice	4th choice	Total (N)
Follow my own judgment					
EPP	73.0	9.5	8.0	9.5	100 (63)
S&D	65.4	27.0	3.8	3.8	100 (52)
ALDE	7.4	14.3	14.3	0.0	100 (28)
Greens/EFA	86.7	6.7	6.7	0.0	100 (15)
Others	52.2	26.1	4.3	17.4	100 (23)
Follow the view of my national party					
EPP	11.1	34.9	23.8	30.2	100 (63)
S&D	0.0	25.0	32.7	42.3	100 (52)
ALDE	3.8	26.9	23.1	46.2	100 (26)
Greens/EFA	0.0	20.0	53.3	26.7	100 (15)
Others	13.0	30.5	43.5	13.0	100 (23)
Follow the view of my national party leadership					
EPP	4.7	21.9	43.8	29.7	100 (64)
S&D	9.6	15.4	44.2	30.8	100 (52)
ALDE	11.5	15.4	38.5	34.6	100 (26)
Greens/EFA	6.7	6.7	26.7	60.0	100 (15)
Others	30.5	17.4	34.8	17.4	100 (23)
Follow the view of my European political group					
EPP	11.1	31.7	27.0	30.2	100 (63)
S&D	25.0	32.7	19.2	23.1	100 (52)
ALDE	15.4	42.3	23.1	19.2	100 (26)
Greens/EFA	6.7	66.7	13.3	13.3	100 (15)
Others	4.3	26.1	17.4	52.2	100 (8)

Note: Others = ECR, EUL/NGL, EFD.

Source: EPRG 2010 MEP Survey.

leadership come as third and fourth choices, respectively. None of the respondents would follow the view of their national party first. This pattern strongly differs from the other groups: 43 per cent of EPP, and 58 per cent of S&D and ALDE MEPs would follow the view of their EP group as first or second choice (against 75 per cent of the Green MEPs). Forty-five per cent of the EPP, 25 per cent of the S&D and 30 per cent of ALDE members would choose the view of their national party as first or second choice in case of conflict, for only 20 per cent of the Greens/EFA. Similarly, only 13 per cent of the Greens put the view of the national party leadership as first or second choice, compared to 25 per cent in the EPP, S&D and ALDE and more than 35 per cent in smaller groups such as EFD, ECR and EUL/NGL.

Table 10.4 indicates that national delegations do not seem to constitute an obstacle to cohesion within the Greens/EFA group. First, national delegations in the EP have incorporated the logics of cohesion into their own logics, to the extent that cohesion *in fine* comes from these delegations (Hix, et al., 2007). If the national party position often differs from the EP group's position, they are not completely independent. They are the results of extensive internal discussions, deliberative processes and compromises (Interviews, Brussels, 26 February 2013 and 7 March 2013). Second, the organisation of the group reflects the balance of power between the national delegations. In the Greens/EFA group, as in other groups, the leadership of the EP party is composed of the leaders of the larger national delegations in that EP group. This eventually entails less policy conflicts for the MEPs from these national parties. Leaders retain control over a large proportion of the group's MEPs. Moreover, large delegations and group leaders influence significantly the policy position of the EP groups. They are therefore more likely to agree on the final position in which they played a major role. Therefore, one can expect to see a correlation between the size of the national delegation of the party group leader(s) and the level of cohesion (Bailer, et al., 2009). The copresidency appears as a specific means for national delegations management. The Greens/EFA group being dominated by the French and the German delegations, its positions are largely traceable to the positions of these national delegations.

Table 10.5 analyses the degree of loyalty of national party delegations toward the EP group line, measured as the frequency to which each national party delegation's positions correspond to the group's political positions. Several elements seem to confirm our expectations. First, the two largest delegations (France and Germany) are in the top four most loyal national delegations, the German delegation being the most loyal national delegation. Second, the seven more loyal delegations are all affiliated to the EGP. In sharp contrast with the Greens, all six EFA national delegations are situated at the bottom half of the ranking. This backs up the idea that the line of the group is assiduously followed (if not mainly spurred) by the larger delegations and by the Green MEPs over EFA members.

Finally, the cohesiveness of the Greens also reflects a deliberate strategy of the group. As Bomberg (2002) demonstrated, the Europeanisation of the Greens has resulted in a 'mellowing' of fundamental Green values rather than the development of a pan-European Green ideology. The Greens have developed a specific strategy aiming at maintaining the group's unity by focusing on noncontentious issues among national delegations. The cohesion of the Greens is related to the ability of the group to shed light on consensual issues, leaving aside more problematic matters (Interview, Brussels, 24 February 2013). These noncontentious issues are the ecology and the integrated approach to environment in other policy fields (transports, energy and economic affairs), peace and more diffuse policies related to 'good governance' (transparency, data protection and so on) (Interview, Brussels, 26 February 2013). To that extent, it is interesting to note that the group displays a remarkably high degree of satisfaction with its political unity: 78.6 per cent of the Greens/EFA respondents agree to some extent to the importance of appearing united, and 85.7 per cent are satisfied with the group's cohesiveness. None is in favour of a loosened unity, which places them far apart from any other EP group.[8]

Table 10.5 Loyalty of National Party delegations toward the Greens/EFA group

Member state	National party	Party at the European level	MEPs (N)	Loyalty (%)
Germany	*Bündnis 90/Die Grünen*	EGP	14	99.8
Austria	*Die Grünen – Die Grüne Alternative*	EGP	2	99.7
Belgium	*ECOLO*	EGP	2	99.5
France	*Europe Écologie*	EGP	15	99.2
UK	*Green Party*	EGP	2	98.8
Finland	*Vihreä liitto*	EGP	2	98.8
Belgium	*Groen*	EGP	1	98.5
Sweden	*Piratpartiet*	Other	2	98.5
Luxembourg	*Déi Gréng – Les Verts*	EGP	1	98.3
Netherlands	*GroenLinks*	EGP	3	98.3
Spain	*Iniciativa per Catalunya Verds*	EGP	1	98.3
Latvia	*Par cilvēka tiesībām vienotā Latvijā*	EFA	1	96.8
France	*Partitu di a Nazione Corsa*	EFA	1	96.8
Greece	*Ecologist Greens*	EGP	1	96.8
Denmark	*Socialistisk Folkeparti*	EGP	1	96.2
Estonia	*Sõltumatu*	Other	1	96,1
UK	*Plaid Cymru – Party of Wales*	EFA	1	95.1
Spain	*Bloque Nacionalista Galego*	EFA	1	93.8
Sweden	*Miljöpartiet de gröna*	EGP	2	87.8
UK	*Scottish National Party*	EFA	2	84.0
Portugal	*Independente*	Other	1	81.1
Belgium	*Nieuw-Vlaamse Alliantie*	EFA	1	75.1

Source: VoteWatch Europe

Overall, cohesion in the Greens/EFA group displays specific features. Discipline is ensured in a relatively loose manner. Deliberative processes, a strong but by no means authoritarian leadership, the incorporation of national delegations in the group's dynamics, constitute the structural engines of cohesion. Conjecturally, green ideologies have been significantly played down by strategies, a phenomenon largely attributable to the organisational (structural) specificities of the group.

Coming back to the two main explanations of cohesion – discipline mechanisms and similar preferences – we find that even when ideological affinities seem to be strong, they are often undermined by a unification strategy. Therefore, we argue that the balance tilts towards discipline over preferences. This does not mean that preferences should be dismissed as explanatory factors; they would certainly deserve more attention and in-depth analyses in future research on Green MEPs.

Conclusion: Challenges and perspectives for the Greens

The Greens have been able to become the most cohesive group in the EP and to remain united in a wide range of policy areas. The organisational specificities of the Greens/EFA group play a significant role in that respect. We have highlighted the particular function of the Bureau and of the Secretariat General as brokers of interest, the importance of the (co-)leadership, the interactions between the group, its members and the national delegations, as well as the strategy of the group to avoid controversial issues. Yet, other explanatory variables would deserve further research. Internally, analysing roll-call initiative strategies would shed further light on leadership–MEPs relations and mutual influence, as a mean to ensure discipline (Corbett, et al., 2011).

Enlargement should also be further studied as an external factor of (un)cohesion (Hix, et al., 2005; Bailer, et al., 2009). The main challenge for the Greens/ EFA group is precisely the development and success of Green parties in Eastern and Southern Europe. The group has benefited less than any other EP group from the last two enlargement rounds. There are also very few representatives of Green parties from the Southern member states. Group members are very much aware of the weakness of their partner parties in these countries and have developed strategies to support them, coaching their leaders, members and officials (Interviews, Brussels, 24 February 2013 and 7 March 2013). Paradoxically, if the relative weakness of Green parties from Eastern and Southern Europe is an important challenge, it also constitutes an asset for the Greens in the EP. It has helped maintain a certain level of homogeneity within the group, contributing to its cohesion, thereby allowing the group to be more influential than its numerical size would suggest.

Despite the attempts of the political parties at the European level and EP political groups to increase the visibility of pan-European issues and EP elections, the 2014 elections remained largely dominated by national parties and national issues. The Greens, as small parties, benefited from these elections and remaind more prominent and successful at the European level than in most national political arenas. They have renewed their alliance with the regionalists and have attracted a few more independents or members of atypical parties such as the Pirate parties. However, they did not manage to maintain their position as the fourth largest EP group. In parallel, seizing the opportunity offered by the new provisions of the Lisbon Treaty regarding the designation of the European Commission President, the European Green Party has put forward a full-fledged candidate selection process. Two leading candidates (among four contenders) have been selected through what was arguably the most ambitious system to date among the political parties at European level: an online primary open to all voters.

Table 10.6 Composition of the group in the EP, 1984–2014

Member State	GRAEL/RBW 1984–1989			GGEP 1989–1994			1994–1999			Greens/EFA 1999–2004			2004–2009			2009–2014*		
	G	R	Other	G	EFA	Other	G	EFA	Other	G	EFA	Other	G	EFA	Other	G	EFA	Other
Austria							1*		0	2	0	0	2	0	0	2	0	0
Belgium	2	2	0	3	0	0	2		0	5	2	0	2	0	0	3	1	0
Denmark	0	0	4	0	0	0	0		0	0	0	0	1	0	0	1	0	0
Estonia													0	0	0	0	0	1
Finland							1*		0	2	0	0	1	0	0	2	0	0
France	0	0	0	9	0	0	0		0	9	0	0	6	0	0	15	1	0
Germany	7	0	0	8	0	0	12		0	7	0	0	13	0	0	14	0	0
Greece	0	0	0	0	0	0	0		0	0	0	0	0	0	0	1	0	0
Ireland	0	0	0	0	0	0	2		0	2	0	0	0	0	0	0	0	0
Italy	1	0	2	7	0	2	3		1	2	0	0	2	0	0	0	0	0
Latvia													0	1	0	0	1	0
Luxembourg	0	0	0	0	0	0	1		0	1	0	0	1	0	0	1	0	0
Netherlands	2	0	0	0	0	0	2		0	4	0	0	2	0	2	3	0	0
Portugal	0	0	0	0	0	0	0		0	0	0	0	0	0	0	0	0	1
Romania													0	1*	0	0	0	0
Spain	0	0	0	0	0	1	0		0	0	4	0	2	1	0	1	1	0
Sweden							4*		0	2	0	0	1	0	0	2	0	2
UK	0	0	0	0	0	0	0		0	2	4	0	2	3	0	2	3	0
Total	**12**	**2**	**6**	**27**	**0**	**3**	**22**		**1**	**38**	**10**	**0**	**35**	**6**	**2**	**47**	**7**	**4**
Group total/Total number of MEPs	**20/434**			**30/518**			**23/567**			**48/626**			**42/732 (43/785)**			**58/754**		

Notes: * Figures represent the number of MEPs at the start of the legislature (incoming Parliament), except: a) for acceding countries, for which MEPs following their first EP elections have been added; b) for the 2009–2014 legislature, for which figures for 2013 are used. G = Greens; R = Regionalists; EFA = members of EFA after 1989; Other = Independent members, other.

Source: European Parliament.

Notes

1   The authors would like to thank the participants of the 'Green Parties in Europe' conference and the anonymous referees for their valuable comments. A special thanks to Emilie van Haute for her suggestions on previous drafts of this chapter.
2   For a concise history of the European Federation of Green Parties, see Dietz, 2000.
3   Some argue that these votes represent less than a third of the votes in the EP and that they are neither a random nor a representative sample. Indeed, group leaders are said to use roll-call votes as a strategy to signal their position or that of a competitor group to citizens or interest groups or to check if their members follow voting instructions. This selection bias would mask the fundamental decisions, which tend not to be taken by roll call, and it would hide dimensions other than the left-right axis.
4   The concept of 'Europarty' is often used as synonymous with 'Political Party at the European Level' or 'transnational party federation'. In this chapter, it is acknowledged that there are three main faces (Katz and Mair, 1993) to these parties: the transnational federation, the national parties and the European Parliamentary group (Calossi, 2012).
5   We follow the categorisation of Costa and Saint Martin (2011) who distinguish large groups (EPP and S&D), intermediate or medium-size group (ALDE) and small groups (Greens/EFA, EUL/NGL, ECR and EFD).
6   EPRG MEP Survey Dataset, 2011. Q5.4 – MEP-group relations: The leader of a European political group should, as far as possible, ensure the unity of that European political group. In doing so, the use of far-reaching means, such as the denial of particular parliamentary posts (for example seats).
7   EPRG MEP Survey Dataset, 2011. Q5.1 – Voting recommendations: Your European political group leadership.
8   EPRG MEP Survey Dataset, 2011. Q5.5 – Opinion on political group unity.

References

Bailer, S., Schulz, T., and Selb, P., 2009. 'What role for the whips' A latent-variable approach to leadership effects on party group cohesion in the European Parliament. *Journal of Legislative Studies*, 15(4), pp. 355–378.

Bardi, L., 2002. Transnational Party Federations, European Parliamentary Groups, and the Building of Europarties. In: R. S. Katz and P. Mair, eds, *How Parties Organize: Change and Adaptation in Party Organizations in Western Democracies*. London: Sage. pp. 357–377.

Bomberg, E., 1996. Greens in the European Parliament. *Environmental Politics*, 5(2), pp. 324–331.

Bomberg, E., 1998. *Green Parties and Politics in the European Union*. London: Taylor and Francis.

Bomberg, E., 2002. The Europeanisation of Green parties: Exploring the EU's Impact'. *West European Politics*, 25(3), pp. 29–50.

Bowler, S., 2000. Parties in Legislatures: Two Competing Explanations. In: R. J. Dalton and M. P. Wattenberg, eds, *Parties Without Partisans: Political Change in Advanced Industrial Democracies*. Oxford: Oxford University Press. pp. 157–179.

Bowler, S., and Farrell, D., 1992. The Greens at the European level. *Environmental Politics*, 1(1), pp. 132–137.

Bowler, S., Farrell, D., and Katz, R. S., 1999. Party Cohesion, Party Discipline, and Parliaments. In: S. Bowler, D. Farrell and R. S. Katz, eds, *Party Discipline and Parliamentary Government*. Columbus: Ohio State University Press. pp. 3–22.

Bressanelli, E., 2012. National parties and group membership in the European Parliament: Ideology or pragmatism? *Journal of European Public Policy*, 19(5), pp. 737–754.

Burchell, J., 2001. Evolving or conforming? Assessing organisational reform within European Green parties. *West European Politics*, 24(3), pp. 113–134.

Calossi, E., 2012. *Europeanisation of Political Parties: The Emergence of Europarties*. Presentation for the *European Union Democracy Observatory (EUDO)*. Metropolitní Univerzita Praha.

Carrubba, C., and Gabel, M., 1999. Roll-call votes and party discipline in the European Parliament: Reconsidering MEP voting behaviour. *European Parliamentary Research Group, Working Paper*, 2.

Carrubba, C., and Gabel, M., 2004. The European Parliament and Transnational Political Representation: Party Groups and Political Conflict. *Europäische Politik Friedrich Ebert Stiftung (FES)*, 3, pp. 1–9.

Carter, N., 1994. The Greens in the 1994 European Parliamentary elections. *Environmental Politics*, 3(3), pp. 445–517.

Carter, N., 2005. Mixed fortunes: The Greens in the 2004 European Parliament election. *Environmental Politics*, 14(1), pp. 103–111.

Cicchi, L., 2011. Party groups in the European Parliament, cohesiveness and MEPs' survey data: New evidence on voting behaviour from a new (simple) methodology. *Interdisciplinary Political Studies*, 1(2), pp. 137–147.

Corbett, R, Jacobs, F., and Shackleton, M., 2011. *The European Parliament*. London: John Harper Publishing.

Costa, O., 2001. *Le Parlement Européen, assemblée délibérante*. Brussels: Éditions de l'Université de Bruxelles.

Costa, O., 2005. Equilibres partisans et comportement parlementaire dans l'Union à vingt-cinq: le Parlement Européen entre continuité et bipolarisation. In: E. Du Réau, C. Manigand and T. Sandu, eds, *Dynamiques et resistances politiques dans le nouvel espace Européen*. L'Harmattan: Paris. pp. 151–159.

Costa, O., and Saint Martin, F., 2009. *Le Parlement Européen*. Paris: La Documentation Française.

Curtice, J., 1989. The 1989 European election: Protest or Green tide? *Electoral Studies*, 8(3), pp. 217–230.

Delwit, P., and De Waele, J-M., 1999. *Les partis verts en Europe*. Bruxelles: Complexe.

Delwit, P., Kuhlaci, E., and Van de Walle, C., 2001. *Les fédérations Européennes de Partis. Organisation et influence*. Brussels: Éditions de l'Université de Bruxelles.

Delwit, P., Kuhlaci, E., and Van de Walle, C., 2004. *The Europarties: Organisation and Influence*. Brussels: Éditions de l'Université de Bruxelles.

De Waele, J.-M., 1999a. La situation des partis verts en Europe centrale et orientale. In: P. Delwit and J.-M. De Waele, eds, *Les partis verts en Europe*. Brussels: Complexe. pp. 221–239.

De Waele, J.-M., 1999b. La structuration partisane interne au Parlement Européen. In: P. Delwit, J.-M. De Waele and P. Magnette, eds, *A quoi sert le Parlement Européen? Stratégies et pouvoirs d'une assemblée transnationale*. Brussels: Complexe. pp. 131–146.

Dietz, T. M., 2000. Similar but different? The European Greens compared to other transnational party federations in Europe. *Party Politics*, 6(2), pp. 199–210.

Doherty, B., 1992. The Fundi-Realo controversy: An analysis of four European Green parties. *Environmental Politics*, 1(1), pp. 95–120.

Faas, T., 2002. Why do MEPs defect? An analysis of party group cohesion in the 5th European Parliament [online]*: European Integration Online Papers (EIoP)*, 6(2002–002). Rochester, NY: Social Science Research Network. Available at: <http://papers.ssrn.com/sol3/papers.cfm?abstract_id=306965> [Accessed 14 February 2013].

Faas, T., 2003. To defect or not to defect? National, institutional and party group pressures on MEPs and their consequences for party group cohesion in the European Parliament. *European Journal of Political Research*, 42(6), pp. 841–866.

Frankland, E. G., 1995. Germany: The rise, fall and recovery of Die Grünen. In: D. Richardson and C. Rootes, eds, *The Green Challenge: The Development of Green Parties in Europe*. London: Routledge. pp. 23–44.

Frankland, E. G., Lucardie, P., and Rihoux, B., 2008. *Green Parties in Transition: The End of Grass-Roots Democracy?* Farnham and Burlington, VT: Ashgate.

Franklin, M. N., and Rüdig, W., 1995. On the durability of Green politics: Evidence from the 1989 European election study. *Comparative Political Studies*, 28, pp. 409–439.

Hazan, R. Y., 2003. Does cohesion equal discipline? Towards a conceptual delineation. *Journal of Legislative Studies*, 9(4), pp. 1–11.

Heidar, K., and Koole, R., 2000. Approaches to the Study of Parliamentary Party Groups. In: K. Heidar and R. Koole, eds, *Parliamentary Party Groups in European Democracies: Political Parties Behind Closed Doors*. London and New York: Routledge. pp. 4–22.

Hines, E. H., 2003. The European Parliament and the Europeanization of Green parties. *Cultural Dynamics*, 15(3), pp. 307–325.

Hix, S., 1996. The Transnational Party Federations. In: J. Gaffney, ed., *Political Parties and the European Union*. London: Routledge. pp. 308–331.

Hix, S., 2001. Legislative behaviour and party competition in the European Parliament: An application of nominate to the EU. *Journal of Common Market Studies*, 39(4), pp. 663–688.

Hix, S., 2006. Dimensions of politics in the European Parliament. *American Journal of Political Science*, 50(2), pp. 494–520.

Hix, S., Kreppel, A., and Noury, A., 2003. The party system in the European Parliament: Collusive or competitive? *Journal of Common Market Studies*, 41(2), pp. 309–331.

Hix, S., Noury, A., and Roland, G., 2005. Power to the parties: Cohesion and competition in the European Parliament, 1979–2001. *British Journal of Political Science*, 35(2), pp. 209–234.

Hix, S., Noury, A., and Roland, G., 2006. Dimensions of politics in the European Parliament. *American Journal of Political Science*, 50(2), pp. 494–511.

Hix, S., Noury, A., and Roland, G., 2007. *Democratic Politics in the European Parliament*. Cambridge: Cambridge University Press.

Hug, S., 2006. Selection effect in roll-call votes. *Centre for Comparative and International Studies Working Paper*, 15, Zürich Swiss Federal Institute of Technology.

Katz, R. S., and Mair, P., 1993. The evolution of party organizations in Europe: The three faces of party organization. *American Review of Politics*, 14, pp. 593–617.

Kitschelt, H., 1988. The rise of left-libertarian parties in Western democracies: Explaining innovation in competitive party systems. *World Politics*, 40(2), pp. 194–234.

Kreppel, A., 2002. *The European Parliament and Supranational Party System: A Study in Institutional Development*. Cambridge: Cambridge University Press.

Kreppel, A., 2004. Moving in the other direction? The impact of domestic party system change on Italian MEPs. *Journal of European Public Policy*, 11(6), pp. 975–999.

Kreppel, A., and Hix, S., 2003. From 'Grand Coalition' to left–right confrontation explaining the shifting structure of party competition in the European Parliament. *Comparative Political Studies*, 36(1–2), pp. 75–96.

Lord, C., 2002. What role for parties in EU politics? *Journal of European Integration*, 24(1), pp. 39–52.

McElroy, G., and Benoit, K., 2010. Party policy and group affiliation in the European Parliament. *British Journal of Political Science*, 40(2), pp. 377–398.

Miller, G. J., 2005. The political evolution of principal-agent models. *Annual Review of Political Science*, 8, pp. 203–225.

Müller, W. C., 2000. Political parties in parliamentary democracies: Making delegation and accountability work. *European Journal of Political Research*, 37, pp. 309–333.

Müller-Rommel, F., 1989. *New Politics in Western Europe: The Rise and Success of Green Parties and Alternative Lists*. Boulder, CO: Westview Press.

Noury, A., 2004. European Parliament as a Research Laboratory. In: P. Magnette, ed., *La Grande Europe*. Brussels: Éditions de l'Université de Bruxelles. pp. 85–95.

O'Neill, M., 1997. *Green Parties and Political Change in Contemporary Europe: New Politics, Old Predicaments*. London: Ashgate.

Poguntke, T., 1993. Goodbye to movement politics? Organisational adaptation of the German Green party. *Environmental politics*, 2(3), pp. 379–404.

Raunio, T., 1999. The Challenge of Diversity: Party Cohesion in the European Parliament. In: S. Bowler, D. Farrell and R. Katz, eds, *Party Discipline and Parliamentary Government*. Columbus: Ohio State University Press. pp. 3–22.

Raunio, T., 2000. Second-Rate Parties? Towards a Better Understanding of the European Parliament's Party Groups. In: K. Heidar and R. Koole, eds, *Parliamentary Party Groups in European Democracies: Political Parties Behind Closed Doors*. London and New York: Routledge. pp. 231–247.

Rüdig, W., 1985. The Greens in Europe: Ecological parties and the European elections of 1984. *Parliamentary Affairs*, 38(1), pp. 56–72.

Rüdig, W., 1990. *Green Politics One*. Edinburgh: Edinburgh University Press.

Rüdig, W., 1996. Green Parties and the EU: Portrait of an Uneasy Relationship. In: J. Gaffney, ed. *Political Parties and the European Union*. London: Routledge. pp. 254–272.

Whitaker, R., and Lynch, P., 2014. Understanding the Formation and Actions of Eurosceptic Groups in the European Parliament: Pragmatism, Principles and Publicity. *Government and Opposition*, 49(2), pp. 232–263.

Part II

Comparative perspective on Green parties in Europe

11 Green parties and elections

Caroline Close and Pascal Delwit

Introduction

Born in the 1980s, Green parties are often presented as the vector of postmaterialist values (Inglehart, 1977), of the *New Politics* ideals (Poguntke, 1993), of the *New Left Policy Agenda* (Kaelberer, 1993) or of the libertarian left (Kitschelt, 1988). They rapidly accessed the parliamentary arenas in a couple of countries: in Switzerland in 1979, in Belgium in 1981, in Germany and in Finland in 1983, in Luxembourg in 1984. During the second half of the 1980s, they entered the legislative assemblies in Austria (1986), in Italy (1987), in Sweden (1988) and in the Netherlands (1989).

Several authors at that time predicted a bright future for Green parties (Galtung, 1986, p. 85). However, looking back at how they have performed in the last decades, the picture appears quite mixed. Analysing the electoral performances of these parties, Mair (1999) has put into question their ability to emerge as relevant actors in the Western political landscape. According to Mair, Green parties in Western Europe have failed to brand themselves as the precursors of a new global realignment and have remained electorally quite marginal. By contrast, Dietz (2001) considers that Green parties have become important electoral political actors at the national level in most EU member states. Fifteen years later, how should we consider the electoral fate of these parties?

In this chapter, we first examine the electoral performances of Green parties in Europe at the national and European levels. Then, we propose a sociological analysis of their electorate. We examine the profile of Green voters in terms of social background, political preferences, form and degree of social and political activism and attitudes towards politics and democratic institutions. Whereas the first part of the chapter highlights the distinct paths that Green parties have followed, the second part insists on the commonalities of the Green electorate across Europe.

Electoral results of Green parties in Europe

Consociational democracies

Consociational democracies (Lijphart, 1981) are characterised by significant fragmentation, a proportional political dynamics and consensus-based decision-making process, in order to ensure 'diversity in unity' (Croisat and Quermonne,

1999, p. 35). In Europe, these democracies present quite high levels of political and economic development. This latter aspect is regularly identified as one of the conditions for the electoral and political development of Green movements. Six consociational democracies are examined here: Austria, Belgium, Germany, Luxembourg, the Netherlands and Switzerland – although the inclusion of Germany in this category has been much discussed in the literature (see Table 11.1).[1] Most of the Green parties in these states were born in the late 1970s or early 1980s.

In five out of six cases – Austria, Belgium, Germany, Luxembourg and Switzerland –, Green parties have initially followed a similar path.[2] They achieved an electoral and political breakthrough in the 1980s (Kitschelt, 1988). This initial success persisted in the 1990s. Rapidly, they became 'relevant' parties (Sartori, 1976) and secured a stable share of the vote (between 5 and 10 per cent). The Netherlands is an exception to this initial common pattern. Two Green organisations have co-existed: a small one – *De Groenen* – and a more important one that resulted from the merger of four parties – *GroenLinks*. *GroenLinks* faced electoral difficulties until the 1998 national election where it succeeded in capturing 7.3 per cent of the votes.

In the late 1990s/early 2000s, the patterns diverged in three different directions. The first pattern is characterised by relative 'stabilisation', as found in Belgium and Germany. There, Green parties reached an electoral peak or 'ceiling' and fluctuated around this peak. In Belgium, *Ecolo* and *Groen* attained their best score at the 1999 national elections: 14.4 per cent of the votes, still today the most remarkable performance among European Green parties. However, *Ecolo* and *Groen* were not able to replicate this success. They endured a severe drop in 2003 following their participation in government (Delwit, 2012). Their score stabilised in the 2007, 2010 and 2014 elections, oscillating between 8 and 9.5 per cent of the votes. In Germany, *Bündnis 90/Die Grünen* reached their ceiling earlier. In 1987, the party secured 8.3 per cent of the vote and then stagnated around this peak in the 1990s and 2000s, even if it managed once to exceed the symbolic threshold of 10 per cent at the 2009 national election. However, comparing the Belgian and German cases is challenging given the German post-reunification context of the 1990s. Indeed, the Greens were less well imbedded politically and electorally in Eastern than in Western Germany (Poguntke, 1998).

The second model is characterised by a relative growth, as in the case of Switzerland, Austria and Luxembourg. The first Green deputy ever was elected in Switzerland; yet the electoral growth of the Green Party of Switzerland (GLP) has been slow. The first time the party managed to exceed the 5 per cent threshold occurred in 1991. This score stabilised during the 1990s. In the 2000s, the party entered a new phase by stabilising its score between 7.4 and 9.6 per cent. The Austrian Greens (*Die Grünen*) experienced an almost linear progression: around 5 per cent in the 1980s, between 5 and 8 per cent in the 1990s and between 10 and 12 per cent in the 2000s. The Austrian Greens have appeared as the democratic alternative on the left side of the political spectrum, especially for those voters who were tired of the grand coalition governments led by the Social Democrats (SPÖ) and the Conservatives (ÖVP). In Luxembourg too, the electoral evolution

Table 11.1 Electoral results of Green parties in consociational democracies (%)

	The Netherlands		Belgium		Switzerland	Austria			Luxembourg			Germany
	De Groenen	GroenLinks	Ecolo	Groen	PES	Die Grunen	VGÖ	ALÖ/GAL	déi gréng	GLEI	GAP	Bündnis 90/Die Grünen
1979					0.6							
1980												1.5
1981			2.5	2.6	1.9							
1983							1.9	1.4				5.6
1984									4.2			
1985			2.5	3.7								
1987			2.6	4.5	4.9	4.8	0.1	0.02				8.3
1989	0.4	4.1								3.7	3.7	
1990						4.8	2.0					5.0
1991		3.5	5.1	4.9	6.1							
1993	0.1											
1994						7.3	0.1		9.9			7.3
1995			4.0	4.8	5.0	4.8						
1998	0.2	7.3	7.4	7.0	5.0							6.7
1999						7.4			9.1			
2002		7.0				9.5						8.6
2003		5.1	3.1	2.5	7.4							
2004									11.5			
2006		4.6				11.1						8.1
2007			5.1	4.0	9.6							
2008						10.4						
2009									11.5			10.7
2010		6.7	4.8	4.4								
2011					8.4							
2012		2.3										
2013						12.4			10.1			8.4
2014			3.3	5.3								

of the Greens appears linear: between 4 and 7.5 per cent in the 1980s, around 9 per cent in the 1990s and an average of 11 per cent in the 2000s. In 2013, these results allowed the Greens to join an unprecedented 'rainbow' coalition that associated the Liberals, the Socialists and the Greens, expelling the Christian Democrats (CVP) in the opposition.[3]

The third model pertains to the evolution of *GroenLinks* in the Netherlands. *GroenLinks* experienced electoral decline. In 2012, it even suffered a bitter defeat with only 2.3 per cent of the vote. On the same side of the political spectrum, the party is challenged by the Socialist Party (SP), a Maoist-rooted organisation that is extremely active, but also by the Party for the Animals (PvdD), which gained two seats in the House of Representatives in 2006.

Thirty years or more after their birth, Green parties in consociational democracies have succeeded in becoming nonmarginal political actors and in acquiring an undeniable relevance in their political system. Nevertheless, even the most successful of them have rarely exceeded 10 per cent of the votes. In some cases, this was a sufficient score to ensure their participation in national government (Belgium, 1999–2003; Germany, 1998–2005; Luxembourg, 2013), but this remains a rare event. While they emerged as the vectors of *New Politics*, Green parties are in some cases challenged on that topic by new or renewed actors, which are mainly situated on the left side of the political spectrum – The Left in Germany, the Socialist Party in the Netherlands, the Workers' Party in Belgium, The Left in Luxembourg. Many of these organisations are entrenched in the eco-socialist project and are more distant than the Greens from power and political institutions.

Scandinavia and Northern Europe

The five Nordic states – Denmark, Finland, Iceland, Norway and Sweden – use proportional electoral rules, which should *a priori* facilitate the emergence of new parties and their access to the parliamentary arena. Nevertheless, these countries differ according to the configuration of their political systems. Historically, and to a certain extent still today, in Denmark, Sweden and Norway, the party system has been dominated by the Social Democrats. However, this has never been the case in Finland and Iceland.

Assessing the performances of Green parties in Denmark is difficult (see Table 11.2). The current member of the European Green Party (EGP) is the Socialist People's Party (SF). This party was founded in 1959 as a split from the Danish Communist Party and was led by its former leader in disgrace, Aksel Larsen. It has long appeared as a communist organisation that developed away from the Soviet legacy and opened itself to new societal issues related to postmaterialism (Gotovitch, et al., 1992). The SF holds the status of observer in the EGP, while being a member of the Nordic Green Left Alliance, in which it connects with organisations like the Left Party of Sweden, the Left Alliance of Finland as well as the Socialist Left Party of Norway. In parallel, a Green party (*De Grønne*) emerged in the early 1980s but was never able to break through. It was expelled from the

Table 11.2 Electoral results of the Nordic Greens in legislative elections (%)

	Denmark		Norway	Sweden	Finland
	SF	De Gronne	MDG	MG	VL
1975	5.0				
1977	3.9				
1979	5.9				
1981	11.3				
1982				1.7	
1983					1.5
1984	11.5				
1985				1.5	
1986					
1987	14.6	1.3			4.0
1988	13.0	1.3		5.5	
1989			0.4		
1990	8.3	0.8			
1991				3.4	6.8
1993			0.1		
1994	7.3			5.0	
1995					6.5
1997			0.2		
1998	7.6			4.5	
1999					7.3
2001	6.4		0.1		
2002				4.6	
2003					8.0
2005	6.0		0.1		
2006				5.2	
2007	13.0				8.5
2009			0.3		
2010				7.3	
2011	9.2				7.3
2013			2.8		
2014				6.8	

EGP because it evolved in the opposite direction of the SF, that is, it reconciled with the radical left. It is therefore necessary to be cautious when interpreting their electoral results. We report the results of the SF, but it would be a mistake to consider its electoral evolution as that of a Green party.

In Norway and Denmark, the two Green parties are totally evanescent political organisations. They have failed to find a niche between the Social Democrats and left parties. However, in 2013, the Norwegian Greens (MDG) won one per cent of the vote and one seat in the House of Representatives for the first time in their history.

There is no Green party *as such* in Iceland. The Left–Green Movement (*Vinstrihreyfingin – grænt framboð*) promotes eco-socialism and locates on the left of Social Democracy. It is also a member of the Nordic Green Left Alliance.

In light of these facts, only two Green parties can be described as 'relevant' in the Nordic countries: the Green Party in Sweden (MG) and the Green League of Finland (VL). The Swedish Green party first crossed the electoral threshold in 1988. With 5.5 per cent of the vote, it gained access to parliamentary representation. However, this performance long remained exceptional. It had to wait until the 2010 election to exceed this level by winning 7.3 per cent of the vote. In-between, the Greens oscillated between 3.4 and 5.2 per cent, flirting with the electoral threshold. In 1991, the Greens did not reach it and were left without parliamentary representation. In 2014, the result was slightly below the 2010 performance (6.8 per cent).

The Finnish Green League, also born in the early 1980s, has a different destiny. The party won its first seat in 1983. Since then, it has experienced a slow but steady increase, reaching 8.5 per cent of the vote in 2007. In the 2011 election, the Green League suffered a significant drop for the first time (−1 percentage point). It is hard to say whether this indicates that the party reached a ceiling or whether this is due to the vicissitudes of a particular election. The Green League has regularly been part of the government coalition since 1995.

Assessing the electoral fate of Green parties in the Nordic states, the picture appears quite disparate. The Greens are absent in Iceland and almost invisible in Norway and Denmark. In Sweden and Finland, the two Green parties have established themselves as parliamentary actors, but with modest electoral profiles.

In the United Kingdom (UK) and Ireland, Green parties face different electoral systems. In the UK, the single-member plurality system raises important barriers to the entry of new outsider parties. Ireland uses the single transferable vote system, which is proportional but operates in low-magnitude districts where the strategy of the parties in terms of voting instructions is important.

The Green Party of the United Kingdom is one of the earliest. In September 1990, the Green Party was split into two organisations acting on different territorial areas: the Green Party of England and Wales (GPEW) and the Scottish Green Party (SGP). Both parties have won only marginal scores in recent British electoral history;[4] roughly between 0.5 and 1 per cent. These scores should be put in perspective given that the Greens do not present candidates in all constituencies. In 2010, for the first time in their history, they were able to gain a seat in the House of Commons. With 16,238 votes compared to 14,986 for the Labour candidate and 12,275 for the Conservative candidate in the constituency of Brighton Pavilion, Catherine Lucas became the first Green MP in the UK history. However, the Green Party is first and foremost a political organisation characterised by extra-institutional activism.

The picture is slightly different at the level of regional assemblies, particularly in the Scottish Assembly.[5] At its first election in 1999, the Scottish Greens won a seat. In 2003, the party reached 6.9 per cent and won six seats. In 2007 and 2011, the party suffered a net decline with a score averaging 4 per cent. In the Welsh Assembly, the Greens usually reach a score between 2.5 and 3.5 per cent, which has never permitted them to access regional representation.

In Ireland, the Green Party is a minor political actor. It has never exceeded 5 per cent of the votes. However, in 1989, it won its first seat and then gradually expanded its parliamentary representation. The six seats it won in 2007 allowed the party to take part in the government for the first time, first with the Progressive Democrats and *Fianna Fáil*, then only with *Fianna Fáil*. However, this experience proved disastrous given the dramatic financial and economic crisis that Ireland faced during this legislature. In the 2011 election, the Green Party lost all its parliamentary representation.

Southern Europe

The situation of Green parties in southern Europe is extremely precarious despite more favourable electoral systems than in the UK (Table 11.3).

The Portuguese Greens (*Partido Ecologista Os Verdes*) participated in all national elections in alliance with the Communist Party (PCP), a much larger organisation. Similarly, in Spain, the Initiative for Catalonia Greens (ICV) participated in national elections on its own only once. At all other elections, the party was a member of the Coalition of the Left (*Izquierda Unida*). Since 2008, the Italian Greens were also part of a coalition 'The Left – The Rainbow' (*La Sinistra – The Arcobaleno*) with the Communist Refoundation Party, the Party of Italian Communists and the Democratic Left. In 2013, they joined the 'Civil Revolution' coalition that gathered the same parties – without the Democratic Left – and was also joined by Italy of Values. Prior to this, the Italian Greens generally ran independently, obtaining minor results (around 2.5 per cent of the votes) but enough to gain 10 to 20 deputies and senators.

In France, the Greens have long achieved inconclusive results. In 1986, although the system of proportional representation was exceptionally introduced, the hope of winning seats did not materialise. In 1993, the Greens reached a substantial score in terms of vote (7.6 per cent) but did not win any seats. In the aftermath of this failure, the party abandoned the so-called 'neither left nor right' strategy and favoured an alliance with the left. This new strategy was first implemented in 1997. It allowed the French Greens to access the National Assembly. Even better, in the context of the plural left, it allowed them to participate in government. Since then, the Greens have maintained this strategy. They obtain low results in national elections – between 3 and 5 per cent of the votes – but manage to win parliamentary seats (17 in 2012). However, these results should be put in perspective given that the Greens do not run candidates in all constituencies.

Table 11.3 Electoral results of Green parties in Southern Europe (%)

	France	Cyprus	Greece	Spain		Italy	Malta
	EELV	KOP	OP	Los Verdes	ICV	Verdi	AD
1981	1.1						
1986	1.2			0.2			
1987						2.5	
1988	0.4						
1989				0.8			
1992						2.8	1.7
1993	7.6			0.8			
1994						2.7	
1995							
1996		1.0		0.3		2.5	1.4
1997	4.1						
1998							1.2
1999							
2000			0.3	0.3	0.5		
2001		2.0				2.2	
2002	4.4						
2003							0.7
2004				0.2			
2006		1.9				2.1	
2007	3.2		1.1				
2008				0.2			1.3
2009			2.5				
2011		2.2					
2012	5.5		2.9				
			0.9				
2013							1.8

In Cyprus, Greece and Malta, Green parties are extremely weak. In Malta, the Democratic Alternative (AD), founded in 1989, has never exceeded 1.8 per cent of the votes and never won a seat. This is partly due to the very low magnitude of the electoral districts. The AD is trapped in a perfect bipartisan system. Therefore, the party can only focus on the 'cultural struggle' since its prospects to enter the parliamentary arena are insignificant. In Cyprus, the Ecological and Environmental Movement (Kinima Oikologon Perivallontiston – KOP) first took part in the national election in 1996 and got 1 per cent of the vote. Since then, it has participated in all elections. Since 2001, the party has been able to win a seat at each election. KOP is still a minor actor, but it can no longer be considered as marginal. In Greece, the Ecologist Greens (OP) first took part in the election of 2000. They achieved their best result at the polls in May 2012, with almost 3 per cent of the vote, but were not able to win seats. A month later, however, the party lost two points as a result of strategic voting in an election where the Conservatives and the Radical Left were neck and neck to win the first place.

Green parties are far from being relevant actors in the southern European countries. With the exception of France, and to a certain extent Italy in the 1990s, Green parties are confined to low electoral scores. In these political landscapes still largely polarised between the left and the right, the Greens are struggling to find a clear positioning and a specific audience. Given the prevalent socio-economic agenda, and because socialist parties are embodying the progressive side of the new societal cleavage, the Greens do not appear as a credible alternative.

Central and Eastern Europe

After the fall of the Berlin Wall, the Czechoslovak Greens represented the best hope for the Green parties during the first democratic elections. However, they only met partial success – 4.1 per cent – and did not win any seat. This initial disappointment was difficult to overcome, and the Czech Greens (SZ), after the split of Czechoslovakia, did not go the polls until 1998. In 1998, the result – 1.1 per cent – was disappointing, to say the least. During the next eight years, the party achieved only modest scores or did not even run for election. In 2006, however, the SZ took everyone by surprise by collecting 6.3 per cent of the vote and six seats. After lengthy negotiations, the Greens took part in a right-wing government, a decision that harmed them. In the 2010 election, the Green Party attracted only 2.4 per cent of the votes and lost all its MPs. Despite a slight increase in 2013, the Greens remain without parliamentary representation. The low relevance of the Slovak Greens (SZ) is even more striking. For the 1994 elections, the small Green party formed a cartel with the Social Democrats and the ex-Communists but then disappeared from the national electoral landscape for two legislatures. In 2002, the party collected 0.99 per cent of the vote then again disappeared until 2012, when it got 0.3 per cent. The fate of the Greens in Poland is not much better. The Green Party (*Zieloni*) was founded in 2003 and has never participated as an independent actor in any national election. In Hungary, the party affiliated to the European Green Party (EGP) does not refer directly to political ecology in its label. Founded in 2009, Politics Can Be Different (LMP) made a remarkable breakthrough in the 2010 election by winning 7.5 per cent of the vote and five seats. In 2014, the party slightly declined – 5.3 per cent.

In Eastern Europe, the Green parties are equally evanescent. In Bulgaria, two Green parties are recognised by the EGP, the Bulgarian Green Party (ZPB) and the Greens (*Zelenite*). The former was established in the second half of the 2000s and has been marginal. It won 0.5 per cent of the vote at the 2009 national elections. In 2013, it was one of the tiny components of the Coalition for Bulgaria, organised around the Bulgarian Socialist Party (BSP). The latter Green organisation is equally insignificant. The Greens took part in the 2013 national elections but gained only 0.7 per cent of the votes and no parliamentarians. In Romania, the Green Party (PV) was established in 2006. It went to the polls on its own in 2008, it collected just 0.3 per cent of the vote. Challenged by the emergence of a rival organisation, the Green Movement (MV), the PV agreed with the latter to both join the 'Social Liberal Union' cartel organised around the Social Democrats and the national Liberals. Each of them won a seat in the House of Representatives. Thereafter, the MV merged into the PV.

What about the states that emerged out of the collapse of Yugoslavia? There, Green parties have only developed in Slovenia and Croatia. In Slovenia, the Green movement was embodied in the Youth Party, later renamed Youth Party – European Greens (SMS – *Zeleni Evrope*). Established in 2000, it immediately managed to enter the House at the 2000 national election, reaching 4.3 per cent of the vote and four seats. However, the SMS could not reiterate this score. In 2004, it dropped to 2.1 per cent and lost its representation. During the 2008 election, it formed as a minor partner in an electoral cartel with the Slovenian people's party. The alliance reached 5.2 per cent and won five seats, none of them for the SMS. Three years later, it won 0.9 per cent of the votes. In 2014, the party did not run for the election. On that occasion, another environmental organisation went to the polls, the Greens of Slovenia (*ZS*), but won only 0.5 per cent of the votes. In Croatia, the Green List (ZL), founded in 2005, recently merged into the Croatian Sustainable Development Party (ORaH). In Serbia, a Green party exists on paper, but it has never taken part in any national election. The same situation applies in Montenegro for the 'Positive Montenegro' party, which is a member of the EGP, and in Macedonia for the Democratic Renewal party.

The situation of Green parties in the Baltic States is contrasted. In Lithuania, the Greens are virtually nonexistent. The Lithuanian Green Party (LZP) only went to the polls in 1992 and won 0.1 per cent of the vote. The party did not participate in the subsequent elections until recently. The picture is quite different in Latvia. At its first election in 1993, the Latvian Green Party (LZP) won 1.2 per cent of the vote. Thereafter, the party launched a strategy of electoral cartels: In 1995, it allied with the National Independence Movement, and the cartel got 6.1 per cent of the votes and eight seats. In 1998, a cartel was created with the Labour Party and the Christian Democratic Union, but it led to a small 2.3 per cent and no seats. From 2002, a new cartel has been established, this time with the Latvian Farmers' Union (LZS). The formula has been much more promising. In 2002, the coalition won 9.4 per cent of the vote and 12 seats. Four years later, it won 16.7 per cent and 18 seats. In 2010, it won 19.7 per cent and no less than 22 seats. With this strategy, the Latvian Green party has become the most relevant party in Central and Eastern Europe (CEE) and an occasional government partner that has even occupied the post of prime minister during a few months. The Estonian Greens (EER), established in 1991, went first to the polls in 1992. Their score was small – 2.6 per cent – but allowed them to win a seat. However, the party could not sustain this performance and remained absent from the electoral scene for 15 years. In 2007, it came back and realised an unexpected breakthrough: 7.1 per cent of the vote, which allowed it to win six seats. But again, the Estonian Greens were not able to consolidate their performance. Four years later, the party only got 3.8 per cent of the vote and consequently lost its parliamentary representation.

Electoral results of Green parties at the European elections

Green parties also compete in European elections. These elections have been qualified as *second-order elections* (Reif and Schmitt, 1980; Reif, 1985), based on four characteristics: a higher level of abstention than in national elections (Delwit, 2002; Koepke and Ringe, 2006); a better result for small parties (including the Greens) due to lower levels of strategic or utilitarian voting and higher levels of 'vot[ing] with the heart' (Hix and Marsh, 2007, p. 497); a sanction vote against governing party(ies) given the national – and not European – focus of these elections (lower for junior coalition partners, see Hix and Marsh, 2007); lower results for government parties as a result of a strengthening of 'vot[ing] with the heart'.

Table 11.4 shows that Green parties do indeed perform better in European elections than in national elections. This is especially striking in the case of the French Greens or the Swedish Greens.

However, these findings have to be nuanced. First, this global picture does not contradict what was observed at the national level. Green parties are mainly relevant in Western Europe and in some Scandinavian countries. Southern and Central-Eastern Europe remain mission lands for the Greens. Second, the results do not take abstentions into account. Since abstention in the European elections is substantially higher than in national elections, performance must be relativised. The Greens not only benefit from the 'vote with the heart' effect, but also from the fact that their electorate has a higher education capital than the average electorate (see below). This segment is, all things being equal, the least affected by the higher level of abstention in the European elections. Third, the dynamic is not linear but rather cyclic, with three electoral breakthroughs: 1989, 1999 and 2009. However, these breakthroughs were not necessarily consolidated in the following election(s).

Overall, this overview of Green parties' electoral performances reveals a mixed record. On the one hand, one can point out that, whatever their degree of success or failure, no Green party has disappeared so far (Rihoux, 2001, p. 21). On the other hand, as was pointed out by Mair (1999), after their electoral breakthrough in the 1980s, Green parties have been struggling to reach new thresholds and new electoral bases. The Greens appear as an electorally stagnant family. However, the failure announced by Mair is not verified.

At the heart of Europe, Green parties have established themselves as political actors that count. Several of them have or have had executive responsibilities at the national or the subnational level, although it remains exceptional. Moreover, their electoral performances fluctuate between 5 and 10 per cent, and Green parties face difficulties to pass the ceiling of 10 per cent. Outside of this heartland, Green parties are characterised by low relevance, with the exception of the Swedish and Finnish Greens.

Table 11.4 Electoral results of Green parties in European elections (%)

	1979	1984	1989	1994	1999	2004	2009	2014
Austria				6.8	9.3	12.9	9.7	14.5
Belgium	3.4	8.2	13.9	11.6	16.0	8.7	13.5	11.0
Bulgaria						0.5		0.9
Croatia								9.4
Cyprus						0.9	1.5	*
Czech Republic						3.2	2.1	3.8
Denmark	4.7	9.2	9.1	8.6	7.1	8.0	15.9	10.9
Estonia						2.7	2.7	0.3
Finland				7.6	13.4	10.4	12.4	9.3
France	4.4	3.4	10.6	2.9	9.7	7.7	17.3	8.9
Germany	3.2	8.1	8.4	10.1	6.4	11.9	12.1	10.7
Greece						0.7	3.5	0.9
Hungary						5.3	5.3	5.0
Ireland		0.5	3.7	7.9	6.7	4.3	1.9	4.9
Italy			3.8	3.2	1.7	2.5		0.9
Latvia						4.3	3.8	8.3
Lithuania								3.6
Luxembourg		6.1	10.5	10.9	10.7	15.0	16.8	15.0
Malta						9.3	2.3	2.9
Netherlands		5.6	7.0	6.1	11.8	7.4	9.1	7.2
Poland						0.3		0.3
Portugal								
Romania						0.4		0.3
Slovakia							2.1	0.5
Slovenia						2.3	1.9	0.8
Spain								
Sweden				18.2	9.5	6.0	11.0	15.3
United Kingdom	0.1	0.5	14.4	3.1	6.4	6.1	8.3	8.3

* The Green Party has made an alliance with the Social Democrats (EDEK).

In 1998, Müller-Rommel isolated eight 'successful Green Parties' in Austria, Belgium, Finland, Germany, Luxembourg, the Netherlands, Sweden and Switzerland (Müller-Rommel, 1998). More than 15 years later, the dynamics haven't changed much with the exception of the Latvian Greens and possibly the French and Hungarian Greens.

The profile of Green voters

This second section looks beyond differences in electoral fates and analyses commonalities of the Green electorate across Europe. More specifically, it explores the distinctiveness of the Green electorate in terms of their social characteristics, political preferences, form and degree of social and political activism and attitudes towards politics and democratic institutions. Analysing attitudinal data from the latest round of the European Social Survey (ESS), the results reveal that the 'Green vote' is mainly determined by voters' social characteristics and political preferences but should also be connected to citizens' preferred forms of political activism. These results give evidence of the relative stability of the Green electorate.

Explaining the Green vote

Because Green parties put the emphasis on 'values that might be important for the survival of mankind instead of promoting the welfare of particular groups' (Dolezal, 2010, p. 537), the Green vote was mostly considered as an issue- or value-based vote that transcended the old 'class-politics' or traditional societal divisions, and the Green electorate was depicted as socio-demographically heterogeneous.

However, more systematic studies have challenged this initial view (Poguntke, 1993; Müller-Rommel, 2002; Dolezal, 2010). Scholars have shown that Green voters share specific sociological characteristics: They are proportionally younger (Franklin and Rüdig, 1992), more female (Knutsen, 2004, pp. 198–200), with a higher level of education (Knutsen, 2004). Support for the Greens is higher among students and housewives and lower among the retired (Dolezal, 2010), and higher among middle-class employees in the public sector (Poguntke, 1993; Müller-Rommel, 2002; Knutsen, 2005). Scholars have also shown that the Green electorate is anchored in traditional cleavages: Green voters would share a left-leaning, state-intervention view on economic issues (Müller-Rommel, 1985; Kitschelt, 1988; Kriesi, 1999); they would clearly adopt progressive positions on issues such as gender equality, same sex marriage, abortion rights, and so forth, and be less integrated in the traditional Christian churches (Dolezal, 2010); and the support for the Greens would be higher among residents of big cities (Kriesi, 1993; Dolezal, 2010), as the Green movement was born in populated, industrial, secular and multicultural areas.

However, the emergence of Green parties in the late 1970s is often related to the emergence of a *new* structuring conflict in Western societies. Inglehart referred to a divide between materialist and postmaterialist values (Inglehart, 1977; Kitschelt, 1989), which resulted in growing environmental concerns among Western citizens. This 'new cultural cleavage' (Kriesi, et al., 2006) would also include other types of values and issues. Hooghe, et al. (2002) conceive this new conflict as an opposition between a Green–Alternative–Libertarian (GAL) pole and a Traditional–Authoritarian–Nationalism (TAN) pole. Kriesi, et al. (2006) add to these dimensions a fundamental opposition between 'demarcation' and 'integration', the demarcation pole being 'characterized by an opposition to the process of European integration and by restrictive positions with regard to immigration' (Kriesi, et al., 2006, p. 924).

Consequently, in terms of political attitudes, Green voters should care a lot about Green issues (Franklin and Rüdig, 1992) and support individuals' autonomy and liberty against any form of domination or cultural regulation; they should display cosmopolitan orientations, be more supportive of international and supranational institutions and be more concerned with the rights of immigrants (Poguntke, 1993).

Our analysis aims at testing whether the Green electorate can still be differentiated on the basis of their social characteristics and political preferences, but also according to the type and degree of social and political activism and their attitudes towards politics and democratic institutions. Since the Greens 'wanted to promote a model of participative democracy' (Villalba, 2005, p. 82) or of 'popular participation' (Kitschelt, 1988, p. 195), we expect Green voters to be more socially and politically active than the rest of the electorate, especially in New Social Movements (Kriesi, 1999) and in unconventional forms of participation (demonstration, petition, boycott, etc.) (Poguntke, 1987). By contrast, we expect Green voters to be less entrenched in traditional forms of political activism such as party membership.

Regarding Green voters' attitudes towards politics and institutions, we expect Green voters to be relatively more interested in politics than other voters, in line with the findings about their educational profile. Second, we formulate two alternative hypotheses regarding their level of trust in institutions and satisfaction with the state of affairs in their country. If the Green vote constitutes a form of protest vote (Kitschelt, 1988), we should find a relatively lower level of trust and satisfaction among Green voters. However, because the Green voters tend to be more entrenched on the 'winner' side of the globalisation process, they could show higher levels of trust and satisfaction than other categories of voters. The analysis allows clarifying which interpretation is the more relevant.

Data and method

The analysis relies on the latest round of the ESS (2012). Green voters are identified with the question asking the respondents which party they voted for in the last national election. Abstainers and respondents who did not answer the question are excluded from the analysis; the statistical models (logistic regression) thus compare Green voters with voters for all other parties.

The original ESS 2012 database includes 29 countries from the European Union and beyond. Our analysis focuses on 15 of these 29 countries in which a Green electorate could be identified (Table 11.5).[6] In many southern European states (Spain, Portugal, Italy), the Greens have taken part in elections in coalition with other parties, which makes the delineation between Green voters impossible. This leaves us with only France and Greece for southern European countries.

Table 11.5 Distribution of Green voters by country (2012 round of the ESS)

Country	Party acronym/short name	Vote for another party	Green vote	Total
Austria	Grüne	1,027	199	1,226
		83.8%	16.2%	100%
Belgium	Groen!/Ecolo	1,162	134	1,296
		89.7%	10.3%	100%
Czech Republic	SZ	1,273	46	1,319
		96.5%	3.5%	100%
Denmark	SF	1,186	141	1,327
		89.4%	10.6%	100%
Estonia	EER	1,248	26	1,274
		98.0%	2.0%	100%
Finland	VL	1,332	166	1,498
		88.9%	11.1%	100%
France	EELV	1,147	66	1,213
		94.6%	5.4%	100%
Germany	Bündnis 90/Die Grunen	1,635	199	1,834
		89.1%	10.9%	100%
Greece	OP	1,172	38	1,210
		96.9%	2.3%	100%
Hungary	LMP	950	52	1,002
		94.8%	5.2%	100%
Ireland	Green Party	1,614	38	1,652
		97.7%	2.3%	100%
Netherlands	GL	1,364	40	1,404
		97.2%	2.8%	100%
Sweden	MG	1,301	140	1,441
		90.3%	9.7%	100%
Switzerland	GPS	632	70	702
		90.0%	10.0%	100%
United Kingdom	GPEW	1,419	19	1,438
		98.7%	1.3%	100%
Total		18,462	1,374	19,836
		93.1%	6.9%	100%

The analysis examines the influence of four sets of independent variables on the Green vote. With regard to socio-demographic characteristics, age is measured as a continuous variable; gender is a dummy variable; education has been recoded in three categories (primary, secondary and higher education). The religion variable is measured with two indicators: religious belonging and practice (measured as frequency of religious service attendance apart from special occasions). The 'occupation' variable includes eight categories: self-employed or independent, private sector employee, public sector employee, student, unemployed, housewife/house husband, retired and others. The type of residence variable distinguishes between rural (countryside or small village), semiurban small town) and urban (big city).

Regarding respondents' political preferences,[7] we use the position of voters on Likert-type questions or indexes related to issues or dimensions. For the socio-economic dimension, we use the proposition 'the government should reduce differences in income level' (a high score indicates a leftist position). For the cultural dimension, we use the proposition 'gays and lesbians should be free to live life as they wish' (a high score indicates a more progressive opinion). For the environmental dimension we use the question on the 'importance they give to caring about the nature and the environment' (a high score indicates a tendency to care much about environmental issues). The position on the libertarian/authoritarian dimension is measured with an additive index based on two propositions: the 'importance that government is strong and ensures safety' and the 'importance to follow traditions and customs' (a high score on the index indicates more libertarian attitudes). For positions on immigration, we use the respondents' opinion about whether immigrants make their country a worse or a better place to live (a low score indicates ethnocentrism). For positions on EU integration, we use a variable measuring the respondents' average trust in the EU parliament (a high score indicates a high level of trust).[8]

Regarding the degree and form of social and political activism, we computed three indexes. The social activism is an additive index of three variables: 'how often socially meet with friends, relatives of colleagues', 'how often take part in social activities compared to others of same age', 'have worked in another organisation or association last 12 months'. The conventional political activism index is an additive index of three variables: party identification or proximity ('feel closer to a particular party'), membership of a union or similar organisation and whether the respondent has worked for a political party in the last 12 months. The unconventional political activism index is an additive index of four variables: 'wore or displayed a campaign badge or sticker', 'signed a petition', 'took part in a lawful public demonstration' and 'boycotted certain products' in the last 12 months.

Lastly, regarding attitudes towards politics and institutions, the level of interest in politics is a four-category variable ('very interested', 'quite interested', 'hardly interested' and 'not at all interested'). Trust in institutions is an additive index of five items: trust in the country's parliament, in the legal system, in politicians, in the police and in the United Nations (a high score indicates a high level of trust). Satisfaction is an additive index of respondents' satisfaction on three items: the present state of the economy in their country, the way democracy works in general and their national government (a high score indicates a high level of satisfaction).

As several studies show that the profile of Green voters differs across countries (Müller-Rommel, 1985), and given the hierarchical structure of the database, we take into account the 'clustered' nature of our database. However, the low number of countries does not permit to conduct a multilevel analysis (Maas and Hox,

2004), and the weak number of Green voters in many countries impedes running the statistical models in each country separately. As a consequence, the logistics models presented in the next section include country 'dummies' in order to control for potential country effects.

The profile of Green voters: A cross-sectional perspective

The multivariate analysis presented in Table 11.6 permits the identification of the marginal effect of each predictor. Five models are displayed. Model 1 tests the effect of socio-demographic variables. Model 2 focuses on issue-based or preference-based explanations. Model 3 looks at the impact of the two other sets of variables (activism and attitudes towards politics and institutions). Model 4 tests simultaneously the effect of all these predictors, while Model 5 controls for country effects.[9]

Model 1 confirms that socio-demographic variables remain determinant in explaining the Green vote, even if the pseudo R^2 are not high. The probability of voting for a Green party is higher for younger age categories, women, urban residents and lower for religion belonging. The frequency of attendance of religious services also reduces the likelihood of voting for the Greens, but the relationship loses its statistical significance after controlling for country effect. Only the effect of occupation contradicts expectations based on previous findings: Employees are not more likely than self-employed to vote for the Greens. The results even give a reverse picture, although the effect is weaker and less significant in the case of employees in the public sector (Models 1 and 5). As expected, the unemployed are less likely to vote for the Greens – thus confirming the idea that Green voters are not on the 'loser' side of the new cleavage – but the relationship hardly reaches the significant level. As far as students – and the retired – are concerned, there might be a problem of collinearity with 'age'. Overall, the effect of occupation is unclear. This could result from a long-term decline of 'class voting' (Clark and Lipset, 2001). This could also indicate that the Green vote transcends classes and thus differs on that aspect from other more 'traditional' parties, as suggested by early studies.

As Model 2 shows, issue-based explanations prove very relevant. Compared to Model 1, the pseudo R^2 are increased, which indicates that the issue-based model has a greater explanatory power than the sociological model. Positions on both the old and the new cleavages appear as significant predictors of the Green vote. The highest coefficient is found for position on the postmaterialist or environmental dimension, followed by positions on the libertarian and cultural progressive dimensions. Interestingly, the position towards the EU shows the weakest (and least significant) coefficient. Green voters might in fact have an ambivalent position towards the EU (Dolezal, 2010, p. 542). On the one hand, they might support the opening of borders and a greater political integration of the EU. On the other hand, they might perceive the EU as being disconnected from citizens and away from the participatory model of democracy that constitutes one of the basic elements of the Greens' programmes; Green voters may also be critical of the EU' neo-liberal economic policies.

Table 11.6 The determinants of the Green vote – Results of logistic regressions

Predictors		Model 1	Model 2	Model 3	Model 4	Model 5
		b (s.e.)	b (s.e.)	b (s.e.)	b (s.e.)	b (s.e.)
Socio-demographics						
Age		−.021***			−.019***	−.016***
		(.002)			(.002)	(.002)
Gender		.509***			.420***	.430***
(ref. male)		(.061)			(.069)	(.070)
Education	Secondary	.891***			.578**	.563**
(ref. 'primary		(.179)			(.202)	(.206)
education')	Tertiary	1.490***			.916***	.986***
		(.183)			(.209)	(.213)
Religion		−.138*			.020	−.158*
		(.069)			(.077)	(.081)
Religious	Sometimes	−.216**			−.114	−.067
attendance		(.067)			(.075)	(.079)
(ref. 'never')	Often	−.587***			−.336**	−.136
		(.107)			(.121)	(.124)
Social/	Private	−.253**			−.237*	−.230*
occupational	sector	(.097)			(.105)	(.108)
classes	employee					
(ref. 'self-	Public	−.118			−.243*	−.191
employed or	sector	(.100)			(.110)	(.113)
independent')	employee					
	Student	.077			.021	−.109
		(.210)			(.235)	(.245)
	Unem-ployed	−.572			−.331	−.344
		(.314)			(.328)	(.339)
	House-wife/husband	−.175			−.194	−.255
		(.185)			(.207)	(.212)
	Retired	.190			.238	.104
		(.175)			(.195)	(.201)
	Other	.083			−.032	−.055
		(.138)			(.158)	(.162)
Residence	Semi	−.252***			−.182*	−.185*
(ref. urban)	urban	(.068)			(.076)	(.078)
	Rural	−.475***			−.396***	−.470***
		(.072)			(.079)	(.083)
Political preferences						
Left socio-economic			.151***		.175***	.138***
			(.029)		(.033)	(.034)

Predictors	Model 1 b (s.e.)	Model 2 b (s.e.)	Model 3 b (s.e.)	Model 4 b (s.e.)	Model 5 b (s.e.)
Cultural progressive		.461*** (.042)		.285*** (.045)	.249*** (.047)
Environment		.588*** (.038)		.607*** (.041)	.589*** (.042)
Libertarian		.434*** (.029)		.361*** (.034)	.320*** (.035)
Proimmigration		.142*** (.015)		.104*** (.017)	.124*** (.018)
Pro-Europe		.042** (.014)		.021 (.020)	.041* (.021)
Social and political activism					
Social activism			.123 (.070)	.020 (.077)	−.024 (.079)
Conventional political activism			−.378** (.121)	−.107 (.137)	−.422** (.146)
Unconventional political activism			2.207*** (.113)	1.070*** (.129)	1.020*** (.137)
Attitudes towards politics and institutions					
Interest in politics (ref. 'Not at all interested') Very interested			−.052 (.144)	−.299 (.159)	−.437** (.164)
Quite interested			−.016 (.129)	−.109 (.139)	−.213 (.143)
Hardly interested			.148 (.130)	.124 (.137)	.054 (.140)
Trust			.050* (.023)	−.045 (.030)	−.028 (.032)
Satisfaction			.072*** (.027)	.080*** (.023)	−.035 (.025)
Intercept	−2.258*** (.233)	−10.328*** (.014)	−3.795*** (.157)	−9.132*** (.443)	−8.644*** (.492)
N	19,600	17,939	17,759	16,634	16,634
Log Likelihood	9209.748	8243.231	8580.528	7284.068	6930.553
Cox & Snell R^2	.033	.056	.026	.078	.097
Nagelkerke R^2	.084	.139	.065	.192	.240

Note: $p \leq 0.1$; *: $p \leq 0.05$; **: $p \leq 0.01$; ***: $p \leq 0.001$.

Dependent variable: 'Vote for Green party'.

The pseudo R^2 found in Model 3 suggest that the respondents' degree and form of activism have a rather weak explanatory power. Regarding social activism, there is no significant and clear tendency. However, the analysis supports the idea that Green voters are entrenched in the New Social Movements, as Models 3, 4 and 5 indicate that the more a respondent is involved in unconventional forms of participation, the more likely s/he is to vote for the Greens. By contrast, the more a respondent is engaged in conventional forms of participation, the less likely s/he is to vote for a Green party (Models 3 and 5).

Surprisingly, the level of interest in politics is not a determinant factor of the Green vote. The relationship even contradicts our hypothesis. When controlling for sociological variables, political preferences, activism and attitudes towards institutions (in Model 5), the level of interest in politics diminishes the probability of voting for the Greens. It might be that Green voters are not interested in politics in general or in conventional politics but are rather mobilised on specific 'niche' issues. This is congruent with the roots of Green parties, which have capitalised on diverse social movements that mobilised around particular matters (environmental, feminist, minorities' movements, etc.); this is also congruent with the unconventional forms of activism adopted by Green voters.

Lastly, Model 3 displays weak but positive relationships between trust and satisfaction with institutions and the Green vote, suggesting that the Green vote has lost its protest function. However, when controlling for other variables (especially the country), the relationships lose their significance. This makes sense since the levels of trust and satisfaction are correlated with the national political and economic contexts. Interestingly, if we compare the electoral success of Green parties with the average levels of trust and satisfaction in the 15 countries, we find that Green parties are more successful in countries with relatively high aggregate levels of trust and of satisfaction.[10] However, the relationship at the individual level is not fully confirmed.

Comparing these results with earlier studies, the Green electorate appears quite stable in its characteristics. Compared to the electorate of other parties, Green voters remain younger, more educated, less religious and more urban; and women are still overrepresented. The effect of occupation is mixed, which suggests that Green parties could be considered as transversal parties. The Green vote still appears as an issue-based vote: individuals' political preferences have a strong predicting power, especially towards the environmental issue. Green voters are also positioned on the left side of the socio-economic political spectrum; they share progressive and libertarian attitudes and promote a culturally open society – although they do not seem to blindly support the EU integration process.

Our analysis suggests that other elements also characterise the Green electorate. This is particularly the case of activism: Green voters are significantly more involved in unconventional forms of political participation than other voters. These results are in line with the *New Politics* ideals brought by the Green movement at its inception. This specific 'activist' profile could partly explain the unexpected relationship between political interest and the Green vote: Green voters do not claim to be interested in politics in general, but they are mobilised around specific issues. Finally, the analysis has revealed mixed results regarding the protest component of the Green vote, which is very much connected to the specific national contexts.

Conclusion

Born in the late 1970s and early 1980s, Green parties in Europe have known very distinctive fates. In the European consociational democracies, Green parties have established themselves as relevant political actors, even if they still rarely cross the 10 per cent threshold. Other countries, mostly Nordic countries, have also faced the emergence of relevant Green parties. Yet, elsewhere in Europe, Green parties have been struggling to perform electorally. In the southern, central-eastern and Baltic countries, Green parties remain weak political organisations, with a couple of exceptions.

If Green parties in Europe have followed distinct electoral paths, their electorate can still be identified as a group sharing specific characteristics that distinguish them from other voters. Sociologically, the young, nonreligious, female, urban and educated individuals are more likely to support the Greens. Besides, the Green vote can be seen as an issue-based vote that transcends the old class politics: values that are related to the new cleavage – whatever its label – are determinant. Lastly, Green voters also have a specific 'activist' profile: they are clearly more involved in new forms of political participation entrenched in the *New Politics* movement.

These characteristics are very similar to those identified in the early years of the Green movement. This reveals the relative stability of Green parties' electoral basis, despite their fluctuating electoral results. What remains unclear is whether Green parties are doomed to lose their initial protest element by collaborating with old traditional parties and institutions – as we have shown, government participation has been quite harmful for the Greens – or whether they will manage to remain the promoters of a societal and political revolution, despite the development of their new challengers – the radical, red-green or eco-socialist parties.

Notes

1 Although the mixed electoral system is completely proportional, the political system dynamic is closer to a majoritarian logic. However, it should be noted that, during the last three legislatures, two 'grand coalition' governments were formed.
2 See Tables 1.1 (Austria and Switzerland), 2.2 (Belgium), 5.1 (Germany) and 6.2 (The Netherlands).
3 This is really an unusual phenomenon in Luxembourg as the Christian Democrats have only been out of government once, between 1974 and 1979.
4 See Chapter 9, Table 9.2 and Table 9.5.
5 See Chapter 9, Table 9.4.
6 For Austria, we use the 2008 round of the ESS, because the data for Austria is missing in the 2012 round; Luxembourg is not included in the 2012 ESS round. For Greece, we use the 2010 round of the ESS, because the data for Greece is missing in the 2012 round. For the Czech Republic, we use the 2010 round of the ESS, because the question on voting behaviour in the 2012 round does not provide a separate category for the SZ.

For Denmark, we examine the voters of the SF with caution. We had to exclude the Latvian Greens since they formed a cartel with the Farmers' Union.

7 Our operationalisation of political preferences is similar to what Dolezal (2010) has proposed.

8 Another question asks the respondents whether they think that the European integration 'should be pushed further' or whether it 'has already gone too far'. However, this variable was not included in the 2010 round. The (Spearman rho) correlation with the question on 'trust in the EU parliament' equals 0.402 (significant at the 0.001 level).

9 The country coefficients are not included in the table for reason of space and clarity. With Sweden as a reference category, the country coefficients are positive for Austria (greatest coefficient, b = 1.003), Belgium, Denmark, Finland, Germany and Switzerland and are negative for the Czech Republic, Estonia, France, Greece, Hungary, Ireland, the Netherlands and the United Kingdom (lowest coefficient, b = −1.701). All the coefficients are statistically significant, except for Hungary.

10 At one extreme, Greece shows very low levels of trust (= 3.05) and satisfaction (= 2.19); at the other extreme, the Scandinavian countries and Switzerland show levels that are twice as high (between 6 and 7 for both variables). The Czech Republic, Hungary, Ireland, Estonia, France and the United Kingdom display aggregate levels that range between 3.9 and 5. Belgium, Austria, Germany and the Netherlands are situated in the middle.

References

Clark, T. N., and Lipset, S. M., eds, 2001. *The Breakdown of Class Politics: A Debate on Post-Industrial Stratification.* Washington, DC: Woodrow Wilson Center Press.

Croisat, M., and Quermonne, J.-L., 1999. *L'Europe et le fédéralisme.* Paris: Montchrestien.

Delwit, P., 2002. Electoral Participation and European Polls: A Limited Legitimation. In: G. Grunberg, P. Perrineau and Colette Ysmal, eds, *Europe at the Polls: The European Elections of 1999.* London and New York: Palgrave-Macmillan. pp. 7–15.

Delwit, P., 2012. *La vie politique en Belgique de 1830 à nos jours.* 3rd edition. Brussels: Editions de l'Université de Bruxelles.

Dietz, T., 2001. Les verts Européens comptent-ils? In: P. Delwit, E. Kulahci and C. Van de Walle, eds, *Les fédérations Européennes de partis: Organisation et influence.* Brussels: Editions de l'Université de Bruxelles. pp. 199–212.

Dolezal, M., 2010. Exploring the stabilization of a political force: The social and attitudinal basis of Green parties in the age of globalization. *West European Politics*, 33(3), pp. 534–552.

Franklin, M. N., and Rüdig, W., 1992. The Green voter in the 1989 European elections. *Environmental Politics*, 1(4), pp. 129–159.

Galtung, J., 1986. The Green movement: A socio-historical exploration. *International Sociology*, 1(1), pp. 75–90.

Gotovitch, J., Delwit, P., and De Waele, J.-M., 1992. *L'Europe des communistes.* Brussels: Editions Complexe.

Hix, S., and Marsh, M., 2007. Punishment or protest? Understanding European Parliament Elections. *The Journal of Politics*, 69(2), pp. 495–510.

Hooghe, L., Marks, G., and Wilson, C. J., 2002. Does left/right structure party positions on European integration? *Comparative Political Studies*, 35(8), pp. 965–989.

Inglehart, R., 1977. *The Silent Revolution: Changing Values and Political Styles Among Western Publics.* Princeton: Princeton University Press.

Kaelberer, M., 1993. The emergence of Green parties in Europe. *Comparative Politics*, 25(2), pp. 229–243.

Kitschelt, H. P., 1988. Left libertarian parties/explaining innovation in competitive party systems. *World Politics*, 40(2), pp. 194–234.

Kitschelt, H. P., 1989. *The Logics of Party Formation: Ecological Politics in Belgium and West Germany*. Ithaca, NY: Cornell University Press.

Knutsen, O., 2004. *Social Structure and Party Choice in Western Europe: A Comparative Longitudinal Study*. Houndmills: Palgrave Macmillan.

Knutsen, O., 2005. The impact of sector employment on party choice: A comparative study of eight West European countries. *European Journal of Political Research*, 44(4), pp. 593–621.

Koepke, J. R., and Ringe, N., 2006. The second-order election model in an enlarged Europe. *European Union Politics*, 7(3), pp. 321–346.

Kriesi, H., 1993. *Political Mobilization and Social Change: The Dutch Case in Comparative Perspective*. Aldershot: Avebury.

Kriesi, H., 1999. Movements of the Left, Movements of the Right: Putting the Mobilization of Two New Types of Social Movements into Political Context. In: H. Kitschelt, P. Lange, G. Marks and J. D. Stephens, eds, *Continuity and Change in Contemporary Capitalism*. Cambridge: Cambridge University Press. pp. 398–423.

Kriesi, H., Grande, E., Lachat, R., Dolezal, M., Bornschier, S., and Frey, T., 2006. Globalization and the transformation of the national political space: Six European countries Compared. *European Journal of Political Research*, 45(6), pp. 921–956.

Lijphart, A., 1981. *Conflict and Coexistence in Belgium: The Dynamics of a Culturally Divided Society*. Berkeley: Institute of International Studies, University of California.

Maas, C. J. M., and Hox, J. J., 2004. Robustness issues in multilevel regression analysis. *Statistica Neerlandica*, 58(2), pp. 127–137.

Mair, P., 1999. Evaluation des performances politiques des partis verts en Europe. In: P. Delwit and J.-M. De Waele, eds, *Les partis verts en Europe*. Brussels: Editions Complexe. pp. 23–42.

Müller-Rommel, F., 1985. The Greens in Western Europe: Similar but different. *International Political Science Review*, 6(4), pp. 483–498.

Müller-Rommel, F., 1998. The new challengers: Greens and right-wing populist parties in Western Europe. *European Review*, 6(2), pp. 191–202.

Müller-Rommel, F., 2002. The Greens in the 1999 European Parliamentary Elections: The Success Story. In: P. Perrineau, G. Grunberg and C. Ysmal, eds, *Europe at the Polls: The European Elections of 1999*. New York: Palgrave Macmillan. pp. 116–129.

Poguntke, T., 1987. New politics and party systems: The emergence of a new type of party? *West European Politics*, 10(1), pp. 76–88.

Poguntke, T., 1993. *Alternative Politics: The German Green Party*. Edinburgh: Edinburgh University Press.

Poguntke, T., 1998. Alliance 90/The Greens in East Germany: From Vanguard to Insignificance? *Party Politics*, 4(1), pp. 33–55.

Reif, K., 1985. Ten Second-Order Elections. In: K. Reif, ed., *Ten European Elections: Campaigns and Results of the 1979/81 First Direct Elections to the European Parliament*. Aldershot: Gower. pp. 1–36.

Reif, K., and Schmitt, H., 1980. Nine second-order national elections – A conceptual framework for the analysis of European election results. *European Journal of Political Research*, 8(1), pp. 3–44.

Rihoux, B., 2001. *Les partis politiques: organisations en changement. Le test des écologistes*. Paris: L'Harmattan.

Sartori, G., 1976. *Parties and Party Systems: A Framework for Analysis*. Cambridge and New York: Cambridge University Press.

Villalba, B., 2005. Ecological Contributions to the European Social Democratic Reform Project. In: P. Delwit, ed., *Social Democracy in Europe*. Brussels, Édition de l'Université de Bruxelles. pp. 79–94.

12 Green parties in government[1]

Conor Little

Introduction

Green parties' first forays into national governments did not augur well for their future beyond the threshold of cabinet participation. In Central and Eastern Europe, they participated in several short-lived transition governments in the early 1990s, only to be absorbed or marginalised as new party systems became established (Rihoux and Rüdig, 2006; Rüdig, 2006). In Western Europe, the Italian Greens' Francesco Rutelli was appointed as Minister for the Environment by Prime Minister Carlo Azeglio Ciampi on 28 April 1993. One day later, Rutelli submitted his resignation (Pasquino and Vassalo, 1995, pp. 68–69; *Parlamento Italiano*, 2013).

Nevertheless, participation in government has become a central objective for Green parties and one that follows from their increased focus on using conventional means – especially parliamentary means – to achieve their goals. Since April 1995, when the Finnish Greens[2] first entered government, Green parties have joined governments in a range of European countries and with an increasing variety of coalition partners. Like their emergence onto the political scene (Müller-Rommel, 1985; Kitschelt, 1988; Hino, 2012, pp. 168–169), their participation in government is a cross-national development that has occurred over a relatively short period.

Despite crossing important developmental thresholds since their emergence, Green parties continue to constitute a coherent and distinctive set of parties in organisational and ideological terms. Many of their core characteristics can be linked to their origins in movement politics. Their policies on the environment, but also on a variety of other issues, remain both similar to one another and distinct from other parties (Burchell, 2002, pp. 151–154; Spoon, 2009, 2011; Carter, 2013). Their organisations are typically characterised by limited professionalisation, collective or amateur leadership structures and formal equality among members, including through their participatory decision-making processes (Rihoux and Frankland, 2008, pp. 266–271).

Government presents a range of new challenges for these parties (Pedersen, 1982, pp. 6–8; Müller-Rommel, 2002, pp. 3–6; Deschouwer, 2008, pp. 3–4). Entering government juxtaposes their participatory structures and culture with the demands of confidential and sometimes rapid decision-making involving a wide variety of actors beyond the party's members. On the other hand, it pitches their policy-oriented activists, seeking rapid change, against entrenched interests and slow-moving bureaucratic and legislative processes (Poguntke, 2002, pp. 142–143). The challenge of government is made all the more complex by the breadth of Green parties' policy goals. They are not single-issue parties (see previous chapters), and therefore, they must make difficult choices between such policy gains as are available across a wide range of policy fields. It is not surprising, then, that government has been a contentious issue within many Green parties and among their supporters.

This chapter provides a comparative overview of Green parties' participation in national governments. Its scope is restricted in a number of respects. First, it focuses on stable parliamentary democracies, thus excluding those cases of Green party participation in transition governments in Central and Eastern Europe in the early 1990s, amongst others.[3] Second, it focuses on conventional Green parties,[4] thus excluding the Latvian Greens (see Auers, 2012) but including the Danish Socialist People's Party (SF). Third, it includes only parties that received senior ministerial positions, thus excluding the case of the Slovak Greens, which held a junior ministerial position from 1998 to 2002; it also ignores the Italian Greens' brush with government in 1993.

The chapter proceeds in a number of steps, addressing Laver and Schofield's (1990) key questions concerning government coalitions: 'Who gets in?', 'Who gets what?' and 'How long does it last?' First, it describes which Green parties have got into government, when and in what circumstances. Second, it asks what they got in coalition: how many ministerial positions, which ministerial positions and did they influence government policy? Third, it describes when and how their spells in government have ended. Going beyond these three issues, it asks, fourth, what has happened to them at and beyond the end of their time in government, with a particular focus on their postincumbency election results. In each step, it describes the parties' outcomes and assesses the role of their distinctive characteristics in their experience of and success in government.

It shows that their time in government has indeed been challenging. This is evident in their limited gains in coalition bargaining, their relatively frequent defection from government coalitions and the electoral costs that they have paid at the end of their time in government. Nonetheless, this must be weighed against policy gains that have gone some way towards forwarding their agenda. Many of the most important factors that have determined their outcomes in government have been beyond their control. However, their typical characteristics – not least their difficulty in placing themselves centrally for the purpose of coalition bargaining, which is accentuated, in some cases, by their participatory organisations – may have compromised their capacity to attain more substantial outcomes.

Getting in

Since 1995, ten Green parties have participated in national governments in nine countries.[5] Green parties' participation in governments has occurred, approximately, in two waves: The first wave lasted from the late 1990s until the early 2000s, and the second wave began in the late 2000s. Figure 12.1 identifies 16 cases of Green parties in government, with several parties (in Finland, Italy, France and Germany) spending more than one spell in government.

In two instances (the French Greens in 1997 and the Czech Greens in 2006–2007), Green parties' entry into government coincided with their crossing the threshold of representation in national parliament for the first time. Nonetheless, in almost all cases, the road to government was a long one. Among the ten parties that have entered government, the median time to doing so is 21 years after crossing the thresholds of declaration and authorisation and 18 years after crossing the threshold of representation (Müller-Rommel, 2002). Some Green parties (for example in Luxembourg and Belgium) had considerable parliamentary experience at the national level by the time they reached government, and the German Greens, further, had several experiences in *Land* governments since the mid-1980s.

Despite their oft-repeated aspiration to be neither left nor right, Green parties have tended to enter government with parties of the centre-left. Several of these coalitions had their origins in electoral alliances that Green parties have joined in order to maximise their parliamentary representation. Some, like those formed in France and Italy, were formal electoral coalitions and appeared necessary if the party were to have any substantial parliamentary representation (Boy, 2002, p. 74; Biorcio, 2002, p. 59; Ignazi, 2007, p. 999), while others (for example in Germany) were less formal yet clearly benefited the Greens electorally (Poguntke, 2003, p. 962; Wüst and Roth, 2006, p. 455).

Recently, some novel government coalitions involving Green parties and the main party of the centre-right have emerged in a number of countries. 2007 was a significant year in this regard: the Czech Greens joined the Civic Democrats and Christian Democrats in government in January; the Finnish Greens joined the Centre Party, the Conservatives and the Swedish People's Party in government in April; and the Irish Greens joined the *Fianna Fáil* party and the Progressive

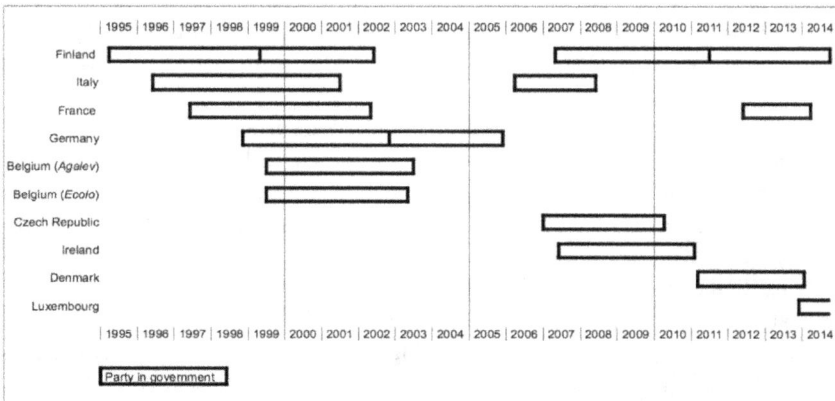

Figure 12.1 Green parties in national governments[6]

Democrats in government in June. In 2011, the Finnish Greens renewed their coalition with the centre-right Conservatives, albeit with the Social Democrats and the Left Alliance taking the place of the Centre Party.

Several of the factors that have contributed to determining whether Green parties enter government or remain in opposition have been beyond these parties' control and are unrelated to their own electoral success (see also Dumont and Bäck, 2006). For example, the Austrian Greens have failed to enter federal government despite their relative electoral strength (see Chapter 1 in this volume), and the German Greens failed to enter government in 2009 despite unprecedented electoral success in a federal election (see Chapter 5 in this volume).

Typically, Green parties' accession to government has depended on the success of its putative coalition partners on the centre-left. The first wave of Green parties' participation in government in particular coincided with a period of dominance by the centre-left in European governments. Meanwhile, the Dutch Greens have failed to enter government due in part to a sustained centre-right majority (see Chapter 6 in this volume) and the Swedish Greens performed strongly in 2010 and would have been part of a Social Democrat-led coalition, had the larger party not performed so poorly (see Chapter 7 in this volume).

The comparison of Finland and Sweden in Chapter 7 further highlights the importance of different environments in determining the office-seeking success of two Green parties that have been relatively successful in electoral terms. The Swedish case illustrates the role of government formation rules (specifically, negative parliamentarism) in keeping the Swedish Greens out of cabinets in 1998 and 2002 (Aylott and Bergman, 2011), and this is lent further support by evidence from the case of the New Zealand Greens (Bale and Blomgren, 2008). It is notable too that, for these support parties, it was not 'power-shyness' (Strøm, 1990) that determined the outcome: in each case, the party wanted to attain office but was successfully excluded by other parties (Little, 2014, pp. 115–116). However, excluding Green parties from government where possible is not the only goal of their potential coalition partners. In Finland in 1995, for example, the Social Democrats invited the Greens to join an already-large coalition in order that their electoral threat might be neutralised and the parliamentary opposition weakened (Jungar, 2011, pp. 141–142). Thus, their participation in government has depended on the strategy of larger parties.

There are also some factors rooted in Green parties' own characteristics that have affected their capacity to accede to government. First, and most obviously, they are small parties. They have rarely exceeded 10 per cent seat share in national parliaments. Second, and more particular to Green parties, they often find themselves 'captive parties' (Bale and Bergman, 2006, p. 193) with limited coalition options. In the presence of their participatory party organisations, their members' antipathy to coalitions with the centre-right has at times prevented them from joining such coalitions or even from setting out an 'open' coalition strategy. This recalls the 'captive' position of the Swedish Greens in 2002 (Aylott and Bergman, 2011); the opposition of the Austrian Greens' members to negotiating with the centre-right in 2002 (Chapter 3); and the Australian Greens' failure to set out a credible 'open' coalition strategy in 2010, despite their leaders' efforts to do so (Williams, 2011). Their 'captivity' is also supported by an electoral logic: as parties that have built their electoral bases to the left of centre, Green parties might quite reasonably fear losing electoral support if they enter government with the centre-right.

Nonetheless, they have recognised that their lack of potential pivotality may be a weakness and have expended some effort on opening up their coalition options in the medium term. Green parties have entered a variety of cooperative arrangements short of government coalition with the centre-right, including in New Zealand in 2009 on home insulation and energy efficiency, in Sweden in 2010 on immigration (see Chapter 7) and in the Netherlands in 2012 on a wider range of budgetary issues (see Chapter 6). Subnational government has been the site of a wider variety of innovative coalitions than national government: the Walloon Greens participated in the 'olive tree' coalition with the Christian Democrats in 2004; the Austrian Greens have governed with both major parties; and the German Greens have been in government with the centre-right in Hamburg and Saarland, for example (see country chapters). However, most Green parties are yet to credibly stake out a potentially pivotal position in their national party systems.

Getting office, getting policy

How successful have Green parties been in securing office and policy in government coalitions? A first and crucial indicator of a party's success in government is how many ministerial offices it attains. While all Green parties that have participated in government have been junior partners, the number and share of ministerial positions that they have received has varied significantly. In half of the 16 cases identified in Figure 12.1, they received one ministerial position upon entering government. On other occasions, they have received between two and four positions, while in one case (the Danish SF in 2011), they received six. Their share of senior ministerial positions has ranged from 3.7 per cent in Italy in 2006 to over one-quarter of senior ministerial positions in Denmark in 2011.

Have these parties punched above their weight? A well-established observation in the literature is that of proportionality in portfolio allocation: parties tend to receive ministerial offices proportional to their contribution to the cabinet coalition. A second observation from that literature is that of small party bias: small parties tend to get more ministerial offices than is their due under a strict proportionality rule (Browne and Franklin, 1973; Warwick and Druckman, 2006). On the basis of these observations, we might expect Green parties to be compensated at least proportionally, if not more generously.

On average, Green parties in government have received a greater-than-proportional outcome. Their mean allocation of ministerial positions is 2 percentage points (pp.) greater than their (lower house) seat contribution to the cabinet coalition (for example a party contributing 13 per cent of the coalition's seats receives 15 per cent of the ministerial positions, on average). However, this mean overcompensation is driven by a small number of cases (especially the Czech and Danish cases); the median Green party's outcome is almost exactly proportional. Moreover, Green parties' overcompensation is substantially less than comparable parties of a similar size (mean = +4.2 pp.; median = +3.7 pp.).[7]

A second aspect of the allocation of ministerial offices to Green parties is the kind of ministerial positions that they have been allocated. In 13 of the 16 cases examined here, Green parties were allocated the environment portfolio. Only in the cases of the Walloon Greens in Belgium in 1999 (when the Flemish Greens got the environment portfolio), the Finnish Greens in 2007 and the French Greens in 2012 did they not receive that portfolio. Among party families, the regularity with which they have been allocated this portfolio (81 per cent of the time) is exceptional (cf. Browne and Feste, 1975; Budge and Keman, 1990). A similar pattern appears to pertain at subnational level (see especially Chapter 5). Other portfolios allocated to Green parties often (although not always) appear to complement their core policy agenda. These have included energy, consumer protection and transport.

One explanation for the regularity with which Green parties are allocated the environment portfolio is, no doubt, Green parties' policy goals and the possibilities for realising these goals that the environment ministry affords them (Bäck, et al., 2011). These preferences are evident from their election manifestos (Carter, 2013) and from the details of individual cases: the Finnish Greens, for example, were disappointed not to receive the environment portfolio in 2007 (personal information). Another potentially complementary explanation is their coalition partners' lack of interest in environmental issues (Falcó-Gimeno, 2014). In at least one case (the French Greens in 1997), there is evidence of the unilateral allocation of the environment ministry to the Greens by their main coalition partner without their being allowed to express a preference for other portfolios (Evrard, 2012, p. 284).

A further factor that surely narrows the range of potential ministerial positions for Green parties is their lack of bargaining power in coalition. This forecloses the possibility of attaining the most weighty ministerial positions. Accordingly, in none of the cases examined here have Green parties held a prime ministerial position or the position of finance minister, and they have only occasionally held the position of deputy prime minister (in the cases of the German Greens and the Walloon Greens, for example) and in the foreign ministry (in Germany, the Czech Republic and Denmark, for example).

A third aspect of coalition payoffs – policy influence – is arguably the most important for Green parties as policy-oriented parties. Have Green parties in government influenced government policy? While policy outputs are difficult to measure and while they are the products of diverse factors, there is evidence for three general observations with regard to the policy influence of Green parties in government.

The first is that Green parties in government have indeed influenced government policy. Some evidence for this observation comes from comparative cross-national research on the influence of Green parties' presence in government on national environmental policy (Knill, et al., 2010; Jensen and Spoon, 2011).

Further evidence – also from beyond the environmental policy field – comes from comparative case studies, which identify Green parties' contributions to influencing policy outputs (Poguntke, 2002, pp. 139–141; Evrard, 2012) and single case studies (for example Biorcio, 2002). Green parties have also influenced policy at European Union (EU) level through their roles in national governments (Bomberg and Carter, 2006). Even in cases of small Green parties in a weak bargaining position, such as the Italian Greens in each of their government coalitions, they influenced policy, including by working with like-minded groups within larger parties (interviews).[8]

The second observation is that these policy gains have been limited. This is not surprising, given Green parties' small size and typically weak bargaining position. Significant compromises are inevitable for these parties. The case of nuclear power policy, described in several of the previous chapters and highlighted in previous studies as a bellwether of Green party influence (Poguntke, 2002), is illustrative of the limits of that influence. The first Red-Green coalition in Germany achieved agreement to close nuclear power plants, but only in the medium term (Chapter 5); in the short term, they had to oversee controversial nuclear waste transports. In France, the Greens' influence on nuclear energy policy was severely limited in their first spell in government (Evrard, 2012). In 2012, the French Greens achieved an agreement not to build new nuclear power plants and to close a number of reactors by 2025 but failed to reach agreement concerning a new third-generation reactor under construction in Normandy (Chapter 4). The limits of the Finnish Greens' influence on nuclear policy while in government have been exposed several times, including when the government pressed ahead with plans to build Finland's fifth nuclear power plant in 2002, when they agreed to build a sixth plant in 2010 and when they issued a licence for building the sixth plant in 2014. In 2002 and 2014, the Greens responded by leaving government. The long-term and path-dependent nature of these large infrastructure projects also highlights a further limitation on Green parties' influence: their role in government has typically been transitory, and this can make it difficult to influence policies in the medium term.

The third observation concerning Green parties' policy influence is that, within these limitations, Green parties' policy gains have varied. Evrard's (2012) comparative case study of the French and German Greens shows how their influence has varied across parties and how, along with national institutions, their professionalisation, the extent to which they were embedded in policy networks and their prioritisation of policy issues have contributed to determining their level of influence. Green parties' influence has also varied across policy areas and types (Poguntke, 2002) and over time within their spells in government. Biorcio's (2002) study of the Italian Greens' first spell in government (1996–2001) shows how the party's policy influence waned with changing political and economic conditions. The case of the Irish Greens, too, illustrates how the party's deteriorating opinion poll standing and the onset of a severe economic recession weakened its bargaining position (despite the party being increasingly necessary for the continuation of the coalition) and the government's capacity for policymaking (Little, 2011).

As with their accession to government, Greens parties' office and policy pay-offs have often depended on circumstances beyond their control. However, as in that case, it is likely that their small size and their typical inability to pivot right and left to form alternative coalitions weakened their bargaining position. One further factor that has influenced their policy payoffs in individual cases is inter-nal dissent and division, culminating at times in leaving government early, with negative consequences for the party's policy payoffs. It is to this outcome – and to Green parties' duration in government more generally – that we next turn.

Getting out

All spells in government come to an end, but the timing and manner of this ending varies. As relatively inexperienced, policy-driven, internally democratic, small parties that risk heavy electoral punishment after being in government, Green parties are expected by some to be unreliable coalition partners (Brancati, 2005, fn. 3; Gahrton and Aylward, 2010, p. 17). Their inexperience may lead them to make poor decisions, including exiting government; their policy-driven nature may mean that they are less attached to office *per se* than other parties; their internally democratic nature increases the pressures on party elites from policy-oriented activists; and their small size makes them more sensitive to potential electoral losses (Bolleyer, 2008), which may have existential consequences. If this is the case, they may be more likely to defect from government, and this may, in turn, cause political instability.

Have these expectations been borne out? In the 15 completed cases that are detailed in Table 12.1, Green parties spent an average of three and a half years in government. In six cases, Green parties remained in government until sched-uled, obligatory elections at the end of the legislative term, which was either four (Finland, Germany, Belgium) or five (Italy, France) years long. These elec-tions occurred in Finland (1999 and 2011), Italy (2001), France (2002), Germany (2002) and Belgium (2003 for the Flemish Greens, *Agalev*). In two cases, early elections were precipitated by factors beyond the influence of the Green parties: once in Germany in 2005, when Chancellor Schroder called an early election due to increasing political competition within and beyond his party and declining prospects for his coalition in parliament, and once in Italy in 2008, when Romano Prodi's government lost its majority in parliament.

On seven occasions, Green parties have withdrawn from government. This is a high rate of defection compared to the wider population of parties in govern-ment (Tavits, 2008, p. 499). In several recent instances, defection appears to have substantially shortened the party's time in government. The Danish SF left the Thorning-Schmidt government in January 2014, after little over two years, over the partial sale of a state-owned energy company to Goldman Sachs, which had given rise to intense conflict within the party. The French Greens left government in March 2014 due to the replacement of Prime Minister Ayrault with the right-leaning Prime Minister Valls. Uniquely, the Finnish Greens have twice defected over the government's nuclear power plans: once from a Social Democrat-led

Table 12.1 The duration of Green parties' spells in government and how they ended

Case	Time in government (years)	How the party's time in government ended*	Electoral result (pp. vote share gain/loss)
Finland, 1995–1999	4.0	Election	+0.8
Italy, 1996–2001	5.1	Election	−0.3
France, 1997–2002	4.9	Election	+0.8
Germany, 1998–2002	4.0	Election	+1.9
Finland, 1999–2002	3.1	Defection	+0.7
Belgium (*Agalev*), 1999–2003	4.0	Election	−4.5**
Belgium (*Ecolo*), 1999–2003	3.8	Defection	−4.2
Germany, 2002–2005	3.1	Early election	−0.5
Italy, 2006–2008	2.0	Early election	−1.4**
Czech Republic, 2007–2010	3.2	Defection	−3.9**
Finland, 2007–2011	4.1	Election	−1.2
Ireland, 2007–2011	3.6	Defection	−2.9**
Denmark, 2011–2014	2.3	Defection	NA
Finland, 2011–2014	3.2	Defection	NA
France, 2012–2014	1.8	Defection	NA

Note: * Election = scheduled election at the end of the legislative term; ** Party lost all seats in parliament; NA: No Answer. Postincumbency elections have yet to take place.

Sources: Döring and Manow (2012); *European Journal of Political Research* (EJPR) data yearbooks; Inter Parliamentary Union (IPU) (2013); various media outlets for recent (2014) events.

coalition in 2002 and once from a Conservative-led coalition in 2014. On both occasions, they did so several months in advance of the next scheduled general election.

However, other defections have taken place in the shadow of an imminent election and have therefore only slightly shortened the Greens' time in government. The Walloon Greens *Ecolo* left government less than two weeks before the 2003 elections, citing the issue of night flights over Brussels (Fitzmaurice, 2004, p. 152). The Czech Greens left government in March 2010, less than two months before scheduled elections, citing disagreement on energy policy and the Prunéřov coal-fired power plant in particular (Hanley, 2013, pp. 10–11). The only Green party defection to date that has precipitated an election was that of the Irish Greens, which left government in early 2011 citing a breakdown of trust within the coalition and the need for an election following the intervention of the EU and International Monetary Fund (IMF) in the country's economic affairs in late 2010. However, it was very likely that an early election would take place soon in any case as the coalition was steadily losing the support in parliament.

Thus, while Green parties have left government early almost half of the time, this has not generally caused wider political instability. Nor, in several cases, have they substantially shortened their own time in office, as they defected in the shadow of an imminent or very likely election. Finally, some of these parties continued to support the policies and even the survival of the government after defecting. Examples include the Danish SF and, for a short period in early 2011, the Irish Greens.

Clearly, external factors such as the timing of obligatory elections and the calling of early elections have played an important role in directly determining how long Green parties remain in government. However, in cases of defection, internal factors have also played a role. First, the strong policy orientation of these parties is frequently reflected in the reasons given for leaving government. In particular, the prevalence of energy policy as a reason for leaving government (in Denmark, the Czech Republic and twice in Finland) is notable. Second, features of their party organisations and leaderships have played a role, at times, in constraining the party to quit government (for example in Denmark in 2014), consistent with Warwick's (2012, p. 279) suggestion that organisational cohesion or responding to activists may play a role in defection decisions. However, the relationship between Greens' participatory organisations or collective leadership styles and their duration in government is not a simple one. In the case of the Irish Greens, for example it seems that defection was delayed precisely due to a culture of collective decision-making within the parliamentary party (Boyle, 2012).

Getting punished?

If proportional portfolio allocation is one rule of coalition government, then postincumbency electoral punishment is another. Green parties might expect to receive even worse results than other parties in government, as small, newly governing and antiestablishment parties incur a greater cost than other parties (Font, 2001; Buelens and Hino, 2008; Van Spanje, 2011). Moreover, they began to join governments at a time when the electoral cost of government was high and rising (Narud and Valen, 2008, pp. 380–381), and in more recent years, the economic crisis has contributed to further electoral volatility.

There are 12 cases in which Green parties have faced the electorate after being in government (Table 12.1). Their outcomes have ranged from heavy losses (−4.5 pp. vote share) to modest gains (+1.9 pp.). Overall, their results have been decidedly negative. They have lost vote share on average (−1.2 pp.) and more often than not (on 8 occasions of 12; median = −0.9 pp.) In four cases, they have been sent back over the threshold of representation, losing all of their seats in parliament. At the same time, these losses are comparable to other new or antiestablishment parties in government. Indeed, it seems that they have not been punished as badly, on average, as these parties (Buelens and Hino, 2008; Van Spanje, 2011).

Part of Green parties' postincumbency losses can be accounted for by the fact that, like other parties, they often enter government on the back of electoral gains. These gains are hard to consolidate, as new voters are weakly habituated to voting for the party (Butler and Stokes, 1969, pp. 55–58; Gomez, 2012, Ch. 3; Little, 2014, Ch. 4). The cases of the Green parties in Belgium are illustrative: they contested their preincumbency election in the context of public concern regarding dioxins in the food chain in 1999. While this is an extreme case of vote gains that were likely to be unsustainable, it is not an isolated case. Of the seven Green parties that have entered government on the back of electoral gains, only one (the unusual case of the Finnish Greens in 2003) made further gains at the postincumbency election.

Another explanation may be that the balancing act between loyalty and distance from government (Poguntke, 2002, pp. 143–144; Rüdig, 2006) is too difficult to sustain, in many cases. As compromise on many issues is inevitable, supporters of a policy-oriented junior partner will be disappointed more often than not. This may be aggravated in cases where Green parties enter government with partners that are distant from their policy preferences, and especially if they leave a major electoral rival in opposition who can offer an alternative to Green party voters. This scenario appears to correspond to some particularly poor results (for example in Ireland in 2011, in Finland in 2011 and, to some extent, in the Czech Republic in 2010).

To date, Green parties that have defected from government have not done well at their postincumbency election. This reflects the fact that these parties – in Belgium (*Agalev*), the Czech Republic and Ireland – have generally defected with very poor electoral prospects. The exception in this regard is the Finnish Greens' defection in 2002, which took place well in advance of the next scheduled election, when the party had positive electoral prospects and over a policy disagreement that was easily comprehensible to voters. They ultimately gained votes. The results of coming general elections in Finland, France and Denmark will provide more data on the electoral results of comparable cases.

Thus, while earlier studies could observe that Green parties' postincumbency electoral outcomes were relatively positive (Buelens and Hino, 2008) and that very few Green parties (and no Green parties in government) had been pushed back over the threshold of representation (Müller-Rommel, 2002, p. 5), these observations have, to a great extent, been overtaken by events. The cost of governing for these parties, while not invariable, is clear. Once Green parties have chosen to enter government, their electoral fate is often decided by forces beyond their control.

Conclusion

Green parties' participation in government continues to pose new challenges for these parties. In facing the choice of joining government or remaining in opposition, they face a trade-off between coalition bargaining goals (office and policy) and electoral goals. Reconciling the compromises inherent in being a junior coalition partner with their policy-oriented support base, which is in turn empowered by their participatory organisational forms, is clearly difficult. Their bargaining power, further, is typically constrained at every stage of the process by the organisational and electoral costs of seeking to occupy a central position in their party systems. These features can be traced back to their origins in new social movements and more broadly to their core policy goals, which have tended to survive strategic and developmental changes. On the other hand, Green parties' 'rootedness' has been important for aspects of Green parties' success before (Bolleyer and Bytzek, 2013) and during government (Evrard, 2012). The costs of governmental participation have been high, while the policy gains have been variable and are more difficult to quantify. Further to the difficulties that they face due to their own characteristics, as small parties, they are often subject to the institutions, political configurations and economic developments that are beyond their control.

However, the picture is not all bleak for Green parties that seek to influence policy from inside government. Contrary to Mair's (2001, pp. 107, 111) prediction that government would spell the end of Green party growth, Green parties have, with few exceptions (for example in Italy), both recovered and continued to grow electorally, even after postincumbency setbacks. Some have returned to regional and national government. Even in Belgium, where both Green parties suffered crushing electoral defeats in 2003, they rejoined regional governments six years later. Their participation in government – and there is little sign that they are deviating from that goal – is becoming a standard feature of many parliamentary democracies, just as their representation in parliament did in earlier years.

Notes

1 This chapter draws on research carried out at the European University Institute in Florence for the author's PhD thesis (Little, 2014).
2 For brevity and clarity, I generally use the terms 'Finnish Greens', 'Italian Greens', 'Flemish Greens' and so on, rather than the parties' official names.
3 This chapter uses Freedom House's (2013) 'Free' status to identify stable democracies. It also excludes the case of the Mauritian Greens in government for lack of data.
4 These are 'parties with a predominantly ecological orientation that are or were recognised by or affiliated to the European Federation of Green Parties (since 2004: the European Green Party)' (Rihoux and Rüdig, 2006, p. 7).
5 As identified here, spells in government end when the party leaves government or when there is a general election. Some of the spells identified in Figure 12.1 encompass changes in the coalition's party composition and changes in prime minister (for example Italy, 1996–2001, and the Czech Republic, 2007–2010), thus spanning several cabinets, as conventionally defined (Müller, et al., 2008, p. 6).
6 This chapter covers the period up to 20 September 2014.
7 The data referred to in this paragraph do not include the recent Luxembourgish case, which had a roughly proportional outcome (contribution = 19 per cent of the cabinet parties' seats; allocation = 20 per cent of senior ministerial positions). Relative to their size, Green parties were overcompensated by a factor of 1.31, while other small parties were overcompensated by a factor of 1.67. The data for the comparison with other small parties refer to 240 small (≤ 9 per cent seat share) parties in government, drawn from Warwick and Druckman's (2006) data. See Little (2014, Ch. 2) for details.
8 These interviews with current and former members of Italian political parties, the trade union movement and environmental nongovernmental organisations (ENGOs) were carried out by the author in 2014 in the framework of the ESRC-funded *Climate Change and Political Parties* project.

References

Auers, D., 2012. The curious case of the Latvian Greens. *Environmental Politics,* 21(3), pp. 522–527.

Aylott, N., and Bergman, T., 2011. When median legislator theory fails: the Swedish Greens in 1998 and 2002. In: R. W. Andeweg, L. De Winter and P. Dumont, eds, *Puzzles of Government Formation: Coalition Theory and Deviant Cases* (1st ed.). London: Routledge. pp. 44–64.

Bäck, H., Debus, M., and Dumont, P., 2011. Who gets what in coalition governments? Predictors of portfolio allocation in parliamentary democracies. *European Journal of Political Research,* 50(4), pp. 441–478.

Bale, T., and Bergman, T., 2006. A taste of honey is worse than none at all?: Coping with the generic challenges of support party status in Sweden and New Zealand. *Party Politics,* 12(2), pp. 189–202.

Bale, T., and Blomgren, M., 2008. Close But No Cigar? Newly Governing and Nearly Governing Parties in Sweden and New Zealand. In: K. Deschouwer, ed., *New Parties in Government: In Power for the First Time.* London: Routledge. pp. 85–103.

Biorcio, R., 2002. Italy. *Environmental Politics,* 11(1), pp. 39–62.

Bolleyer, N., 2008. The Organizational Costs of Public Office. In: K. Deschouwer, ed., *New Parties in Government: In Power for the First Time.* London: Routledge. pp. 17–44.

Bolleyer, N., and Bytzek, E., 2013. Origins of party formation and new party success in advanced democracies. *European Journal of Political Research,* 52(6), pp. 773–796.

Bomberg, E. E., and Carter, N., 2006. The Greens in Brussels: Shaping or shaped? *European Journal of Political Research,* 45, pp. S99–S125.

Boy, D., 2002. France. *Environmental Politics,* 11(1), pp. 63–77.

Boyle, D., 2012. *Without Power or Glory: The Green Party in Government in Ireland, 2007–2011.* Dublin: New Island.

Brancati, D., 2005. Pawns take queen: The destabilizing effects of regional parties in Europe. *Constitutional Political Economy,* 16(2), pp. 143–159.

Browne, E. C., and Feste, K. A., 1975. Qualitative dimensions of coalition payoffs. *American Behavioral Scientist,* 18(4), pp. 530–556.

Browne, E. C., and Franklin, M. N., 1973. Aspects of coalition payoffs in European Parliamentary democracies. *The American Political Science Review,* 67(2), pp. 453–469.

Budge, I., and Keman, H., 1990. *Parties and Democracy: Coalition Formation and Government Functioning in Twenty States.* Oxford: Oxford University Press.

Buelens, J., and Hino, A., 2008. The Electoral Fate of New Parties in Government. In: K. Deschouwer, ed., *New Parties in Government: In Power for the First Time.* London: Routledge. pp. 157–174.

Burchell, J., 2002. *The Evolution of Green Politics: Development and Change Within European Green Parties.* London: Earthscan.

Butler, D., and Stokes, D. E., 1969. *Political Change in Britain: Forces Shaping Electoral Choice.* London: Macmillan.

Carter, N., 2013. Greening the mainstream: Party politics and the environment. *Environmental Politics,* 22(1), pp. 73–94.

Deschouwer, K., ed., 2008. *New Parties in Government: In Power for the First Time.* London: Routledge.

Döring, H., and Manow, P., 2012. Parliament and government composition database (ParlGov): An infrastructure for empirical information on political institutions – Version 12/10. Available at: <http://www.parlgov.org/>.

Dumont, P., and Bäck, H., 2006. Why so few, and why so late? Green parties and the question of governmental participation. *European Journal of Political Research*, 45, pp. S35–S67.

Evrard, A., 2012. Political parties and policy change: Explaining the impact of French and German Greens on energy policy. *Journal of Comparative Policy Analysis: Research and Practice*, 14(4), pp. 275–291.

Falcó-Gimeno, A., 2014. The use of control mechanisms in coalition governments. The role of preference tangentiality and repeated interactions. *Party Politics*, 20(3), pp. 341–356.

Fitzmaurice, J., 2004. Belgium stays 'purple': The 2003 federal election. *West European Politics*, 27(1), pp. 146–156.

Font, J., 2001. Dangerous coalitions (for small parties): The electoral consequences of government in Spanish regions and municipalities. *South European Society and Politics*, 6(2), pp. 71–96.

Freedom House, 2013. *Country Status and Ratings By Region, 1973–2013*. Available at: <http://www.freedomhouse.org/sites/default/files/Country%20Status%20and%20Ratings%20By%20Region%2C%201973–2013_0.xls>.

Gahrton, P., and Aylward, A., 2010. *Greens in Government: The Experience of European Green Parties' Involvement in Government*. Stockholm: Cogito.

Gomez, R., 2012. *Changing Choices, Changing Elections: A Study of Volatility and Vote-switching in six Western European Countries.* Florence: European University Institute.

Hanley, S., 2013. Unexpected consequences of an unexpected Prime Minister? The 2009–10 Fischer administration in the Czech Republic. Presented at the *EUSA Thirteenth Biennial Conference*, Baltimore, MD. Available at: <http://euce.org/eusa/2013/papers/6h_hanley.pdf>.

Hino, A., 2012. *New Challenger Parties in Western Europe: A Comparative Analysis*. London: Routledge.

Ignazi, P., 2007. Italy. *European Journal of Political Research*, 46(7–8), pp. 993–1004.

Inter-Parliamentary Union, 2013. PARLINE database on national parliaments. *Inter-Parliamentary Union*. Available at: <http://www.ipu.org/parline-e/parlinesearch.asp> [Accessed 10 June 2013].

Jensen, C. B., and Spoon, J.-J., 2011. Testing the 'Party Matters' thesis: Explaining progress towards Kyoto protocol targets. *Political Studies*, 59(1), pp. 99–115.

Jungar, A.-C., 2011. The Rainbow Coalition: A Surplus Majority Coalition in Finland. In: R. W. Andeweg, L. De Winter and P. Dumont, eds, *Puzzles of Government Formation: Coalition Theory and Deviant Cases*. 1st edition. London: Routledge. pp. 129–146.

Kitschelt, H. P., 1988. Left-libertarian parties: Explaining innovation in competitive party systems. *World Politics*, 40(2), pp. 194–234.

Knill, C., Debus, M., and Heichel, S., 2010. Do parties matter in internationalized policy areas? The impact of political parties on environmental policy outputs in 18 OECD countries, 1970–2000. *European Journal of Political Research*, 49(3), pp. 301–336.

Laver, M., and Schofield, N., 1990. *Multiparty Government: The Politics of Coalition in Europe*. Oxford: Oxford University Press.

Little, C., 2011. The general election of 2011 in the republic of Ireland: All changed utterly? *West European Politics*, 34(6), pp. 1304–1313.

Little, C., 2014. *Politics on the Margins of Government : A Comparative Study of Green Parties in Governing Coalitions*. Florence: European University Institute.

Mair, P., 2001. The Green challenge and political competition: How typical is the German experience? *German Politics*, 10(2), pp. 99–116.

Müller, W. C., Bergman, T., and Strøm, K., 2008. Coalition Theory and Cabinet Governance: An Introduction. In: K. Strom, W. C. Müller and T. Bergman, eds, *Cabinets and*

Coalition Bargaining: The Democratic Life Cycle in Western Europe. Oxford: Oxford University Press. pp. 1–50.

Müller-Rommel, F., 1985. The Greens in Western Europe: Similar but different. *International Political Science Review*, 6(4), pp. 483–499.

Müller-Rommel, F., 2002. The lifespan and the political performance of Green parties in Western Europe. *Environmental Politics* 11(1), pp. 1–16.

Narud, H. M., and Valen, H., 2008. Coalition Membership and Electoral Performance. In: K. Strom, W. C. Müller and T. Bergman, eds, *Cabinets and Coalition Bargaining: The Democratic Life Cycle in Western Europe*. Oxford: Oxford University Press. pp. 369–402.

Parlamento Italiano, 2013. *I Governo Ciampi*. Parlamento Italiano. Available at: <http://storia.camera.it/governi/i-governo-ciampi#nav>.

Pasquino, G., and Vassalo, S., 1995. The Government of Carlo Azeglio Ciampi. In: C. Mershon and G. Pasquino, eds, *Italian Politics: Ending the First Republic*. Boulder, CO: Westview Press. pp. 55–73.

Pedersen, M. N., 1982. Towards a new typology of party lifespans and minor parties. *Scandinavian Political Studies*, 5(1), pp. 1–16.

Poguntke, T., 2002. Green parties in national governments: From protest to acquiescence? *Environmental Politics*, 11(1), pp. 133–145.

Poguntke, T., 2003. Germany. *European Journal of Political Research*, 42(7–8), pp. 957–963.

Rihoux, B., and Frankland, E. G., 2008. Conclusion: The Metamorphosis of Amateur-Activist Newborns into Professional-Activist Centaurs. In E. G. Frankland, P. Lucardie and B. Rihoux, eds, *Green Parties in Transition: The End of Grass-Roots Democracy?* Farnham, England: Ashgate.

Rihoux, B., and Rüdig, W., 2006. Analyzing Greens in power: Setting the agenda. *European Journal of Political Research*, 45, pp. S1–S33.

Rüdig, W., 2006. Is government good for Greens? Comparing the electoral effects of government participation in Western and East-Central Europe. *European Journal of Political Research*, 45, pp. S127–S154.

Spoon, J.-J., 2009. Holding their own: Explaining the persistence of Green parties in France and the UK. *Party Politics*, 15(5), pp. 615–634.

Spoon, J.-J., 2011. *Political Survival of Small Parties in Europe*. Ann Arbor: University of Michigan Press.

Strøm, K., 1990. *Minority Government and Majority Rule*. Cambridge: Cambridge University Press.

Tavits, M., 2008. The role of parties' past behavior in coalition formation. *American Political Science Review*, 102(4), pp. 495–507.

Van Spanje, J., 2011. Keeping the rascals in: Anti-political-establishment parties and their cost of governing in established democracies. *European Journal of Political Research*, 50(5), pp. 609–635.

Warwick, P. V., 2012. Dissolvers, disputers, and defectors: The terminators of parliamentary governments. *European Political Science Review*, 4(2), pp. 263–281.

Warwick, P. V., and Druckman, J. N., 2006. The portfolio allocation paradox: An investigation into the nature of a very strong but puzzling relationship. *European Journal of Political Research*, 45(4), pp. 635–665.

Williams, P., 2011. House divided: The Australian general election of 21 August 2010. *Australian Journal of Political Science*, 46(2), pp. 313–329.

Wüst, A. M., and Roth, D., 2006. Schröder's last campaign: An analysis of the 2005 bundestag election in context. *German Politics*, 15(4), pp. 439–459.

13 Green party ideology today

Divergences and continuities in Germany, France and Britain

Gareth Price-Thomas

Introduction[1]

In much of Western Europe, Green parties have persisted for three decades or more. Many of these parties have undergone a series of transformations. Some have achieved significant electoral successes and have even participated in national government; others have remained on the fringes of national political life; many have lost several aspects of their organisational distinctiveness in the process of their development. Nevertheless, it is still possible to speak of a partial continuity across time in terms of party membership and organisation (see other chapters in this volume). However, what of Green party ideology? Today, is it appropriate to speak of a single Green 'party family' in ideological terms?

'Ideology' is one of the four approaches to the classification of party families, as theorised by Mair and Mudde (1998). However, in recent years in particular, Green party ideology has received little scholarly attention. There have been some studies that draw on the results of the Comparative Manifesto Project, which provide a useful aggregate picture of where Green parties stand today (Bukow and Switek, 2012; Carter, 2013). However, it is difficult to gain a particularly deep insight into the nuances of party ideology through such quasi-quantitative approaches. This chapter addresses precisely this gap in the literature. It consists of a close qualitative textual analysis of recent manifestos and press releases produced by three Western European Green parties, and it considers to what extent these documents reflect the preoccupations and emphases that have been known to mark Green party ideology over the past 30 years.

In the first section of this chapter, I explain the basis of my approach via a brief analysis of the relevant literatures. I affirm the existence of a distinct ideology and follow the terminology of Thomas Poguntke in classifying this as 'new politics'. In the second section of the chapter, I study the content of this ideology in closer detail. I move between its most significant themes one-by-one, explaining the significance of each in the history of Green party development and testing its continuing salience in recent party documents. In the final section, I suggest that one can indeed speak of Greens as forming a distinct party family, at least inasmuch as ideology is concerned. Finally, I offer some reflections on the ambiguities which surround this conclusion, and on possible future directions for Green party ideology.

'Party families' and Green party ideology

The purpose of this chapter is to answer the question as to whether contemporary Green parties may be understood as comprising a single party family along ideological lines. The concept of the 'party family' thus provides the rationale for the study, as well as the prism through which the parties' modes of thought will be analysed.

The concept of the party family is a broad one, and Mair and Mudde argue that it is to some extent still 'under-theorised' (1998, p. 214). Nevertheless, in the same article, the authors emphasise the continuing importance of the concept for the classification of political parties via their ideological characteristics (p. 224). What is more, there are already several examples of ideological theorisations of the party family that identify the Greens as a distinct type, though these are rather cursory in their engagement with the question as to what Green party ideology actually is (Gallagher, et al., 1995; Ware, 1996) or are by now rather outdated (von Beyme, 1985). Conversely, the term 'party family' itself crops up quite frequently within the literature on Green parties (Bomberg, 2002; Belchior, 2010; Carter, 2013). This testifies to the popularity of the notion that Greens across Europe, which act within quite different political environments, nevertheless possess a mode of thought that is both relatively homogeneous across the different parties and relatively distinct from the ideologies of other types of political parties. In this broad sense of the ideological 'party family', it can be argued that the concept underlies all discussions of a posited transnational Green party ideology; and it is to these which I now turn.

There is, of course, no academic or social consensus as to the nature of 'ideology' itself (Williams, 1988, pp. 153–157). It is therefore unsurprising to discover that there is no consensus within the literature on Green party ideology as to how it should best be theorised. The problem is perhaps accentuated in the case of Green parties, for two reasons. First, Green parties are 30 years young as well as 30 years old. They have shown themselves to be a relatively enduring phenomenon of the later postwar period in Europe, certainly, but this is hardly a *longue durée* when compared to the centuries of experience accumulated by Conservative, Liberal and Socialist parties. The second reason is related to Greens' preference for open forms of party organisation and mistrust of political elites. Greens shun explicit appeals to intellectual orthodoxy and have made little attempt to develop a canon of 'great thinkers'; they have no 'Mill, Marx, or Freud' (Freeden, 1996, p. 546). This is suggested in the 2002 party programme of *Die Grünen* where it is claimed that '[w]e are united . . . by a set of basic values, not by an ideology' (2002, p. 9).[2]

Approaches to the theorisation of Green party ideology range from the narrow ('ecologist') to the broad ('left-libertarianism'). At the one end of this continuum, one finds interpretations that are highly specific, conceiving of the ideology at hand as a form of radical environmental thought and as deriving from principles inherent in nature itself; the 'environmental' aspect of the ideology is, therefore, emphasised above all others. Such analyses tend to favour terms such as 'ecologism' or 'green ideology' to refer to the object of study. Some of these approaches tend to be political theoretical in nature and offer a complex analysis of the ideology at hand but place rather less emphasis on the sociological and political context of its elaboration (Freeden, 1996; Talshir, 2002). There are also works that do discuss the provenance of the ideology in more detail (Young, 1992), some of which do not adopt a fully 'ecologist' interpretation of the ideology's structure (Doherty, 2002), but which still conceive of it as deriving from the environmental movement in particular.

On the other end of the spectrum, the environmental aspect of the parties' thought is acknowledged, but it does not receive as great an emphasis. Instead, the ideology is understood to be comprised of multiple central themes, most of which are related to the concerns of the 'new left' or the 'new social movements' in general rather than the environmental movement in particular. Generally speaking, such accounts are more sociological than political theoretical in approach and place greater emphasis on the common demographic qualities that marked participants of many of the new social movements, and not just those of the environmental movement, and that still characterise much of the electorate of Green parties today. Dolezal (2010) offers one recent empirical study of note. The two most influential theoretical accounts, though, are that of Poguntke, who refers to Green party ideology as 'new politics ideology' (1993), and of Kitschelt, who prefers the term 'left-libertarianism' (1988).

I adopt the term 'new politics' for two reasons. First, it is quite clear that Green parties are ideologically united by more than just their concern for the natural world, and it is therefore too narrow to speak of just 'green' or 'ecologist' ideology. Second, by contrast, I find the term 'left-libertarianism' of Kitschelt to be too broad in scope. While the term is fitting, it could equally be applied to many other political currents in history, to the point where the distinctive nature of the positions taken by Green parties is lost. The term 'new politics', by contrast, allows for a multiplicity of components within the ideology and simultaneously highlights its relative novelty. It might be added that the term has a great deal of currency outside of Poguntke's own writings (Jahn, 1993; Faucher, 1999b, p. 487; Burchell, 2001; Bomberg and Carter, 2006, p. 105; Spoon, 2009) and continues to inspire theoretical debate (Blühdorn, 2013).

Empirical analysis

Method

It will be noted that I have not as of yet offered a definition of the new politics ideology. This task will be accomplished in the course of the empirical analysis that follows. I have selected six themes for close analysis, which are grouped under the three major fields of this mode of thought: ecology, radical democracy and egalitarianism.[3] In each sub-section of the empirical analysis, I first clarify the nature of each field of the ideology, providing an assessment of the role that its themes have played in the history of the new politics ideology. In more detail, I then test each theme's continuing salience in documents produced by contemporary Green parties, in order to gauge whether this theme continues to preoccupy Greens today.

Finally, in the chapter's concluding section, I consider what this empirical study reveals about the nature of the Greens in party family terms.

I draw primarily on recent manifestos of the German, French and British Green parties.[4] In manifestos, parties have to formulate an integral plan of action, one that encompasses all fields of political planning and that goes beyond the more narrow significance of individual policy areas. This is especially so in the case of Green parties, which overall still possess a holistic approach to policy-writing (Doherty, 2002, p. 70) and which – at least in the case of the three parties under study – still produce manifestos that possess an explicitly ideological tone. Mair and Mudde are, however, correct to highlight the fact that manifestos are 'explicitly designed in the context of election campaigns' (1998, p. 219). It is for this reason that, where relevant, I draw also on party press releases from a broader time period around the publication of these manifestos (between 2008 and 2012) as an additional window into Green party thought.

These parties were selected because of the rather different positions they occupy within the party system. *Bündnis 90/Die Grünen* (DG) is the prototypical case of the successful Green party; *Europe Écologie – Les Verts* (EELV) has achieved a measure of influence, but only via dependency on its centre-left rival;[5] and the Green Party of England and Wales (GPEW) remains on the fringes of national politics, having only recently won its first Member of Parliament (MP). In Pedersen's terminology (1982), they occupy different positions within the lifespan of the political party. What is more, the three countries in which these party systems are situated possess three distinct political cultures. Hence, if there is a reasonable degree of ideological continuity across these three parties, it seems fair to posit the existence of an ideological Green party family more generally, at least in Western Europe.[6]

In the course of the analysis, I show that this is indeed the case: that Green parties today do form a party family, in ideological terms. One certainly cannot speak of an ideological homogeneity, as there are some divergences between the parties. Nevertheless, in the aggregate, there are sufficient 'family resemblances' (to borrow a phrase of Wittgenstein's) to be able to speak of a relatively coherent collection of ideological tendencies that distinguish the Greens from rivals on the left and right of the parliamentary spectrum.

Field 1: Ecology

It is important not to reduce the new politics ideology to its most obvious component, but it is still appropriate to begin any analysis with this same topic. After all, it is precisely 'Green' parties that are under discussion; the names of the vast majority of members of the European Green Party, for example, contain a word that implicitly or explicitly relates to the environment. Of course, the health of the natural world is not a new concern, in historical terms (Worster, 1994), and concern about environmental degradation has become increasingly widespread within and beyond late capitalist societies (Inglehart, 1995). Even among political parties, Greens cannot claim exclusive ownership of the ecological issue (Gallagher, et al., 1995, p. 189; Markovits and Silvia, 1997, p. 59; Carter, 2013). Nevertheless, Green party ideology has long been understood to entail a particularly radical perspective on nature (Poguntke, 1993, pp. 36–37; Talshir, 2002).

The most fundamental elaboration of such a perspective can be found in O'Riordan's concept of 'ecocentrism' (O'Riordan, 1976, pp. 1–11; Eckersley, 1992). An ecocentric position entails an appreciation of the natural world for its own intrinsic value and a conception of the human being as just one part of earth's broader ecology. This stands in contrast to more 'anthropocentric' approaches, which calculate the environment's worth on the basis of its utility to humankind and see humans as distinct from and possibly superior to the habitats in which they live. The corollary of the ecocentric viewpoint is that human interests may on occasion have to take secondary status next to the overall wellbeing of nature as a whole (Poguntke, 1993, p. 36). This, in turn, is at the heart of the distinctively Green rejection of economic growth (Kitschelt, 1988, p. 195; Poguntke, 1993, p. 36; Barry and Doherty, 2001, p. 601; Doherty, 2002, p. 70; Talshir 2002, p. 15). Contrary to the received wisdom of the postwar era, Greens understand growth to be deleterious to the wellbeing of the planet as well as to human beings. In the following analysis, I gauge whether each of these two themes of the new politics ideology – an appreciation for the intrinsic value of nature and an antigrowth stance – may be said to endure among Green parties today.

The conception of nature

The three parties share a very similar conception of nature, which is marked by a degree of new politics radicalism. All three gesture, at least sporadically, towards an ecocentric positioning. In the most straightforward formulation of this stance, and relating to a specific aspect of environmental policy, the German Greens claim that they 'tirelessly support the protection of biological diversity *for its own sake*' (my emphasis) (DG, 2009a, p. 49). More generally and rather more explicitly, *Les Verts* argue that '[i]n opposition to a purely utilitarian vision of nature . . . human beings must redefine their place in the equilibrium of the living world' (EELV, 2012, p. 30). The first part of the citation explicitly rejects the wholly anthropocentric conception of the natural world, while the second asks the manifesto's readers to question their assumptions about their relation to nature; it also lends a kind of agency to nature as a system that is self-regulating ('equilibrium').

These examples aside, there are also many instances within the manifestos that indicate the appreciation of nature from a utilitarian – and therefore specifically human – perspective. The national election manifesto of *Die Grünen* contains a chapter devoted to environmental policy that is titled, 'An intact environment: Preserving that which preserves us' (DG, 2009b, p. 131). This turn of phrase suggests a very pragmatic reason for the protection of the natural world: we humans could not survive without it. Similarly, the French party can be seen to translate its aforementioned concern for nature in itself into a concern for nature as a mechanism for the fulfilment of social and economic policies. Its electoral documents refer to the 'irreplaceable services which nature provides [humanity] with' (Europe Écologie (EE), 2009, p. 61), as well as the importance of these 'services' for the sustenance of 'the world economy' (EELV, 2012, p. 29).

This is not to argue that the clear ecocentric streak indicated above should be ignored. But it does suggest that the three parties have become caught between the more radical aspirations that one might have attributed to Green parties in their early years and the practical necessities of representing one's ideological position to mass publics that are by no means ecocentric in orientation. This conclusion is in accordance with Andrew Dobson's reflections that the concept of ecocentrism may itself have lost ground within the broader environmental movement in recent years, to the benefit of 'pragmatic environmentalism' (Dobson, 2010). Today, Greens are trying to have their cake and eat it, a position that is aptly depicted in couplets that indicate both ecocentrism and anthropocentrism simultaneously, such as the British party's claim that '[w]e must protect our wildlife and landscape and their diversity, both for their own sake and ours' (GPEW, 2010a, p. 41). In other words, even if you do not believe in the intrinsic value of nature, you will commit yourself to its defence – if you know what is good for you.

Growth

I turn now to the question of growth. This, incidentally, allows an insight into the parties' economic as well as environmental positioning. Again, the parties under study do partially retain a distinctively new politics character. The British party states in its 2010 national election manifesto that 'size matters: if the economy gets too big it will grow beyond its ecological limits' (GPEW, 2010a, p. 8). Here, then, the document appeals explicitly to environmental boundaries that objectively dictate that the growth paradigm must be brought to an end. Rather more poetically, the French Greens claim at the very beginning of a chapter on economic policy that '[o]ur goal is not to increase the size of a cake which is more and more poisonous . . . for the planet' (EELV, 2012, p. 59). The party is similarly emphatic in a press release issued at the height of the financial crisis where it rejects the notion of 'green growth' put forward by then President Sarkozy, claiming that his use of this oxymoronic term calls into question 'his ecological virtues' (2008).

However, these individual instances of antigrowth sentiment cannot be said to receive particular emphasis. In the case of the French party, the references to the matter are extremely few and far between. The British party refers to the matter more often, but it gently qualifies this stance on many occasions, such as where the party refers critically to the current 'obsession with growth' (GPEW, 2010a, p. 8), to 'indiscriminate growth' (GPEW, 2009, p. 8) and to 'growth-as-usual' (GPEW, 2009, p. 8). Does the party oppose growth outright, or simply an excess of growth? In these instances, one cannot be entirely sure. Most strikingly, while *Die Grünen* does imply a certain scepticism towards the concept of economic growth on a few occasions (2009a, p. 111; 2009b, p. 25), it also shows indications that it might be on the cusp of abandoning an antigrowth position altogether. At one point, it adopts the very concept that *Les Verts* had rejected in its critique of Sarkozy, that of green growth: '[e]nvironmental protection is a global growth market. Invest- ments made today into technologies and jobs are the prerequisite for the export successes of tomorrow'. (DG, 2009b, p. 30) Whereas an antigrowth position is usually predicated on the existing processes of environmental degradation, here the German Greens present the logic of growth as a strategy for avoiding such damage in future.

In this case, therefore, it can be stated that the parties have retained an aspect of their new politics distinctiveness, but that the radicalism of their claims has softened a good deal. In the case of the German party, the party expresses its traditionally antigrowth stance in such a weak and ambiguous form that it might go unnoticed by the layperson. One might speculate that this is the result of the comparatively deep integration of *Die Grünen* within the party system in which it operates.

Field 2: Radical democracy

The second broad component of new politics ideology – which I need not split into various distinct themes and instead engage with in its integrity – is a radical conception of democracy. Like ecology, this theme is not solely the purview of new politics ideology; one thinks in particular of the older-established ideology of anarchism. Nevertheless, from the beginning of the scholarship, it has been recognised that Greens call for greater public participation in politics and for the decentralisation of power in all of its forms (Poguntke, 1993, pp. 37–38; Doherty, 2002, p. 72). Indeed, Kitschelt's early studies made this radical democratic aspect of Green thought visible in the very term he constructed to denote it: 'left-*libertarianism*' (1988, 1989). Today, too, Green parties are still frequently studied for their still relatively grassroots forms of organisation (see Rihoux in this volume). This institutional framework derives from a particular tenet of new politics ideology: namely that all of society ought to have a greater say in the making of decisions that affect society as a whole.

On this topic, again, it is clear that Green parties have retained at least some significant aspects of their traditional aspirations. There is a full chapter in both German Green manifestos that engages with related topics (2009a, pp. 112–133; 2009b, pp. 161–172). In the case of the GPEW, the theme is also prominent. There is within the national election manifesto the call for the creation of a 'citizen culture', which is accompanied by the claim that '[c]reating a fair and sustainable society is a job for government at all levels – but also a job for us as citizens' (GPEW, 2010a, pp. 28–29). This same sentiment regarding citizen duty is advanced within the European manifesto also: 'a job for every member of the community' (2009, p. 26).

It is this last citation that indicates a related ideological facet of the British Greens, which serves to ground their radical democratic tendencies: localism. Localism refers to the advocacy of smaller units of political organisation, geographically decentralised and therefore closer to those who are on the receiving end of political decisions. The emphasis on local forms of political organisation is an emphatic concern of the British party, as is indicated by the fact that the word 'community' arises 30 and 25 times in the national and European manifestos, respectively. Hence, more decentralised, participatory forms of democratic engagement are never far from the concerns of the GPEW, and while they do not receive as consistent an emphasis, similar localist tendencies may be found within the German party ('the communes are important germination points of democratic society and of citizen participation', 2009b, p. 164).

Like the German and British parties, *Les Verts* displays a marked radical democratic tendency. This is evident both in its policy – calls to support the use of citizen-initiated referenda and for other such democratic experiments (EELV, 2012, p. 161) – and in the way the party conceives of itself. In the national manifesto, it claims to be part of a broader 'movement' (2012, p. 12), in such a way as to imply that 'political ecology' (the party's term for its ideology) is concerned not only with institutional politics but also with more direct forms of political activity. This aspect of the party's ideology can also be seen in visual terms within the European election manifesto, as every other page bears a stylised image of a crowd of protestors, implying that the party continues to self-identify with the radically democratic movement politics from which it was originally formed.

On the other hand, the French Greens do not possess the same localist streak as may be found within the German or, especially, the British party. It does speak of the need for decentralisation, but this is couched in terms of 'a new, federal form of state organisation' which argues in favour of granting further autonomy to the 'regions' of France (2012, p. 158). These proposals would amount to a French Republic that in terms of its institutional framework, looks rather like the German state as it is configured today. The degree of ideological radicalism on display here is more modest than that of the other two parties, though when one takes the context into account – the French Greens are part of a particularly centralised political system – then it is clear that *Les Verts* is at least tending in the same direction as the other two parties. It is unsurprising that differences in national political culture should strongly influence how Greens concern themselves with the reform of existing political procedures. In sum, one can still identify a series of shared preoccupations that may be said to identify the parties under study as a part of a broader family.

Field 3: Egalitarianism

The final broad component of the new politics ideology is egalitarianism or an insistence on social justice for all groups of society (Kitschelt, 1988, p. 195; Poguntke, 1993, pp. 37–38; Doherty, 2002, p. 71). Unlike other ideologies that have a similar emphasis on the equality of all human beings – most notably, socialism and classical anarchism – the new politics does not emphasise the exploitation of the working class more than it does any other demographic. Instead, there is a relatively high degree of attention given to the rights of women, migrants, sexual minorities and the inhabitants of developing countries.

In this section, I first consider the extent to which Green parties today might be broadly understood as feminist parties. Given the influence of the women's movement in the historical development of Green parties (Kolinsky, 1988; Doherty, 2002, pp. 54–55), it is important to ask whether these parties still place particular emphasis on the maintenance and expansion of women's rights. Second, given the Greens' defence of migrants' rights (Poguntke, 1987, p. 78) and of ethnic minorities (Kitschelt, 1989, p. 93; Poguntke, 1987, p. 78), I study how the three parties conceive of issues of migration. Finally, as a further indicator of whether the Greens may be seen as egalitarian on a global scale – and because it is a topic that cannot be bypassed in any study of new politics ideology – I look at the extent to which the German, French and British Greens express pacifist concerns. Green parties took up the cause of peace in Europe and beyond from a very early point (Kolinsky, 1984; Bomberg and Carter, 2006: 103; Carter, 2013: 75) and, as a part of this, advocated unilateral disarmament in opposition to the arms race between the American and Soviet powers (Poguntke, 1993, p. 39).

Women's rights

On the topic of women's rights, it is difficult to speak of ideological consistency across the three parties. The French party is the most straightforwardly new politics of the three cases. Consider, for example, the breadth of forms of discrimination against women discussed by the party: political under-representation, economic hardship, physical violence and so on. Consider also the radicalism that the tone of the documents sometimes takes. For Greens, it is argued:

> A solidaristic world can only be constructed if the social relations between women and men change considerably [. . .] From school to work, it is all of society which must be transformed to make possible respect [for women] via a feminist approach.
>
> (EELV, 2012, p. 131)

A radically systemic conceptualisation of gender inequality is suggested elsewhere in both manifestos, as well as in press releases issued by the party. It is claimed in one release that 'acts of violence against women are not individual problems' but are instead the result of 'a society where women-men relations . . . still rest on a dominant-dominated basis linked to the patriarchal system' (EELV, 2010b).

In the case of *Die Grünen*, the question of women's rights receives even greater emphasis. It raises its head throughout the manifestos and not merely in specific policy chapters. Furthermore, press releases issued by the federal party (*Bundespartei*) on the topic far outnumber those produced over the same period by the French and British parties. The content of its feminism, however, is a little different. At times, the tone struck is indeed radically new politics ('[w]e Greens stand in the tradition of the women's movement', DG, 2011a). However, undoubtedly, there is also a strong bourgeois streak to the party's feminism. Unlike in the case of the French party, *Die Grünen* gives particular emphasis to the economic status of women, the need to move away from the 'model of the sole male bread-winner' (2009b, p. 180). So, for example, the very first section within the chapter on women's rights is called 'Equal opportunities in the labour market' (2009b, pp. 181–182). But apart from the emphasis on women's economic position in general, there is an explicitly careerist element that is articulated from time to time, where the party discusses the need for more women in leading positions within companies and other institutions (2009b, pp. 49–50, 181; 2009a, pp. 123–124) and in scientific and academic roles (2009b, p. 110).

Lastly, and interestingly, it is important to note that the British party's manifestos devote no particular space to the topic. Instead, it is referred to in passing, within the context of other policy fields (for example GPEW 2009, pp. 15, 27; 2010a, pp. 12, 25, 31). The point is true also of the party's press releases, of which very few are devoted to the question of women's rights. This is not to say that the British party ignores questions of gender; to take a current example, its two most prominent leadership roles must be allocated according to principles of gender parity. Nevertheless, based on this analysis, women's rights do not form a central aspect of the party's ideology. As such, and given the somewhat different approaches to the topic espoused by *Les Verts* and *Die Grünen*, with the latter adopting a rather liberal feminist stance, it would seem that Green parties today cannot straightforwardly be identified by a new politics, radical position on women's rights. Though, certainly, one might still argue that their aggregate position is still reasonably distinct from that of other types of political party.

Migration

On the subject of migration, there are certainly clear areas of overlap in the positions taken by the parties. All three are highly critical of existing policies that are being deployed at the European and national levels in order to curb immigration. The French Greens, for example, are forthright on this point in their statement that '[W]e refuse Fortress Europe' (EE, 2009, p. 48). In opposition to this, the party claims the need for 'an immigration policy which is open and humanist, and which permits another approach to North-South relationships than the war on migrants which the European Union is currently leading' (EELV, 2012, p. 139).

Die Grünen places an even more continual emphasis on the rights of migrants. The question arises continually throughout the manifestos. Like *Les Verts*, the party is highly critical of existing immigration policy, as it castigates the conception of the European Union as a "fortress" against refugees' (2009a, p. 115); and, furthermore, it advocates 'a society which is open for immigration and which makes possible integration through participation' (2009a, p. 115). It goes perhaps even further in its cosmopolitan stance than the French Greens, though, as it speaks of the outright cultural necessity of migration for the creation of a diverse national culture: most strikingly, it speaks of the need to 'advance integration and to democratically create multicultural reality' (2009b, p. 147). There is one subtle

aspect in which *Die Grünen* differs, however, and this is in the relative importance placed on the economic integration of migrants ('[t]he labour market is a
key to integration', 2009b, p. 148). This process is essential not just for migrants
themselves but also for national economic productivity ('[l]egal immigration is a
way of meeting the labour market's demands for skilled labour', 2009a, p. 115).
To some extent, then, this mirrors the party's somewhat bourgeois approach to
feminism noted in the discussion of the previous theme and further implies an
integration of the ideological concerns of the German Greens into more mainstream, liberal discourse.

Finally, the GPEW mirrors the preoccupations of the French and German parties, for the most part. It is similar to the multicultural position taken by *Die
Grünen* where it claims that '[m]uch of our language, culture and way of life
have been enriched by successive new arrivals [of migrants] over two thousand
years' (2010a, p. 45). Furthermore, the party seeks to enforce the notion of 'British
Citizens' as themselves migrants, both historically and in the present ('[w]e in the
[United Kingdom] are part of the pattern of global migration', 2009, p. 30). There
is, though, a slight distinction regarding the British party's approach to the topic of
migration. The party is not absolutely new politics in its approach; at one point, it
shows a gentle ambivalence towards the effects of migration (2010a, p. 45), and
it would appear to do so partly on the basis of the localist position indicated in
the above analysis of the party's stance on radical democracy. The point should
not be overemphasised because, for the most part, its arguments are close to those
of the other two parties. But to a similar – if slightly lesser – degree as with the
previous theme, I have shown that there are differences in the parties' positions
on migration, even if Green parties still can in general be thought of as staunch
defenders of migrants' rights.

Pacifism

This final topic proves to be the least helpful of all six themes in the identification
of a Green party family. Of the three parties, it is the GPEW that perhaps makes the
greatest case to be qualified as pacifist. Unlike the other two parties, it demands
the immediate recalling of its national troops from Afghanistan. This is made clear
in the manifestos (2010a, p. 42) and in press releases ('[t]here is no military solution to this conflict', 2010b). However, the party does not explicitly claim to oppose
the use of military force in all circumstances; and, furthermore, where it argues
against it, it sometimes does so through a language of pragmatism rather than one
of morality. For example, the 'invasions of Iraq and Afghanistan' are said to be
'counterproductive' (2010a, p. 42), and the document here claims that '[i]t is now
absolutely clear that our security has been compromised, not improved' as a result
of these actions. Here, then, the wars are partly criticised from the standpoint of
efficacy, implying that 'our security' was and remains the central question at stake.

The German and French parties are even less easily qualified as pacifist. It is
well known that *Die Grünen* underwent a rather tumultuous stage in its development shortly after acceding to national office when German air forces participated

in the North Atlantic Treaty Organisation (NATO) military actions in the former Yugoslavia (Rüdig, 2002, p. 95). Interestingly, the party implicitly refers to this series of events in its European manifesto, in the introductory section to the chapter on foreign policy:

> With the end of the confrontation between the two blocs and the flaring up of new wars and civil wars, ethnic cleansings and massacres against the civilian population, the majority of the party has brought itself to a reappraisal of the military.
>
> (2009a, p. 146)

The text here denies that the party has changed its position in disavowing pacifism. It is, instead, the world that has become more violent, and the party has simply adapted its perspective to accommodate this new geopolitical context. The party thus presents itself as unrepentant regarding the Balkan episode. In more recent terms, and in quite stark contrast with the British party, *Die Grünen* claims that some meaningful successes have been won in Afghanistan – 'the liberation of a great part of the population from the despotism and terror of the Taliban, better access to education and opportunities for economic development' – even though this is heavily qualified with reference to the suffering that the war has also entailed (DG, 2011c).

As for the French party, *Les Verts* does at one point in the manifestos make an explicit statement in favour of '[n]onviolence', which 'as a mode of resolution of international crises represents a constitutive value of political ecology' (2012, p. 184). Yet this reads as somewhat paradoxical in the face of some of the party's policy positions. Like *Die Grünen* (DG 2011c), though unlike the GPEW, the French party is not in favour of an immediate withdrawal of national troops from Afghanistan (EELV, 2010a). More strikingly, the party was in full favour of a multilateral military action against the Gaddafi regime in Libya for the creation of a 'no-fly' zone (EELV, 2011a; 2011b), the party's rationale being that this would protect civilians against airstrikes by the regime's forces. The prospects of such an action received a much more ambiguous appraisal by both the British and German parties (DG, 2011b; GPEW, 2011).

In sum, none of the parties is in principle opposed to the use of military force under specific circumstances. Two of the three – likely not coincidentally, those that were in national government at the time of the military actions in the former Yugoslavia and in Afghanistan – explicitly talk of the benefits of the intervention of armed forces in recent historical events. Based on this analysis, it would seem that Green parties today cannot be identified as 'pacifist' parties.

Conclusion

What, then, are the results of this study? To come to the point, it would seem plausible to conclude that Green parties today do indeed constitute an ideological party family, at least within Western Europe. I premise this conclusion on two claims. First, the three parties under study – which have enjoyed very different levels of success, and which function within three rather different national political cultures – have been shown to possess a great many commonalities across the six themes studied. Second, these commonalities suggest an ideology that is sufficiently distinctive from that of other types of party. But the question remains: is it as straightforward to speak of a Green party family today as it was 30 years ago? The remainder of the essay engages with this very issue.

On the first point, as to the degree of ideological overlap evident between Green parties, it is clear that the picture is not one of absolute homogeneity. Differences have arisen in the course of the analysis, most prominently within the themes of economic growth, feminism and pacifism. Furthermore, the German and British parties in particular have indicated multiple divergences from the historical model of the new politics ideology. Why should this be the case? On the part of the German Greens, its relative integration into the party system within the *Bundestag* is surely the most plausible explanation. The ideological distinctions within the British party might best be understood as a result of the somewhat different origins of the GPEW, whose relation to the new social movements were at the time of its foundation rather more indirect (Faucher, 1999a). Furthermore, in the case of all three parties, national differences in political culture must also provide part of the explanation, and these have been referred to in the individual thematic analyses above. Perhaps, then, Green parties are becoming increasingly heterogeneous over time.

But this is likely not the case. It must be remembered that I have been comparing individual party ideologies against an aggregate model of new politics ideology and that, in fact, Green parties have never been ideologically homogeneous (Müller-Rommel, 1985; Müller-Rommel and Poguntke, 1989). Furthermore, the specific influences on Green parties, considered immediately above, are not new. Green parties across Europe have always been partially divided by their differing levels of integration into their national political systems. Their origins have tended to be similar, but they have never been precisely the same in any two cases. In addition, of course, Greens have been exposed to the pressures of distinct national political cultures from their foundation. Indeed, to some extent, it can be said that each Green party has grown out of its own particular nation-state, even as it has argued against the inadequacies of a solely national politics in the face of contemporary environmental and social crises. Party family approaches to ideological classification have always had to consider such factors and to make allowances for them.

However, regarding the distinctiveness of Green party ideology, the last 30 years have taken their toll. The thematic analysis above has shown that while all the parties advocate more direct forms of democratic participation, the state is tacitly accepted as the principal lever of social change, as is reflected in the texts as well as in the primarily electoral strategy of most Green parties. While the Greens under study here have a partially radical view of nature, they compromise and understand the environmental partly in utilitarian terms, even if they do so primarily to attract more votes. Their egalitarianism is still very much in view, but the parties do not overall approach discrimination against women and migrants in a radically systemic fashion. Finally, they say little of their opposition to economic growth, and they can scarcely be thought of as pacifist, often adopting positions compatible with 'liberal humanitarianism', even if the parties remain on the sceptical edge of this philosophy of military activity.

In sum, Green parties have lost some of their radical edge. The aggregate Green party ideology discovered in the analysis above has partially shifted away from the historical model of new politics, and one can no longer easily speak of them as 'antiparty' parties, neither in the organisational nor the ideological sense. This is very likely so because over a period of 30 years they all, including the more marginal amongst them, have become relatively established institutions seeking national political influence. All Green parties have undergone a greater or lesser degree of integration within the existing party system. Herein lies a potential challenge for future attempts to classify party families by ideology. If even the newest challenger group within European party systems has lost some of its ideological distinctiveness, and if this process of incorporation into the political mainstream continues, then this suggests that we must be prepared to adopt a more subtle approach than in the past. We must acknowledge that, in general, the gaps between party family ideologies are becoming less substantial than in past years.

However, it is by no means certain that Green parties will continue on their trajectory of integration and deradicalisation. Thirty years on, Green parties endure and occasionally still achieve considerable electoral successes. But one cannot speak today of an upwards trajectory of Green parties comparable to that which was in evidence in the 1980s and 1990s. It is now rather difficult to believe that Greens will achieve political influence comparable to that of the older-established party families, at least in the foreseeable future and in the absence of any sudden increase in the salience of environmental degradation among voting publics. To take a dramatic example, the German Greens have recently (as of the time of writing) suffered a disappointing result in the federal elections of 2013, despite their considerable successes in recent years (Rüdig, 2012) and discussions of the possibility that they might become a new catch-all party (Kroh and Schupp, 2011; Probst, 2011; Schneider and Winkelmann, 2012) and, furthermore, despite the possibilities granted by the increase in public opposition to nuclear technology in the aftermath of the nuclear disaster at Fukushima.

Green parties that remain on the relative fringes of their national political systems might decide that further ideological moderation is needed if they are ever to appeal to greater swathes of the public. On the other hand, their role of permanent opposition – or at best junior coalition partner – might incite them to emphasise their ideological distinctiveness. This could contribute to a phase of ideological stability or even reradicalisation, as they continue to find greater support among those sympathetic to the social movements from which they originated than they do among voters inhabiting the middle ground of society. One thing is for sure. If the Greens' 'long march through the institutions' has indeed been halted, then making any accurate guesses at the future development of Green party ideology is a difficult task.

Notes

1 I would like to thank the James Pantyfedwen Foundation for its support of my PhD studies, from which the research that forms this contribution is derived. I would also like to thank Emilie van Haute for her editorial guidance; the participants of the 'Green Parties in Europe: A Comparative Perspective' conference (Brussels, 28–29 March 2013), at which the earliest draft of this chapter was presented; and Ingolfur Blühdorn, who as discussant provided me with helpful comments on a subsequent draft, presented at the 2013 ECPR General Conference (Bordeaux, 4–7 September 2013).
2 This and all further citations from German- and French-language documents are of my own translation.
3 These three overarching fields were selected on the basis of the analysis of Doherty (2002) that, despite its (in my opinion) too narrow conceptualisation of Green party thought as 'green ideology', presents the most accurate general structure of the ideology under study.
4 For the sake of brevity, I often refer to the Green Party of England and Wales (GPEW) as the 'British' party. I acknowledge that this is not strictly accurate, given that there has been a separate Scottish Green Party since 1990.
5 For the sake of economy, I will at times continue to refer to the party by its former, briefer name of *Les Verts*.
6 The Green parties of Central and Eastern European countries are known to differ from their Western European counterparts in ideological terms, though they are considerably more marginal. For more detail, see Frankland's contribution, Chapter 3 in this volume.

References

Barry, J., and Doherty, B., 2001. The Greens and social policy: Movements, politics and practice? *Social Policy and Administration*, 35(5), pp. 587–607.

Belchior, A. M., 2010. Are Green political parties more post-materialist than other parties? *European Societies*, 12(4), pp. 467–492.

Blühdorn, I., 2013. *Simulative Demokratie nach der postdemokratischen Wende*. Berlin: Suhrkamp Verlag.

Bomberg, E., 2002. The Europeanisation of Green parties: Exploring the EU's impact. *West European Politics*, 25(3), pp. 29–50.

Bomberg, E., and Carter, N., 2006. The Greens in Brussels: Shaping or shaped? *European Journal of Political Research*, 45, pp. 99–215.

Bukow, S., and Switek, N., 2012. Die grüne Parteienfamilie. In: U. Jun and B. Höhne, eds, *Parteienfamilien: Identitätsbestimmend oder nur noch Etikett?* Opladen: Verlag Barbara Budrich. pp. 185–219.

Bündnis 90/Die Grünen, 2009a. *Volles Programm mit WUMS! Für ein besseres Europa: Europawahlprogramm 2009*. [pdf] Berlin: Bündnis 90/Die Grünen. Available at: <http://www.gruene.de/fileadmin/user_upload/Dokumente/Europawahlprogramm/ Europawahlprogramm.pdf> [Accessed 13 September 2012].

Bündnis 90/Die Grünen, 2009b. *Der grüne neue Gesellschaftsvertrag: Bundestagswahlprogramm 2009*. [pdf] Berlin: Bündnis 90/Die Grünen. Available at: <http:// www.gruene.de/fileadmin/user_upload/Dokumente/Wahlprogramm/BTW_Wahl programm_2009_290609.pdf> [Accessed 15 December 2012].

Bündnis 90/Die Grünen, 2011a. *100. Internationaler Frauentag – Grund zum Feiern, Anlass zum Weiterstreiten*. [Press release] (Published 7 March 2011) Available at: <http://www.gruene.de/presse/100-internationaler-frauentag-grund-zum-feiern-anlass- zum-weiterstreiten.html> [Accessed 17 June 2013].

Bündnis 90/Die Grünen, 2011b. *Keine einfache Entscheidung*. [Press release] (Published 18 March) Available at: <http://www.gruene.de/presse/keine-einfache-entscheidung. html> [Accessed 31 May 2013].

Bündnis 90/Die Grünen, 2011c. *10 Jahre Afghanistan-Einsatz: Aufbau und Rückschläge*. [Press release] (Published 7 October) Available at: <http://www.gruene.de/presse/10-jahre-afghanistan-einsatz-aufbau-und-rueckschlaege.html> [Accessed 29 May 2013].

Burchell, J., 2001. Evolving or conforming? Assessing organisational reform within European Green parties. *West European Politics*, 24(3), pp. 113–134.

Carter, N., 2013. Greening the mainstream: Party politics and the environment. *Environmental Politics*, 22(1), pp. 73–94.

Dobson, A., 2010. Ecocentrism: A response to Paul Kingsnorth. *Open Democracy*. Available at: <http://www.opendemocracy.net/andrew-dobson/ecocentrism-response-to-paul-kingsnorth> [Accessed 5 October 2013].

Doherty, B., 2002. *Ideas and Actions in the Green Movement*. London: Routledge.

Dolezal, M., 2010. Exploring the stabilisation of a political force: The social and attitudinal basis of Green parties in the age of globalisation. *West European Politics*, 33(3), pp. 534–552.

Eckersley, R., 1992. *Environmentalism and Political Theory: Toward an Ecocentric Approach*. London: UCL Press.

Europe Écologie, 2009. *Elections Européennes du 7 juin 2009: le contrat écologiste pour l'Europe*. (Personal communication with French party member and 2009 European campaign activist Simon Persico, 21 January 2013).

Europe Écologie – Les Verts, 2010a. *Afghanistan: trouver une solution politique à la conférence de Londres*. [Press release] (Published 21 January 2010) Available at: <http://lesverts.fr/spip.php?article4997> [Accessed 29 May 2013].

Europe Écologie – Les Verts, 2010b. *25 novembre: journée internationale pour l'élimination des violences à l'égard des femmes: encore une année de trop*. [Press release] (Published 24 November 2010) Available at: <http://feminisme.eelv.fr/2010/11/24/25-novembre-journee-internationale-pour-l%E2%80%99elimination-des-violences-a-l%E2%80%99egard-des-femmes-encore-une-annee-de-trop> [Accessed 17 June 2013].

Europe Écologie – Les Verts, 2011a. *L'Union Européenne doit agir pour le peuple libyen*. [Press release] (Published 9 March 2011) Available at: <http://eelv.fr/2011/03/09/lunion-europeenne-doit-agir-pour-le-peuple-libyen> [Accessed 1 June 2013].

Europe Écologie – Les Verts, 2011b. *Libye: la chance d'une nouvelle ère pour le droit international*. [Press release] (Published 18 March 2011) Available at: <http://eelv.fr/2011/03/18/libye-la-chance-dune-nouvelle-ere-pour-le-droit-international> [Accessed 1 June 2013].

Europe Écologie – Les Verts, 2012. *Vivre mieux: vers une société écologique*. Paris: Europe Écologie – Les Verts. Available at: <http://eelv.fr/wp-content/uploads/2012/03/projet-pdf.pdf> [Accessed 8 December 2012].

Faucher, F., 1999a. L'impossible développement des verts britanniques. In: P. Delwit and J.-M. De Waele, eds, *Les partis verts en Europe*. Paris: Editions Complexe. pp. 197–219.

Faucher, F., 1999b. Party organisation and democracy: A comparison of Les Verts and the British Green Party. *GeoJournal*, 47, pp. 487–496.

Freeden, M., 1996. *Ideologies and Political Theory: A Conceptual Approach*. Oxford: Oxford University Press.

Gallagher, M., Laver, M., and Mair, P., 1995. *Representative Government in Modern Europe*. 2nd edition. London: McGraw-Hill.

Green Party of England and Wales, 2009. *'It's the Economy, Stupid': The Green Party Manifesto for the European Parliament Elections 2009*. London: Green Party of England and Wales. Available at: <http://www.greenparty.org.uk/assets/files/EU_Manifesto_2009.pdf> [Accessed 14 September 2012].

Green Party of England and Wales, 2010a. *General Election Manifesto 2010: Fair is Worth Fighting for.* London: Green Party of England and Wales. Available at: <http://www.greenparty.org.uk/assets/files/resources/Manifesto_web_file.pdf> [Accessed 15 December 2012].

Green Party of England and Wales, 2010b. *Caroline Lucas to Speak at Public Meeting on Afghanistan.* [Press release] (Published 8 September 2010) Available at: <http://greenparty.org.uk/news/08-09-2010-afghanistan-meeting-parliament.html> [Accessed 29 May 2013].

Green Party of England and Wales, 2011. *Parliamentary Vote Needed Before Any Libyan Action.* [Press release] (Published 11 March 2011) Available at: <http://greenparty.org.uk/news/11-03-2011-parliamentary-vote-libya.html> [Accessed 31 May 2013].

Inglehart, R., 1995. Public support for environmental protection: Objective problems and subjective values in 43 societies. *PS: Political Science and Politics*, 28(1), pp. 57–72.

Jahn, D., 1993. The rise and decline of new politics and the Greens in Sweden and Germany: Resource dependence and new social cleavages. *European Journal of Political Research*, 24, pp. 177–194.

Kitschelt, H. P., 1988. Left-libertarian parties: Explaining innovation in competitive party systems. *World Politics*, 40(2), pp. 194–234.

Kitschelt, H. P., 1989. *The Logics of Party Formation: Ecological Politics in Belgium and West Germany.* London: Cornell University Press.

Kolinsky, E., 1984. Ecology and peace in Western Germany: An uneasy alliance. *Journal of Area Studies Series 1*, 5(9), pp. 23–28.

Kolinsky, E., 1988. The West German Greens: A women's party? *Parliamentary Affairs*, 41(1), pp. 129–148.

Kroh, M., and Schupp, J., 2011. Bündnis 90/Die Grünen auf dem Weg zur Volkspartei? *Wochenbericht des DIW Berlin*, 12/2011. Available at: <http://www.diw.de/documents/publikationen/73/diw_01.c.369952.de/11-12-1.pdf> [Accessed 4 October 2013].

Mair, P., and Mudde, C., 1998. The party family and its study. *Annual Review of Political Science*, 1, pp. 211–229.

Markovits, A. S., and Silvia, S. J., 1997. Changing shades of Green: Political identity and alternative politics in united Germany. *Debatte: Journal of Contemporary Central and Eastern Europe*, 5(1), pp. 49–66.

Müller-Rommel, F., 1985. The Greens in Western Europe: Similar but different. *International Political Science Review*, 6(4), pp. 483–499.

Müller-Rommel, F., and Poguntke, T., eds, 1989. The Unharmonious Family: Green Parties in Western Europe. In: E. Kolinsky, ed., *The Greens in West Germany: Organisation and Policy-Making.* Oxford: Berg. pp. 11–29.

O'Riordan, T., 1976. *Environmentalism*. London: Pion.

Pedersen, M. N., 1982. Towards a new typology of party lifespans and minor parties. *Scandinavian Political Studies*, 5(1), pp. 1–16.

Poguntke, T., 1987. New politics and party systems: The emergence of a new type of party? *West European Politics*, 10(1), pp. 76–88.

Poguntke, T., 1993. *Alternative Politics: The German Green Party*. Edinburgh: Edinburgh Press.

Probst, L., 2011. Bündnis 90/Die Grünen auf dem Weg zur "Volkspartei"? Eine Analyse der Entwicklung der Grünen seit der Bundestagswahl 2005. In: O. Niedermayer, ed., *Die Parteien nach der Bundestagswahl 2009*. Wiesbaden: VS Verlag für Sozialwissenschaften. pp. 131–156.

Rüdig, W., 2002. Germany. In: F. Müller-Rommel and T. Poguntke, eds, *Green Parties in National Governments*. London: Frank Cass. pp. 78–111.

Rüdig, W., 2012. The perennial success of the German Greens. *Environmental Politics*, 21(1), pp. 108–130.

Schneider, S. H., and Winkelmann, R., 2012. Die Grünen: eine Volkspartei? Eine quantitative Analyse des Zeitraums 2000 bis 2009. *Mitteilungen des Instituts für Parteienrecht und Parteiforschung*, 18, pp. 86–98.

Spoon, J.-J., 2009. Holding their own: Explaining the persistence of Green parties in France and the UK. *Party Politics*, 15(5), pp. 615–634.

Talshir, G., 2002. *The Political Ideology of Green Parties: From the Politics of Nature to Redefining the Nature of Politics*. Basingstoke: Palgrave Macmillan.

Von Beyme, K., 1985. *Political Parties in Western Democracies*. Aldershot: Gower, 1985.

Ware, A., 1996. *Political Parties and Party Systems*. Oxford: Oxford University Press.

Williams, R., 1988. *Keywords: A Vocabulary of Culture and Society*. Revised and expanded edition. London: Fontana Press.

Worster, D., 1994. *Nature's Economy: A History of Ecological Ideas*. 2nd edition. Cambridge: Cambridge University Press.

Young, S. C., 1992. The different dimensions of green politics. *Environmental Politics*, 1(1), pp. 9–44.

14 Green party organisations

The difficult path from amateur-activist to professional-electoral logics

Benoît Rihoux

Introduction

In the early 1980s, when some Green parties gained their first parliamentary seats, they were very much perceived as 'unconventional' parties. In 1981, the first Belgian Green Members of Parliament (MPs) from *Ecolo* and *Agalev* arrived at the Parliament building on bicycles, some of them wearing long beards and rough wool sweaters. Two years later, the first German *Grünen* federal MPs walked in procession through the streets of Bonn to the *Bundestag*, carrying a dead tree in protest against the 'productivist society'. They then regularly used the federal parliament as an arena to voice protest and presented themselves as 'loudspeakers' for various radical new social movements and as an 'antiparty party'. They had no party president, rather a rotating group of 'spokespersons'.

Thus, besides ideological preferences, the 'Greenness' of Green parties also had to do with their political style – and some deeper organisational logics. Therefore, the first analysts of Green parties considered their organisational features as one of the core definitional aspect of Green parties besides ideology, constitutive to a particular form of 'New Politics' parties (for example Poguntke, 1993, p. 36ff; revisited by Hino, 2012).

Three decades later, there is something much more conventional about the Greens' political style. Winfried Kretschmann, who became the first Green minister-president of a German *Land* (Baden-Württemberg) in 2011, is dressed up like any regular politician. So are most Green MPs and party leaders nowadays. Many Green parties have a regular party president, often experienced as a professional career politician.

Beyond these appearances, rituals and dress codes, does this also mean that Green parties have been transformed in-depth as organisations? A simple view would be to argue that their gradual institutionalisation has also led to their gradual mainstreaming. This is, of course, too simply put, because institutionalisation, as shall be argued below, is not a linear phenomenon. Besides, not all Green parties have institutionalised to the same extent.

In this chapter, the organisational transformation of European Green parties will be surveyed across the whole 'lifespan' (Pedersen, 1982) of these parties, which is across more than three decades for some of them. The initial or 'genetic'

(Panebianco, 1988) organisational features of those parties will first be systematically described. Then, in a second major section, their main organisational transformations will be empirically analysed across the numerous cases. Further, the main explanatory factors – or, rather, combinations of such factors – leading to those transformations will be identified through a comparative analysis. This will lead, in conclusion, to an interrogation on the current nature of Green party organisation, caught in between different and largely contradictory logics.

The genetic organisational features of Green parties

It is not overstated to argue that Green parties have long been characterised by a distinctive organisational style. Indeed the way they organised in their early years is tightly linked to their ideology and to the process that led to their creation.

European Green parties are to a more or less large extent the children of the New Social Movements (NSMs). The latter, which developed especially in the 1960s and 1970s, were characterised by a specific ideological-organisational project – that is: the NSMs' ideology and the way they structured themselves were intertwined. Among the NSMs' organisational features were the relatively low level of formalisation, the emphasis on amateur activists (vs. professionals), a preference for direct participation of rank-and-file members (vs. more hierarchical representative procedures), limitations in the prerogatives of the leaders and frequent leadership rotation (Kitschelt, 1989). This specific organisational style of the NSMs was not only instrumental, that is geared towards political efficacy; rather, it was seen by the NSM proponents as a sort of *avant-garde* that would transform society: the organisational form was 'a goal in itself. . . . The medium, the movement itself as a new medium, is the message' (Melucci, 1984, p. 830).

There is broad evidence, in most national settings, that Green parties were gradually born, first as temporary lists, then as protoparties and then more durable parties, as prolongations of different segments of NSMs: environmentalists, deeper ecologists, peace movements, feminists, antinuclear, radical federalists and so on, (for example Müller-Rommel, 1985; Rootes, 1992; see also the country chapters in this volume). Indeed not only did their ideology stem from these movements; the large majority of the leaders, activists and members of these parties were first socialised within the NSMs. In fact, many of them continued to be active in those movements while being politically active in the new parties – a textbook case of 'multiple activism' (Rihoux, 1995; see also below).

Following Panebianco (1988, p. 53), it is to be expected that a party's initial organisational features (its 'genetic model' as an organisation) be strongly influenced by the ideology and prior experiences of the party's founders. In concrete terms, it is fair to say that the literature has concentrated very much on the case of the German *Grünen* and that some other national cases are much less well documented. However, there is a quite broad agreement among scholars with regard the core, specific and initial organisational features that were shared to a large extent by Green parties and that also defines them as a specific party 'family' besides their ideology (see Chapter 13). The ideal-typical genetic organisational

Table 14.1 List of ideal-typical genetic organisational features of Green parties

---

Collective leadership

Imperative mandate (strong control of the mandate holders by the party members)

Rotation of leadership positions (binding rotation rules)

Openness (for example free access to meetings for party members)

Local autonomy and priority given to the lowest organisational level

Separation of party office positions and parliamentary mandates

Various forms of direct participation by the party members

Absence of fully professionalised leadership (amateur politics)

Gender parity rules

Guaranteed representation for minority groups

Limitations in financial income for mandate holders (for example Members of Parliament [MPs])

Source: Author's own compilation.

features of Green parties are listed in Table 14.1; this list stems from the core grassroots democratic traits of the *Basisdemocratie* model of the German *Grünen* (Poguntke, 1993, pp. 136–148), complemented by other specific traits surveyed by Rihoux (2001, p. 26).

Note that such an organisational model goes along with a form of antileadership and anti-'professional politics' bias also found in many NSMs (Poguntke, 1993, pp. 36–40) – a form of challenge to the classical prediction of Michels (1962) that all parties are inevitably due to follow a similar path towards informal concentration of power and oligarchy (Lucardie and Rihoux, 2008, p. 3). This other organisational model is in fact a sort of 'movement/party' model, in conjunction with a Left-libertarian ideology (see Chapter 13), and characterised by a 'negative consensus on ideological questions, a heterogeneous clientele, open membership, a weak centralised organisation, and loose networks of grassroots support' (Gunther and Diamond, 2003, pp. 188–189).

It is difficult to examine empirically each one of the 11 features listed in Table 14.1 across many parties in their first years of existence. The level of formalisation of these parties is bound to be quite low at that stage – as most of these parties remained extraparliamentary and rather small for quite a number of years before ultimately gaining access to institutions and to more resources (see also below). Therefore, a pragmatic approach is to narrow down the analysis to some core features. For each party, the material that has been used is the first comprehensive party statutes officially validated by the party structures, often complemented by other more or less binding regulatory documents (for example *règlement d'ordre intérieur* in French). Table 14.2 surveys the actual presence of 5 core, grassroots, democratic and 'movement/party' organisational features across 14 Green parties in their first years of existence (Rihoux,

Table 14.2 Presence or absence of core 'movement/party' organisational features in the founding years of Green parties*

Party* & year of statutory text	Collective leadership	Rotation rules	Separation of office & mandate	Amateur leadership	Gender parity rules
Die Grünen (Germany) (80)	X	X	X	X	
GroenLinks (Netherlands) (91)		X	X		
De Groenen (Netherlands) (93)	X			X	
Ecolo (Belgium) (81)	X		X	X	
Agalev (Belgium) (82)	X			X	
Comhaontas Glas (Eire) (83)	X			X	
Green Party of England and Wales (United Kingdom) (77)				X	
Vihreä Liitto (Finland) (87)	X	X			
Die Grünen (Austria) (87)	X	X	X		X
Les Verts (France) (85)	X	X	X	X	
Miljöpartiet (Sweden) (82)	X	X	X	X	X
Federazione dei Verdi (Italy) (86)	X			X	X
Fédération des Partis Verts de Suisse (Switzerland) (83)		X		X	
Gréng Alternativ Partei (Luxembourg) (83)	X	X		X	

Note: * Party label as the party was founded.

Source: Author's own compilation.

2001, pp. 174–178). More precisely, the five features have been operationalised as follows:

(1) Collective leadership: collective nature of the presidential function
(2) Rotation rules: presence of binding rules for internal positions and/or external mandates
(3) Separation of office and mandate: presence of binding rules for internal positions and/or external mandates
(4) Amateur leadership: amateur (not fully paid) party executive
(5) Gender parity rules: presence of binding rules for the party executive and/or for electoral lists

The evidence from Table 14.2 appears rather mixed, but 7 out of the 14 parties do meet at least 3 features of the ideal-type. However, the criteria that were used are quite demanding (binding texts), and it may be that, for some parties, a given feature is *partly* met even if it is not (yet) explicitly provisioned as a binding rule – for example in terms of gender parity practices. Thus we may consider that most of these parties, in their founding years, displayed at least some core features of the 'movement/party' ideal-type, bearing in mind that some of these features are really specific to Green parties and observed in virtually no other party (for example collective nature of the presidential function or rotation rules for MPs). In some specific cases, some rules were particularly radical – for instance, in the French *Les Verts* and the Luxembourg *Gréng*, there was initially a mid-mandate rotation rule, according to which MPs had to step down and be replaced by another person in the middle of the legislature.

It also appears that the UK Green party is much more distant from the movement/party ideal-type, as it only features an amateur leadership, and none of the other ideal-typical traits. In fact, this particular feature is not surprising, as this party was largely marginal and had very little resources in the 1970s and therefore could not afford to pay a salary to its leaders. In fact, a similar reasoning can be made for a few other extrainstitutional Green parties – that is those that did not quickly gain national parliamentary representation, such as the Irish, French and Italian Greens. In other words, the fact that some Green parties kept an amateur leadership was not necessarily the result of an (ideological) choice, rather more the result of a low level of resources. Some features were not systematically observed in Green parties, in particular rotation rules and the separation of office and mandate. In fact, it is quite logical that some Green parties, especially those with very few or no MPs, did not *yet* see the use of such rules and hence had not included these *yet* in their party statutes.

In spite of this rather nuanced picture, the bottom line is that most Green parties did bear a 'family resemblance' in terms of their genetic organisational features – besides also displaying some common ideological principles and a relatively small size in terms of membership figures.

Broadening the picture, those specific features of Green parties are, thus, the result of deliberate efforts of (former) NSM activists and cadres to create parties that allow them a maximum of power, probably at the expense of electoral success and impact on policy-making processes. This is why Harmel and Janda (1994) have defined Green parties, at least in their phase of emergence, as 'democracy-seeking' parties, which are prioritising internal party democracy over vote- and office-seeking. Hence, Green party activists endeavoured to control both the party executive and the parliamentary party when they began to emerge – through devices like rotation, imperative mandates or the separation of office and mandates, as analysed above. For the same reason, they preferred collective leadership and opposed professionalisation (Lucardie and Rihoux, 2008, p. 7). This central position of activists has lead Lucardie and Rihoux (2008) to suggest that Green parties, at least in their younger years, largely corresponded to an 'amateur-activist' party type (see Table 14.3).

This 'amateur-activist' type, which is very distant from the earlier 'elite cadre', 'mass' or 'people's party' types (Lucardie and Rihoux, 2008, pp. 7–8), can be conceived as a sort of counter-model *vis-à-vis* the prevailing trend towards professional-electoral parties as defined by Panebianco (1988). On the one hand, both amateur-activist parties and electoral-professional parties do share a few

Table 14.3 Features of the 'amateur-activist' vs. 'professional-electoral' party types

Party type	Professional-electoral party	Amateur-activist party
Origin	Private initiative	New social movements
Ideology	Eclectic	Partial/modular
Relation to civil society	No ties	Informal ties
Relation to state	Close ties	Distance
Member–voter ratio	Low	Low
Leadership	Personal	Collective amateur
Candidate selection	Central	Local or regional
Relation between Member of Parliament (MP) and party	MP in control	Party in control
Main locus of power	Party leader and staff	Activists (congress)
Basic unit	Electoral district	Regional or local branch
Relation of basic unit to top	Direct support	Direct delegation
Role of member	Applause and donations	Total participation
Funding	Donations and subsidies	Member fees
Party apparatus	Professional staff	Volunteers (mainly)

Source: Adapted from Lucardie and Rihoux, 2008, p. 8, with updates.

common 'post-mass party era' characteristics, such as a low member–voter ratio or more fluid ties with civil society. On the other hand, though, these two types follow two rather opposed organisational logics: that of the amateur-activist party is much more decentralised and participatory, much less capital- and staff-intensive and much less geared towards vote maximisation. Indeed Rihoux and Frankland (2008) have demonstrated that Green parties did indeed stand close to the amateur-activist ideal-type in their formative years (see also next section).

Finally, with regard to the linkage with (new) social movements, even when the Green parties became formally independent organisations, they maintained numerous forms of informal ties with the social movements. This happened in two predominant ways: overlapping directorates between the parties and linked social movement structures (for example Kitschelt and Hellemans, 1990), and multiple activism by the party members, remaining simultaneously active is several NSM organisations (Rihoux, 1995). Incidentally, the multiple backgrounds of Green party activists also exerted a strong impact on the ideology of those parties: rather than a complete ideology, the parties embraced 'segments' of ideologies from different movements, in the form of a mixture of ecologism, pacifism or feminism as well as some other NSM topics.

Which transformations – and why?

Obviously Green parties were created outside of the political institutions. Stemming from NSMs, they were first protest, nonconventional, extrainstitutional political movements that gradually crystallised into political parties. For several of them, the process was quite swift because of their quick access to parliamentary representation. A case in point is that of the Belgian (Flemish) Greens of *Agalev* (now *Groen*) who surprisingly obtained a few parliamentary seats in 1981, which literally forced them to transform their political movement into a party in 1982.

However, entry into parliaments (for some Green parties at least) is only one facet of a deeper transformation of Green party organisations. Here transformation is defined as much more than incremental changes, rather as a more profound change – a change in nature – of those party organisations. Indeed quite a deep transformation of Green party organisations was to be expected over the last three decades, for several reasons. First, according to the 'lifespan' model (Pedersen, 1982, 1991), those parties have passed several successive thresholds in the course of their development, each one of these thresholds being a sort of 'qualitative leap' forcing some organisational changes (Rihoux, 2001, pp. 124–127). Indeed, the possible institutionalisation process of Green parties is not linear; it goes through leaps and bounds. Second, most Green parties remained small in terms of membership size (with the notable exception of the German Greens), and precisely because of this smaller size and relatively scarce (financial) resources, they are likely to be more sensitive to variations in membership size. In particular, because of their strong direct participatory inclination (see above), a significant increase in membership figures (say, from a few hundreds to a few thousands) is very likely to lead to organisational adaptations in the direction of more representation and delegation (*versus* direct participation of all members). Third, those relatively small parties with relatively volatile electorates (see Chapter 11 in this volume) are likely to experience strong variations in terms of their (financial) resources. Indeed, gaining access to (or exiting) parliament or gaining (or losing) a few seats does mean a lot for such parties in terms of financial resources and the possibility (or not) to stabilise a party structure with permanent paid staff. In other words, Green parties are expected to be more sensitive to internal or external 'shocks' as defined by Harmel and Janda (1994), first, because of the specific features detailed above. Second, because of their more limited and unstable resources as compared to other types of parties (the opposite situation being that of the mass parties with strong ancillary organisations and a broad membership base), Green parties are expected to be more sensitive to internal or external 'shocks' as defined by Harmel and Janda (1994).

Hence, a whole range of factors is expected to push for significant changes in the organisational shape, procedures (including major statutory changes), style and practices of Green parties. These potential factors can be placed into at least four categories, from broader, system-level factors to more intraparty factors. Several authors have suggested more or less integrated models encompassing and ordering a certain number of these factors, such as Harmel and Janda (1994), Panebianco (1988) or Kitschelt (1989), more specifically with regard to Green parties for the latter author. Each one of these authors considers that there is a core 'causal mechanism' or core factor triggering organisational change – in short, an external or internal 'shock' (for Harmel and Janda), a change in the 'dominant

Table 14.4 Main potential factors pushing for organisational change in Green parties

System-level changes	Party-political competition level changes	Party-level changes	Intraparty-level changes
Regime change Change in the electoral system Change in the legislation on parties Change in the public financing of parties	Rise/decline of a direct competitor	Electoral victory/defeat Entry in/ exit from Parliament Access to/ exit from Government	Leadership change Change in balance of power between factions Generational turnover of activists/members Change in organisational size Change in social composition of activists/members

Source: Adapted from Lucardie and Rihoux (2008).

coalition' within the party (for Panebianco) or a change in coalitions between different types of party activists (for Kitschelt). Rihoux (2001) and Lucardie and Rihoux (2008) have, however, argued in favour of a more open approach, envisaging a broader range of factors, not *a priori* considering one single factor as being more central. Those factors can be ordered in four categories, as shown in Table 14.4 – with an emphasis on a fundamental distinction between those factors that lie out of control of the party players (left-hand side) and those that can to some extent be influenced by within-party players.

According to a quite logical scenario, Green party organisations would be expected to shift more or less rapidly away from the 'movement/party' logic as they become increasingly institutionalised and professionalised. Yet, this has not really been the case, at least not until the late 1990s. Table 14.5 re-examines the presence or absence of core 'movement/party' organisational features in Green parties by 1998, which is after around 15–20 years of existence of those parties. This table is to be compared with Table 14.2 (situation in the founding years).

What Table 14.5 shows is a surprising persistence or even reinforcement of 'Green' movement/party features, at least up to the late 1990s – and in spite of the relative institutionalisation and 'parliamentarisation' (Ismayr, 1985) of most of these parties. The main observation is that, by the late 1990s, most Green parties have converged towards a more or less similar set of features, from left to right in Table 14.5:

(1) Collective leadership, most frequently in the form of a 'joint presidency' between a male and a female copresident or co-chair (wo)man or cospokesperson – but often refraining from using the 'presidential' terminology.
(2) Rotation rules, quite systematic but less radical than the initial very strict rules (for example mid-term rotation; see above), for instance with a limitation to two consecutive mandates. An increasing number of parties have also started to provision some exceptions to the rule. So, on the whole, the whole

rotation principle has become (much) more flexible, even if it has not (yet) been suppressed.

(3) Rules in terms of the separation of office and mandate: these rules became rather systematic but did become less drastic in a number of parties (for example allowing one to combine a national executive position with a local councillor position, etc.).

(4) Gender parity rules: there has been a mainstreaming of such binding rules, especially for electoral lists but also for most party bodies, usually in the form of strict parity, beyond the legal obligations.

Note that this relative convergence does *not* equate with maintaining a 'deep Green', very unconventional and nonhierarchical, direct democratic political style in Green party organisations. In fact, between the early 1980s and late 1990s, those parties did follow a trend of professionalisation and relative concentration of power. For instance, the institution of two 'copresidents' does mean that the party's top has become more narrow and more stable, a stark contrast with the

Table 14.5 Presence or absence of core 'movement/party' organisational features in Green parties* by 1998

Party*	Collective leadership	Rotation rules	Separation of office & mandate	Amateur leadership	Gender parity rules
Bündnis 90/Die Grünen (Germany)	X	X	X		X
GroenLinks (Netherlands)		X	X		
De Groenen (Netherlands)	X	X	X	X	X
Ecolo (Belgium)	X	X	X		
Agalev (Belgium)	X	X	X		
Green Party/Comhaontas Glas (Eire)	X	X	X		X
Green Party of England and Wales (UK)	X	X	X		X
Vihreä Liitto (Finland)		X	X		X
Die Grünen (Austria)		X			X
Les Verts (France)	X	X	X		X
Miljöpartiet de Gröna (Sweden)	X	X	X		X
Federazione dei Verdi (Italy)			X		
Parti Ecologiste Suisse (Switzerland)	X	X			X
Dei Gréng (Luxembourg)	X	X	X		X

Note: * Party label by 1998.

Source: Rihoux, 2001.

initial situation in which there was in fact no real presidency function – or rather, this function was shared across a large group of members of the executive board. Besides, rotation rules did not prevent the stabilisation of a group of professional party leaders, through forms of 'horizontal rotation' between the MP and top party apparatus positions (Kitschelt, 1989). During this same period, from the creation of these parties until 1998, most parties debated and implemented a rather large number of organisational reforms. In fact the culture of 'activist debate' on the organisational form itself prevailed, with the implementation of significant reforms every three or four years on average (Rihoux, 2001, p. 183). This also means that Green parties, for a long time, have devoted a lot of time and energy to those internal organisational issues.

Note also one other core finding in Table 14.5: the end of the 'amateur leadership' era for Green parties (except for the Dutch *De Groenen*, simply because it remained a micro-party). In other words, the executives of all Green parties became fully (5 out of 13 parties) or predominantly (8 out of 13 parties) professional, with full salaries. As significantly, by 1998, the same held for the broader party councils.

Thus, in spite of the prolongation of some specific 'Green' elements of organisation culture, and in spite of the resistance of more radical party activists ('ideologues', in Kitschelt's terms [1989]), the over-arching picture is one of growing control of the party by fully paid professionals (MPs, party apparatus officials and a growing support staff). Besides, there is a diminishing influence of amateur activists even if the latter remain very active and sometimes voice protest and dissent in assemblies or congresses. Besides, at the local level, amateur 'localists' (Kitschelt, 1989) still constitute the bulk of the party on the ground. Considering the Green parties at the national level, it is clear that, as they grew as increasingly professionalised organisations, their dependence on public funding increased. Note that the institutionalisation and organisational growth of Green parties also coincided, in many European countries, with the passing of pieces of legislation increasing the public funding of parties in the 1980s and 1990s (Alexander, 1989). Therefore, they became ever more dependent on their electoral results. Does this mean that Green parties have shifted gradually (or fully?) from amateur-activist logic to a professional-electoral logic?

In order to tackle this broader question, Table 14.6 summarises the evolution of the relative proximity of Green parties *vis-à-vis* the amateur-activist and professional-electoral party types (as defined above), from their founding year to 2008 (data compiled from Rihoux and Frankland, 2008, pp. 261–271). The sequence of parties is identical to that of previous tables (without the Italy and Luxembourg cases that are not covered by this part of the analysis).

The first clear indication from Table 14.6 is that a majority of Green parties, which used to stand very close to the amateur-activist type, have become somewhat more distant from that model. In fact, one may distinguish two more contrasted clusters of parties. On the one hand, the Dutch *Groenen* as well as the UK, French and Irish Greens have remained relatively close to amateur-activist party dynamics. Note that these also stood among the least institutionalised Green

Table 14.6 Relative proximity of Green parties vis-à-vis the amateur-activist and professional-electoral party types

Party	Founding year		2008	
	Amateur-activist score (out of 14)	Professional-electoral score (out of 14)	Amateur-activist score (out of 14)	Professional-electoral score (out of 14)
Bündnis 90/Die Grünen (Germany)	14	2	6	4
GroenLinks (Netherlands)	9	4	8	6
De Groenen (Netherlands)	13	2	11	2
Ecolo (Belgium)	13	2	7	4
Groen! (Belgium)	14	2	8	6
Green Party/Comhaontas Glas (Eire)	10	2	10	4
Green Party of England and Wales (UK)	7	4	8	2
Vihreä Liitto (Finland)	13	2	8	6
Die Grünen (Austria)	10	2	7	5
Les Verts* (France)	13	2	11	4
Miljöpartiet de Gröna (Sweden)	14	2	8	4
Parti Ecologiste Suisse (Switzerland)	11	2	7	5

Note: * Party label by 2008.

Source: Author's own compilation

parties in Western Europe (at least until 2008). On the other hand, the German, Belgian (both *Ecolo* and *Groen!*), Finnish and Swedish Greens have witnessed the strongest move away from the amateur-activist type. By no coincidence, those five parties have taken part in national government coalitions or coalition-type (toleration) agreements and have been long-lasting parliamentary parties.

Secondly, there has been a general trend – albeit still an incomplete one – towards more proximity *vis-à-vis* the professional-electoral model. In particular, in most Green parties, the MPs have gained a lot of autonomy *vis-à-vis* both the grassroots activists and the party apparatus, as the parliamentary groups are most often organisationally stronger than the party central offices. Altogether, the top political personnel (party presidents, members of the executive, MPs) of these parties has also become much more stable, now constituting a stratum of professional politicians. This also means that the mechanism of overlapping directorates, which initially enabled strong linkages with various NSM organisations (see above), has largely disappeared, not least because of the willingness of the latter organisations to remain free from any party-political control. The distance increased further when some Green parties joined national governments. For instance, when the Belgian Green (*Ecolo*) secretary of state for energy and sustainable development, a former Greenpeace cadre, proudly announced in 1999 that an agreement had been reached by the coalition for a (long-term and conditional) phasing out of nuclear power plants, it immediately spurred protest from Greenpeace, deeming the decision as fragile and insufficient.

In addition, the party apparatus (at the national level at least) has become almost exclusively professional in most Green parties. It is fair to say that a rather stable core of professional cadres has developed in most parties; to this core, depending on the electoral (mis)fortunes and attached variations in financial resources, a second circle of more temporary professionals has also developed. It would be an overstatement to conclude that some Green parties have become professional-electoral parties; however, the more institutionalised ones have indeed followed a trend towards the professional-electoral logic.

Note also that the Greens have kept, throughout their lifespan, a (very) low member–voter ratio (see also other chapters in this volume) – this feature is compatible both with the amateur-activist and professional-electoral types. However, this state of affairs is not the result of a deliberate strategy from the Green strategists; it is simply the consequence of inability to grow as membership organisations (Rihoux and Frankland, 2008, p. 270). This also means that the level of secure financial resources through the membership base is (very) low for most of these parties, which makes them particularly vulnerable in case of electoral defeat.

How is it possible to account for these shifts – albeit still incomplete – away from the 'purist' movement/party logics and amateur-activist party type? A detailed analysis of the complex causal mechanisms leading to organisational changes in Green parties is beyond the reach of this chapter – thus, what are the over-arching points? To put it more analytically: among the potential explanatory factors or stimuli for organisational change, which ones have proven to play a stronger role? To sum up, one may conclude that five determinants have played a stronger – or more direct or traceable – role:

(1) change in organisational size (sharp increase or sharp decrease in size);
(2) major electoral victory or defeat;
(3) entry into/exit from parliament;
(4) entry into/exit from government; and
(5) major factional change (Rihoux, 2001; Rihoux, 2006; Rihoux and Frankland, 2008).

Obviously the first four factors are pretty much intertwined, or rather, they often operate in a sequence of 'shocks' (referring to Harmel and Janda's terminology, 1994), which constrain Green parties in some particular conjunctures to follow predominantly a path of organisational adaptation (Panebianco, 1988), in spite of the reluctance of the grass-roots and some activists.

One of the most frequent or typical scenarios is that of a stark electoral defeat (an 'external shock'), which is perceived both by the party leadership and by the activists as a major failure. Then, as a result of this defeat, the party's financial resource base (decrease in direct and indirect public funding) is significantly affected, which leads to a stark decrease in the size of the party's (professional) apparatus, the infrastructure, paid expertise and so on, it can afford. This in turn provides a strong push for organisational change, or rather adaptation (in Panebianco's sense), that is a form of mainstreaming to ultimately increase the party's efficiency in vote- and office-seeking. Here comes frequently into play a major factional change: a shift in favour of a more '*Realo*' or moderate faction also seeking to make the party more efficient in the electoral competition. There have been many such episodes, such as the German *Grünen* following their 1990 defeat and quasi-exit from the federal parliament or the Belgian *Ecolo* following their 2003 defeat.

A less frequent but regularly observed scenario is that of a major electoral progress, which, on the one hand, generates a form of organisational stress or 'growth crisis'. For instance, the Swedish and German Greens, in the 1990s especially, reached a stage in which they gained so many seats at the local level that it became practically impossible to implement their initial rotation rules. Obviously as well, a first electoral breakthrough that leads to the formation of a first parliamentary group constitutes a 'qualitative leap' (see above) in terms of professionalisation, party size in terms of resources and actual functioning of the party organisation, which eventually forces some organisational reforms. On the other hand, an electoral success as such rarely suffices for those parties to actually implement organisational reform or adaptation: the latter needs to be pushed by a 'modernizing' or 'moderate/*Realo*' faction that is indeed most often reinforced by the electoral success. Thus, a shift in favour of such a faction often proved to be a major facilitator or catalyst.

Quite similarly in fact, access to/exit from government also proved to be a strong push for further adaptation and mainstreaming (Rihoux, 2006; Rihoux and Rüdig, 2006). In those circumstances, Green party leaders and cadres quickly reconsidered their participatory, and therefore rather slow, decision-making procedures, as well as some of their organisational features (typically the absence of a single-party president who is able to bargain with the other coalition partner). As for exit from government, it has most often been the result of a relative electoral defeat and has operated as a negative shock on the party structure (Rihoux, 2006), adding to the pressure from the electoral defeat itself (see above).

Summing up, the two core factors that most frequently led – in conjunction – to major organisational reforms in Green party organisations have been:

(1) Organisational 'shocks' that produce a strong and sudden increase or decrease in organisational size (that is in terms of resources: members, activists, finance, paid staff) and that placed those parties in potential situations of 'slack innovation' (growth crisis) or 'distress innovation' (degrowth crisis) (Rihoux, 2001, p. 222).
(2) Leadership change or, more frequently, factional change in favour of a more moderate or pragmatic faction, pushing for further mainstreaming so as to

ensure more political efficacy in the institutions and in a context of electoral competition. This finding is in fact a clear rejoinder to Panebianco's (1988) suggestion that there needs to be a prior shift in the 'power map' of a party organisation for it to be in a further stage of organisational adaptation.

Conclusion

Over the last three decades, Green party organisations have undergone deep trans-formations. Their sheer increase in size (even though they are still relatively small parties), their more or less durable entry in the political institutions (in particular their parliamentarisation) and durability has gone along with a process of internal differentiation. In their founding years, those (proto)parties were mainly operated by social movement activists, freshly involved in politics, '[sharing] a common culture and common goals [and operating] on a fairly equal footing' (Rihoux and Frankland, 2008, p. 280). Three decades later, even if most of these parties do not regularly have access to governmental participation, they now feature pretty dif-ferentiated party 'circles' (following Katz and Mair's terminology, 2002): a party in public office (mainly the parliamentary group or groups), a party central office and a party on the ground (the local party units and their activists).

Over the years, the first two circles, in most if not all Green parties, have clearly shifted from a 'logic of constituency representation' (along with an unconven-tional organisational style) to a 'logic of electoral competition', as Kitschelt (1989, p. 41) had already concluded in the late 1980s about the German and Belgian Greens. Therefore, as demonstrated in this chapter, most parties have moved away from the initial 'amateur-activist' grassroots democratic type. This has reinforced a logic of mainstreaming or organisational adaptation within these parties. How-ever, in contrast, a significant proportion of the (unpaid) members and activists who constitute the 'party on the ground' still adhere to the amateur-activist model with its grassroots democratic practices.

Thus, the situation after three decades of development and (partial) institution-alisation is that the core of Green party organisations now operate as relatively conventional parties, with a stable core of leaders and professionals, whereas the periphery (the local party members and activists, the party congress) are still pretty much in line with the initial predicaments in terms of organisational style. Green parties have hence become increasingly stratified, with frequent tensions and mis-understandings between the two main strata – as suggested by Lauber (in Rihoux and Frankland, 2008, p. 281): they can be portrayed as 'centaurs', that is mythical creatures with a human head and animal limbs, in this case a 'professional-electoral, efficiency-seeking head, but still amateur-activist, participation-seeking bodies'. This makes these parties particularly difficult to steer also given the high qualification of Green party activists – indeed, in such parties, there is no differen-tial in terms of cultural capital between party rank and file members, party cadres and party leaders. This means that Green party leaders and cadres always face resistance when trying to push for further organisational adaptations to achieve better 'political efficacy'.

All things considered, the Green case(s) tell us that there is indeed something like an 'iron law of party institutionalisation' (Ignazi, 1998) according to which parties are increasingly constrained to adapt to their environment, such as the mass media, the political institutions, and not least the demands of the other, larger and more powerful parties. And yet, most Green parties have resisted full mainstreaming and have kept some of their original features – mostly under the pressure of the party rank and file. Many aspects of the Greens' political culture (and ideology, see other chapter) prevent them from becoming fully professional-electoral. However, the story is not over, as the intraparty debates on the 'genuinely Green' organisational features continue. A recent illustration is that of the 'copresidency' in the Belgian francophone Green party (*Ecolo*), currently held by one male and one female copresident. Following the major electoral defeat of this party at the May 2014 general election, one of the first discussion points within the party has been to envisage full mainstreaming, that is accepting to finally (after 33 years as a stable parliamentary party) go for a 'normal', single-party president.

Putting this into a longer-term perspective: Green party organisations, founded in the late 1970s and early 1980s, were the children and inheritors of the NSMs. The latter were deeply libertarian, antiauthority, with a strong bias against hierarchies and leadership. Hence, the grassroots democratic features of Green parties are also a heritage from this particular period. Three to four decades later, it seems that the successive generations of Green party activists have not (yet?) challenged fundamentally this heritage. And yet: today's Green party organisations, at least the most institutionalised ones, also display some features of 'professional cadre parties' (as suggested – and advocated – by Raschke (1993)) or 'modern cadre parties' (Koole, 1992). Such a party type is compatible with a stronger party leader, even if some participatory elements are maintained in the intraparty procedures. It is a fact that a strong party leader becomes an increasingly important factor of electoral success in European democracies, in a context of a growing personalisation of politics (Karvonen, 2010). Established parties as well as new protest parties, including radical left-wing parties or 'progressive' parties partly in competition with the Greens' electorate, are often led by strong an charismatic leaders. Given that most Green parties are now firmly engaged in a logic of electoral competition, will this be the next phase in the difficult mainstreaming of Green party organisations?

References

Alexander, H. E., ed., 1989. *Comparative Political Finance in the 1980s*. Cambridge: Cambridge University Press.

Gunther, R., and Diamond, L., 2003. Species of political parties: A new typology. *Party Politics*, 9(2), pp. 167–199.

Harmel, R., and Janda, K., 1994. An integrated theory of party goals and party change. *Journal of Theoretical Politics*, 6(3), pp. 259–287.

Hino, A., 2012. *New Challenger Parties in Western Europe: A Comparative Analysis.* New York: Routledge.

Ignazi, P., 1998. The iron law of party institutionalization. *ECPR Joint Sessions of Workshops.* Warwick, 23–28 March 1998.

Ismayr, W., 1985. Die Grünen im Bundestag: Parlamentarisierung und Basisanbindung. *Zeitschrift für Parlamentsfragen,* 16(3), pp. 299–321.

Karvonen, L., 2010. *The Personalisation of Politics: A Study of Parliamentary Democracies.* Wivenhoe: ECPR Press.

Katz, R. S., and Mair, P., 2002. The Ascendancy of the Party in Public Office: Party Organizational Change in Twentieth-Century Democracies. In: R. Gunther, J. R. Montero and J. J. Linz, eds, *Political Parties: Old Concepts and New Challenges.* New York: Oxford University Press. pp. 113–135.

Kitschelt, H., ed., 1989. *The Logics of Party Formation: Ecological Politics in Belgium and West Germany.* London and Ithaca, NY: Cornell University Press.

Kitschelt, H., and Hellemans, S., eds, 1990. *Beyond the European Left: Ideology and Political Action in the Belgian Ecology Parties.* Durham and London: Duke University Press.

Koole, R., ed., 1992. *De opkomst van de moderne kaderpartij: Veranderende partijorganisatie in Nederland 1960–1990: De ontwikkelling van de Nederlandse politieke partijen aan het begin van de jaren zestig tot de moderne kaderpartijen.* Utrecht: Het Spectrum.

Lucardie, P., and Rihoux, B., 2008. From Amateur-Activist Parties to Professional-Electoral Machines? On the Organizational Transformation of Green Parties in Western Democracies. In: E. G. Frankland, P. Lucardie and B. Rihoux, eds, *Green Parties in Transition: The End of Grass-Roots Democracy?* Farnham and Burlington, VT: Ashgate. pp. 3–16.

Melucci, A., 1984. An end to social movements? An introductory paper to the session on 'new movements and change in organizational forms'. *Social Science Information,* 23(4–5), pp. 819–835.

Michels, R., ed., 1962. *Political Parties: A Sociological Study of the Oligarchical Tendencies of Modern Democracy.* New York: The Free Press.

Müller-Rommel, F., 1985. New social movements and smaller parties: A comparative perspective. *West European Politics,* 8(1), pp. 41–54.

Panebianco, A., ed., 1988. *Political Parties: Organization and Power.* Cambridge: Cambridge University Press.

Pedersen, M. N., 1982. Towards a new typology of party lifespans and minor parties. *Scandinavian Political Studies,* 5(1), pp. 1–16.

Pedersen, M. N., 1991. The Birth, Life and Death of Small Parties in Danish Politics. In: F. Müller-Rommel and G. Pridham, eds, *Small Parties in Western Europe: Comparative and National Perspectives.* London; New Delhi and Newbury Park, CA: Sage. pp. 95–114.

Poguntke, T., ed., 1993. *Alternative Politics: The German Green Party.* Edinburgh: Edinburgh University Press.

Raschke, J., ed., 1993. *Die Grünen: wie sie wurden, was sie sind.* Köln: Bund-Verlag.

Rihoux, B., 1995. Ecolo et les 'nouveaux mouvements sociaux' en Belgique francophone: frères de sang ou lointains cousins? *Res Publica,* 37, pp. 443–460.

Rihoux, B., 2001. *Les partis politiques: Organisations en changement: Le test des écologistes.* Paris: L'Harmattan.

Rihoux, B., 2006. Governmental participation and the organisational adaptation of Green parties: On access, slack, overload and distress. *European Journal for Political Research,* 45(Supplement 1), pp. S69–S98.

314   *Benoît Rihoux*

Rihoux, B., and Frankland, E. G., 2008. Conclusion: The Metamorphosis of Amateur-Activist Newborns Into Professional-Activist Centaurs. In: E. G. Frankland, P. Lucardie and B. Rihoux, eds, *Green Parties in Transition: The End of Grass-Roots Democracy?* Farnham and Burlington, VT: Ashgate. pp. 259–288.
Rihoux, B., and Rüdig, W., 2006. Analyzing Greens in power: Setting the agenda. *European Journal of Political Research,* 45(Supplement 1), pp. S1–S33.
Rootes, C., 1992. The new politics and the new social movements. Accounting for British exceptionalism. *European Journal of Political Research,* 22(2), pp. 171–191.

Conclusion

Green parties in Europe: Which family ties?

Emilie van Haute

The primary goal of this volume has been to address two central questions: (1) is the concept of party family applicable and relevant for the study of Green parties in Europe? and, (2) if it is, how can we characterise the Green party family today?

The concept of party family has been used as overarching analytical framework to allow for a multi-dimensional approach of Green parties. Indeed, the existing comparative exercises tend to focus on one specific dimension of Green party politics: their emergence (Müller-Rommel, 1989; Richardson and Rootes, 1995; O'Neill, 1997), electoral fortunes (Kitschelt, 1988; Müller-Rommel, 1994), organisational developments (Kitschelt, 1989; Poguntke, 1989; Rihoux, 2001), ideological positioning (Burchell, 2001) or relation to power (Müller-Rommel and Poguntke, 2002). This volume's ambition was to combine these dimensions, using the concept of party family as analytical framework.

To examine these issues, this volume has brought together a group of prominent country experts as well as comparativists. The volume is organised in two distinct parts, one dedicated to case studies and the other to comparative perspectives.

The case studies cover 14 Western European democracies and 11 Central and Eastern European (CEE) democracies, as well as the European level.[1] The comparative chapters cover an additional 5 countries,[2] which brings the geographical scope to a total of 30 countries. In terms of parties, the volume mentions no less than 70 movements or parties and provides longer developments and analyses on 37 of them.

This strategy has allowed for an analysis of Green parties through various angles and dimensions. More specifically, four dimensions have been systematically looked at: (1) the origins and the development of Green parties, including their life-cycle patterns, electoral developments and relationship to power; (2) the sociological composition of their electorates; (3) their ideological and programmatic positions and (4) their organisational structures.

In this conclusion, we bring together the most important findings from the various chapters in an attempt to provide an answer to our overarching questions. The structure of the conclusion mirrors that which was adopted in the book.

Origins and life-cycle

The classification of parties based on their origins refers to the idea of a common conflict on which they originated. These common roots are clearly visible in the case of Green parties, at least for some of the parties considered. As shown in the country chapters in this volume, in Western Europe, there was a clear trend towards the emergence of new political issues revolving around environmental concerns and opposition to nuclear energy policy but also around pacifism, human rights and radical democracy. These issues initially pushed forward by environmental movements or groups were progressively politicised, as they were not adequately addressed by existing parties. It opened up the political space for the emergence of Green parties. In that sense, most Green parties have roots outside parliament, with notable exceptions such as *GroenLinks* in the Netherlands.

With their roots outside parliament, the transformation of groups or movements into parties was in most cases a matter of debate and generated some tensions. The threshold of declaration was not easy to overcome, as some parts of the movements were reluctant to form parties and to enter the political game. In most countries, the establishment of a political party was preceded by one or more attempts to organise politically. As summarised in Table 15.1, Green parties first emerged in the late 1970s in the UK, France, Germany and Belgium. The trend expanded to Sweden, Ireland, Portugal and Spain in the early 1980s and then to Austria, Switzerland and Finland. The Netherlands, Italy and Greece have seen their Green parties develop in the late 1980s. In most cases, the threshold of authorisation (participation in national elections) was passed less than three years after the foundation of the party, with the exception of *GroenLinks*, which first passed the threshold of authorisation and participated in elections before being officially established as a political party, and of the Greek and Portuguese Greens.

In Central and Eastern Europe, environmental groups and parties emerged quite rapidly after 1989; yet, they faced rapid decline. As emphasised in Chapter 3, this can be explained by a combination of factors: the politicisation of their core issues faced more difficulties due to the predominance of economic questions, the absence of postmaterialist values and the integration of environmental issues by other competing actors. Furthermore, establishing a party and participating in elections are much more regulated in these countries (Pilet and van Haute, 2012). Consequently, even the thresholds of declaration and of authorisation have been difficult to pass on a structural basis, and some parties have simply not been able to consistently participate in elections (see for example the interruptions in Bulgaria, Czech Republic, Estonia, Latvia or Slovenia).

Once established, Green parties have known very distinctive electoral fates across Europe. In Northern and Western Europe, they have established themselves as relevant electoral actors, even if they still rarely cross the 10 per cent mark.

Elsewhere, Green parties struggle to perform electorally and remain weak political organisations, with some exceptions. Especially in Central and Eastern Europe, Green parties have been marginalised (with the notable exception of Latvia), despite the second wave of party creation in the 2000s.

Table 15.1 Life-cycle of Green parties at the national level

		Origins (declaration)[1]	Authorisation[2]	Representation[3]	Relevance[4]
AT	Grüne	1982 (pre-), 1986	1983 (pre-), 1986	1986 (28)	(only at the Land level)
BE	Groen	1982	1981	1981 (22), 2007 (7)	1999 (4)
BE	Ecolo	1974 (pre-), 1980	1977 (pre-), 1981	1981 (33)	1999 (4)
CH	GPS	1983 (pre-), 1987	1979 (pre-), 1987	1979 (pre-), 1987 (27)	(only at the cantonal level)
CH	GLP	2004 (pre-), 2007	2007	2007 (7)	–
DE	DG	1979 (pre-), 1980	1980	1983 (31)	1998 (8)
EL	OP	1988 (pre-), 2002	1990 (pre-), 2007	NO	–
ES	LV	1984	1986	2004 (4)	–
FI	VL	1988	1983 (pre-), 1991	1983 (pre-), 1991 (23)	1995 (8), 2007 (8)
FR	EELV	1973 (pre-), 1984	1973 (pre-), 1986	1997 (17)	1997 (5), 2012 (2)
IE	Green Party	1981	1982	1989 (22)	1997 (4)
IT	FV	1986 (pre-), 1990	1987 (pre-), 1992	1987 (21)	1993 (in alliances)
NL	GL	1990	1989	1989 (25)	(only at the local and occasionally provincial levels)
PT	PEV	1982	1987	1987 (27)	–
SE	MP	1981	1982	1988 (3), 1994 (20)	(but deals from outside government)
UK	GPEW	1973 (pre-), 1985	1974 (pre-), 1987	2010 (1999 in Scottish Parliament)	–
BG	Zelenite	2008	2009	–	–
BG	ZPB	1989	1990 (interruption 2009–2013)	1990 (1), 1997 (2)	–
BG	PC Eco-glasnost	1990	1990	1990 (1), 1995 (6)	–
CZ	SZ	1989, 1993	1990 (interruption 1996–1998)	1992 (4), 2006 (4)	–
EE	ER-EER	1989 (pre-), 1991	1992 (interruption 1999–2007)	1992 (4), 2007 (4)	

(Continued)

Table 15.1 (Continued)

		Origins (declaration)[1]	Authorisation[2]	Representation[3]	Relevance[4]
HR	ZL-ORaH	2004, 2013	2007	–	–
HR	*HSZ*	1996	1996	–	–
HR	*ZS*	1996	1996	–	–
HR	*ZH*	2001	2003	–	–
HU	LMP	2009	2010	2010 (4)	–
HU	*MZP*	1989	1990	–	–
HU	*ZA-ZDS-ZB*	1993	1994	–	–
LT	LZP	1989	1990 (interruption 1996–2011)	1990 (2), 2012	1990 (2)
LT	*LVŽS*	2001 (pre-), 2012	2004 (pre-), 2012	2012 (2)	–
LV	LZP	1990	1993	1995 (3), 2002 (12)	1993 (6), 2002 (9)
PL	Zieloni	1988 (pre-), 2003	1991 (pre-), 2005	–	–
RO	PER		1992	1992 (8)	–
RO	PV-MVDA	2006, 2009, 2011	2008	–	–
RO	*MER-FER*	1990	1990	1990 (2), 1996 (4)	1991 (2)
SI	ZS	1989	1990	1990 (3)	1990 (3)
SI	SMS-Zeleni	2000	2000 (interrupted in 2014)	2000 (4)	–
SI	*ZA*	1995	1996	–	–
SI	*TRS*	2011	2011	–	–

Notes: (pre-) denotes that the threshold was passed that year with a pre-existing political organisation; 1: Year of foundation of the party at the national level; 2: Year of first participation in national elections; 3: Year of first seats in national parliament (lower chamber) – number of years of uninterrupted presence in parliament between brackets (end 2014 as reference point); 4: Year of first governmental participation at the national level – number of consecutive years in government between brackets.

Electoral fates are related to the sociological composition of their electoral basis (see below) but are also linked to the capacity of parties to enter the parliamentary game, as voters may be deterred to vote for parties that have low chances of getting a seat in parliament. In most cases in Northern and Western Europe, the delay between the first participation in national elections and the first seats in parliament was null or below 5 years. In other cases, it took longer for the Greens to gain parliamentary representation, as in Ireland, Sweden, France especially, the UK and Spain (not to mention Greece where the Greens have not passed this threshold yet).

The delay between the first participation to elections and the first seats in national parliament (threshold of representation) very much depends on the rules of the electoral game in the various countries (type of electoral system, presence of a threshold, etc.). In countries applying proportional representation or two-round runoff voting (where Green parties can benefit from electoral alliances), Green parties were much more successful in entering national parliaments and re-entering them after severe electoral defeats, than in first-past-the-post systems such as the UK. In these cases, Green parties often passed the threshold of representation at infra- (e.g. *Land* level in Germany in 1979 vs. federal level in 1983) or supra-national (European) levels first, since some countries adopt more proportional systems at these levels. In Northern and Western Europe, if most parties have managed to secure a constant presence in parliament since their entry, severe electoral setbacks can also mean a step backwards in the lifespan model. In Italy, Spain or Ireland, Green parties have lost their parliamentary representation in the 2000s and have not (yet?) managed to regain it, contrary to Belgium (for *Groen*) and Sweden.

In most Central and Eastern European countries, gaining parliamentary representation is still the exception rather than the norm, with the notable outlier Latvia, where the Greens experienced 12 steady consecutive years of parliamentary representation.

Lastly, the threshold of relevance is connected to the capacity of parties to have an input on policies from within or outside government. The question of power has been and still is a matter of debate for most Green parties, as was the question of movement versus party in the early days. It is especially the case at the national level, as several Green parties have successfully passed the threshold of relevance at the sub-national or local levels (e.g. in Austria, Switzerland and the Netherlands). In the cases of governmental participation, given their modest electoral size, the Green parties in Northern and Western Europe were often placed in a situation of potential junior coalition partner. It has put them in an uncomfortable bargaining position, making it hard to reconcile with their policy-oriented support base. Policy gains related to governmental participation have been variable and difficult to quantify, as shown in Chapter 12. Yet, the costs of governmental participation have been high for most Green parties and have been a major reason of electoral setback and parliamentary exit. However, Green parties in Western Europe have, with few exceptions, recovered electorally from their postincumbency major setbacks. Their participation in government is becoming more of a standard feature, just as their representation in parliament did in earlier years.

In Central and Eastern Europe, short-lived governmental participation has been achieved in the early days but has not been experienced since (again, with the exception of Latvia).

Sociological composition

If Green parties in Europe have followed distinct electoral paths, Chapter 11 demonstrates that their electorate shares specific characteristics that distinguish them from voters of other parties. Sociologically, the ideal-typical Green voter is young, nonreligious, female, urban and educated. Besides, the Green vote can be seen an issue-based vote that transcends old politics: Values that are related to new politics are determinant. Lastly, Green voters also share an 'activist' profile: they tend to be more involved in new forms of political participation, which reflects the original anchorage of Green parties in new social movements.

Green voters today share the same characteristics as the Green electorate in the early years of Green parties. This points toward a relative stability of the Green parties' core electoral basis, despite fluctuating electoral results. As Chapter 11 has shown, what remains less clear is the capacity of Green parties to maintain the protest component in the Green vote. With a normalisation of Green parties' governmental participation and the emergence of new challengers trying to capitalise on protest sentiments, are Green parties doomed to lose their protest element, or will they manage to remain the promoters of a societal and political revolution?

Ideological and programmatic positions

The country chapters in this volume have highlighted commonalities in terms of ideology or policy positions among Green parties. As emphasised in Chapter 13, Green parties have never been ideologically homogeneous (Müller-Rommel and Poguntke, 1989). Yet, they share some distinctive features.

As expected, the environment is clearly the most salient issue for Green parties. Yet, some parties emerged as single-issue parties (UK Greens), while others developed from the very start a comprehensive programme and project (e.g. *Ecolo* or *Groen* in Belgium). The environmental issue is still the most salient issue for Green parties today, and they tend to own the issue over the other parties. However, the proportion of their manifesto dedicated to the issue has tended to decrease over time leaving more space to other issues. Similarly, on the issue itself, the Greens have tended to adopt more pragmatic positions (e.g. EELV in France or *GroenLinks* in the Netherlands). In Central and Eastern Europe too, sustainability, ecology and environmental issues are at the core of the Green parties' manifestos. This is especially the case among the newly founded parties of the 'second wave' (see Chapter 3) that receive clear support from the EGP in designing manifestos in exchange for membership.

Most Green parties were initially reluctant to position themselves on a left–right scale, which was considered as 'old' politics. Yet, their position on issues revealed in most cases a clear left anchorage that was progressively more assumed to the point that electoral or governmental alliance with (centre-)right parties is more taboo than in some Social-Democratic parties. Over time, the left anchorage has shifted to the centre in some cases (e.g. Germany) or further to the left in other cases (e.g. UK Greens), mainly guided by the party's place in its national context. There are a few exceptions to the left anchorage, mainly in the chief of Central and Eastern European parties. For example, the Estonian or Latvian Greens tend to be located to the right of the centre, as is the PER in Romania. In their manifesto, this translates to support of entrepreneurship, private property, national identity or more conservative positions. These positions are very much connected to the place of the party in the national political system.

On socio-economic issues, individual chapters in this volume emphasise that Green parties tend to favour issues related to social justice, welfare and solidarity over issues connected to the economy *stricto sensu* (again, with some of the above-mentioned CEE exceptions). Finally, the position of Green parties on Europe illustrates a clear shift in most parties from anti-EU toward more moderate or even supportive positions (with the exception of the Finnish and the Belgian Greens). The pro-EU stances are exacerbated in some cases where the competition for recognition by the EGP is fierce, as emphasised in Chapter 3.

As shown in Chapter 13, 30 years of political competition and integration within their party systems has had an impact on Green parties' ideology. They have lost part of their radical edge or protest component. They are less critical of the state even if they still do promote more direct forms of democratic participation; they do not oppose economic growth but remain sceptical of military activity. However, electoral setbacks and disappointing participation to power may raise internal debate as to the ideological route in which to engage.

Organisational structure

Over the last three decades, Green party organisations have undergone deep transformations toward institutionalisation, professionalisation and 'normalisation', mainly in Western and Northern Europe. With the expansion of party goals from policy-oriented to increased vote- and office-seeking goals, Green parties in these countries have in parallel evolved from movements to proto-parties or amateur-activist parties, to fully fledged organisations that look more like conventional parties. As emphasised in Chapter 14, the Green case(s) could be taken as an illustration of the 'iron law of party institutionalisation' (Ignazi, 1998). Yet, Green parties have kept some of their initial features. The grassroots are still attached to the initial predicaments of policy-seeking goals and the amateur-activist model, antiauthority and antihierarchy. This inner dilemma is not without generating tensions, especially when Green parties face hard choices such as governmental participation or compromises on policies or new electoral competitors.

Final considerations

Green Parties in Europe aimed at investigating how Green parties have evolved over time, in a comparative perspective.

Previous works have pointed toward the existence of a distinct Green party family. After the emergence of Green parties in the late 1970s and 1980s, scholars have tried to explain the birth of these new parties in what appeared at the time as 'frozen' party systems in Western Europe. Quite rapidly, the literature linked this birth to the diminished saliency of old cleavages and the emergence of a new conflict dimension (Müller-Rommel, 1989; Poguntke, 1989; for a counter-argument, see Seiler, 1999). Using Lipset and Rokkan's (2008) cleavage theory, it pointed toward the emergence of 'new politics' as opposed to 'old politics' and the development of new issues and values (see Müller-Rommel, 1989, p. 5). Social movements carrying these issues progressively turned into parties as 'old' parties failed to integrate these issues (Müller-Rommel, 1994). Therefore, the emergence of Green parties has been interpreted as the first sign of the 'defreezing' of party systems (Dalton, et al., 1984). In line with this interpretation, Green parties have been classified as a new party family. Poguntke (1989) stresses that Green parties are by no means alike, but he argues that they share a distinct new politics feature that translates in their organisation, programme and electoral base. He identifies two sub-groups in the 'new politics' family: the moderates and the fundamentalists. O'Neill (1997) identified four types of Green parties based on ideology (eco-socialists vs. pure Greens) and behaviour in the system (antiparty vs. pragmatic).

This volume mobilised a large number of criteria and dimensions on which to assess the existence of a distinct party family. Ultimately, the developments in this volume point at common origins, as well as strong similarities in the sociological composition of Green parties. These are two crucial elements that directly refer to Lipset and Rokkan's (1967, 2008) classic conception of party family.

Yet, any comparative or classification exercise cannot make abstraction of the fact that Green parties have grown out of their respective national contexts and have been exposed to these contexts from their foundation. This volume has demonstrated that context does affect the fate of Greens parties, especially in their capacity to overcome the threshold of representation and governmental participation. This is crucial, as presence in parliament or government in return strongly affects what Green parties are, how they organise and how they position themselves ideologically. Ideologically and organisationally, Green parties may thus be more diverse. Nevertheless, Chapters 13 and 14 have emphasised core basic organisational features and positions on issues that could be considered as part of the ideal-type or the genes of Green parties. We would therefore argue that the concept of party family is applicable and relevant for the study of Green parties in Europe.

As to how to characterise the Green parties family today, one could identify three circles in the family. The first circle corresponds to the core, nuclear, Green party family composed of Northern and Western Green parties (excluding Denmark but including Italy and Latvia). They are the backbone of family gatherings that take form of transnational federations and groupings, in particular the European Green Party (EGP) and the Greens/EFA group in the EP. The second circle is composed of the Southern Greens, which could be considered as the young nephews in the family. They do not seem to have reached full adulthood yet. They are invited to family gatherings (EGP), but they can also be expelled like turbulent teenagers, as in the case of *Los Verdes* in Spain. Finally, the third circle is composed of Central and Eastern European Green parties, which could be viewed as distant cousins (they do not always share the same names – party labels – or participate in the EGP) or even in some cases as the adopted children (adoption of a name and platform to be recognised by the EGP).

To get back to Mair and Mudde's (1998) method to identify a party family, party labels and especially transnational links reveal the place of each party in the Green family tree. This can be a source of tensions: Some members are banned (*Los Verdes* in Spain), while others compete for recognition (Zelenite vs. ZPB in Bulgaria; LMP vs. ZB in Hungary). Tensions can also arise when some get recognition while others do not, as in Denmark, Romania, Slovenia or Croatia, where several parties claiming to belong to the Green family coexist, but only one gets the recognition of the EGP.

In that sense, looking at party labels and transnational links would mean looking at the effects or consequences of underlying power struggles within the family. Conversely, investigating the origins, the social base and the ideological orientations of parties has highlighted common roots despite these family disagreements. As pointed out earlier, national contexts are crucial in shaping the evolution of Green parties. It could pull the nuclear family apart or bring cousins closer together.

Notes

1 Belgium, France, Germany, the Netherlands, Austria, Switzerland, Sweden, Finland, Italy, Greece, Portugal, Spain, the United Kingdom, Ireland, Bulgaria, Croatia, Czech Republic, Estonia, Hungary, Latvia, Lithuania, Poland, Romania, Slovakia and Slovenia.
2 Cyprus, Denmark, Luxembourg, Malta and Norway.

References

Burchell, J., 2001. Evoloving or conforming? Assessing organisational reform within European Green parties. *West European Politics*, 24(3), pp. 113–134.

Dalton, R., Flanagan, S., and Beck, P. eds, 1984. *Electoral Change in Advanced Democracies*. Princeton: Princeton University Press.

Ignazi, P., 1998. The Iron Law of Party Institutionalization. Paper presented in the Workshop 'Challenges to Established Party Organization? Theory and Practice of Green and Alternative Left Party Organization'. *ECPR Joint Sessions of Workshops*: Warwick.

Kitschelt, H., 1989. *The Logics of Party Formation: Ecological Politics in Belgium and West Germany*. New York: Cornell University Press.

Kitschelt, H., 1988. Left-libertarian parties: Explaining innovation in competitive party systems. *World Politics*, 1(1), pp. 194–234.

Lipset, S. M., and Rokkan, S., 1967. *Party Systems and Voter Alignments: Cross-National Perspectives*. Toronto: The Free Press.

Lipset, S. M., and Rokkan, S., 2008. *Structures de clivages, systèmes de partis et alignement des électeurs: une introduction*. Brussels: Editions de l'Université de Bruxelles, coll. UBLire.

Mair, P., and Mudde, C., 1998. The party family and its study. *Annual Review of Political Science*, 1, pp. 211–229.

Müller-Rommel, F., 1994. Green parties under comparative perspective. *ICPS Working Papers* 99.

Müller-Rommel, F., ed., 1989. *New Politics in Western Europe: The Rise and Success of Green Parties and Alternative Lists*. London and Boulder, CO: Westview Press.

Müller-Rommel, F., and Poguntke, T. eds, 2002. *Green Parties in National Governments*. London and Portland, OR: Frank Cass.

O'Neill, M., 1997. *Green Parties and Political Change in Contemporary Europe*. Aldershot: Ashgate.

Pilet, J.-B., and van Haute, E., 2012. Criteria, conditions, and procedures for establishing a political party in the Member states of the European Union. *Report to the European Parliament*, Policy Department C (PE 431.512).

Poguntke, T., 1989. The 'new politics dimension' in European Green Parties. In: F. Müller-Rommel, ed., *New Politics in Western Europe: The Rise and Success of Green Parties and Alternative Lists*. London and Boulder, CO: Westview Press. pp. 175–194.

Richardson, D., and Rootes, C., 1995. *The Green Challenge: The Development of Green Parties in Europe*. London and New York: Routledge.

Rihoux, B., 2001. *Les partis politiques: Organisations en changement: Le test des écologistes*. Paris: L'Harmattan.

Seiler, D.-L., 1999, Comment classer les partis verts en Europe? In: P. Delwit and J.-M. De Waele, eds, *Les partis verts en Europe*. Bruxelles: Complexe. pp. 43–70.

Index

326   *Index*

For Product Safety Concerns and Information please contact our EU
representative GPSR@taylorandfrancis.com
Taylor & Francis Verlag GmbH, Kaufingerstraße 24, 80331 München, Germany